Ultimate Microsoft Power Automate for Business Automation

Design, Automate and Optimize Business Processes with Microsoft Power Automate Integrating AI Copilot and Enterprise Connectors

Ankesh Sinha

www.orangeava.com

First Published: December 2025

Published By: Orange Education Pvt Ltd, AVA®

Address: 9, Daryaganj, Delhi, 110002, India

275 New North Road Islington Suite 1314 London,
N1 7AA, United Kingdom

ISBN (PBK): 978-93-49888-22-7

ISBN (E-BOOK): 978-93-49888-91-3

Scan the QR code to explore our entire catalogue

www.orangeava.com

Dedicated To

My Beloved Parents,
Shri S. N. Sinha and Smt. Prabha Sinha,
Whose Unwavering Support and Guidance
Have Been the Foundation of My Journey.

My Cherished Wife, Preeti Singh
And My Precious Daughter, Avni,
Who Inspire Me Every Day
To Reach New Heights.

About the Author

Ankesh Sinha is the owner and principal architect at Prudent Autolytics, where he leads digital transformation initiatives for organizations across diverse industries. With over 18 years of experience in the IT industry, Ankesh has established himself as a recognized authority in business process automation, Microsoft Power Platform solutions, and enterprise architecture.

As a three-time Microsoft Power Platform Super User, Ankesh has been instrumental in helping thousands of professionals navigate the complexities of Power Automate, Power Apps, and the broader Microsoft ecosystem. His expertise extends beyond technical implementation to strategic business transformation, making him a sought-after consultant for organizations looking to maximize their automation investments.

Ankesh's commitment to knowledge sharing is evident through his extensive contributions to the technology community. He is a frequent book contributor and conference speaker, having presented at major industry events across the globe. His presentations consistently receive high ratings for their practical insights and actionable strategies that attendees can immediately implement in their organizations.

His selection for Microsoft, particularly for Startups Founders Hub program reflects his innovative approach to product development and his success in growing businesses on the Azure platform. This recognition has enabled him to work closely with Microsoft's product teams, providing valuable feedback that has influenced the development of Power Automate and related services.

At Prudent Autolytics, Ankesh has successfully delivered automation solutions for complex business cases across various sectors including finance, healthcare, manufacturing, and retail. His ability to translate intricate business requirements into elegant automation solutions has earned him the trust and loyalty of clients who continue to rely on his expertise for their most challenging projects.

Beyond his professional achievements, Ankesh is passionate about democratizing automation technology. He believes that powerful automation tools should be accessible to all business professionals, not just technical experts. This philosophy drives his approach to education and training, where he focuses on empowering citizen developers to create their own automation solutions.

When not architecting automation solutions or speaking at conferences, Ankesh enjoys exploring emerging technologies, contributing to open-source projects, and mentoring the next generation of automation professionals. His vision for the future includes a world where intelligent automation eliminates mundane tasks, allowing humans to focus on creative and strategic work that drives innovation and growth.

About the Technical Reviewer

Digesh Tailor is the Founder and Managing Director of **Digital Cloud UK**, a leading digital transformation consultancy specializing in Microsoft technologies, with a core focus on Microsoft Dynamics 365, Power Platform, Microsoft 365, and cloud-based CRM solutions. With over 15 years of experience at the intersection of technology, strategy, and operations, Digesh has built a reputation for delivering impactful, user-centric solutions that drive efficiency, growth, and innovation across sectors.

His journey began with a strong technical foundation in software development and systems integration, which quickly evolved into consultancy and strategic leadership roles. Recognizing the growing need for intelligent, scalable solutions tailored to modern business challenges, Digesh established Digital Cloud UK to bridge the gap between enterprise-level technology and the unique needs of SMEs, charities, and public sector organizations.

Under Digesh's leadership, Digital Cloud UK delivers successful digital transformation projects for a wide range of clients, including charities, education, local authorities, and commercial businesses. Beyond his commercial work, he demonstrates a strong commitment to social impact, notably as the founder of Grassroots to Glory, an initiative leveraging technology to elevate youth sports, reflecting his belief in inclusive and accessible technology.

Whether leading high-value CRM implementations, advising on digital strategy, or mentoring his growing team, Digesh remains driven by a clear vision: to make technology a true enabler of progress, efficiency, and meaningful outcomes.

Acknowledgments

There are a few people I want to thank for the continued and ongoing support they have given me during the writing of this book. First and foremost, I would like to thank my wife for continuously encouraging me for writing this book–I could have never completed this book without her support.

I extend my heartfelt gratitude to those who have been my pillars of strength throughout this journey. My brother, Arindam Sinha, whose unwavering belief in my abilities has been a constant source of motivation. Suresh Chaparala (Suresh Sir), Sameer Kumar Mandal, Amol Nemade, Ajit Kumar Pradhan, and Rahul Koul, who provided invaluable encouragement, mentorship, and guidance that has shaped not only this book but my professional growth. Their continuous support and faith in my vision have been instrumental in bringing this project to fruition.

I owe a debt of gratitude to all the Power Automate content creators out there. I have learned so much from their books, videos, blogs and presentations that this book simply would not exist without them. Throughout the book, I have added links to various additional resources created by many of the people I have learned from. There are also those who have inspired me to push myself past the point of procrastination, and into the world of action. Often these people do not realize that they lead by example, that they inspire others, and that they make all our lives a little bit better, each day.

All those moments acknowledging that I have something useful to share, encouraged me to write this book.

Thanks to Microsoft for building an awesome product, and for listening to my feedback. The continuous evolution of Power Automate and the responsiveness of the Microsoft team to community feedback has made this platform truly exceptional.

I would also like to thank my clients who came up with complex business cases which my team and I were able to provide solutions, using Power Automate, and retained their faith in this powerful tool by Microsoft. These real-world challenges have shaped much of the practical content in this book.

Thank you for all the hidden support provided. I gratefully acknowledge Digesh Tailor for his kind technical scrutiny for this book.

My gratitude also goes to the publishing team for being supportive enough to provide me quite a long time to finish this comprehensive guide, and for understanding the complexity of covering such a rapidly evolving platform.

To conclude, a grateful shout-out to the editorial team at Orange Education Pvt. Ltd. for publishing this book, and patiently answering my questions throughout the process.

Preface

In today's rapidly evolving business landscape, the ability to automate repetitive tasks and streamline complex workflows has become not just an advantage, but a necessity for organizations seeking to remain competitive. The book, ***Ultimate Microsoft Power Automate for Business Automation*** stands at the forefront of this automation revolution, empowering businesses of all sizes to transform their operations through intelligent process automation.

This book represents a comprehensive journey through the world of Power Automate, designed to take readers from fundamental concepts to advanced enterprise-scale automation strategies. Hence, whether you are a business analyst seeking to eliminate manual processes, an IT professional looking to implement robust automation solutions, or a citizen developer aiming to create powerful workflows without extensive coding knowledge, this guide provides the practical expertise and real-world examples, you need to succeed.

The importance of business process automation extends far beyond simple task elimination. In an era where digital transformation drives competitive advantage, the ability to systematically automate workflows, integrate disparate systems, and create intelligent business processes provides organizations with the agility and efficiency needed to thrive. From automating approval processes to orchestrating complex data synchronization across multiple platforms, Power Automate has become the backbone of modern business operations.

This book takes a distinctly practical approach, focusing on real-world applications and industry-tested methodologies. Rather than merely presenting theoretical concepts, each chapter builds upon hands-on examples that demonstrate how Power Automate solves actual business challenges. You will discover how Microsoft's comprehensive automation platform, combined with its seamless integration capabilities and AI-powered features, makes it the ideal choice for automation projects of any complexity.

The comprehensive structure of this book ensures a logical progression from basic automation concepts to advanced enterprise implementations. We begin with Power Automate fundamentals, ensuring that readers have a solid foundation in the platform's core capabilities and interface. From there, we explore workflow design principles, data manipulation techniques, and desktop automation—all essential skills for building robust automation solutions.

The latter chapters delve deep into advanced topics, covering everything from AI Builder integration to enterprise-scale deployment strategies. We examine the best practices for error handling, performance optimization, and governance, providing detailed guidance on implementing automation frameworks that can handle complex, mission-critical scenarios.

Throughout this journey, we maintain a focus on practical applications. Each concept is reinforced with step-by-step tutorials, real-world case studies, and troubleshooting guides that reflect the challenges you will encounter in actual implementation scenarios. This approach ensures that you not only understand how Power Automate works, but also how to apply it effectively in your specific business context.

The Power Automate ecosystem is constantly evolving, with Microsoft regularly introducing new features, connectors, and capabilities. This book captures the current state of the platform, while providing insights into emerging trends and future developments. By understanding both the current capabilities and the strategic direction of Power Automate, you will be better positioned to make informed decisions about your automation strategy.

As you embark on this automation journey, remember that the goal is not just to eliminate manual tasks, but to reimagine how work gets done. Power Automate provides the tools to create more intelligent, responsive, and efficient business processes that can adapt to the changing requirements, and scale with your organization's growth.

So, welcome to the world of Ultimate Microsoft Power Automate—where manual processes become automated workflows, and business efficiency reaches new heights. The book has been divided into following chapters:

Chapter 1: Getting Started with Power Automate

Chapter 2: Creating Your First Flow

Chapter 3: Expanding Your Workflow with Connectors

Chapter 4: Working with Conditional Logic

Chapter 5: Understanding and Setting Triggers

Chapter 6: Actions in Power Automate for Workflows

Chapter 7: Navigating Data Operations

Chapter 8: Expressions and Functions in Power Automate

Chapter 9: Error-Free Power Automate Workflows

Chapter 10: Debugging Your Automations

Chapter 11: Using Copilot to Develop Power Automate Flows

Chapter 12: Security Measures in Power Automate

Chapter 13: AI Builder in Power Automate

Chapter 14: Building Custom Connectors

Chapter 15: HTTP Requests and API Integration

Chapter 16: Real-World Case Studies

Get a Free eBook

We hope you are enjoying your recently purchased book! Your feedback is incredibly valuable to us, and to all other readers looking for great books.

If you found this book helpful or enjoyable, we would truly appreciate it, if you could take a moment to leave a short review with a 5 star rating on Amazon. It helps us grow, and lets other readers discover our books.

As a thank you, we would love to send you a free digital copy of this book, and a **30%** discount code on your next cart value on our official websites:

www.orangeava.com

www.orangeava.in (For Indian Subcontinent)

☑ Here's how:

Leave a review for the book on Amazon.

Take a screenshot of your review, and send an email to **info@orangeava.com** (it can be just the confirmation screen).

Once, we receive your screenshot, we will send you the digital file, within 24 hours.

Thank you so much for your support – it means a lot to us!

Downloading the code bundles and colored images

Please follow the links or scan the QR codes to download the
Code Bundles and Images of the book:

https://github.com/OrangeAVA/Ultimate-Microsoft-Power-Automate-for-Business-Automation

The code bundles and images of the book are also hosted on
https://rebrand.ly/1840a2

In case there's an update to the code, it will be updated on the existing GitHub repository.

Errata

We take immense pride in our work at **Orange Education Pvt Ltd,** and follow best practices to ensure the accuracy of our content to provide an indulging reading experience to our subscribers. Our readers are our mirrors, and we use their inputs to reflect and improve upon human errors, if any, that may have occurred during the publishing processes involved. To let us maintain the quality and help us reach out to any readers who might be having difficulties due to any unforeseen errors, please write to us at :

errata@orangeava.com

Your support, suggestions, and feedback are highly appreciated.

DID YOU KNOW

Did you know that Orange Education Pvt Ltd offers eBook versions of every book published, with PDF and ePub files available? You can upgrade to the eBook version at **www.orangeava.com** and as a print book customer, you are entitled to a discount on the eBook copy. Get in touch with us at: **info@orangeava.com** for more details.

At **www.orangeava.com**, you can also read a collection of free technical articles, sign up for a range of free newsletters, and receive exclusive discounts and offers on Print Books and eBooks.

PIRACY

If you come across any illegal copies of our works in any form on the internet, we would be grateful if you would provide us with the location address or website name. Please contact us at **info@orangeava.com** with a link to the material.

ARE YOU INTERESTED IN AUTHORING WITH US?

If there is a topic that you have expertise in, and you are interested in either writing or contributing to a book, please write to us at **business@orangeava.com**. We are on a journey to help developers and tech professionals to gain insights on the present technological advancements and innovations happening across the globe and build a community that believes Knowledge is best acquired by sharing and learning with others. Please reach out to us to learn what our audience demands and how you can be part of this educational reform. We also welcome ideas from tech experts and help them build learning and development content for their domains.

REVIEWS

Please leave a review. Once you have read and used this book, why not leave a review on the site that you purchased it from? Potential readers can then see and use your unbiased opinion to make purchase decisions. We at Orange Education would love to know what you think about our products, and our authors can learn from your feedback. Thank you!

For more information about Orange Education, please visit **www.orangeava.com**.

Table of Contents

CHAPTER 1

Getting Started with Power Automate

Part I: Laying the Foundation

Introduction

Welcome to the first chapter of our journey into Microsoft Power Automate. In this chapter, we will lay the foundation to understand this powerful automation tool. Whether you are a business professional looking to streamline your daily tasks, an IT administrator aiming to improve organizational workflows, or simply someone curious about the world of low-code automation, this chapter will provide you the essential knowledge to get started.

We will begin by exploring what Power Automate is and how it has evolved, while highlighting the key benefits it offers to both businesses and individuals. You will learn how to access Power Automate, navigate its user-friendly interface, and understand the different types of flows you can create.

By the end of this chapter, you will have a clear grasp of Power Automate's capabilities and be ready to create your first flow. We will walk you through a simple example, demonstrating how easy it is to automate a common task without any prior knowledge of coding.

This chapter will be your stepping stone into the world of Power Automate as it will prepare you for more advanced concepts and techniques explored in later chapters. Let us begin our journey to unlock the potential of automation in your work and life.

Structure

This chapter will address the following topics:

- Introduction to Power Automate
- Overview of the Power Automate Portal
- Understanding the Power Automate Interface
- Types of Power Automate Flows
- Creating your First Flow: A Simple Example
- Best Practices for Creating Flow with Power Automate
- Power Automate versus Traditional Programming
- Power Automate versus Custom Coding
- Industry-Based Case Studies

Introduction to Power Automate

Power Automate, formerly known as Microsoft Flow, is a cloud-based service that allows users to create and automate workflows and tasks across multiple applications and services, without requiring any developer assistance. It is a powerful tool that enables businesses and individuals to streamline repetitive tasks, improving efficiency and productivity.

Brief History and Evolution

Launched in 2016 as Microsoft Flow, the service was rebranded to Power Automate in 2019. This change reflected its deeper integration with the Microsoft Power Platform, which includes Power Apps, Power BI, and Power Virtual Agents. Over the years, Microsoft has continuously enhanced Power Automate's capabilities, adding features like AI-driven automation and Robotic Process Automation (RPA) through Power Automate Desktop.

Power Automate has evolved significantly since its launch. Understanding its evolution will help us appreciate its current capabilities that are explained in the following figure:

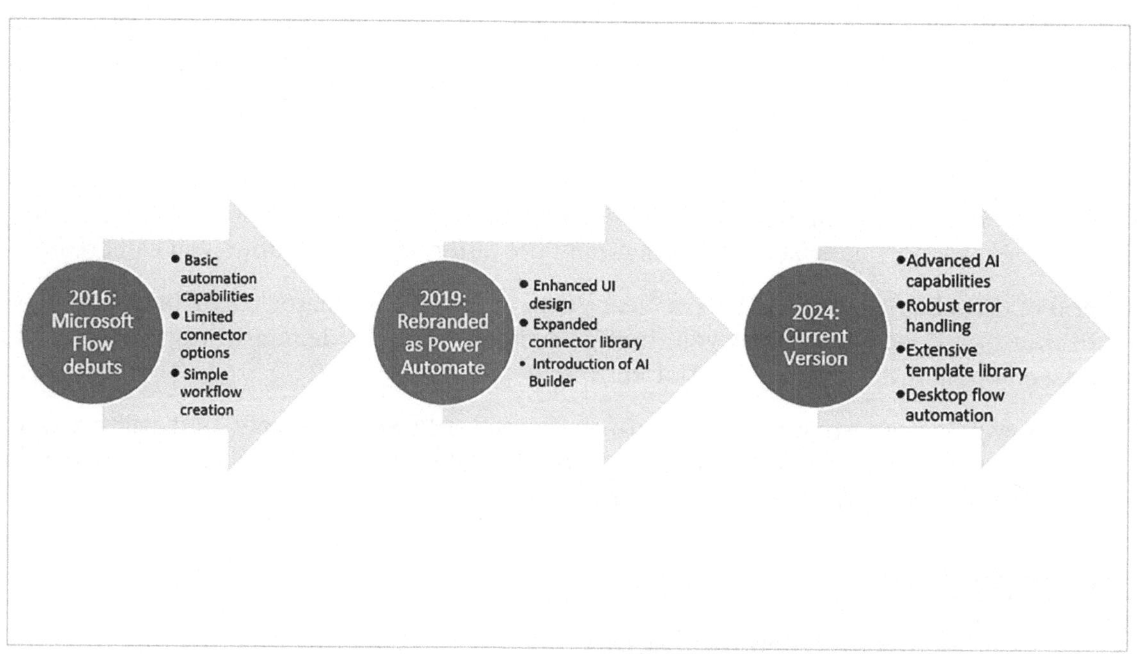

Figure 1.1: *Evolution of Power Automate Features over Time*

2016: Microsoft Flow Debuts

- Basic automation capabilities
- Limited connector options
- Simple workflow creation

2019: Rebranded as Power Automate

- Enhanced User Interface design
- Expanded connector library
- Introduction of AI Builder

2024: Current Version

- Advanced AI capabilities

- Robust error handling
- Extensive template library
- Desktop flow automation

Key Benefits for Businesses and Individuals

Power Automate delivers significant advantages across organizations of all sizes, from individual users seeking to streamline personal workflows to large enterprises implementing complex automation strategies.

- **Time saving:** Automate repetitive tasks to focus on more valuable work
- **Improved accuracy:** Reduce human errors in routine processes
- **Enhanced productivity:** Streamline workflows across multiple applications
- **Accessibility:** No coding skills required for many automations
- **Scalability:** Easily adapt flows as business needs change
- **Integration:** Connect with a wide range of Microsoft and third-party services
- **Cost-effectiveness:** Reduce manual labour costs and improve resource allocation

Accessing Power Automate

Getting started with Power Automate is straightforward, but understanding the different access methods and requirements ensures a smooth onboarding experience. This section will guide you through the various ways to access Power Automate and what you need to know before creating your first flow.

Sign-in Requirements and Account Types

Power Automate can be accessed using different types of Microsoft accounts, each with a different level of functionality. You can sign in using a work or school account (which is typically provided by your organization through Microsoft 365 or Azure Active Directory), a personal Microsoft account (such as outlook.com, hotmail.com, or live.com), or create a new Microsoft account specifically for Power Automate.

Work or school accounts generally provide the most comprehensive access to Power Automate features, including premium connectors and advanced administrative controls. Personal Microsoft accounts offer access to core Power Automate functionality with a few limitations on premium features and connectors.

Primary Access Methods

The most common way to access Power Automate is through the web portal at make.powerautomate.com. This web-based interface provides complete access to all Power Automate features, including flow creation, editing, monitoring, and administrative functions. The web portal is compatible with modern browsers including Microsoft Edge, Google Chrome, Mozilla Firefox, and Safari.

Power Automate is also available as a mobile application for both iOS and Android devices. The mobile app allows you to create simple flows, monitor existing flows, receive notifications, and approve requests on the go. While the mobile app is convenient for basic tasks and monitoring, complex flow creation is best executed through the web interface.

Additionally, as Power Automate is integrated within other Microsoft 365 applications, a user may create flows directly from SharePoint lists, Microsoft Teams, Outlook, and other Office applications.

This integration enables context-aware automation without requiring the user to exit their primary work environment.

Licensing and Subscription Considerations

Power Automate is a part of most Microsoft 365 subscriptions and provides access to standard connectors and basic automation capabilities. It might have some specific features that are available depending on a particular subscription level. Business and enterprise subscriptions typically include more generous limits on flow runs and access to additional connectors.

Some advanced features and premium connectors require additional licenses. Premium connectors include connections to on-premises systems, third-party services like Salesforce, and specialized business applications. If an organization requires these premium features, it might need to purchase separate Power Automate licenses or upgrade its existing Microsoft 365 subscription.

Initial Setup and Environment Configuration

When accessing Power Automate for the first time, you will be placed in a default environment corresponding to your account type and organizational setup. Environments in Power Automate provide isolation for flows, connections, and data, thereby allowing organizations to separate development, testing, and production workloads.

Individual users typically work in their default environment, while organizations may have multiple environments for different purposes. Your system administrator might have configured specific environments for your team or department, and you might have to switch between environments as per your role and responsibilities.

Understanding the Interface

The Power Automate web interface is organized into several key sections that you would use regularly. The main navigation includes "`Home`" for quick access to recent flows and templates, "`My flows`" for managing your created flows, "`Create`" for starting new flows, "`Templates`" for pre-built automation patterns, and "`Connectors`" for browsing available integrations.

The home page provides a dashboard view of your automation activities, recent flows, and suggested templates based on usage patterns. This central hub makes it easy to resume work on the existing flows or discover new automation opportunities.

Prerequisites and Technical Requirements

Before creating your first flow, ensure that you have a stable internet connection and are using a supported browser after enabling JavaScript. Power Automate works best with modern browsers with the latest web standards. While basic flows can be created on tablets and mobile devices, complex flow development is optimized for desktop and laptop computers.

If you plan to integrate with on-premises systems or use premium connectors, your organization might need to install and configure additional components, such as the on-premises data gateway. Check with your IT department about any organizational requirements or restrictions that may affect your Power Automate usage.

Getting Started Checklist

Before creating your first flow, take a moment to explore the interface and familiarize yourself with the available templates and connectors. Review any organizational policies regarding automation and data access and consider starting with simple workflows to build your confidence before tackling more complex automation scenarios.

As you have understood these access methods and requirements, you can begin creating automated workflows to streamline your daily tasks and improve productivity across your organization.

Licensing options

- **Office 365 subscriptions:** Many plans include Power Automate
- **Power Automate per user plan:** For users needing access to full capabilities
- **Power Automate per flow plan:** For organizations automating high-volume processes
- **Power Automate RPA attended and unattended plans:** For desktop automation

How to sign up and log in:

1. Visit make.powerautomate.com
2. Click "`Sign in`" or "`Sign up free`" if you don't have an account
3. Enter your work or school account or create a new account
4. Follow the prompts to complete the sign-up process

Overview of the Power Automate Portal

The Power Automate portal is organized into several key sections that provide intuitive access to all the tools and resources you need to create, manage, and monitor your automated workflows.

- **Home page:** Displays your recent flows, recommendations, and quick access to templates
- **My flows:** Lists all your created flows
- **Templates:** Pre-built flows for common scenarios
- **Connectors:** Shows available connections to various services
- **AI Builder:** Access to AI models for intelligent automation

Understanding the Power Automate Interface

The Power Automate interface is designed to be intuitive, but understanding its components is crucial for effective use.

Navigating the Portal

The Power Automate portal is organized into several key areas:

- **Home Dashboard**
    - Recent flows
    - Popular templates
    - Quick creation buttons
    - Activity feed
- **My Flows Section**
    - Cloud flows
    - Desktop flows
    - Shared flows

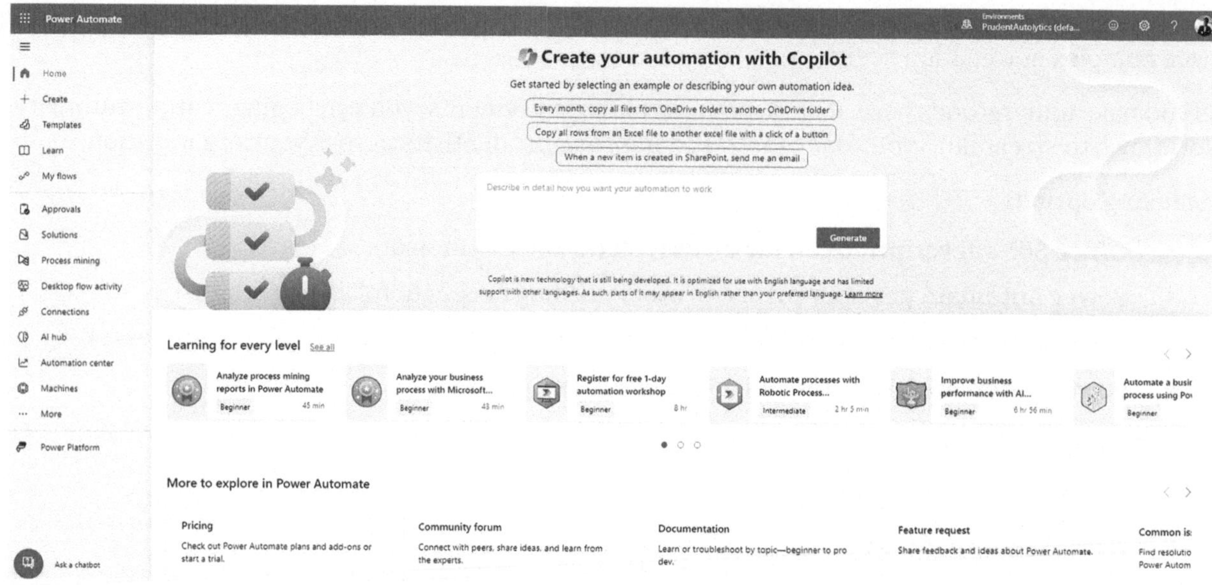

Figure 1.2: *Power Automate Home Screen*

- **Dashboard overview**
  - **Recent flows:** Quick access to your most used flows
  - **Learning resources:** Tutorials and guides to help you get started
  - **Templates:** Suggested templates based on your usage and popular flows
  - **Create new flow:** Button to start creating a new automation
- **Main menu options**
  - **Home:** Return to the main dashboard
  - **My flows:** View and manage your created flows
  - **Templates:** Browse and use pre-built flow templates
  - **Connectors:** Explore and manage connections to various services
  - **AI Builder:** Access AI capabilities for your flows
  - **Process advisor:** Analyze and improve your business processes
  - **Solutions:** Manage collections of flows for specific business solutions
  - **Data:** Access and manage data sources used in your flows
- **Creating a new flow**
  - Click "`Create`" on the left sidebar
  - Choose the type of flow you want to create
  - Select a template or start from scratch
  - Configure your flow using the visual designer

Understanding Power Automate Fundamentals

Think of Power Automate like a digital domino chain—when one domino falls, it triggers a sequence of actions leading to a desired outcome. Let us break this down in simple terms.

The Basic Principle: Trigger-Action-Outcome

Imagine that you have to brew a cup of your morning coffee. The alarm clock ringing in the morning will be your trigger that prompts you to make the coffee. This action is followed by an outcome where a steaming cup of joe is there on your table. Power Automate works in the same way, just digitally.

Let us use a real-world example:

```
Morning Routine Analogy:
Trigger: Alarm rings at 7 AM
Action 1: Get out of bed
Action 2: Make coffee
Action 3: Pack lunch
Outcome: Ready for work

Power Automate Example:
Trigger: New email arrives
Action 1: Save attachment to SharePoint
Action 2: Send notification to Teams
Outcome: Document stored and team notified
```

Figure 1.3: *Visual Representation of the trigger-action-outcome Principle*

Understanding Triggers

A trigger is like a pistol being fired to signal the beginning of a race as it sets everything in motion.

Types of Triggers

- **Schedule-Based Triggers:** Think of these like an alarm clock:

```
Example:
- Every Monday at 9 AM
- Daily at lunch time
- First day of each month
```

Figure 1.4: *Schedule-Based Triggers*

- **Event-Based Triggers:** These are like a doorbell—something happens, and your flow responds as follows:

```
Example:
- New email arrives
- File is modified
- Form is submitted
```

Figure 1.5: *Event-Based Triggers*

- **Manual Triggers:** These function like a light switch-you decide when to initiate the flow:

```
Example:
- Button press on your phone
- Clicking a button in Teams
- Starting the flow from a website
```

Figure 1.6: *Manual Triggers*

Understanding Actions

Actions are the steps taken by the flow after it is triggered. These actions are like items on a to-do list.

Common Actions

Let us look at this through a simple office task:

```
Example: Processing a New Invoice
1. Save the invoice (Action: Save File)
2. Extract the amount (Action: Parse PDF)
3. Create approval request (Action: Start Approval)
4. Send notification (Action: Send Email)
```

Figure 1.7: *Example of Actions*

Each action is a mini-task that contributes to the larger goal. For example, how you might divide a single goal like cooking breakfast into smaller steps like "toast the bread," "fry or scramble eggs," and "pour juice."

Understanding Connectors

Connectors are like universal translators as they help different applications interact with each other. Imagine if you could only speak English but needed to talk to someone who only speaks French. A translator (connector) would help you communicate. It acts as a bridge between two applications.

Working of Connectors

When you create a flow in Power Automate, connectors facilitate the exchange of data and commands between different services by handling authentication, data formatting, and communication protocols behind the scenes.

```
Example: Sharing News on Social Media
Without Connector:
- Copy text from email
- Open Twitter
- Paste text
- Post manually

With Connector:
- Email connector reads the message
- Twitter connector posts automatically
- Everything happens seamlessly
```

Figure 1.8: *Understanding Connectors*

Putting It All Together

Let us look at an example of how the trigger-action-outcome framework plays out in a real business scenario.

Example: Expense Report Processing

Consider a common workplace scenario where employees submit expense reports that require review, approval, and systematic tracking across multiple systems.

- Trigger:
    1. Employee submits expense report through a form
- Actions:
    1. Save receipt images to SharePoint
    2. Calculate total amount
    3. Check if amount > $1000
    4. If yes, route to manager
    5. If no, auto-approve
    6. Update expense tracking system
- Outcome:
    1. Expense report processed
    2. Appropriate approvals obtained
    3. Records updated

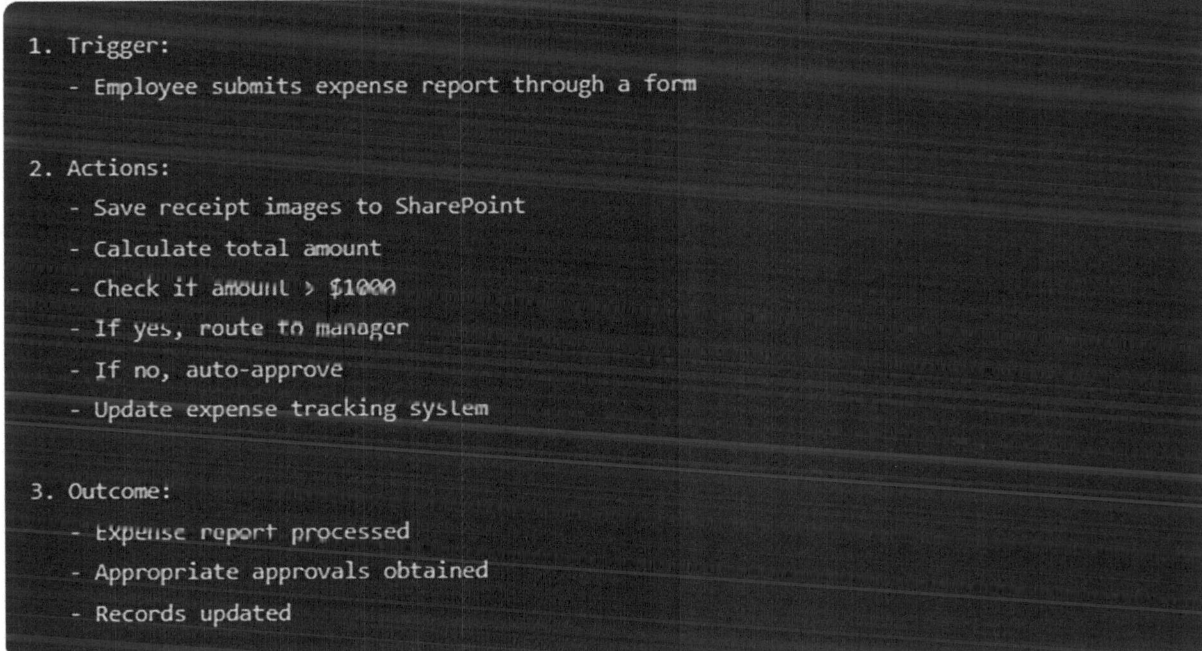

```
1. Trigger:
   - Employee submits expense report through a form

2. Actions:
   - Save receipt images to SharePoint
   - Calculate total amount
   - Check if amount > $1000
   - If yes, route to manager
   - If no, auto-approve
   - Update expense tracking system

3. Outcome:
   - Expense report processed
   - Appropriate approvals obtained
   - Records updated
```

Figure 1.9: *Expense Report Processing Automation Flow*

Breaking Down Processes

You can break down any business process using this principle. Let us look at another example:

```
1. Trigger:
   - Employee submits expense report through a form

2. Actions:
   - Save receipt images to SharePoint
   - Calculate total amount
   - Check if amount > $1000
   - If yes, route to manager
   - If no, auto-approve
   - Update expense tracking system

3. Outcome:
   - Expense report processed
   - Appropriate approvals obtained
   - Records updated
```

Figure 1.10: *Complete Flow Showing Trigger, Actions and Outcome*

This structure helps you organize even complex processes into manageable pieces. Think of it as creating a clear roadmap where you can identify exactly what starts your automation, what steps it performs, and what results it delivers.

Tips for Identifying Components

While creating your own flows, ask yourself these questions:

- For Triggers:
  - What starts this process?
  - When does this need to happen?
  - What event signals the beginning?
- For Actions:
  - What steps are needed?
  - What order do they need to be executed in?
  - What information is needed at each step?
- For Outcomes:
  - What should be the result?
  - How will I know it worked?
  - What needs to be updated or notified?

Remember, just like a recipe needs ingredients (connectors), steps (actions), and a starting point (trigger) to create a meal (outcome), Power Automate uses these components to create automated processes that make work easier and more efficient.

Types of Power Automate Flows

Power Automate offers several distinct types of flows, each designed to address specific automation scenarios and business requirements. Understanding the differences between these flow types is essential for selecting the right automation approach for your particular use case. The choice of flow type depends on factors such as how the automation should be triggered, whether it involves cloud services or desktop applications, and the level of complexity required. Let us explore each flow type and understand when to use them effectively.

Automated Cloud Flows

Automated cloud flows are event-driven automations that respond to specific triggers without requiring any manual intervention from users.

- **Trigger:** Starts automatically based on a specified event
- **Use case:** Send a notification when a new file is added to SharePoint
- **Key feature:** Can run in the background without user intervention

```
Trigger: New email with attachment
Actions:
1. Save attachment to SharePoint
2. Create task in Planner
3. Notify team in Teams
```

Figure 1.11: *Automated Cloud Flow*

Instant Cloud Flows

Instant cloud flows provide on-demand automation that users can trigger manually whenever they need to perform a specific task or action.

- **Trigger:** Manually started by the user
- **Use case:** Submit a vacation request with a button click
- **Key feature:** Often used for on-demand tasks or approvals

```
Button Click Trigger
Actions:
1. Get current location
2. Log work hours
3. Update timesheet
```

Figure 1.12: *Instant Cloud Flow*

Scheduled Cloud Flows

Scheduled cloud flows operate on a time-based schedule, executing automated tasks at predetermined intervals or specific times.

- **Trigger:** Runs at specified intervals or times
- **Use case:** Generate a weekly report every Monday at 9 AM
- **Key feature:** Perfect for recurring tasks or batch processing

```
Trigger: Daily at 9 AM
Actions:
1. Open legacy application
2. Enter data from Excel
3. Generate report
4. Save to shared drive
```

Figure 1.13: *Scheduled Cloud Flow*

Describe It to Design It

This innovative AI-powered capability allows users to create flows using natural language descriptions, making automation accessible even to those without technical expertise.

- **Purpose:** Describe what you want to automate, and AI will help you make it happen.
- **Use case:** You simply describe the automated workflow you want in everyday language.
- **Key feature:** This AI-powered feature uses a language model to create a cloud flow from a description. The model understands natural language input and writes the code for the flow.

Desktop Flow

Desktop flows extend Power Automate's capabilities beyond cloud services to automate tasks directly on your computer, including legacy applications and systems that lack modern API integration.

- **Purpose:** Desktop flows in Microsoft Power Automate are designed to automate tasks on legacy or desktop applications that do not have APIs or easy web integration capabilities.
- **Use case:** Desktop flows are particularly useful for automating repetitive tasks in applications like legacy ERP systems, desktop-based data entry tools, or any software that doesn't offer direct integration with cloud services. For example, automating data entry from an Excel spreadsheet into a legacy desktop application.
- **Key feature:** A key feature of Desktop flows is its ability to record and replay user actions on the desktop, including mouse clicks, keyboard inputs, and interactions with UI elements, allowing for the automation of tasks that would typically require manual intervention.

Process Mining

Process mining provides analytical capabilities that help organizations discover, monitor, and improve their actual business processes by extracting insights from system event logs.

- **Purpose:** Process mining in Microsoft Power Automate is designed to analyse and visualize business processes based on event logs from various systems, helping organizations understand and optimize their workflows.
- **Use case:** Process mining is particularly useful for identifying inefficiencies, bottlenecks, and deviations in business processes. For example, it can be used to analyse order-to-cash processes, revealing delays in order processing, identifying frequently skipped steps, or highlighting variations in how different teams handle similar tasks.
- **Key feature:** A key feature of process mining in Power Automate is its ability to automatically generate process maps and analytics from raw event data, providing insights into actual process execution without the need for manual process documentation or interviews.

Power Automate Licensing

Understanding licensing options is crucial for planning your automation strategy.

License Types

Power Automate offers several licensing options:

- **Free License**
  - Basic connectors
  - Personal automation
  - Limited runs per month
- **Premium License**
  - Premium connectors
  - AI Builder
  - Unlimited flows
  - RPA capabilities

Choosing the Right License

Consider these factors when selecting a license:

Business Needs Assessment:

```
Questions to Ask:
1. How many flows do you need?
2. Which connectors are required?
3. Do you need RPA features?
4. What's your automation budget?
```

Figure 1.14: *Business Needs Assessment, Questions to Ask*

Security and Compliance

Security is paramount when automating business processes. Power Automate incorporates enterprise-grade security features to protect your data and ensure that automated workflows comply with organizational policies and regulatory requirements. Understanding these security and compliance capabilities is essential for implementing automation solutions that meet your organization's governance standards.

Power Automate leverages Microsoft's robust security infrastructure, including data encryption both in transit and at rest, multi-factor authentication, and role-based access controls. These features ensure that only authorized users can create, modify, or execute flows, while sensitive data remains protected throughout the automation lifecycle.

Compliance is equally critical, particularly for organizations operating in regulated industries such as healthcare, finance, or government. Power Automate supports various compliance certifications including GDPR, HIPAA, ISO 27001, and SOC 2, enabling organizations to automate processes while maintaining adherence to industry-specific regulations. The platform also provides data loss prevention (DLP) policies that administrators can configure to prevent sensitive information from being shared inappropriately across different connectors and services.

Additionally, Power Automate offers comprehensive audit logging and monitoring capabilities, allowing administrators to track flow execution history, identify potential security incidents, and maintain detailed records for compliance reporting. These audit trails provide visibility into who created or modified flows, when they were executed, and what data was accessed, ensuring accountability and traceability across all automated processes.

Security Features

Power Automate includes robust the following security measures:

- **Data Protection**
  - Encryption at rest
  - Encryption in transit
  - Role-based access
  - Data loss prevention
- **Compliance Standards**
  - ISO 27001
  - GDPR compliance
  - SOC 1 and SOC 2
  - Industry-specific compliance

Understanding Copilot in Power Automate

Copilot is an AI-powered assistant within Power Automate and helps users create and modify flows using natural language instructions. Think of it as having a knowledgeable colleague who can understand your automation needs and translate them into working flows.

Working of Copilot in Power Automate

While interacting with Copilot, you can describe what you want to achieve in simple language. Copilot then interprets your request and suggests appropriate actions and logic to create the flow. For example, you might say "Create a flow that saves email attachments to SharePoint and notifies me in Teams," and Copilot will construct the necessary steps accordingly.

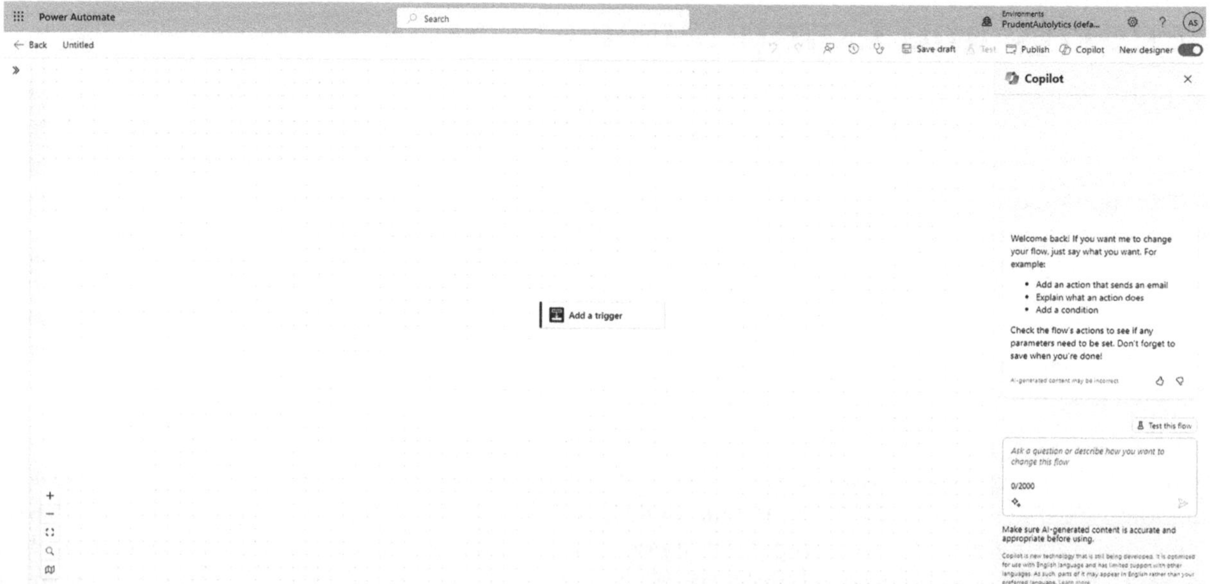

Figure 1.15: *Copilot Interface Showing Natural Language Input and Suggested Flow*

Natural Language Processing Capabilities

Copilot understands various ways in which automation needs are expressed. For instance:

Simple Request: "Send me a daily email with today's tasks"

Complex Request: "When someone uploads a document to SharePoint, check if it is larger than 5MB, and if it is, send an approval request to my manager and notify me in Teams"

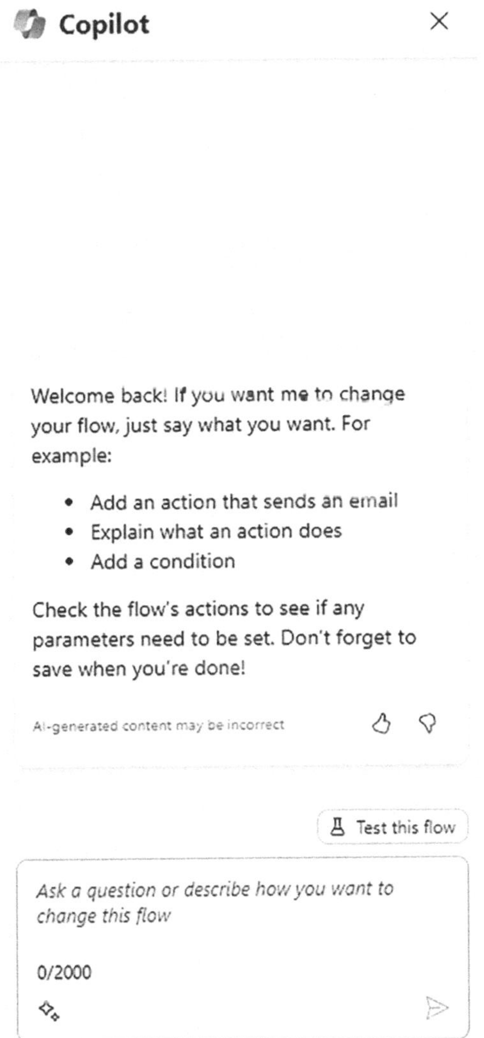

Figure 1.16: Copilot in Power Automate

Practical Applications of Copilot

Let us explore real-world scenarios where Copilot proves to be particularly valuable:

Document Management Automation

You might tell Copilot: "I need to automatically organize documents based on their content"

Copilot would create a flow that:

1. Analyses document content using AI
2. Creates appropriate folders

3. Moves documents to relevant locations
4. Sends confirmation notifications

Meeting Follow-up Automation

Natural language request: "Create a flow that handles post-meeting tasks"

Copilot generates a flow that:

1. Extracts meeting notes from Teams
2. Creates action items in Planner
3. Sends summary emails to attendees
4. Schedules follow-up meetings if needed

Advanced Features of Copilot

Beyond basic flow creation, Copilot in Power Automate offers sophisticated capabilities that enhance productivity, streamline troubleshooting, and enable users to work more efficiently with complex automation scenarios. These advanced features leverage artificial intelligence to provide intelligent assistance throughout the entire automation lifecycle, from initial design to ongoing optimization.

One of the most powerful advanced features is Copilot's ability to explain existing flows in natural language. When you encounter a complex flow created by another team member or inherited from a previous project, Copilot can analyze the flow's structure and provide a clear, step-by-step explanation of what the flow does, how it works, and why specific actions were configured in a particular way. This dramatically reduces the time needed to understand and maintain existing automations.

Copilot also excels at troubleshooting and debugging flows. When a flow fails or produces unexpected results, you can describe the issue to Copilot, and it will analyze the flow's execution history, identify potential problem areas, and suggest specific corrections. This intelligent debugging assistance helps users resolve issues faster without needing deep technical expertise in flow architecture or connector configurations.

Another advanced capability is flow optimization and refactoring. Copilot can review your existing flows and suggest improvements to make them more efficient, reliable, or maintainable. This might include recommendations to consolidate redundant actions, implement better error handling, optimize conditional logic, or replace deprecated connectors with more current alternatives. These suggestions help ensure your automations follow best practices and perform optimally.

Copilot's advanced features also include intelligent connector recommendations. When building flows, Copilot can suggest the most appropriate connectors and actions based on your described requirements, even if you're not familiar with all available options. It considers factors such as data types, authentication requirements, and performance characteristics to recommend solutions that best fit your specific automation needs.

Furthermore, Copilot can assist with creating complex expressions and formulas within your flows. Instead of manually constructing intricate logic using Power Automate's expression language, you can describe what you want to accomplish, and Copilot will generate the appropriate expressions, complete with proper syntax and functions. This feature is particularly valuable when working with data transformations, date calculations, or conditional logic that would otherwise require significant technical knowledge.

Flow Modification and Enhancement

Copilot can modify existing flows. For example: "Add error handling to my expense approval flow"

Copilot will:

1. Analyze the current flow
2. Suggest appropriate error handling steps
3. Add notification mechanisms
4. Implement retry logic where appropriate

Complex Logic Creation

Copilot excels at creating sophisticated conditional logic:

Request: "Create a customer support ticket routing system based on priority and category"

Copilot builds:

```
If (Priority = "High" AND Category = "Technical")
    Route to Senior Technical Team
    Set 4 hour SLA
    Notify Department Head
Else If (Priority = "Medium")
    Route to Standard Support Queue
    Set 8-hour SLA
Else
    Route to General Support
    Set 24-hour SLA
```

Figure 1.17: *Using Copilot to Create and Generate Complex Power Automate Flow*

Best Practices for Using Copilot

To maximize the benefits of Copilot in Power Automate and ensure you receive the most accurate and useful assistance, it is important to follow certain best practices when interacting with this AI-powered tool. These guidelines will help you communicate more effectively with Copilot, receive better recommendations, and create more robust and maintainable automation solutions.

Clear Communication Tips

To get the best results from Copilot:

- **Be Specific:** Instead of: "Create a notification flow" Better: "Create a flow that sends me a Teams message when high-priority emails arrive"
- **Provide Context:** Include relevant details about your business process and requirements when describing your needs
- **Review and Refine:** Always review Copilot's suggestions and make necessary adjustments

Common Use Cases and Solutions

Effective scenarios for Copilot:

- **Data Collection and Processing:** "Create a flow that collects survey responses and generates a weekly summary report"
- **Approval Workflows:** "Build an approval process for purchase requests over $1000 with multiple approval levels"
- **Integration Flows:** "Create a flow that syncs customer data between Salesforce and SharePoint"

Troubleshooting with Copilot

When your flows need adjustment, Copilot can help diagnose and fix issues:

- **Flow Analysis:** Ask Copilot to review your flow and suggest improvements
- **Error Resolution:** Describe the error you are encountering, and Copilot can suggest potential solutions
- **Performance Optimization:** Request Copilot to analyse your flow for efficiency improvements

Through these various capabilities and applications, Copilot serves as a powerful tool for both beginners and experienced users in Power Automate. It simplifies the process of creating and maintaining flows while helping users learn best practices for automation design.

Starting with Templates: Your Training Wheels

Templates in Power Automate are like cooking recipes for beginners - they provide a tested formula that you can follow and modify as you learn.

Value of Templates for Beginners

Think of templates as learning from experienced chefs rather than trying to create recipes from scratch. They offer several advantages:

- Learning by Example:

```
Benefits:
- See how experienced users structure flows
- Understand best practices
- Learn common patterns
- Discover available features
```

Figure 1.18: *Benefits of Using Templates in Power Automate*

- Quick Wins:

```
Advantages:
- Get working flows quickly
- Build confidence
- Show immediate value
- Learn while doing
```

Figure 1.19: *Using Templates in Power Automate for Quick Wins*

Finding the Right Template

Power Automate template library is organized to help you find relevant solutions:

- Popular Templates:
  - Email notifications
  - File handling
  - Approval processes
  - Team notifications
- Industry-Specific Templates:
  - Sales processes
  - Customer service
  - Project management
  - Document handling

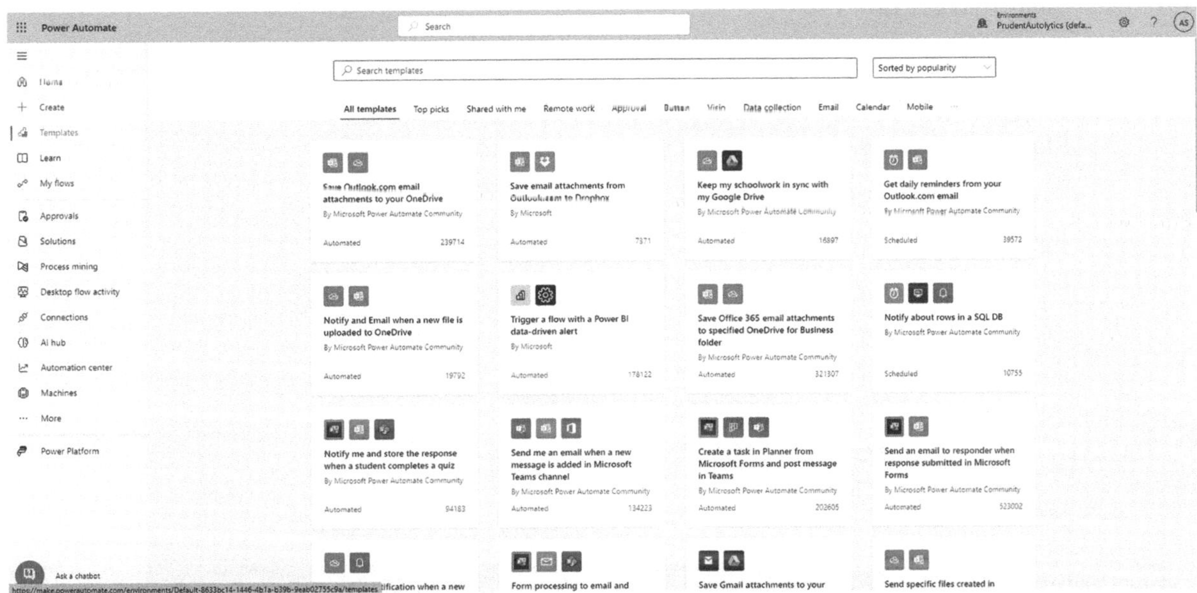

Figure 1.20: *Templates Screen in Power Automate*

Customizing Templates

Modifying templates is like adjusting a recipe to your taste that includes elements like:

- Basic Modifications:

```
Start Simple:
- Change email addresses
- Modify message text
- Adjust timing
- Update file locations
```

Figure 1.21: *How to Use Templates in Power Automate*

- Advanced Customization:

```
As You Learn:
- Add new actions
- Modify conditions
- Enhance error handling
- Integrate additional services
```

Figure 1.22: *Advanced Usage of Templates in Power Automate*

Best Practices for New Users

As you begin your Power Automate journey, keep these guidelines in mind:

Starting Small

- Begin with simple flows:
  - Single trigger flows
  - Basic notifications
  - Simple file operations
  - Standard approvals
- Gradually increase complexity:
  - Add conditions
  - Include multiple actions
  - Integrate more services
  - Handle exceptions

Building Your Knowledge

Create a learning path that builds your skills progressively:

```
Week 1-2:
- Explore templates
- Create basic flows
- Learn interface navigation

Week 3-4:
- Modify existing flows
- Add simple conditions
- Use common connectors

Week 5-6:
- Create custom flows
- Implement error handling
- Use advanced features
```

Figure 1.23: *Plan to Master Power Automate*

Environment Setup Checklist

Before you start creating flows, ensure that you have:

- Access Requirements:
  - Valid Microsoft account
  - Appropriate license level
  - Necessary permissions
- Technical Setup:
  - Modern web browser
  - Stable internet connection
  - Required connectors configured
- Resource Access:
  - SharePoint sites (if needed)
  - Team permissions
  - Database connections

Remember, starting with Power Automate is like learning to ride a bicycle, where you begin with training wheels (templates), practice in a safe environment (test flows), and gradually build up to more complex manoeuvres (custom flows). Take your time to understand each component, and do not hesitate to experiment with templates to build your confidence and knowledge.

Creating Your First Flow: A Simple Example

Step-by-step guide to creating a basic automated flow:

1. From the Power Automate dashboard, click "**`Create`**" then "**`Automated flow`**"
2. Name your flow (for example, "New email notification")
3. In the "**`Choose your flow's trigger`**" field, search for and select "**`When a new email arrives (V3)`**"
4. Click "**`Create`**"

Choosing a trigger

- In this example, we are using the "**`When a new email arrives (V3)`**" trigger
- Configure the trigger by specifying conditions such as folder, importance, or sender

Adding an action

1. Click "**`+ New step`**"
2. Search for and select "**`Send me a mobile notification`**"
3. In the "**`Text`**" field, add dynamic content by clicking the lightning bolt icon
4. Select relevant fields from the trigger, such as "**`Subject`**" and "**`From`**"
5. Customize the notification message (for example, "New email from {From} about {Subject}")

Testing and activating the flow

1. Click "**`Save`**" to save your flow

2. Click "`Test`" in the top right corner
3. Choose "`I will perform the trigger action`"
4. Send yourself a test email
5. Check your mobile device for the notification
6. If successful, close the test pane
7. Your flow is now active and will run automatically

The above example demonstrates the basics of creating a flow, right from selecting a trigger to adding an action and testing the result. As users become more comfortable with Power Automate, they can create more complex flows with multiple actions, conditions, and integrations with various services.

Best Practices for Creating Flow with Power Automate

Creating effective and reliable automation workflows requires more than just technical knowledge, it demands careful planning, thoughtful design, and adherence to established best practices. Following proven guidelines helps ensure your flows are maintainable, scalable, performant, and resilient to errors. Whether you are building simple automations or complex enterprise workflows, applying these best practices from the start will save time, reduce troubleshooting efforts, and result in more robust solutions that deliver long-term value to your organization.

Naming Conventions

When creating flows in Power Automate, consistent and clear naming conventions are crucial. Consider the following guidelines:

- **Use descriptive names:** Your flow names should clearly indicate their purpose. Example: "Weekly Sales Report Email" instead of "Report Flow"
- **Include the trigger or main action:** Start the name with the trigger or primary action. Example: "When a new email arrives - Move to folder"
- **Use Pascal Case or spaces for readability:** Example: "NewEmployeeOnboarding" or "New Employee Onboarding"
- **Include the department or team if applicable:** Example: "HR - New Employee Onboarding"
- **For actions within flows, use consistent verb-noun structure:** Example: "Get Sales Data", "Send Email Notification"

Documentation

Proper documentation is essential for maintaining and troubleshooting your flows. Remember the following measures to do so:

- **Use flow descriptions:** Provide a brief overview of the flow's purpose and functionality in the description field.
- **Add comments to actions:** Use the notes feature to explain complex logic or important steps.
- **Maintain a flow inventory:** Keep a spreadsheet or document listing all your flows, their purposes, and owners.

- **Version control:** Document major changes to flows, including the date and reason for changes.
- **Create process diagrams:** For complex flows, consider creating visual diagrams to illustrate the workflow.

Testing and Troubleshooting Basics

Effective testing and troubleshooting are crucial for reliable automations:

- **Start with small tests:** Begin with simple test cases and gradually increase complexity.
- **Use test data:** Create a set of test data that covers various scenarios, including edge cases.
- **Monitor flow runs:** Regularly check the run history to identify and address any failures.
- **Use try/catch actions:** Implement error handling to make your flows more robust.
- Leverage Power Automate's built-in troubleshooting tools:
  - Flow checker for identifying potential issues
  - Run history for detailed execution logs
  - Real-time debugging for step-by-step flow execution

Power Automate versus Traditional Programming

Understanding the relationship between Power Automate and traditional programming approaches helps clarify when to use each method and how they can complement one another in modern automation strategies. While both Power Automate and traditional programming aim to automate tasks and solve business problems, they differ significantly in their approach, required skill sets, development speed, and ideal use cases. This comparison is not about determining which approach is superior, but rather about understanding the strengths and limitations of each so you can make informed decisions about the right tool for your specific automation needs.

Development Approach and Accessibility

Traditional programming requires writing code in languages such as Python, C#, Java, or JavaScript, demanding substantial technical expertise, understanding of programming concepts, and familiarity with development environments and tools. Developers must handle syntax, logic structures, error handling, and often complex infrastructure considerations. In contrast, Power Automate uses a visual, low-code approach where users build automations by selecting pre-built connectors and actions through a graphical interface. This visual paradigm makes automation accessible to business users, analysts, and citizen developers who may lack formal programming training but possess deep understanding of business processes that need automation.

Time to Value and Development Speed

Power Automate excels in rapid development and deployment of automations, particularly for integrating existing cloud services and applications. What might take days or weeks to code, test, and deploy using traditional programming can often be accomplished in hours with Power Automate, especially for common integration scenarios. The platform provides ready-made connectors to hundreds of services, eliminating the need to write authentication logic, API calls, and data transformation code from scratch. However, traditional programming offers more flexibility for highly customized solutions, complex algorithms, or scenarios that fall outside the capabilities of available connectors.

Maintenance and Scalability

Flows created in Power Automate are generally easier for non-technical users to understand and modify, as the visual representation clearly shows the sequence of actions and logic. This accessibility reduces dependency on specialized IT resources for routine updates and troubleshooting. Traditional code, while more powerful and flexible, requires programmers to maintain and often benefits from version control systems, formal testing frameworks, and deployment pipelines. For enterprise-scale solutions processing massive data volumes or requiring microsecond-level performance optimization, traditional programming may offer advantages in fine-tuning and resource management that low-code platforms cannot match.

Integration Capabilities

Power Automate shines in scenarios requiring integration between multiple SaaS applications, Microsoft services, and cloud platforms. Its extensive connector library handles the complexity of authentication, API versioning, and data formatting automatically. Traditional programming is more suitable when you need to integrate with legacy systems lacking modern APIs, require direct database access, or need to implement custom protocols and communication methods. Many organizations adopt a hybrid approach, using Power Automate for standard integrations while employing traditional development for specialized or complex system interactions.

Cost Considerations

The cost structure differs significantly between these approaches. Power Automate operates on a subscription or per-flow licensing model with predictable costs and minimal infrastructure overhead, as Microsoft manages the hosting and maintenance. Traditional programming requires investment in developer salaries, development tools, hosting infrastructure, and ongoing maintenance resources. For smaller-scale automations or departmental solutions, Power Automate often proves more cost-effective. For large-scale, mission-critical applications with unique requirements, the initial investment in custom development may be justified by greater long-term flexibility and control.

Governance and Control

Traditional programming offers complete control over every aspect of the application, from architecture to security implementation to performance optimization. Development teams can implement custom logging, sophisticated error handling, and fine-grained security measures. Power Automate, while offering robust governance features through data loss prevention policies, environment management, and audit logging, operates within the framework and limitations of the platform. Organizations must balance the desire for complete control against the benefits of standardization and reduced complexity that platforms like Power Automate provide.

The Complementary Approach

Rather than viewing Power Automate and traditional programming as competing alternatives, forward-thinking organizations recognize them as complementary tools in their automation toolkit. Power Automate empowers business users to automate routine processes quickly while freeing professional developers to focus on complex, custom applications that truly require programming expertise. Many sophisticated solutions combine both approaches, using Power Automate for user-facing workflows and integrations while calling custom APIs or Azure Functions written in traditional code for specialized processing, complex calculations, or system integrations that exceed Power Automate's native capabilities.

Understanding these differences enables you to select the appropriate approach for each automation opportunity, maximize the value of both platforms, and build a comprehensive automation strategy that leverages the strengths of each method while mitigating their respective limitations.

Advantages of Low-Code/No-Code Platforms

Low-code and no-code platforms like Power Automate have revolutionized the automation landscape by democratizing technology and making sophisticated capabilities accessible to a broader range of users within organizations.

- **Rapid Development:** Create automations quickly without extensive coding knowledge
- **User-Friendly Interface:** Intuitive drag-and-drop interface makes it accessible to non-technical users
- **Pre-built Connectors:** Easy integration with a wide range of applications and services
- **Reduced Maintenance:** Automatic updates and maintenance handled by the platform
- **Cost-Effective:** Lower development and maintenance costs compared to custom solutions
- **Scalability:** Easily scale automations as business needs grow
- **Collaboration:** Facilitate collaboration between business users and IT teams

Selecting Between Power Automate and Custom Coding

Use Power Automate when:

- Automating simple to moderately complex business processes
- Integrating multiple Microsoft 365 or third-party applications
- Rapid prototyping or proof of concept is needed
- The automation doesn't require complex algorithms or data processing

Consider custom coding when:

- Highly complex business logic is required
- Performance optimization is critical
- Deep system-level integrations are needed
- Custom user interfaces or experiences are required
- Dealing with large volumes of data that exceed Power Automate's limits

Use Cases and Examples

Common Scenarios Where Power Automate Shines

- **Approval Workflows:** Automating document or request approvals across departments
- **Data Collection and Processing:** Gathering data from various sources and consolidating it into reports
- **Notification Systems:** Sending automated alerts based on specific triggers or conditions
- **Social Media Management:** Scheduling posts and monitoring social media activity
- **Customer Service Automation:** Routing customer inquiries and automating responses
- **Employee Onboarding:** Streamlining the new hire process with automated tasks and notifications
- **Inventory Management:** Tracking stock levels and triggering reorder processes

Industry-Based Case Studies

- **Healthcare:** A hospital can use Power Automate to streamline patient appointment scheduling. When a new appointment is created in their system, it triggers a flow that sends a confirmation email to the patient, adds the appointment to the doctor's calendar, and updates the hospital's capacity planning spreadsheet.

- **Retail:** A clothing retailer can automate their inventory management process. When stock levels drop below a certain threshold, a flow is triggered to generate a purchase order, send it to the supplier, and update the inventory management system.
- **Education:** A university can use Power Automate to simplify the grade submission process. When professors submit grades through a SharePoint form, a flow automatically updates the student information system, sends notifications to students, and generates reports for the academic office.
- **Finance:** An accounting firm can automate their invoice processing. When a new invoice is received via email, a flow extracts the relevant information, creates an entry in their accounting software, and routes it to the appropriate person for approval.

Power Automate vs. Traditional Automation Tools

Let us examine how Power Automate stands when compared to other major players in the automation space, like UiPath, Automation Anywhere, and Zapier. Each tool has its strengths, but Power Automate offers unique advantages in several key areas.

Integration Capabilities

Power Automate's deep integration with Microsoft 365 sets it apart. When automating tasks within the Microsoft ecosystem, Power Automate provides seamless connectivity that other tools cannot match. For example, while Zapier needs multiple steps to process a SharePoint document and update Teams, Power Automate can do this natively with better performance and reliability.

Consider this scenario:

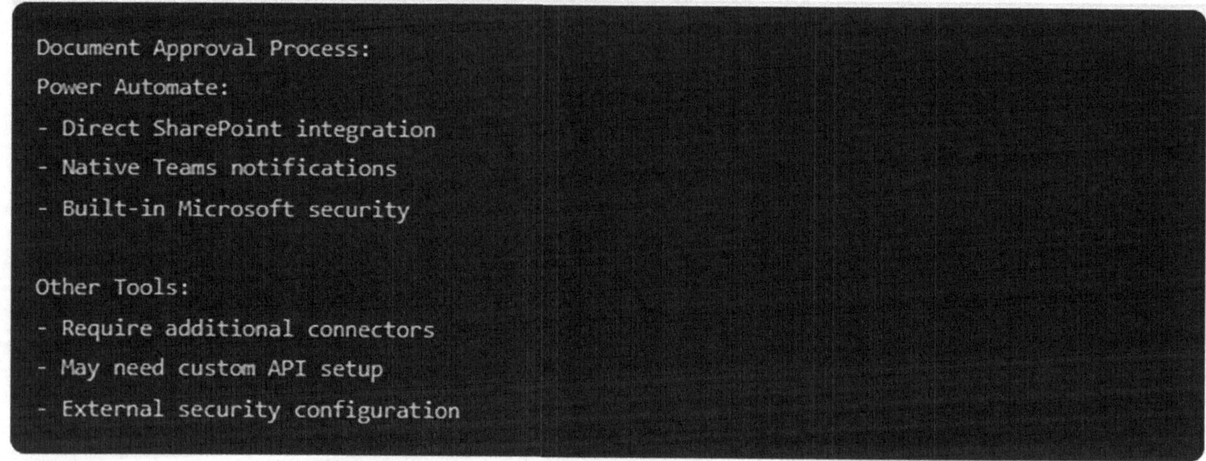

```
Document Approval Process:
Power Automate:
- Direct SharePoint integration
- Native Teams notifications
- Built-in Microsoft security

Other Tools:
- Require additional connectors
- May need custom API setup
- External security configuration
```

Figure 1.24: *Power Automate Integration Capabilities*

Cost-Effectiveness

Power Automate often provides better value, especially for organizations already using Microsoft 365. Let us break down the cost structure:

Power Automate:

- Included in many Microsoft 365 licenses
- Per-user pricing for additional features

- No per-bot charges
- Unlimited flow runs (within fair use)

Traditional RPA Tools:

- Separate licensing costs
- Per-bot pricing models
- Additional costs for advanced features
- Runtime limitations

Development Experience

Power Automate offers a more accessible development experience while maintaining its powerful capabilities such as:

Low-Code Experience: Power Automate provides an intuitive visual designer that helps users create flows without extensive coding knowledge. The platform uses natural language descriptions and clear visual cues to guide users through the automation process.

Other platforms might offer similar visual designers but often require more technical expertise:

UiPath:

- Requires more programming knowledge
- Steeper learning curve
- More complex deployment process

Automation Anywhere:

- More technical interface
- Requires specialized training
- Complex bot management

AI and Machine Learning Integration

Power Automate's AI Builder provides significant advantages like:

- Built-in AI models
- Easy model training
- Native form processing
- Image and text analysis
- Seamless integration with flows

Competing Platforms:

- Often require third-party AI services
- More complex integration
- Additional costs for AI features
- Limited pre-built models

Security and Compliance

Power Automate provides robust security through Microsoft's enterprise-grade infrastructure such as:

- Azure Active Directory integration
- Data Loss Prevention policies

- Role-Based Access Control
- Compliance with global standards
- Regular security updates

Other Platforms:

- May require additional security setup
- Third-party identity management
- Separate compliance certifications
- Variable update schedules

Unique Power Automate Advantages

Several features like the following give Power Automate a distinct edge:

- Power Platform Integration: Power Automate works seamlessly with other Power Platform tools:
- Power Apps for custom applications
- Power BI for data analytics
- Power Virtual Agents for chatbots
- Dataverse for data management
- Hybrid Capabilities: Power Automate uniquely bridges cloud and on-premises systems:
- Cloud flows for online services
- Desktop flows for legacy applications
- Gateway connections for local resources
- Mixed-mode operations
- Collaborative Features: Power Automate excels in team environments:
- Shared flows
- Solution management
- Version control
- Team development features

Industry-Specific Considerations

Different industries might use Power Automate for the specific advantages it offers:

- Healthcare:
    - HIPAA compliance
    - Electronic Health Record integration
    - Patient data security
- Financial Services:
    - SOX compliance
    - Banking connector support
    - Transaction security
- Manufacturing:
    - IoT integration

- Supply chain automation
- Quality control workflows

Scalability and Enterprise Readiness

Power Automate provides robust enterprise scalability through the following features:

- CoE toolkit
- Environment management
- Admin analytics
- Global deployment
- Cross-region support

While other platforms may offer enterprise features, Power Automate's integration with Microsoft's enterprise ecosystem provides a more cohesive experience for large organizations.

In this section, we can see that while each automation platform has its strengths, Power Automate offers a unique combination of accessibility, integration capabilities, and enterprise-ready features. Its position within the Microsoft ecosystem, besides its robust feature set and competitive pricing, makes it a compelling choice for organizations of all sizes.

Critical Thinking Scenarios

- A colleague suggests creating separate flows for each department in your organization. What factors would you consider when deciding whether to implement this approach?
- Your team frequently modifies shared flows, leading to version control issues. How would you establish best practices for collaborative flow development?
- An automated flow occasionally fails during peak business hours. How would you approach optimizing the flow for better performance and reliability?

Problem-Solving Exercises

- Create a diagram showing how you would automate a document approval process using Power Automate. Include all necessary triggers, actions, and connectors.

Conclusion

In this chapter, we have covered the fundamentals of Power Automate, including best practices, comparisons with traditional programming, real-world use cases, and resources for further learning.

As you continue your journey, consider experimenting with creating your own flows based on your specific needs and exploring the various connectors available in Power Automate. Joining the Power Automate community will allow you to learn from and share with others, while keeping up with new features and updates through official Microsoft channels, ensuring that you are leveraging them efficiently.

In the next chapter, we will dive deeper into creating more complex flows and explore advanced features of Power Automate.

Resources for Learning

Official Microsoft Documentation

- Power Automate Documentation: https://docs.microsoft.com/en-us/power-automate/ Comprehensive guides, tutorials, and reference materials.
- Microsoft Learn for Power Automate: https://docs.microsoft.com/en-us/learn/powerplatform/power-automate Free, structured learning paths and modules.

Community Forums and Resources

- Power Automate Community: https://powerusers.microsoft.com/t5/Power-Automate-Community/ct-p/MPACommunity Official forum for asking questions and sharing knowledge.
- Power Automate Blog: https://flow.microsoft.com/en-us/blog/ Latest news, updates, and best practices.

Training and Certification Options

- **Microsoft Certified:** Power Automate Associate Official certification demonstrating proficiency in Power Automate.
- **Instructor-led Training:** Available through Microsoft Learning Partners.
- **Online Courses:** Platforms like Udemy, Coursera, and LinkedIn Learning offer Power Automate courses.
- **Power Platform Virtual Training Days:** Free online training events hosted by Microsoft.

CHAPTER 2
Creating Your First Flow

Introduction

Microsoft Power Automate represents a powerful shift in how organizations approach workflow automation, transforming manual, time-consuming processes into efficient, automated solutions. In the previous chapters, we explored the foundational concepts of Power Automate, including its core components, the difference between various flow types, and how to navigate the Power Automate interface. We also examined the extensive library of connectors and triggers that make Power Automate a versatile automation platform, setting the stage for practical implementation.

In this chapter, we will guide you through the process of creating your first flow in Microsoft Power Automate, moving from theory to hands-on practice. You will learn how to design a complete automation workflow from start to finish, including selecting appropriate triggers, configuring actions, implementing error handling, and testing your flow to ensure optimal performance. We will cover essential concepts such as dynamic content, expressions, and flow logic that form the backbone of effective automation solutions.

By the end of this chapter, you will be able to develop a functional automation that serves as more than just a learning exercise. It will be a practical tool you can immediately deploy in your work environment. More importantly, this foundational flow will become your template for creating more sophisticated automations in the future. The step-by-step approach followed here will give you the confidence and practical knowledge to tackle increasingly complex automation challenges, thereby transforming how you approach repetitive tasks and workflow optimization in your organization.

Structure

In this chapter, we will cover the following topics:

- Planning Your First Flow
- Accessing the Power Automate Portal
- Understanding Flow Types in Detail
- Choosing the Right Flow Type for Your Scenario
- Creating Your Automated Flow Step-by-Step
- Selecting a Trigger
- Implementing Conditional Logic
- Adding Actions
- Advanced Configuration Options
- Monitoring and Maintenance
- Best Practices for Long-term Success

Planning Your First Flow

Before diving into the technical aspects of flow creation, it is essential to understand the planning phase that precedes any successful automation project. Proper planning is the foundation of effective workflow automation and can save significant time and effort during implementation and maintenance phases.

Understanding Business Requirements

The first step in creating any flow is to clearly define what you want to achieve. This involves identifying the manual process you wish to automate, understanding its current pain points, and defining success metrics. In this chapter, we will address a common business need as an example: staying informed about document changes in SharePoint without constantly monitoring the site manually.

Consider the frequency of the task, the number of people involved, and the potential time savings. Document these requirements clearly, as they will guide your technical decisions throughout the flow creation process. A well-defined requirement might be: "Notify the project team within 5 minutes whenever a new document is added to the project folder, including relevant file details and a direct link to the document."

Identifying Stakeholders and Impact

Before implementing any automation, consider who will be affected by your flow. Stakeholders might include people who are currently performing the manual task, those who will receive notifications, and managers overseeing the process. Understanding the impact on each stakeholder group ensures that your automation enhances the existing workflows, instead of disrupting them.

In our SharePoint notification example, the list of stakeholders includes document contributors who upload files, team members who need to stay informed about new documents, and project managers who need to track document activity. Each group has different needs and expectations from automation.

Defining Success Criteria

Establish clear metrics for measuring the success of your automation. These include response time improvements, error rate reduction, user satisfaction scores, or time savings calculations. Having concrete success criteria helps you evaluate the effectiveness of your flow and provides due justification for automation initiatives.

Success criteria for our example flow might include: notification delivery within 2 minutes of file upload, zero missed notifications, positive user feedback on notification content usefulness, and measurable reduction in time spent manually checking for new documents.

Introduction to Flow Creation

Before we dive into the practical steps, let us understand what we want to achieve in this chapter.

Creating a flow in Power Automate is like building a digital assembly line for your data and tasks. Each flow starts with a trigger, which is an event that sets things in motion. The trigger is followed by a series of actions that process and move your data along, much like stations on an assembly line.

In this chapter, we will create a simple yet practical flow for an automated email notification system. This flow will send you an email whenever a new file is added to a specific SharePoint folder. This type of automation can be incredibly useful for staying on top of document updates without constantly checking your SharePoint site.

Accessing the Power Automate Portal

To begin creating your flow, you need to access the Power Automate portal. Understanding how to access and navigate the Power Automate portal is fundamental to your automation journey. The portal serves as your central hub for creating, managing, and monitoring all your flows. Here is how to do it:

1. Open your web browser and navigate to https://make.powerautomate.com/
2. Click "**`Sign in`**" on the top right corner
3. Enter your Microsoft account credentials (usually your work or school email)
4. Once logged in, you will see the Power Automate homepage

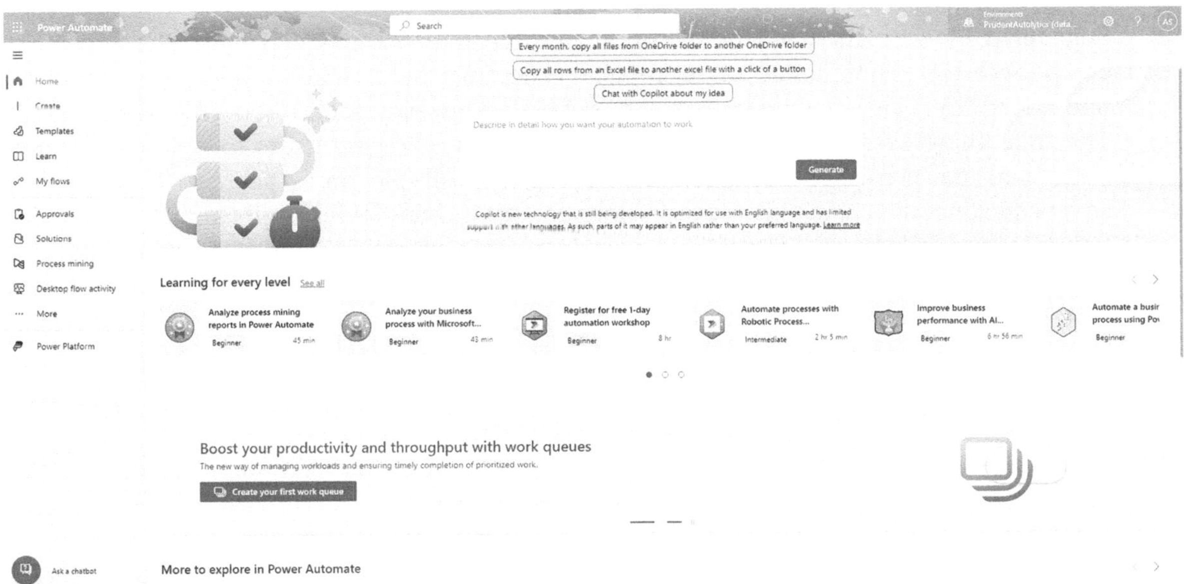

Figure 2.1: *Power Automate Homepage*

Note: *Bookmark the Power Automate portal for easy access in the future. You will be visiting it often as you create and manage your flows.*

Understanding Flow Types in Detail

Power Automate offers several types of flows, each designed for specific automation scenarios. Understanding these types thoroughly will help you choose the right approach for each automation challenge.

Types of Flows

Power Automate primarily offers four types of flows:

- **Automated Flows**: Automated flows are the most common type of Power Automate workflow. They are triggered automatically when specific events occur in connected systems. The trigger events can include receiving an email to updating a SharePoint list item, posting on social media, and making changes in database records. The power of automated flows lies in their ability to respond to events in real-time without human intervention. Once configured and activated, these flows continuously monitor for their trigger conditions and execute their defined actions whenever those conditions are met. This makes them ideal for notification systems, data synchronization tasks, and approval workflows. For our SharePoint file notification example, we are creating an automated flow that triggers whenever a new file is added to a specific folder. This approach ensures immediate notification without requiring anyone to manually check for new files or remember to send notifications.

- **Instant Flows**: Instant flows, also known as button flows, are designed for on-demand execution. These flows do not run automatically but are triggered manually by users when needed. They are particularly useful for tasks that need human judgment about when to execute or for processes that do not have clear automated trigger points. Instant flows can be triggered from various interfaces, including the Power Automate mobile app, SharePoint lists, or custom applications through Power Apps. They often include input parameters, which allow users to provide specific information when triggering the flow. Common use cases for instant flows include approval requests, data collection, status updates, and ad-hoc reporting. For example, you might create an instant flow that gathers team status updates and compiles them into a summary email for management.
- **Scheduled Flows**: Scheduled flows run at predetermined times and intervals. These flows are perfect for maintenance tasks, regular reporting, data cleanup, and batch processing operations. You can schedule flows to run once, daily, weekly, monthly, or at custom intervals. The scheduling system in Power Automate is robust, allowing users to deal with complex scheduling patterns. You can specify exact times, multiple times per day, or even create advanced schedules using cron expressions for maximum flexibility. Examples of scheduled flows include daily backup operations, weekly report generation, monthly data archiving, and quarterly compliance checks. These flows often process large amounts of data or perform system maintenance tasks during off-peak hours.
- **Desktop Flows (RPA):** Desktop flows represent the Robotic process Automation (RPA) capabilities of Power Automate. These flows can interact with desktop applications, legacy systems, and any software interface that does not have API connectivity. Desktop flows record your actions and can replay them automatically or on schedule. Although we will not create desktop flows in this chapter, understanding their existence is important for comprehensive automation strategies. Desktop flows bridge the gap between modern cloud services and legacy applications, enabling end-to-end automation across your entire technology stack.

Choosing the Right Flow Type for Your Scenario

Selecting the appropriate flow type is crucial for automation success. This decision impacts performance, maintenance requirements, and user experience. Let us explore the decision-making process in detail.

Analyzing Your Automation Requirements

The first step in choosing a flow type is analyzing your specific requirements. Consider the trigger mechanism: Does your automation need to respond to events, run on a schedule, or execute on demand? The answer to this question typically points you toward the appropriate flow type.

For event-driven processes, automated flows are usually the best choice. These scenarios include responding to emails, file changes, form submissions, or database updates. The real-time nature of automated flows makes them ideal for processes where timing is critical.

For tasks that need to run at specific times regardless of external events, scheduled flows are appropriate. These might include report generation, data synchronization between systems, or maintenance tasks that should occur during specific time windows.

Considering User Interaction Requirements

Some automations require human input or decision-making at execution time. In these cases, instant flows provide the necessary flexibility while maintaining the benefits of automation for the subsequent steps. Users can provide context-specific information when triggering the flow, making the automation more intelligent and relevant.

You must also know the technical skills of your users in this regard. Instant flows triggered from familiar interfaces like SharePoint or mobile apps are more accessible to non-technical users than complex automated flows with multiple conditions and branches.

Evaluating Performance and Resource Requirements

Different flow types have varying performance characteristics and resource requirements. Automated flows must be designed to handle the expected frequency of trigger events without overwhelming connected systems. If you expect high-frequency triggers, you will need to factor in any throttling and error handling strategies. Scheduled flows allow for more predictable resource usage but need to be designed to handle the full volume of data they process. Consider the processing time requirements and available time windows when designing scheduled flows. We will be using an Automated Flow in our example of creating an email notification whenever a new file is added to SharePoint.

Creating Your Automated Flow Step-by-Step

Now that we know about the planning and decision-making aspects, let us dive into the practical steps of creating our automated flow. We will build a comprehensive SharePoint file notification system that demonstrates key Power Automate concepts. Let us create our new automated flow via the following steps:

1. From the Power Automate homepage, click "**`Create`**" in the left sidebar
2. Select "**`Automated cloud flow`**" from the options presented

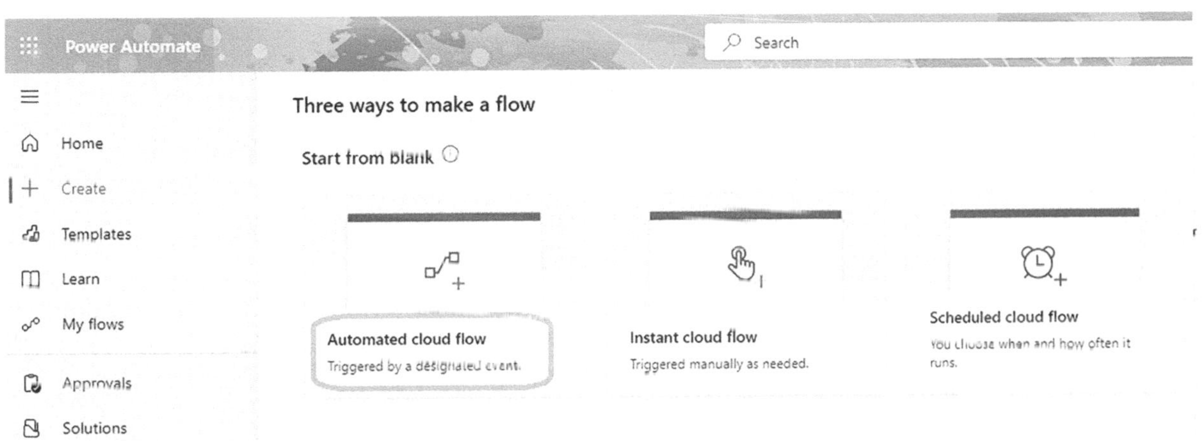

Figure 2.2: *Creating a New Automated Cloud Flow*

3. In the pop-up window, give your flow a name. For this example, Let us call it "**`SharePoint File Notification`**"
4. In the search bar, type "**`SharePoint`**" and select "**`When a file is created in a folder`**" as your trigger
5. Click "**`Create`**"

Note: *Choose descriptive names for your flows. A good name will help you quickly identify the purpose of each flow when you have many.*

The automated flow creation dialog presents you with options for naming your flow and selecting an initial trigger. Give your flow a descriptive name such as "`SharePoint Document Notification System`" or "`Project Files Alert Flow`." Good naming conventions become increasingly important as your automation library grows.

In the trigger search field, type "`SharePoint`" to filter the available triggers to SharePoint-related events. You will see various options including file creation, modification, and deletion triggers. For our example, select "`When a file is created in a folder`" as this matches our requirement exactly.

After selecting your trigger, click the "`Create`" button to initialize your flow. Power Automate will create the basic flow structure and open the flow designer interface where you will configure the details.

Configuring the SharePoint Trigger

The flow designer opens with your selected trigger as the first step. Click the trigger box to expand its configuration options. The SharePoint trigger requires several configuration parameters to function correctly.

The first parameter is "`Site Address`," which specifies which SharePoint site to monitor. Click the dropdown menu to see available sites. If your target site does not appear in the list, you can type its URL directly. Ensure you have appropriate permissions to access the selected site, as the flow will fail if authentication is insufficient.

The "`Folder Id`" parameter specifies which folder within the site to monitor. Click the folder icon to browse the site structure and select the appropriate folder. Take care to select the correct folder, as the flow will only trigger for files added to this specific location.

The "`Include Subfolders`" option determines whether the flow should also trigger for files added to subfolders within the selected folder. For most scenarios, leaving this set to "`No`" provides more predictable behavior, but set it to "`Yes`" if you need comprehensive monitoring of the entire folder structure.

Understanding Dynamic Content

Before adding actions to your flow, it is important to understand dynamic content, which forms the backbone of intelligent automation in Power Automate. Dynamic content represents all the information from previous steps in your flow that can be used in subsequent actions.

When you select the SharePoint file trigger, Power Automate automatically makes various pieces of information available as dynamic content. This includes the file name, file size, file path, creation time, and other metadata about the newly created file.

Dynamic content appears in the right panel of the flow designer when you are configuring actions. You can click dynamic content items to insert them into action parameters to make your flow responsive to the specific files that trigger it.

The power of dynamic content becomes apparent when you realize that each flow run can produce different results based on the specific trigger event. A flow triggered by a PDF file will include the PDF's filename in notifications, while the same flow triggered by an Excel file will include the Excel filename instead.

Adding and Configuring Email Notifications

With your trigger configured, it is time to add the email notification action. Click "`New step`" below your trigger to open the action selection interface. In the search bar, type "`Send an email`" to find email-related actions.

Now, select "`Send an email (V2)`" from the Office 365 Outlook connector. This action provides the most comprehensive email functionality, including support for rich text formatting, attachments, and advanced delivery options.

The email action configuration panel opens with several fields to complete. The "`To`" field specifies the recipient of the notification. You can enter a specific email address, use dynamic content to send to the file creator, or use a distribution list for team notifications.

For the subject line, create a descriptive message that includes dynamic content. A good subject might be: “New file added to [Folder Name]: [File Name]”, where the bracketed items are replaced with appropriate dynamic content from your trigger.

Crafting Effective Email Content

The email body is where you can provide comprehensive information about the new file. Start with a clear, friendly greeting and explanation of why the recipient is receiving the notification. This context is particularly important in organizations where people receive many automated emails.

Include relevant file details using dynamic content. Essential information might include the file name, size, creation date, and creator (if available). Consider also including a direct link to the file using the "`Link to item`" dynamic content, which allows recipients to access the file directly without navigating through SharePoint.

Format your email for readability using HTML formatting if supported. Use headings, bullet points, and clear sections to organize information. Remember that recipients might be viewing the email on mobile devices, so keep formatting simple and content concise.

Consider including actionable next steps in your email. If the file requires review, mention the reviewer and the deadline by which they can do so. If it is solely informational, make that clear beforehand. Providing context about expected actions reduces confusion and improves the overall effectiveness of your automation.

Selecting a Trigger

The trigger is the event that starts your flow. In our case, we have already selected "`When a file is created in a folder`" as our trigger. Now, let us configure it.

Configuring the SharePoint Trigger

Now that we have selected our trigger, the next critical step is to configure it properly to ensure it monitors the correct location and responds to the right events. Proper trigger configuration is essential for your flow to work reliably and efficiently.

The flow designer opens with your selected trigger as the first step. Click on the trigger box to expand its configuration options. The SharePoint trigger requires several configuration parameters to function correctly.

1. In the trigger configuration box, click the dropdown menu for "`Site Address`" and select the SharePoint site you want to monitor.

2. For "`Folder Id`", click the folder icon and navigate to the specific folder you want to watch.
3. Leave the "`Include Subfolders`" option as "`No`" for now.

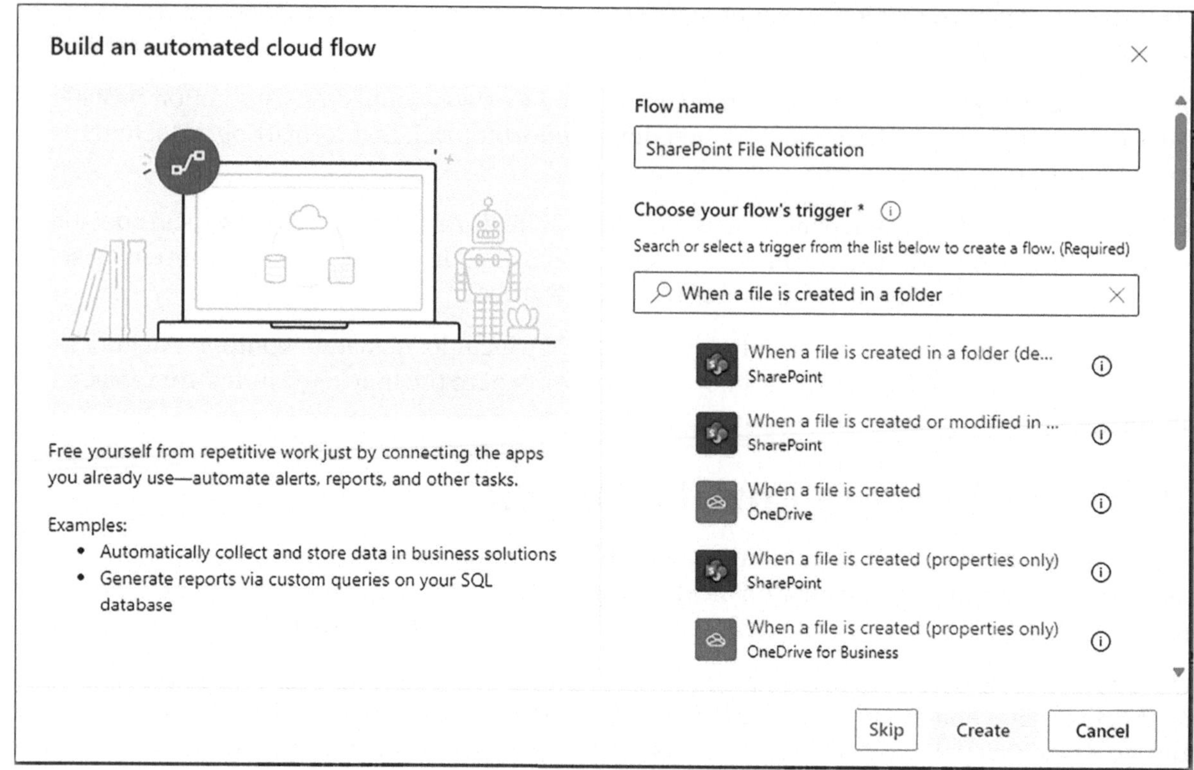

Figure 2.3: *Configuring the SharePoint Trigger*

Note: *Create a connection to the same Sharepoint site if you frequently work with it to save time during future flow creations.*

Adding Actions

Now that we have our trigger set up, it is time to add an action. Actions are the tasks that are performed when your flow is triggered.

Adding an Email Action

For our flow, we want to send an email notification. Here is how to add this action:

1. Click "`New step`" below your trigger
2. In the search bar, type "`Send an email`"
3. Select "`Send an email (V2)`" from the options

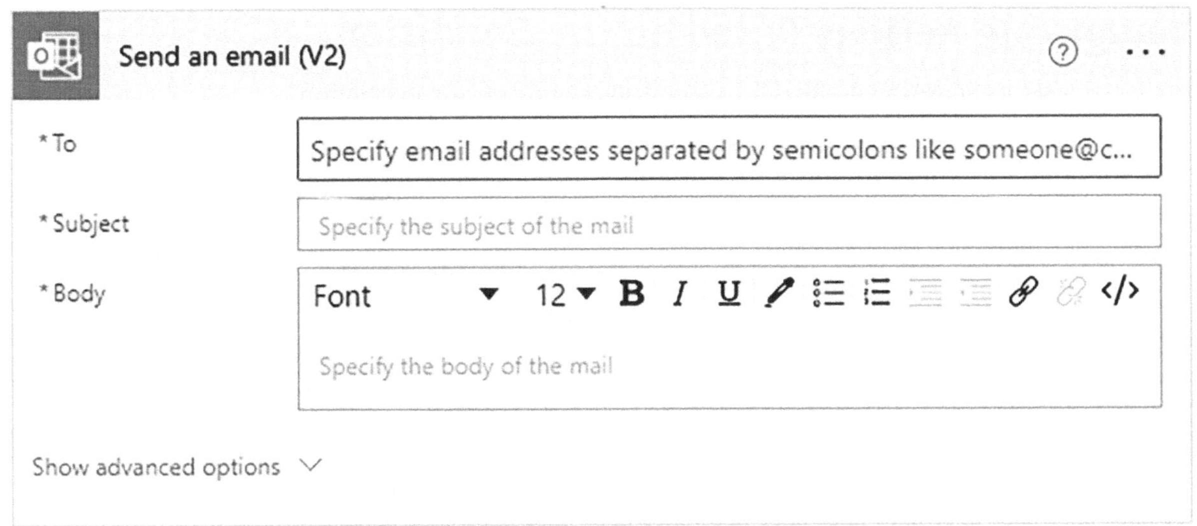

Figure 2.4: *Adding the Email Action to Your Flow*

Configuring the Email Action

Now, let us set up the email notification:

1. In the "**`To`**" field, enter your email address.
2. For the "**`Subject`**", type "**`New file added to SharePoint:`**" and then click "**`Add dynamic content`**" button.
3. From the dynamic content list, select "**`File name`**" to include the name of the new file in the subject line.
4. In the "**`Body`**" field, you can craft your message.
5. Replace the placeholders in curly braces {} with the corresponding dynamic content from the list on the right.

Tip: *Using dynamic content allows your flow to include specific information about the triggering event, making your notifications more informative and useful.*

Configuring Flow Logic

Let us add some basic logic to make our currently functional flow more versatile.

Adding a Condition

To add a condition to only send notifications for files over a certain size:

1. Click "**`New step`**" after your email action
2. Search for "**`Condition`**" and select it
3. In the condition setup, choose "**`File size`**" from the dynamic content list
4. Set the condition to "**`is greater than`**"
5. Enter a file size threshold, like 5000000 (5MB in bytes)

Configuring Actions Based on the Condition

Now, we will set up different actions for when the condition is true or false:

1. In the "**`If yes`**" branch, move your existing "**`Send an email`**" action
2. In the "**`If no`**" branch, add a new "**`Send an email`**" action with a different message for smaller files

This way, you will receive different notifications based on the size of the new file.

Note: *Using conditions allows you to create more sophisticated flows that respond differently to various scenarios.*

Testing Your Flow

Before activating your flow, it is crucial to test it to ensure it works as expected. Testing serves as your quality assurance checkpoint, allowing you to validate that each component of your automation functions correctly and produces the desired results. A well-tested flow not only prevents errors and disruptions in your production environment but also gives you confidence that your automation will reliably serve its intended purpose when deployed.

Using the Built-in Test Feature

Power Automate provides a comprehensive built-in testing mechanism that allows you to validate your flow's functionality in a controlled environment before deploying it to production. This testing feature enables you to trigger the flow manually, observe its execution in real-time, and identify any issues before they affect your users.

1. Click "**`Test`**" on the top right corner of the flow editor
2. Choose "**`I will perform the trigger action`**"
3. Click "**`Test`**" and then go to your SharePoint folder and upload a new file
4. Return to Power Automate and click "**`Run flow`**"
5. Check the run results to see if each step succeeded

Troubleshooting Common Issues

If your flow does not work as expected, here are some common issues to check:

- Ensure all connections (SharePoint, Office 365) are valid
- Double-check the SharePoint site and folder path
- Verify that the email address is correct
- Check if any dynamic content is missing or incorrectly placed

Note: *Always test your flows thoroughly before activating them. It is easier to fix issues during the testing phase than after the flow is live.*

Saving and Activating Your Flow

If you are satisfied with your flow and it passes the tests, it is time to save and activate it via the following steps:

Saving Your Flow

1. Click "**Save**" on the top right corner of the flow editor
2. Review the flow details one last time

Activating Your Flow

1. After saving, you will see a toggle switch at the top of the page
2. Click this switch to turn your flow on
3. Confirm the activation when prompted

Note: *Consider the potential impact of your flow before activating it, especially in a business environment. Ensure it will not overwhelm systems or users with notifications.*

Monitoring Your Flow

Once your flow is active, it is important to monitor its performance to ensure it continues to work correctly.

Accessing Flow Run History

Once your flow is active and running in production, the run history becomes your primary tool for monitoring performance, diagnosing issues, and verifying successful executions. This historical record provides comprehensive details about every instance your flow has executed, making it invaluable for ongoing maintenance and troubleshooting.

1. From the main Power Automate page, find your flow in the "**My flows**" list
2. Click your flow name to open its details page
3. Navigate to the "**28-day run history**" tab

Interpreting Run Statuses

Understanding the different status indicators in your flow run history is essential for quickly assessing the health and performance of your automation. Each status provides specific information about how the flow executed, enabling you to identify patterns, diagnose problems, and take appropriate action when necessary.

- **Succeeded:** The flow ran without any errors
- **Failed:** The flow encountered an error and couldn't complete
- **Skipped:** The flow was triggered but skipped due to conditions not being met

Note: *Regularly check your flow's run history to catch and address any recurring issues promptly.*

Example: Creating a Simple Notification Flow

Let us recap the flow we have created in this chapter:

- **Trigger:** When a new file is created in a specific SharePoint folder
- **Condition:** Check if the file size is greater than 5MB
- **Action (If yes):** Send a detailed email notification
- **Action (If no):** Send a basic email notification

This flow demonstrates the basic principles of automation in Power Automate: triggering on an event, applying logic, and taking actions.

Best Practices for Flow Creation

As you continue creating flows, keep these best practices in mind:

1. Name your flows descriptively for easy identification
2. Document your flows with comments and descriptions
3. Use clear, consistent naming conventions for variables and actions
4. Test thoroughly before activation
5. Monitor performance regularly
6. Update and refine your flows as needs change

Note: *Creating effective flows is an iterative process. Do not be afraid to revise and improve your flow over time.*

Implementing Conditional Logic

To make your flow more intelligent and reduce unnecessary notifications, you can add conditional logic that determines when notifications should be sent. Click "`New step`" after your email action and search for "`Condition`" in the actions list.

Conditions in Power Automate use a simple interface for creating logical comparisons. You can compare dynamic content values against static values or other dynamic content. For our example, let us create a condition that only sends notifications for files larger than a certain size.

In the condition configuration, select "`File size`" from the dynamic content list as your first value. Choose "`is greater than`" as your comparison operator. For the comparison value, enter a file size in bytes (for instance, 1000000 for files larger than approximately 1MB).

This condition creates two branches in your flow: "`If yes`" for when the condition is true, and "`If no`" for when it is false. You can configure different actions for each branch, allowing your flow to respond appropriately to different scenarios.

Handling Different Scenarios with Branching Logic

Move your existing email action into the "`If yes`" branch by dragging it or using the "`...`" menu options. This ensures that the full notification email is only sent for files that meet your size criteria.

In the "`If no`" branch, you might add a different action or no action at all. If you want to log small file additions without sending email notifications, you could add a "`Create item`" action that logs the event to a SharePoint list for tracking purposes.

Consider adding additional conditions for different file types, creation times, or other criteria relevant to your organization. Power Automate supports nested conditions and parallel branches, which enables the creation of sophisticated logic to handle various scenarios appropriately.

Error Handling and Resilience

Building robust flows requires considering the next course of events if things go wrong. Power Automate provides several mechanisms to handle errors gracefully and ensure that flows continue to operate even when individual steps fail.

Configure timeout settings for actions that might take varying amounts of time to complete. Sending emails, for example, might occasionally take longer than usual due to network conditions or server load. Setting appropriate timeout values prevents your flow from failing unnecessarily.

Add "**`Configure run after`**" settings to critical actions. This feature specifies whether subsequent actions should run if previous actions succeed, fail, are skipped, or time out. For non-critical actions, you might configure subsequent steps to run even if the previous step fails.

Consider implementing retry logic for actions that might fail temporarily. Some connectors support automatic retry with exponential backoff, while others might require a manual retry configuration. Understanding these options helps create more resilient automations.

Testing Your Flow Thoroughly

Testing is a critical phase that many automation creators rush through, which often gives rise to problems in production. Power Automate provides several testing mechanisms to validate your flow before activation.

Use the built-in test feature by clicking the "**`Test`**" button in the flow designer. Choose "**`I will perform the trigger action`**" to manually trigger your flow during testing. This approach gives you complete control over the test conditions and allows you to observe the flow's behavior in real-time.

Create test files of different sizes and types to validate your conditional logic. Upload files that should trigger notifications and files that shouldn't, verifying that your conditions work as expected. Pay particular attention to edge cases, such as files exactly at your size threshold.

Review the test results carefully, examining each step's output and execution time. Look for any warnings or errors, even if the overall flow succeeds. Address any issues before activating your flow, as problems during testing often become more significant in production.

Advanced Testing Scenarios

Beyond basic functionality testing, consider testing your flow under various conditions that might occur in your real environment. This includes testing during high-activity periods, with different user accounts, and with various file types and sizes.

Test the flow's behavior when SharePoint is experiencing performance issues or when email services are temporarily unavailable. While you cannot simulate all possible failure scenarios, testing a few common ones ensures that your flow behaves predictably in adverse conditions.

Document your testing process and results. This documentation becomes valuable when troubleshooting future issues or when explaining the flow's behavior to other team members. Include information about what was tested, what scenarios were covered, and any limitations discovered during testing.

Advanced Configuration Options

As you become more comfortable with basic flow creation, exploring advanced configuration options allows you to create more sophisticated and efficient automations.

Working with Multiple Connectors

While our basic example uses only SharePoint and Outlook, real-world scenarios often integrate multiple systems. Power Automate excels at connecting disparate systems and creating unified workflows across your technology ecosystem.

Consider expanding your file notification flow to include other systems. You might send notifications to Microsoft Teams channels for immediate team awareness, log events to a database for reporting purposes, or trigger additional workflows in other systems for downstream processing.

When working with multiple connectors, pay attention to authentication requirements. Each connector might require different authentication methods, from basic username/password to OAuth tokens or service principal authentication. Plan your authentication strategy carefully, especially for flows that would run unattended.

Implementing Parallel Branches

Power Automate supports parallel execution of actions, allowing your flows to perform multiple tasks simultaneously rather than sequentially. This capability can significantly improve flow performance and user experience.

To implement parallel branches, use the "`Add a parallel branch`" option when configuring actions. This creates multiple execution paths that run concurrently, rejoining when all branches complete or at specified synchronization points.

Parallel branches are particularly useful when performing multiple independent actions, such as sending notifications to different systems, updating multiple databases, or performing various validation checks. Be cautious with parallel branches that modify the same data, as this can lead to conflicts or inconsistent results.

Using Expressions for Advanced Logic

While dynamic content handles most scenarios, Power Automate expressions provide powerful capabilities for data transformation and advanced logic. Expressions use a formula syntax similar to Excel functions and can perform complex calculations, string manipulations, and data transformations.

Common expression scenarios include formatting dates for display, extracting information from file names using string functions, performing mathematical calculations, and creating conditional logic that's more complex than simple conditions can handle.

Learn the most commonly used expression functions: `concat()` for string concatenation, `formatDateTime()` for date formatting, `substring()` for text extraction, and `if()` for inline conditional logic. These functions form the base for more advanced expression usage.

Optimizing Flow Performance

As your flows become more complex, performance optimization becomes increasingly important. Poorly designed flows can consume excessive resources, fail under load, or provide poor user experience due to slow execution times.

Minimize the number of calls to external systems by batching operations whenever possible. Instead of making individual API calls for each item in a list, use batch operations or bulk APIs when available. This approach reduces network overhead and improves overall performance.

Consider the timing of your flows carefully. Flows that run during peak business hours should be optimized for speed, while maintenance flows that run overnight can prioritize thoroughness over speed. Adjust your design approach based on these timing considerations.

Monitoring and Maintenance

Creating a flow is only the beginning; ongoing monitoring and maintenance ensure continued effectiveness and reliability of your automations.

Understanding Flow Analytics

Power Automate provides comprehensive analytics about your flows' performance, usage patterns, and error rates. Regular review of these analytics helps identify optimization opportunities and potential issues before they become significant problems.

The flow analytics dashboard shows key metrics including run frequency, success rates, average execution time, and error patterns. Pay particular attention to trends over time, as gradual changes might indicate developing issues that need attention.

Use the analytics data to validate your original success criteria. If you defined specific performance targets during the planning phase, regular monitoring helps ensure those targets continue to be met as usage patterns and data volumes change.

Setting Up Monitoring and Alerts

Configure monitoring alerts for critical flows to receive immediate notification of failures or performance degradation. Power Automate supports various alerting mechanisms, from email notifications to integration with monitoring platforms.

Create separate flows dedicated to monitoring your primary automation flows. These monitoring flows can spot specific error patterns, validate that critical flows have run recently, and alert you to unusual patterns in flow execution.

Document your monitoring strategy and ensure that appropriate team members have access to monitoring information. Consider creating dashboards or reports that provide visibility into automation performance for stakeholders who need oversight but not detailed technical information.

Troubleshooting Common Issues

Even well-designed flows occasionally encounter issues. Developing strong troubleshooting skills helps you quickly identify and resolve problems, thereby minimizing disruptions in business processes.

Connection failures are among the most common flow issues. These can result from expired credentials, changed permissions, or temporary service outages. Develop a systematic approach to checking and refreshing connections when troubleshooting flow failures.

Data-related issues often stem from unexpected changes in source systems. Field name changes, data format modifications, or structural changes in connected systems can cause flows to fail. Regular coordination with system administrators helps anticipate and prepare for such changes.

Performance issues might develop gradually as data volumes increase or as connected systems experience changing load patterns. Regular performance monitoring helps identify these trends before they become serious problems.

Best Practices for Long-term Success

Establishing good practices early in your Power Automate journey sets the foundation for long-term success with workflow automation.

Documentation and Knowledge Management

Document your flows comprehensively, including their purpose, configuration details, dependencies, and maintenance requirements. Good documentation becomes invaluable when troubleshooting issues, training new team members, or modifying flows months after creation.

Create standardized templates for flow documentation that include sections for business requirements, technical specifications, testing procedures, and maintenance notes. Consistent documentation across all flows makes information easier to find and understand.

Establish a knowledge sharing process within your team or organization. Regular reviews of automation successes and challenges build collective expertise and help users avoid repeating common mistakes.

Version Control and Change Management

Treat your flows like any other business-critical system, implementing appropriate change management processes. Before modifying production flows, test changes thoroughly in development environments and document all modifications.

Power Automate automatically maintains version history for flows, but establishing your own change management process provides additional protection and documentation. Consider implementing approval processes for changes to critical flows.

Create backup copies of important flows before making significant modifications. While Power Automate's version history provides some protection, manual backups give you additional control over rollback processes.

Scaling Your Automation Program

As you gain experience with Power Automate, you will likely identify additional automation opportunities. Plan to scale your automation program systematically rather than creating ad-hoc solutions.

Establish governance processes for automation creation, including guidelines for times when automation is appropriate, standards for flow design and documentation, and procedures for ongoing maintenance and support.

Consider the skills and resources needed to support a growing automation program. This might include training additional team members, establishing centers of excellence, or engaging with external expertise for complex scenarios.

Conclusion

In this comprehensive chapter, we have walked through the complete process of creating your first flow in Power Automate. You have learned how to access the Power Automate portal effectively and navigate its various sections with confidence. We covered the critical decision-making process of choosing appropriate triggers and configuring them for optimal performance, along with detailed guidance on adding and configuring actions that meet your specific business requirements.

The chapter explored implementing sophisticated logic with conditions and dynamic content, transforming simple workflows into intelligent automation systems that respond appropriately to different scenarios. We emphasized the importance of thorough testing procedures and established methodologies for identifying and resolving common issues before they impact production operations. Additionally, we covered the essential processes of saving, activating, and monitoring flows to ensure continued effectiveness and reliability.

Throughout this journey, we established fundamental best practices that will serve as the foundation for your ongoing Power Automate development. These practices encompass planning and requirements gathering, systematic testing and validation, comprehensive documentation and maintenance procedures, and strategic approaches to scaling your automation initiatives.

The practical example we built together demonstrates how these concepts integrate to create real business value through workflow automation.

As you become more familiar with these foundational concepts and techniques, you will be able to tackle increasingly complex automation challenges that can streamline your work processes and enhance organizational efficiency. In Chapter 3: Expanding Your Workflow with Connectors, we will build upon this foundation by exploring the vast ecosystem of connectors available in Power Automate. You will learn about integrating multiple systems seamlessly, working with popular connectors like Microsoft Teams, OneDrive, Excel and other third-party services, and creating sophisticated workflows across your entire technology stack. The chapter will also cover connector authentication methods, data transformation between different systems, and advanced techniques for building enterprise-grade automation solutions.

Mastering Power Automate is fundamentally an iterative process that improves through practice and experimentation. The confidence to create test flows and explore different triggers and actions will accelerate your learning and help you discover innovative solutions to business challenges. Every automation you create builds upon previous experience, while gradually expanding your capabilities and enabling you to address more sophisticated business requirements. The key to long-term success lies in maintaining curiosity about new possibilities as you apply the systematic approaches and best practices mentioned in this chapter.

Key Terms

- **Triggers** are the events that initiate flow execution. They can be based on schedules, external events, or manual activation. Understanding different trigger types and their characteristics is fundamental for designing effective flows.
- **Actions** are the tasks that flows perform, from sending emails to updating databases to calling external APIs. Each connector provides various actions, and understanding the capabilities and limitations of different actions helps you design comprehensive solutions.
- **Dynamic Content** refers to data from previous flow steps that can be used in subsequent actions. This data makes flows intelligent and responsive to the specific events that trigger them.
- **Expressions** are formula-based functions that perform data transformation and advanced logic within flows. They extend Power Automate's capabilities beyond simple point-and-click configuration.
- **Connectors** are the interfaces between Power Automate and external systems. Understanding the available connectors and their capabilities helps you identify integration opportunities and design comprehensive solutions.
- **Conditions** are logical tests that create branching in flows, allowing different actions based on various scenarios. They make flows more intelligent and reduce unnecessary processing.

Points to Remember

- Several critical concepts deserve emphasis as you continue your Power Automate journey. Planning remains the most important factor in automation success, so always define clear requirements and success criteria before beginning technical implementation.
- Testing should be thorough and systematic, covering normal operations, edge cases, and error scenarios. Problems discovered during testing are much easier and less expensive to fix than issues that appear in production environments.

- Documentation and monitoring are ongoing responsibilities, not one-time tasks. Establish regular review processes to ensure your flows continue meeting business needs and performing optimally.
- Start simple and add complexity gradually. It is better to create a basic working flow that you can enhance over time than to attempt overly complex automation that fails to work reliably.
- Consider the impact of your automations on other people and systems. Well-designed automation enhances workflows rather than creating new problems or confusion for users.

CHAPTER 3
Expanding Your Workflow with Connectors

Introduction

Understanding connectors is crucial for creating powerful and versatile workflows in Power Automate. In this chapter, we will explore how connectors serve as bridges between different services and applications, thereby enabling seamless automation across your digital workspace. Building upon the foundations established in *Chapter 1: Getting Started with Power Automate* and *Chapter 2: Creating Your First Flow*, where you learned about the Power Automate interface and created your first flows, we will now witness the vast ecosystem of applications and services that can be integrated into your automation solutions. Connectors represent the true power behind Microsoft Power Automate, transforming it from a simple workflow tool into an enterprise-grade integration platform.

Throughout this chapter, you will discover the rich landscape of standard and premium connectors available in Power Automate, from Microsoft 365 applications to third-party services and custom APIs. We will examine how to authenticate and configure various connectors, understand their triggers and actions, and troubleshoot common connectivity issues. You will learn the strategies to select the right connector for specific business needs and combine multiple connectors into sophisticated workflows to transform your organization's productivity. These skills will elevate your automation capabilities beyond simple department-level processes to enterprise-wide solutions.

By mastering the concepts presented in this chapter, you will be equipped to implement cross-platform workflows that were previously impossible without custom code. Imagine automatically creating tasks in Planner when specific emails arrive, generating documents from database entries, or synchronizing information across disconnected systems—all without writing a single line of code. The practical examples and hands-on exercises will give you the confidence to start connecting your digital ecosystem immediately, unlocking new possibilities for automation that can save your organization countless hours of manual work while ensuring data consistency across platforms.

Structure

This chapter covers the following topics:

- Understanding Power Automate Connectors
- Essential Built-in Connectors
- Premium Connectors Deep Dive
- Creating Custom Connectors
- Advanced Connector Scenarios
- Security and Governance
- Troubleshooting Connector Issues

- Real-World Examples
- Best Practices and Tips

Understanding Power Automate Connectors

Connectors are the foundation of Power Automate's integration capabilities. They function as pre-configured API wrappers that abstract away the complexity of direct system integration. Rather than writing custom code to authenticate, format requests, and parse responses for each service you want to connect, connectors provide a standardized interface that handles these technical intricacies automatically. This means you can focus on designing the logic of what should happen when data moves between systems, rather than wrestling with how to make that movement possible.

Defining Connectors

Connectors in Power Automate are pre-built integrations that provide a way to connect your workflows with various applications and services. They handle complex authentication and API interactions behind the scenes, allowing you to focus on building your workflow logic.

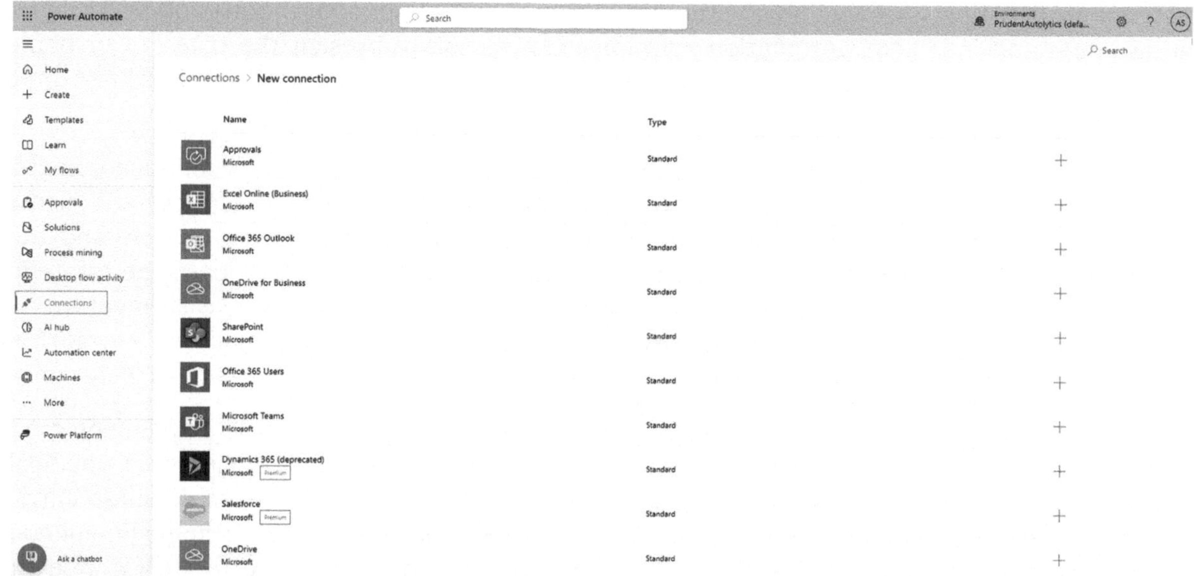

Figure 3.1: *Connectors/Connections Page in Power Automate Showing Various Available Connectors*

Types of Connectors

Power Automate offers the following types of connectors, with each serving different purposes:

Standard Connectors

- Available with any Office 365 license
- Include common services such as SharePoint, Outlook, and Teams
- No additional cost to use

Premium Connectors

- Require a Premium license
- Connect to services such as Salesforce, DocuSign, and Adobe
- Enable more advanced automation scenarios

Custom Connectors

- Created for specific needs
- Connect to internal systems or unique APIs
- Require development knowledge to create

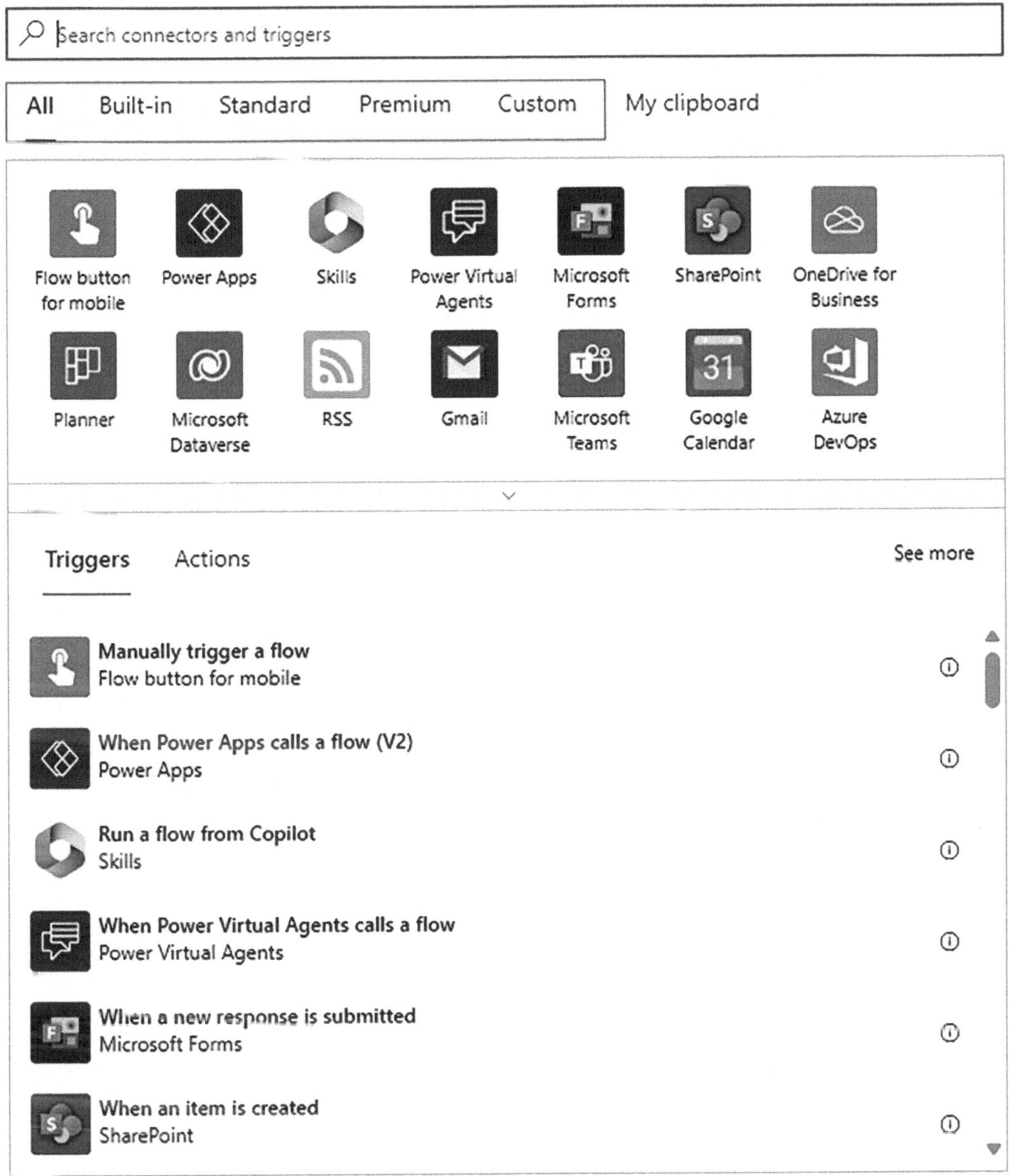

Figure 3.2: *Different Connector Types Available in Power Automate*

Essential Built-in Connectors

Let us explore some of the most used built-in connectors and how they can enhance your workflows.

Microsoft 365 Connectors

The following connectors integrate with core Microsoft 365 services:

Outlook Connector

Example Use Case: Automatic Email Processing

1. **Trigger:** When a new email arrives
2. **Filter:** Contains specific keywords
3. **Action:** Create a task in Planner
5. **Action:** Save attachment to SharePoint

Figure 3.3: *Configuring the Outlook Connector in a Flow*

Teams Connector

Example Use Case: Automated Team Notifications

1. **Trigger:** When a file is modified
2. **Action:** Post message to Teams channel
3. **Include:** File link and modifier's name

SharePoint Connector

Example Use Case: Document Processing

1. **Trigger:** New file in document library
2. **Action:** Extract file properties
3. **Action:** Update SharePoint list

Note: *When working with Microsoft 365 connectors, use connection references to make your flows more portable between environments.*

Data Connectors

Data connectors help you work with various data sources:

Excel Connector

Example Use Case: Automated Reporting

1. **Trigger:** Scheduled (daily)
2. **Action:** Get rows from Excel file
3. **Action:** Process data using expressions
4. **Action:** Update dashboard

The Excel Online (Business) connector provides a comprehensive suite of actions that enable seamless data manipulation and worksheet management within Power Automate flows.

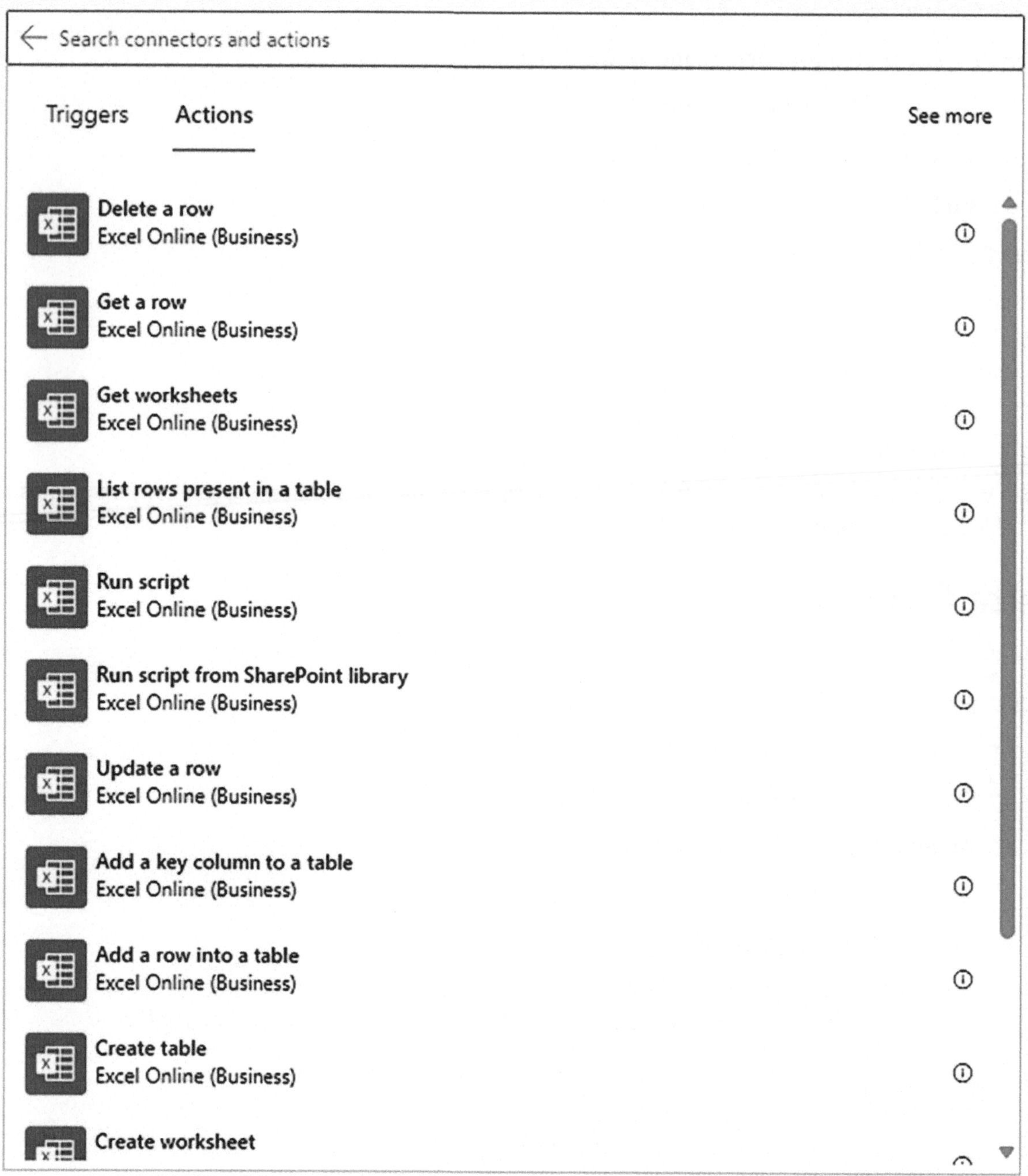

Figure 3.4: *Using the Excel Connector to Automate Data Processing*

Figure 3.4 displays the Actions tab for the Excel Online (Business) connector, showing the extensive range of operations available for automating Excel-based processes. The interface presents various data management capabilities including row operations (Delete a row, Get a row, Update a row, Add a row into a table), table management (List rows present in a table, Add a key column to a table, Create table), worksheet operations (Get worksheets, Create worksheet), and advanced scripting functions (Run script, Run script from SharePoint library). Each action is clearly labeled with the Excel Online (Business) designation and includes information icons for additional details. This comprehensive action set demonstrates how Power Automate enables users to perform complex Excel operations programmatically, from basic data entry and retrieval to advanced worksheet manipulation and custom script execution, thus making it possible to fully automate Excel-based business processes without manual intervention.

SQL Connector

Example Use Case: Database Operations

1. **Trigger:** When a record is modified
2. **Action:** Query related data
3. **Action:** Update connected systems

Premium Connectors Deep Dive

While standard connectors provide excellent integration capabilities within the Microsoft ecosystem, many organizations need to extend their automation reach beyond these boundaries. Premium connectors open advanced automation possibilities across various business systems, enabling you to connect Power Automate with enterprise-grade platforms like Salesforce, DocuSign, Adobe, and hundreds of other third-party services. This expanded connectivity transforms Power Automate from a departmental productivity tool into a true enterprise integration platform capable of orchestrating complex, cross-platform business processes.

Popular Premium Connectors

While the premium connector catalog is extensive, a handful of connectors stand out for their ability to unlock transformative automation scenarios that directly impact revenue, customer satisfaction, and operational efficiency.

Salesforce Connector

Example Use Case: Lead Management

1. **Trigger**: New lead in Salesforce
2. **Action**: Create contact in Microsoft 365
3. **Action**: Schedule follow-up tasks
4. **Action**: Send notification to sales team

The Salesforce connector demonstrates the power of premium connectors by offering robust CRM integration capabilities that enable comprehensive customer relationship management automation.

Figure 3.5: *Integrating Salesforce with Microsoft 365 Using Power Automate*

Figure 3.5 illustrates the Actions tab for the Salesforce connector, highlighting its status as a premium connector, where each action is clearly marked with a "PREMIUM" label. The interface showcases a wide array of CRM-focused operations including record management (Create record, Get records, Delete record, Get a Record by External ID), job processing capabilities (Create a job, Close or abort a job, Delete a job, Get all jobs, Get job info), and advanced query functionality (Execute SOSL search query, Execute a SOQL query). All actions are branded with the distinctive Salesforce logo and a blue color scheme, emphasizing the professional-grade integration capabilities. This premium connector enables organizations to seamlessly integrate their Salesforce CRM data with other business systems through Power Automate, facilitating automated lead management, customer data synchronization, and complex sales process workflows that would otherwise require custom development or manual data entry.

DocuSign Connector

Example Use Case: Contract Processing

1. **Trigger:** When envelope is completed
2. **Action:** Save signed document to SharePoint
3. **Action:** Update contract tracking system
4. **Action:** Send confirmation emails

Working with Premium Connectors

Here are the best practices for implementing premium connectors:

- Plan authentication requirements
- Test in non-production environment first
- Monitor usage and performance
- Implement proper error handling

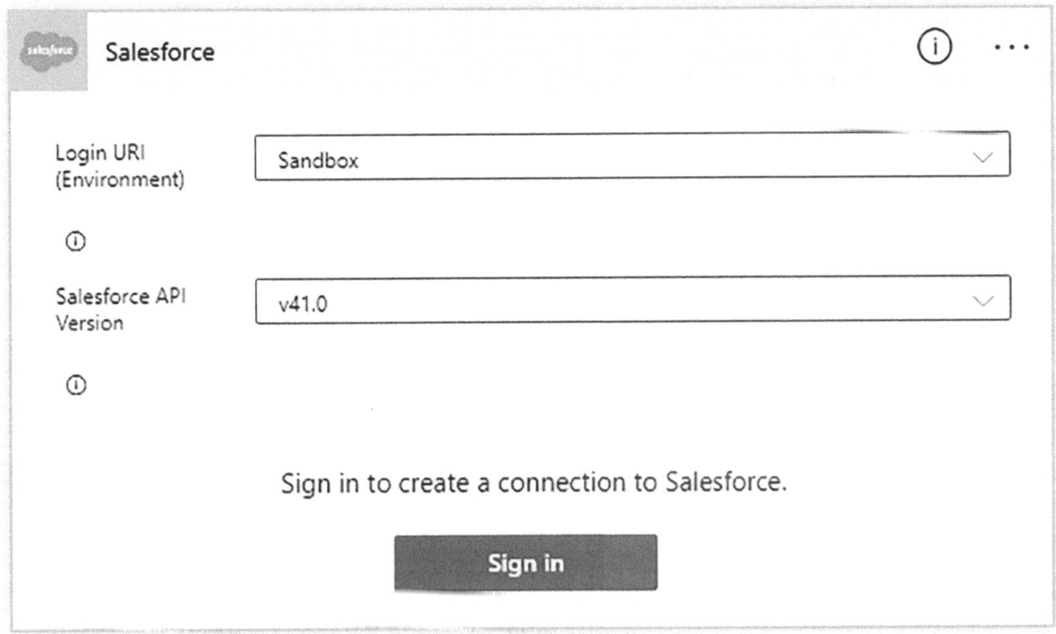

Figure 3.6: *Setting up Authentication for a Premium Connector*

Creating Custom Connectors

When built-in connectors do not meet your needs, you can create custom connectors to integrate with any REST API.

Custom Connector Development Process

Steps to create a custom connector:

1. **Define the API:**

```
{
    "swagger": "2.0",
    "info": {
        "title": "My Custom API",
        "version": "1.0"
    },
    "host": "api.example.com",
    "basePath": "/v1"
}
```

Figure 3.7: *Define API*

2. **Configure Authentication:**
    a. Choose authentication type (OAuth 2.0, API Key, and so on)
    b. Set up security definitions
    c. Test authentication flow
3. **Define Operations:**
    a. Specify available actions and triggers
    b. Configure request/response parameters
    c. Add test examples

Testing and Debugging Custom Connectors

Implement thorough testing procedures:

- Test each operation individually
- Verify error handling
- Validate response parsing
- Check performance under load

Advanced Connector Scenarios

Let us explore some advanced ways to use connectors in your workflows:

Combining Multiple Connectors

Single connectors automate tasks, but combining multiple connectors automates entire business processes, eliminating the manual handoffs and context switching that consume hours of your team's valuable time each day.

Example: Customer Onboarding Automation

1. **Trigger:** New customer in CRM
2. **Actions:**
    a. Create SharePoint site (SharePoint connector)
    b. Set up Teams channel (Teams connector)

c. Generate welcome documents (Word connector)
d. Send for signature (DocuSign connector)
e. Update customer record (CRM connector)

Error Handling with Connectors

Implement robust error handling with the following steps:

Try-Catch Pattern

1. Configure run after conditions
2. Add parallel branches for error handling
3. Implements retry policies
4. Log errors appropriately

Security and Governance

Understanding security implications when working with connectors is crucial. Every connector you add to your environment creates an authenticated pathway that extends your security perimeter beyond your organization's direct control, often into third-party cloud services. Without proper governance, a connector configured by one department could unintentionally share confidential financial data with a marketing automation platform, or a developer's test connector could remain active in production with full administrative privileges. Real-world breaches have occurred when organizations failed to audit connector permissions regularly, allowing former employees' connections to remain active or test accounts with weak credentials to persist in production environments.

Connection Security

Follow these best practices for secure connector usage:

- Use managed identities where possible
- Regularly rotate credentials
- Implement least privilege access
- Monitor connection usage

Data Loss Prevention (DLP)

Implementing DLP policies:

- Classify connectors by risk level
- Define business data policies
- Monitor and audit connector usage
- Enforce compliance requirements

Troubleshooting Connector Issues

Here are some common connector issues and their solutions:

Connection Problems

Here are some troubleshooting steps to follow when you encounter connection issues:

1. Verify authentication status
2. Check permission levels
3. Validate network connectivity
4. Review service health

Performance Optimization

Follow these tips for optimal connector performance:

- Implement pagination for large datasets
- Use batch operations where available
- Optimize polling intervals
- Cache frequently used data

Real-World Examples

Let us examine some practical applications of connectors in business scenarios.

HR Process Automation: Developing Employee On-boarding Flow

Example: Employee On-boarding Flow

1. **Trigger:** New employee record in HR system
2. **Actions:**
    a. Create user accounts (Azure AD connector)
    b. Set up workstation (ServiceNow connector)
    c. Schedule orientation (Outlook connector)
    d. Generate paperwork (SharePoint connector)

```
Example: Employee Onboarding Flow
1. Trigger: New employee record in HR system
2. Actions:
   - Create user accounts (Azure AD connector)
   - Set up workstation (ServiceNow connector)
   - Schedule orientation (Outlook connector)
   - Generate paperwork (SharePoint connector)
```

Figure 3.8: *Trigger and Actions for Employee On-boarding Flow*

Sales Process Integration: Developing power automate flow for Lead to Order Process

Example: Lead to Order Process

1. **Trigger:** New lead in CRM
2. **Actions:**
   a. Enrich lead data (LinkedIn connector)
   b. Create opportunity (Salesforce connector)
   c. Schedule follow-up (Teams connector)
   d. Generate quote (PDF connector)

```
Example: Lead to Order Process
1. Trigger: New lead in CRM
2. Actions:
   - Enrich lead data (LinkedIn connector)
   - Create opportunity (Salesforce connector)
   - Schedule follow-up (Teams connector)
   - Generate quote (PDF connector)
```

***Figure 3.9:** Trigger and Actions for Lead to Order Process Flow*

Best Practices and Tips

Conclude with the following best practices to work with connectors:

- Documentation and Naming:
  - Use clear, consistent naming conventions
  - Document connector configurations
  - Maintain connection inventory
- Performance and Scalability:
  - Monitor usage patterns
  - Implement error handling
  - Use batch operations where possible
- Security and Compliance:
  - Regular security reviews
  - Audit connector usage
  - Maintain compliance requirements
- Maintenance and Updates:
  - Regular connection testing
  - Version control for custom connectors
  - Update monitoring and management

Conclusion

In this chapter, we explored the powerful world of connectors in Power Automate and how they serve as the foundation for comprehensive workflow automation. From essential built-in connectors for Microsoft 365 services, to premium connectors for enterprise applications and even custom connectors for specialized needs, you now know about integrating diverse systems into your automation strategy. We have examined real-world scenarios in HR and sales processes, discussed security considerations, and provided troubleshooting techniques to help you overcome common challenges. By implementing the best practices outlined for documentation, performance optimization, security compliance, and ongoing maintenance, you can create robust, scalable automation solutions that connect your organization's digital ecosystem seamlessly and reliably.

As we move forward to *Chapter 4, Working with Conditional Logic*, you will learn about adding intelligence to your connected workflows by implementing decision-making capabilities. You will also discover how to create flows that can evaluate conditions, take different paths based on data values, and handle complex business rules—transforming your automations from simple sequential processes into adaptive solutions that respond dynamically to changing scenarios. The conditional logic skills you will gain will perfectly complement your connector knowledge, allowing you to build even more sophisticated automations that connect systems, while making smart decisions about how information flows between them.

Multiple Choice Questions

1. What role do connectors play in Power Automate?
   a. Store workflow templates
   b. Act as bridges between different services and applications
   c. Create visual dashboards
   d. Manage user permissions
2. Which connector type requires NO additional licensing fees?
   a. Premium Connectors
   b. Custom Connectors
   c. Standard Connectors
   d. Enterprise Connectors
3. You want to automatically create Planner Tasks when specific emails arrive. Which connector combination would you use?
   a. Teams + SharePoint
   b. Outlook + Planner
   c. Excel + Word
   d. Salesforce + DocuSign
4. What is the biggest advantage of Premium Connectors over Standard ones?
   a. They are faster
   b. They connect to enterprise services like Salesforce and DocuSign

   c. They are easier to configure
   d. They work offline

5. When should you create a Custom Connector?
   a. When you want to save money
   b. When standard connectors are too slow
   c. When you need to connect to your company's unique internal system
   d. When you want better security

6. In error handling, what does the "try-catch" pattern help you achieve?
   a. Faster workflow execution
   b. Automatic retry when things go wrong
   c. Better user interface
   d. Reduced licensing costs

7. What is the FIRST step when troubleshooting a connector that will not work?
   a. Restart Power Automate
   b. Create a new flow
   c. Check if authentication/login is still valid
   d. Contact Microsoft support

8. For handling large datasets efficiently, you should:
   a. Create multiple flows
   b. Use pagination to process data in chunks
   c. Increase the polling frequency
   d. Switch to premium connectors

9. Which security practice is most important for enterprise connector usage?
   a. Using the same password for all connections
   b. Sharing connector credentials across teams
   c. Using managed identities where possible
   d. Storing passwords in Excel files

10. What makes Power Automate truly powerful according to the chapter?
    a. Its user-friendly interface
    b. The vast ecosystem of connectors that transform it into an enterprise integration platform
    c. Its low cost
    d. Its Microsoft branding

Answers

1. b
2. c
3. b
4. b
5. c
6. b
7. c
8. b
9. c
10. b

CHAPTER 4
Working with Conditional Logic

Introduction

In Power Automate, conditional logic is the decision-maker in your flows and determines how your automation should respond to different situations. This chapter will explore how to implement intelligent decision-making in your flows through various conditional logic techniques. Building on the foundations established in previous chapters where we explored the Power Automate interface, creating basic flows, and connecting to various data sources, we will now learn about adding conditional intelligence to your automations.

Throughout this chapter, you will learn essential conditional structures including condition cards, switch statements, and apply to each loop that form the backbone of complex business logic. We will examine how to create expressions that evaluate multiple conditions, work with various data types in comparisons, and implement nested decision paths. These techniques will enable you to build flows that can adapt dynamically to changing business requirements and handle exceptions gracefully.

By mastering the concepts presented in this chapter, you will be equipped to implement sophisticated decision-making capabilities in your workflows. You will be able to create automations that intelligently route documents based on content, send notifications only when specific criteria are met, and process records differently depending on their attributes. These skills will transform your Power Automate solutions from simple sequential processes into intelligent systems capable of handling the complexity of real-world business scenarios.

Structure

This chapter covers the following topics:

- Understanding Conditional Logic in Power Automate
  - Basic Principles of Conditional Logic
  - Types of Conditions
  - Implementing Basic Conditions
    - Single Condition Flows
    - Multiple Conditions
  - Advanced Conditional Logic
    - Nested Conditions
    - Switch Statements
  - Working with Expressions in Conditions
    - Basic Expressions
    - Complex Expressions

    - Error Handling in Conditional Logic
        - Try-Catch Patterns
        - Condition-Based Error Handling
    - Real-World Applications
        - Document Management System
        - Customer Service Automation
    - Performance Optimization
        - Condition Ordering
        - Reducing Complexity
    - Testing and Troubleshooting
        - Test Scenarios
        - Debugging Techniques
    - Best Practices and Guidelines
        - Design Principles
        - Implementation Guidelines
- Performance Optimization and API Consumption
    - Understanding API Consumption
    - Common API Consumption Pitfalls
    - Optimization Strategies
    - Monitoring and Managing API Usage
    - Cost-Effective Design Patterns
    - Real-World Optimization Example
- Mastering Compose and Related Actions
    - Understanding the Compose Action
    - Strategic Uses of Compose
    - Advanced Compose Techniques
    - Related Actions
        - Initialize Variable
        - Set Variable
    - Using Parse JSON Action
    - Debugging Strategies Using Compose
    - Best Practices for Using Compose

Understanding Conditional Logic in Power Automate

Conditional logic is important as it creates dynamic and responsive flows. Think of it as teaching your flow to make decisions, much like how a traffic controller directs vehicles based on different conditions.

Basic Principles of Conditional Logic

At its core, conditional logic in Power Automate evaluates conditions and executes different actions based on whether these conditions are true or false. Let us understand this with a simple example:

```
Example: Email Priority Handling

If (Email Priority = "High")
    Then: Send immediate notification to manager
    Create urgent task
Else:
    Add to regular processing queue
```

Figure 4.1: *Basic Conditional Logic Structure in Power Automate*

This simple example demonstrates how a flow can take different paths based on a single condition. However, real-world scenarios often require more complex decision-making.

Types of Conditions

Power Automate supports various types of conditions to handle different scenarios:

- Simple Conditions:
    - Equal to
    - Not equal to
    - Greater than
    - Less than
    - Contains
    - Starts with
    - Ends with
- Complex Conditions:
    - Multiple conditions using AND/OR
    - Nested conditions
    - Dynamic expressions

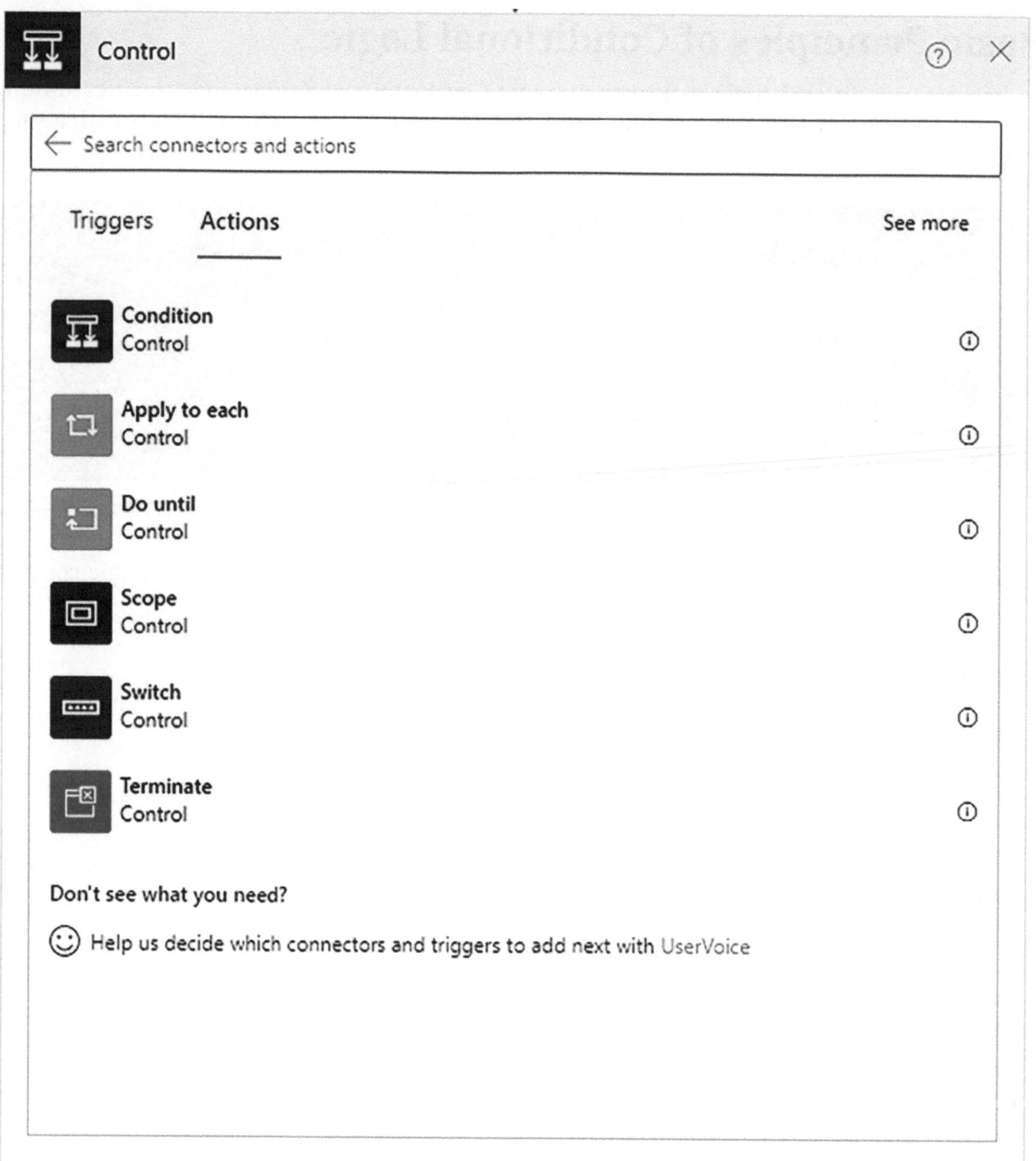

Figure 4.2: *Basic Conditional Actions in Power Automate*

Implementing Basic Conditions

Conditional logic forms the foundation of intelligent workflow automation, enabling your flows to make decisions and adapt their behavior based on specific criteria. Let us explore how to implement basic conditional logic in your flows through practical examples.

Understanding how to structure and implement conditions properly is essential for creating effective automated workflows. Basic conditions allow you to evaluate data, compare values, and direct your flow's execution path based on whether certain criteria are met or not. These fundamental building blocks enable you to create workflows that respond dynamically to different scenarios, handle exceptions gracefully, and automate complex decision-making processes that would otherwise require manual intervention.

Single Condition Flows

Single condition flows represent the simplest form of conditional logic, where your workflow evaluates one specific criterion and takes action based on whether that condition is true or false. These straightforward decision points are ideal for scenarios where you need to check a single value, status, or attribute before proceeding with subsequent actions.

In single condition implementations, the workflow follows a binary decision path: if the condition evaluates to true, one set of actions executes; if it evaluates to false, either an alternative set of actions runs or the workflow simply continues without taking the conditional action. This basic pattern forms the building block for more complex conditional logic and is commonly used for tasks such as validating input data, checking approval statuses, verifying user permissions, or confirming that required fields contain values before processing.

Mastering single condition flows provides the foundation you need to build more sophisticated multi-condition workflows and nested decision structures.

Example: Document Approval Process

```
Scenario: Route documents based on file size
If (File Size > 5MB)
    Then: Route to senior approver
    Send notification about large file
Else:
    Route to regular approver
```

Figure 4.3: *Single Conditional Actions in Power Automate*

Implementation Steps:

1. Add a Condition control
2. Configure the condition expression
3. Set up "**If yes**" actions
4. Set up "**If no**" actions

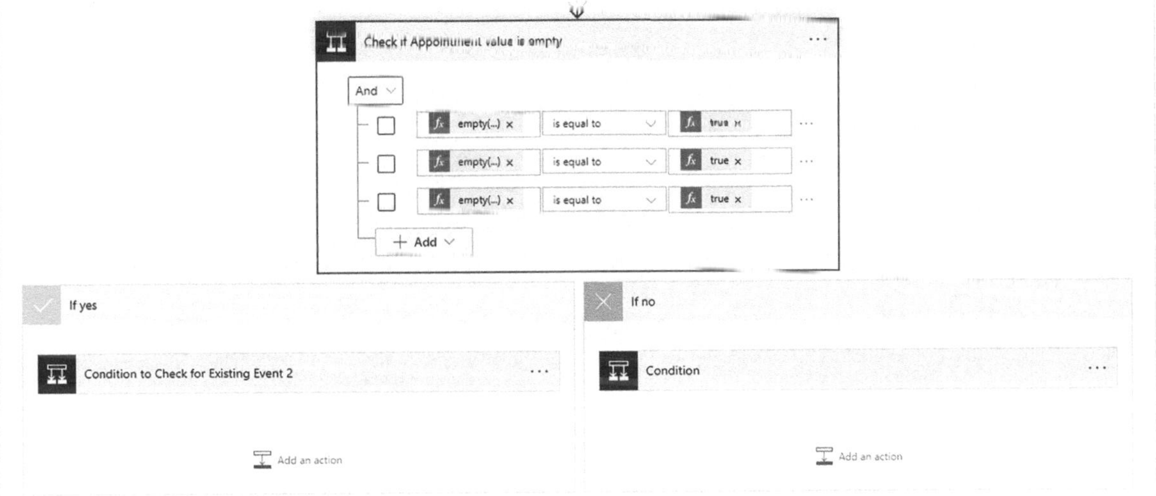

Figure 4.4: *Setting up a Single Condition in Power Automate*

Note: *Always test your conditions with edge cases to ensure robust handling.*

Multiple Conditions

Sometimes you need to evaluate multiple conditions simultaneously as in the following figure:

```
Example: Expense Approval Workflow

If (Amount > 1000 AND Department = "Sales")
    Then: Route to Sales Director
Else If (Amount > 500)
    Then: Route to Department Manager
Else
    Auto-approve and notify manager
```

Figure 4.5: *Implementing Multiple Conditions in a Flow*

Advanced Conditional Logic

As your workflows grow in complexity, you'll encounter scenarios where simple true/false conditions aren't sufficient. You may need to evaluate multiple criteria, handle various outcomes, or create hierarchical decision trees that adapt to different combinations of conditions.

Nested Conditions

Nested conditions are conditions within conditions, allowing users to create more complex decision trees, like in the following figure:

```
Example: Customer Support Ticket Routing

If (Priority = "High")
    If (Category = "Technical")
        Route to Tech Support Level 2
        Send immediate notification
    Else If (Category = "Billing")
        Route to Finance Team
        Create urgent case
Else
    If (Category = "Technical")
        Route to Tech Support Level 1
    Else
        Route to General Support
```

Figure 4.6: *Implementing Nested Conditions in Power Automate*

Switch Statements

Switch statements are ideal when you need to evaluate multiple possible values. This is shown in the following figure:

```
Example: Invoice Processing

Switch (Invoice.Status)
    Case "Draft":
        Send to reviewer
        Set reminder for 24 hours
    Case "Review":
        Check approval threshold
        Route to appropriate approver
    Case "Approved":
        Process payment
        Send confirmation
    Default:
        Log exception
        Notify admin
```

Figure 4.7: *Using Switch Statements for Multiple Conditions*

Working with Expressions in Conditions

Expressions add powerful capabilities to your conditional logic, paving the way for more complex evaluations. Here are some types of expressions:

Basic Expressions

Basic expressions use simple functions and operators to evaluate single pieces of data or perform straightforward comparisons. These expressions typically involve fundamental operations such as comparing values, checking string content, performing arithmetic calculations, or evaluating dates. They form the building blocks of conditional logic by allowing you to transform and assess data before making decisions.

The following figure demonstrates a practical example of using date comparison expressions within conditional logic to determine due date status:

```
Example: Date Comparison Expression

if(equals(formatDateTime(utcNow(), 'yyyy-MM-dd'),
        formatDateTime(triggerBody()?['dueDate'], 'yyyy-MM-dd')),
    'Due Today',
    'Not Due')
```

Figure 4.8: *Using Basic Expressions in Conditions*

Complex Expressions

Complex expressions combine multiple functions, operators, and logical conditions into a single evaluation statement. These sophisticated expressions allow you to assess several criteria simultaneously, nest functions within one another, and create compound logical tests that evaluate multiple data points at once. By chaining functions together, you can build powerful conditional statements that handle intricate business rules and multi-factor decision-making scenarios without requiring multiple separate condition blocks.

The following figure shows an example of combining multiple functions and logical operators within a single conditional statement to evaluate email content and length simultaneously:

```
Example: Advanced String Manipulation

if(and(contains(variables('emailBody'), 'urgent'),
       greater(length(variables('emailBody')), 100)),
   'Priority Processing',
   'Standard Processing')
```

Figure 4.9: *Implementing Complex Expressions in Conditions*

Error Handling in Conditional Logic

Handling errors properly is crucial for robust flows. The example shown below demonstrates a complete error handling workflow where the system attempts to process a file, handles success and failure scenarios differently, captures any unexpected errors, and ensures cleanup operations are performed regardless of the outcome. This pattern prevents workflow failures and provides clear visibility into processing results.

Try-Catch Patterns

The following figure illustrates a comprehensive try-catch-finally pattern that demonstrates how to structure conditional logic for robust file processing with proper error handling at each stage:

```
Example: File Processing with Error Handling

Try:
    Process File
    If (Success)
        Move to Processed Folder
    Else
        Log Error
Catch:
    Send Error Notification
    Move to Error Folder
Finally:
    Update Processing Log
```

Figure 4.10: *Implementing Try-catch Patterns in Power Automate*

Condition-Based Error Handling

The preceding figure demonstrates how to implement sophisticated error handling using conditional logic based on HTTP status codes. This approach allows for granular response management, where different error conditions trigger specific handling procedures.

In this API response handling example, the workflow evaluates the status code and routes execution accordingly: successful responses (200) proceed with normal processing, client errors like "not found" (404) trigger resource-specific error handling, server errors (500+) initiate retry mechanisms with proper logging, and any unexpected status codes fall through to generic error handling. This pattern ensures that your workflow can handle various API response scenarios gracefully while providing appropriate feedback and recovery options for each type of error condition.

The conditional approach is particularly valuable in integration scenarios, where different error types require distinct remediation strategies to maintain workflow reliability and user experience.

```
Example: API Response Handling

If (Status Code = 200)
    Process Response
Else If (Status Code = 404)
    Handle Missing Resource
Else If (Status Code >= 500)
    Retry Logic
    Log Server Error
Else
    Generic Error Handling
```

Figure 4.11: *Using Conditions for Error Handling*

Real-World Applications

Let us examine some practical applications of conditional logic in business scenarios:

Document Management System

The preceding figure illustrates an intelligent document routing system that uses a nested conditional logic to automatically direct contracts through appropriate approval workflows based on document type and monetary value.

This example demonstrates a hierarchical decision-making process where the system first identifies the document type as a "Contract," then applies progressive value-based routing rules. High-value contracts exceeding $100,000 are automatically escalated to the Legal Department for thorough review due to their significant financial impact and potential legal complexity. Medium-value contracts between $10,000 and $100,000 are routed to Department Managers who have the authority to handle standard business agreements within this range. Lower-value contracts below $10,000 follow a streamlined path to Team Leaders for quick approval, enabling faster processing of routine transactions.

This conditional routing system optimizes organizational efficiency by ensuring that document reviews are handled at the appropriate authorization level, reducing bottlenecks while maintaining proper oversight for high-risk or high-value agreements. The nested structure creates clear escalation paths and complies with internal approval policies.

```
Example: Intelligent Document Routing

If (Document.Type = "Contract")
    If (Contract.Value > 100000)
        Route to Legal Department
        Create High-Value Contract Review
    Else If (Contract.Value > 10000)
        Route to Department Manager
        Set Standard Review
    Else
        Route to Team Leader
        Set Quick Review
```

Figure 4.12: *Document Management Flow with Conditional Logic*

Customer Service Automation

The preceding figure demonstrates an intelligent support ticket prioritization system that uses conditional logic to automatically route and escalate customer issues based on customer tier and issue severity.

This automated workflow showcases a sophisticated decision-making process that prioritizes premium customers while ensuring critical system issues receive immediate attention. When a premium customer reports a system outage, the system automatically creates a Priority1 (P1) incident, immediately notifies the support manager for executive oversight, and starts the Service Level Agreement (SLA) timer to ensure contractual response times are met. For other premium customer issues that aren't system-critical, the workflow creates a Priority2 (P2) ticket and assigns it directly to the specialized Premium Support team, ensuring these valuable customers receive expedited service.

Standard customers follow the default ticket processing workflow, which maintains efficient service delivery while allowing premium customers to receive the enhanced support experience they expect. This conditional approach helps organizations balance resource allocation, meet different service commitments across customer segments, and ensure that business-critical issues are handled with appropriate urgency regardless of customer tier.

The automation reduces manual triage work, minimizes response delays, and helps maintain consistent service quality standards across different customer categories.

```
Example: Support Ticket Prioritization

If (Customer.Tier = "Premium")
    If (Issue.Category = "System Down")
        Create P1 Incident
        Notify Support Manager
        Start SLA Timer
    Else
        Create P2 Ticket
        Assign to Premium Support
Else
    Standard Ticket Processing
```

Figure 4.13: *Customer Service Automation with Conditions*

Performance Optimization

The way you structure your conditional statements directly impacts workflow performance, with small optimizations often yielding significant improvements in execution speed and system responsiveness.

Condition Ordering

Proper condition ordering means structuring your if-else chains so that the most common scenarios are checked first, reducing computational overhead and improving overall workflow response times.

```
Example: Optimized Condition Chain

// Most frequent condition first
If (Common_Case)
    Handle Common Case
// Less frequent conditions follow
Else If (Special_Case)
    Handle Special Case
Else
    Handle Rare Case
```

Figure 4.14: *Optimizing Condition Order for Performance*

The preceding figure illustrates a fundamental performance optimization technique: ordering conditional statements based on execution frequency to minimize unnecessary evaluations and improve workflow efficiency.

This optimized condition chain demonstrates the principle of placing the most frequently encountered conditions at the beginning of the evaluation sequence. By checking for "`Common_Case`" first, the system can quickly resolve the majority of scenarios without having to evaluate subsequent conditions. When the common case is met, the workflow immediately executes the appropriate logic and exits, thus avoiding the computational overhead of checking less likely conditions.

The structure then progresses to "**Special_Case**" scenarios, which occur less frequently but still need proper handling, and finally addresses "**Rare_Case**" situations at the end of the chain. This ordering strategy significantly reduces average execution time because most workflow runs will complete after evaluating only the first condition, rather than processing through multiple unlikely scenarios.

This approach is particularly valuable in high-volume environments where workflows execute frequently, as the cumulative time savings from optimized condition ordering can result in substantial performance improvements and reduced system resource consumption. The technique applies the statistical reality that in most business processes, a small number of scenarios account for the majority of actual occurrences.

Reducing Complexity

When conditional logic becomes too complex with multiple levels of nesting, refactoring it into simpler, more readable structures enhances both workflow performance and long-term maintainability.

```
Example: Simplified Logic

// Instead of nested conditions
If (A AND B AND C)
    Action 1
Else If (A AND B)
    Action 2
Else If (A)
    Action 3

// Use switch or parallel branches
Switch (True)
    Case (A AND B AND C): Action 1
    Case (A AND B): Action 2
    Case A: Action 3
```

Figure 4.15: *Simplifying Complex Conditional Logic*

The preceding figure demonstrates two effective strategies for simplifying complex conditional logic: using compound logical operators and implementing switch statements with parallel branches.

The first approach shows how to replace deeply nested if-else structures with streamlined compound conditions using logical operators (AND, OR). Instead of creating multiple layers of nested conditions that are difficult to read and maintain, the simplified version evaluates multiple criteria within single conditional statements. This reduces the amount of cognitive load for developers by making the logic flow more transparent and easier to debug.

The second approach illustrates using switch statements or parallel branching structures to handle multiple condition scenarios more elegantly. Rather than chaining lengthy if-else sequences, the switch pattern makes way for cleaner organization of different condition combinations, with each case clearly mapped to its corresponding action. This approach is particularly effective when dealing with multiple discrete conditions that do not require complex nesting.

Both techniques significantly improve code readability, reduce the likelihood of logical errors, and make maintenance easier. They also tend to perform better than deeply nested structures because they reduce the number of conditional evaluations needed to reach a decision. These optimization patterns are especially valuable in complex business workflows, where multiple criteria must be evaluated simultaneously to determine the appropriate course of action.

Testing and Troubleshooting

Here are some effective testing strategies for conditional logic implementations:

Test Scenarios

Thorough testing of conditional logic requires creating test cases that cover all possible paths through your workflow, including both expected scenarios and edge cases. Comprehensive test scenarios help identify logical errors, validate decision paths, and ensure your conditions handle unexpected data gracefully

```
1. Happy Path Testing
   - Test most common scenarios
   - Verify expected outcomes

2. Edge Case Testing
   - Test boundary conditions
   - Verify error handling

3. Negative Testing
   - Test invalid inputs
   - Verify error messages
```

Figure 4.16: *Setting up Test Scenarios for Conditional Logic*

Debugging Techniques

Implementing proper debugging strategies from the start makes it significantly easier to troubleshoot conditional logic issues, diagnose unexpected behavior, and validate that your workflows are making correct decisions.

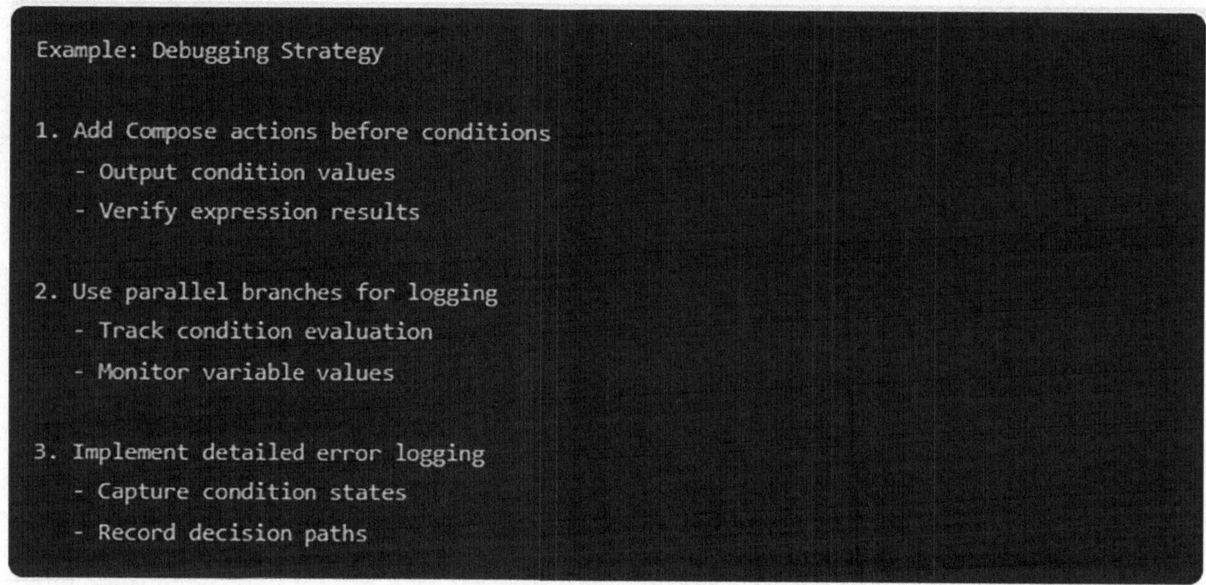

```
Example: Debugging Strategy

1. Add Compose actions before conditions
   - Output condition values
   - Verify expression results

2. Use parallel branches for logging
   - Track condition evaluation
   - Monitor variable values

3. Implement detailed error logging
   - Capture condition states
   - Record decision paths
```

Figure 4.17: *Debugging Conditional Logic in Flows*

The preceding figure outlines a comprehensive three step debugging strategy specifically designed for troubleshooting conditional logic issues in workflow automation systems.

The first technique involves strategically placing compose actions or logging statements immediately before conditional evaluations to capture and output the values being tested. This approach allows developers to verify that variables contain expected data and that expressions are producing correct results before they are evaluated in conditions. By outputting condition values and verifying expression results in real-time, you can quickly identify whether logic failures stem from incorrect data or faulty conditional statements.

The second strategy recommends implementing parallel branches dedicated to logging condition evaluation processes. These logging branches run alongside your main workflow logic to track how conditions are being evaluated and monitor variable values as they change throughout execution. This technique provides visibility into the decision-making process without disrupting the primary workflow functionality.

The third approach focuses on implementing comprehensive error logging that captures detailed information about condition states and records the specific decision paths taken during workflow execution. This creates an audit trail that helps users identify patterns in logic failures and provides context for understanding why certain conditions succeeded or failed during different workflow runs.

Together, these debugging techniques provide multiple layers of visibility into conditional logic behavior and allow the user to easily identify, diagnose, and resolve complex workflow issues.

Best Practices and Guidelines

Here are some essential best practices to follow when working with conditional logic:

Design Principles

Effective conditional logic design balances functionality with readability, ensuring that your workflows not only work correctly today but remain understandable and adaptable for future requirements. These core principles guide you in creating sustainable automation that stands the test of time.

- Keep conditions simple and clear

- Use meaningful names for conditions
- Document complex logic
- Plan for scalability
- Consider maintenance requirements

Implementation Guidelines

Following systematic implementation guidelines helps you transform conditional logic requirements into robust, production-ready workflows while avoiding common pitfalls. This methodical approach ensures each stage of development is completed thoroughly before moving forward, reducing rework and debugging time.

- Start with pseudo-code
- Build incrementally
- Test thoroughly
- Monitor performance
- Document decisions

Performance Optimization and API Consumption

Performance optimization in Power Automate is crucial to maintain speed and manage API calls effectively. Let us understand why this matters and how can we implement efficient solutions:

Understanding API Consumption

When your flow executes, each action typically makes one or more API calls to interact with various services. Power Automate has specific limits on API calls, and exceeding these limits can lead to throttling or increased costs.

Let us examine a common scenario:

```
Example: Inefficient Customer Data Processing

// This approach makes an API call for each customer
ForEach (Customer in CustomerList)
    Get Customer Details (API Call 1)
    Get Orders (API Call 2)
    Get Preferences (API Call 3)
    Update Profile (API Call 4)
```

Figure 4.18: *Comparison of API Calls between Inefficient and Optimized Approaches*

In this example, for just 100 customers, you are making 400 API calls. Now let us see an optimized version:

```
Example: Optimized Customer Data Processing

// Batch API calls for efficiency
Get All Customer Details (Single API Call)
Get Bulk Orders (Single API Call)
Get Bulk Preferences (Single API Call)
Batch Update Profiles (Single API Call)
```

Figure 4.19: *Comparison of API Calls between Efficient and Optimized Approaches*

Common API Consumption Pitfalls

Let us explore situations that often lead to excessive API usage:

- Nested Loops:

  Nested loops represent one of the most common causes of exponential API call growth, where each iteration of an outer loop triggers multiple iterations of an inner loop, rapidly multiplying the total number of API requests. This pattern can quickly exhaust API rate limits and significantly degrade workflow performance.

```
// Inefficient - Multiple nested API calls
ForEach (Department in Departments)
    ForEach (Employee in Employees)
        Get Employee Details (API Call)
        Update Department Records (API Call)
```

Figure 4.20: *Excessive API Usage due to Nested Loops*

- Redundant Data Retrieval:

  Redundant data retrieval occurs when workflows repeatedly fetch the same information from APIs multiple times instead of storing and reusing the data from the initial call. This wasteful pattern unnecessarily consumes API quota, increases execution time, and can lead to rate limiting when the same data is requested over and over.

```
// Inefficient - Repeated API calls for same data
ForEach (Transaction in Transactions)
    Get Customer Info (Same customer multiple times)
    Get Product Details (Same product multiple times)
```

Figure 4.21: *Excessive API Usage Redundant Data Retrieval*

Optimization Strategies

Here are effective strategies to reduce API consumption:

- Data Caching:

  By capturing API responses in variables immediately after retrieval and referencing those variables whenever the data is needed again, you eliminate redundant API calls while maintaining access to the information. Caching is one of the most effective ways to reduce API consumption, as it transforms multiple requests into a single call with multiple reuses.

```
// Store frequently accessed data in variables
Initialize Variable: CustomerData
Set Variable: CustomerData = Get Customer Details (Single API Call)
ForEach (Transaction in Transactions)
    Use CustomerData variable instead of new API calls
```

Figure 4.22: *Reducing API Usage Using Data Caching*

- Batch Processing:

  Batch processing in Power Automate involves using actions like 'Apply to each' with batch-enabled connectors or collecting multiple items into arrays before making a single API call, rather than triggering separate connector actions for each individual item. Many Power Automate connectors support batch operations that allow you to create, update, or retrieve multiple records in one action, dramatically reducing the total number of API calls consumed.

```
// Instead of checking status every minute
Original Approach:
    Check status every 60 seconds (60 API calls per hour)

Optimized Approach:
    Start with 5-minute intervals
    If status changes, reduce interval
    If no change after 3 checks, increase interval
```

Figure 4.23: *Reducing API Usage Using Batch Processing*

- Intelligent Polling:

  Instead of configuring Power Automate flows to check for updates at constant intervals regardless of activity, intelligent polling uses conditional logic to vary polling frequency based on factors like time of day, previous activity patterns, or specific triggers. This strategy significantly reduces API consumption during idle periods while ensuring timely responses when activity is expected.


```
// Instead of checking status every minute
Original Approach:
    Check status every 60 seconds (60 API calls per hour)

Optimized Approach:
    Start with 5-minute intervals
    If status changes, reduce interval
    If no change after 3 checks, increase interval
```


Figure 4.24: *Reducing API Usage by Doing Intelligent Polling*

Monitoring and Managing API Usage

Understanding API consumption patterns and actively monitoring usage is essential for maintaining healthy, sustainable Power Automate workflows. Without proper visibility into how your flows consume API calls, you risk hitting rate limits, experiencing unexpected failures, and incurring unnecessary costs. Proactive monitoring and management ensures your automation remains reliable and operates efficiently within established quotas.

- Implementation of Usage Tracking:

  Implementing usage tracking means adding increment variables or compose actions throughout your Power Automate flows to count connector calls, then writing these totals to a centralized tracking system like Dataverse or a SharePoint list at the end of each flow execution. This custom tracking complements Power Automate's built-in analytics by providing granular, flow-specific data about API consumption patterns that helps you identify which workflows or actions need optimization.

```
// Add monitoring actions
Start with compose action to log start time
Track API calls using variables
Log completion time and total calls
```

Figure 4.25: *Managing API Consumption by Implementing Usage Tracking*

- Setting Up Alerts:

  Alerts in Power Automate can be implemented by building monitoring flows that periodically check your usage tracking data and trigger notifications when API consumption exceeds predetermined thresholds or shows unusual spikes. These alert mechanisms use conditional logic to evaluate current usage against your established baselines and automatically notify administrators through email, Teams, or Azure Monitor when intervention is needed.

```
If (Daily API Calls > Threshold)
    Send Alert to Admin
    Log Usage Pattern
    Trigger Optimization Review
```

Figure 4.26: *Managing API Consumption by Setting up Alerts*

Cost-Effective Design Patterns

Let us examine patterns that help manage API consumption costs:

- Intelligent Batching:

  Intelligent batching in Power Automate means dynamically grouping items into optimally-sized collections before processing them, rather than using fixed batch sizes or processing items individually. This approach uses conditional logic to determine the ideal batch size based on factors like API limits, item complexity, or data volume—for example, collecting items in an array variable until reaching 100 records or a 5-minute timeout, then processing that batch through a bulk connector action before starting the next batch.

```
Example: Invoice Processing

// Instead of processing each invoice immediately
Collect invoices throughout the day
Process in batches during off-peak hours
Use single bulk API call for processing
```

Figure 4.27: *Managing API Consumption by Intelligent Batching*

- Conditional Execution:

  Conditional execution in Power Automate involves using condition actions and expressions to determine whether specific connector actions should run at all, preventing unnecessary API calls when certain criteria aren't met. By implementing checks that evaluate whether data has actually changed, whether required fields contain values, or whether sufficient time has elapsed since the last update, you avoid making API calls that would produce no meaningful results or redundant operations.

```
// Only make API calls when necessary
If (LastUpdateTime > 24hours)
    Perform Update (API Call)
Else
    Use Cached Data
```

Figure 4.28: *Managing API Consumption by Conditional Execution*

Real-World Optimization Example

Let us look at a complete optimization case study:

```
Original Flow: Sales Order Processing

ForEach (Order in NewOrders)
    Get Customer Details (API Call)
    Get Product Information (API Call)
    Get Inventory Levels (API Call)
    Update Order Status (API Call)
    Send Confirmation (API Call)
    Update Analytics (API Call)

// 6 API calls per order
// For 100 orders = 600 API calls
```

Figure 4.29: *Managing API Consumption Case Study*

Optimized Version:

The optimized Power Automate flow restructures the entire processing logic to leverage batch operations and strategic data consolidation, reducing API consumption from 600 calls down to just 7 calls for the same workload. This implementation collects all new orders into an array first, then uses Power Automate's batch-capable connector actions–such as 'Get rows' with filter queries for multiple customers at once, bulk product information retrieval, and batch update operations for order statuses–to process the entire order collection efficiently. By eliminating the 'Apply to each' loop that triggered individual API calls and instead working with arrays and bulk connector methods, this optimized approach demonstrates how thoughtful workflow restructuring in Power Automate can achieve dramatic efficiency gains while delivering identical business outcomes.

```
// Batch Processing Implementation
1. Collect all new orders in array
2. Get all customer details in single call
3. Get all product information in bulk
4. Check inventory levels in batch
5. Batch update order statuses
6. Send confirmations in bulk
7. Update analytics in single call

// 7 total API calls regardless of order count
```

Figure 4.30: *Optimized API Consumption Version*

This detailed explanation of API consumption and optimization strategies helps readers understand the methodology and the reasons behind performance optimization in Power Automate. It provides practical examples and clear implementation strategies that can be applied to real-world scenarios.

Remember, effective API consumption management results in:

- Reduced costs
- Better performance
- Higher reliability
- Improved scalability
- Better user experience

Mastering Compose and Related Actions

The Compose action, along with other similar data manipulation actions, is as a powerful tool for managing data flow and debugging in Power Automate. Understanding how to use these actions effectively can significantly improve your flow development and troubleshooting processes.

Understanding the Compose Action

The Compose action acts like a notepad within your flow, allowing you to temporarily store and manipulate data. Think of it as creating checkpoints in your flow where you can examine and verify data.

Basic Usage Example:

Basic Compose action usage in Power Automate involves adding the action to your flow, providing an input value or expression in the Inputs field, and then referencing its output in later steps using dynamic content selection or the outputs() function. Common basic examples include storing a user's email address, combining first and last names into a full name, or calculating a simple arithmetic result that will be used multiple times downstream.

```
// Store a simple value
Compose Action:
Input: "Hello World"

// Store a complex object
Compose Action:
Input: {
    "customerName": "@variables('customerDetails').name",
    "orderTotal": "@variables('orderAmount')",
    "processDate": "@utcNow()"
}
```

Figure 4.31: *Basic Implementation of Compose Section*

Strategic Uses of Compose

Let us explore various ways to use Compose actions effectively:

- Debugging Complex Expressions:

  When working with intricate formulas or nested functions in Power Automate, Compose actions allow you to break down complex expressions into smaller, testable pieces and view the output of each component separately. By placing Compose actions at intermediate steps in your expression logic, you can verify that each part evaluates correctly before combining them into the final expression, making it easier to identify where errors or unexpected results originate.

```
// Break down complex expressions
Compose Action 1:
Input: "@variables('dateString')"

Compose Action 2:
Input: "@formatDateTime(variables('dateString'), 'yyyy-MM-dd')"

Compose Action 3:
Input: "@greater(variables('orderAmount'), 1000)"
```

Figure 4.32: *Implementation of Complex Compose Action*

- Data Transformation Checkpoints:

  Compose actions serve as verification points in Power Automate flows where you can inspect data after transformations like parsing JSON, filtering arrays, or formatting dates to ensure the operations produced the expected results. By strategically placing Compose actions after each transformation step–such as after using `split()`, `join()`, or `formatDateTime()`

functions—you create a visual audit trail that shows exactly how data evolves through your flow, making troubleshooting significantly easier.

```
// Track data changes through the flow
Compose (Initial Data):
Input: "@triggerBody()"

Compose (After Processing):
Input: "@variables('processedData')"

Compose (Final Format):
Input: "@variables('outputData')"
```

Figure 4.33: *Using Compose Actions as Transformation Checkpoints*

Advanced Compose Techniques

Here are some sophisticated ways to use Compose:

- Dynamic Expression Testing:

  Compose actions in Power Automate provide a safe environment to test and validate dynamic expressions and functions before incorporating them into critical connector actions or conditions that consume API calls. By building and testing expressions like `utcNow()`, `addDays()`, or custom formulas in Compose actions first, you can verify their outputs through the flow run history without risking errors in production operations or wasting API quota on failed attempts.

  ```
  // Test multiple conditions
  Compose (Condition Test):
  Input: {
      "condition1": "@equals(variables('status'), 'active')",
      "condition2": "@greater(variables('amount'), 1000)",
      "combinedResult": "@and(equals(variables('status'), 'active'),
  greater(variables('amount'), 1000))"
  }
  ```

- Array Manipulation Verification:

  When using array functions like `filter()`, `select()`, `union()`, or `intersection()` in Power Automate, Compose actions let you preview the resulting arrays and confirm they contain the expected items and structure before passing them to loops or bulk operations. This verification step is crucial because array manipulation errors can cause 'Apply to each' loops to process incorrect data or skip items entirely, and using Compose actions to check array contents first prevents these costly mistakes from propagating through your workflow.

  ```
  // Track array operations
  Compose (Array Operations):
  Input: {
      "originalArray": "@variables('inputArray')",
      "filteredArray": "@filter(variables('inputArray'), item => equals
  (item.status, 'active'))",
      "arrayLength": "@length(variables('inputArray'))"
  }
  ```

Related Actions: Initialize Variable and Set Variable

These actions work in conjunction with Compose for more complex data handling:

- Initialize Variable for Complex Objects:

  The Initialize Variable action in Power Automate creates a named, typed variable (String, Integer, Boolean, Array, or Object) that persists throughout the entire flow execution and can be updated multiple times, unlike Compose actions which create static, immutable outputs. This is particularly useful for complex scenarios where you need to build or modify data structures incrementally–such as accumulating items in an array variable within a loop or maintaining a counter that tracks processing status across multiple conditions and branches.

```
Initialize Variable (CustomerData):
Type: Object
Value: {
    "personalInfo": {},
    "orderHistory": [],
    "preferences": {}
}

Compose (Verify Structure):
Input: "@variables('CustomerData')"
```

Figure 4.34: *Initialize Variables for Complex Objects*

- Set Variable with Transformed Data:

  The Set Variable action in Power Automate updates the value of a previously initialized variable with new or transformed data, allowing you to maintain dynamic state throughout your flow execution that changes based on conditions or loop iterations. This action is commonly used in conjunction with Compose actions where you first use Compose to test and verify a transformation expression, then use Set Variable to store that validated result in a persistent variable that subsequent flow actions can reference and modify as the workflow progresses.

```
Set Variable (ProcessedData):
Value: "@json(outputs('Compose'))"

Compose (Verify Transform):
Input: "@variables('ProcessedData')"
```

Figure 4.35: *Combining Variable Actions with Compose*

Using Parse JSON Action

The Parse JSON action complements Compose for structured data handling like shown in the following figure:

```
// Sample workflow
Compose (Raw Data):
Input: "@triggerBody()"

Parse JSON:
Content: "@outputs('Compose')"
Schema: {
    type: "object",
    properties: {
        id: { type: "string" },
        amount: { type: "number" }
    }
}

Compose (Parsed Data):
Input: "@body('Parse_JSON')"
```

Figure 4.36: *Implementing Parse JSON with Compose*

Debugging Strategies Using Compose

Here are some effective debugging approaches using Compose:

- Flow Path Tracking:

  In Power Automate, you can use Compose actions strategically placed in different branches of conditions, switches, or parallel paths to mark which execution route your flow took during a specific run. By adding Compose actions with descriptive outputs like 'Approved Path Executed' or 'Error Handler Triggered' at key decision points, you can quickly review the flow run history and identify exactly which conditional branches were followed without having to trace through complex nested logic.

```
// Track execution path
Compose (Path Tracker):
Input: {
    "currentStep": "Processing Order",
    "timestamp": "@utcNow()",
    "flowPath": "@variables('executionPath')"
}
```

Figure 4.37: *Flow Path Tracking*

- Error Condition Monitoring:

  Compose actions in Power Automate can capture and display the values of variables or expressions at the moment an error occurs or when specific conditions are met, providing crucial diagnostic information for troubleshooting. By placing Compose actions immediately before critical operations or within the 'Configure run after' settings to execute on failure, you can log the state of your data—such as variable values, API response codes, or expression results–at the exact point where problems arise, making it much easier to diagnose why flows fail or behave unexpectedly.

```
// Monitor potential error conditions
Compose (Error Check):
Input: {
    "errorPossible": "@empty(variables('customerData'))",
    "errorDetails": {
        "step": "Customer Data Retrieval",
        "timestamp": "@utcNow()",
        "data": "@variables('customerData')"
    }
}
```

Figure 4.38: *Error Condition Monitoring*

Best Practices for Using Compose

Follow these guidelines for effective Compose action usage:

1. Naming Conventions:

   Establishing consistent naming conventions for Compose actions in Power Automate–such as prefixing them with 'Compose -' or 'Debug -' followed by descriptive names like 'Compose - Customer Full Name' or 'Debug - Order Total Calculation'–makes your flows significantly easier to understand and maintain. Clear, descriptive names help you and other team members quickly identify the purpose of each Compose action in the flow designer and locate specific outputs in the run history without having to open each action to see what it contains.

```
// Use descriptive names
Compose (Customer_Data_Initial)
Compose (Customer_Data_Processed)
Compose (Customer_Data_Final)
```

Figure 4.39: *Naming Convention- Use Descriptive Naming*

2. Data Structure Verification:

   Using Compose actions in Power Automate to verify data structures means capturing and displaying complex objects, arrays, or JSON responses at critical points in your flow to confirm they contain the expected properties, array lengths, and nested values before processing them further. This practice is especially important after parsing JSON, receiving webhook data, or building custom objects, as it allows you to validate that the data structure matches your expectations and contains all required fields before passing it to subsequent actions that depend on specific property paths or array elements.

```
// Verify data structure at key points
Compose (Structure_Check):
Input: {
    "hasRequired": "@not(empty(variables('requiredFields')))",
    "dataFormat": "@variables('dataFormat')",
    "validation": "@variables('validationResults')"
}
```

Figure 4.40: *Data Structure Verification*

This detailed exploration of Compose and related actions provides readers with a comprehensive understanding of how to effectively use these tools in their flows. The examples demonstrate practical applications while the best practices ensure optimal implementation.

Remember to use these actions strategically to:

- Improve flow debugging
- Verify data transformations
- Track execution paths
- Monitor potential issues
- Document flow behavior

Conclusion

In this chapter, we have explored the powerful world of conditional logic in Power Automate, from fundamental principles to advanced implementation strategies. You have learned how to create basic and advanced conditions, work with expressions to enhance your flow's decision-making capabilities, and implement robust error handling for smooth-running automations. We have also covered important aspects of performance optimization and testing techniques to help you build professional-grade flows. These conditional logic skills form the cornerstone of creating intelligent automations that can adapt to changing business requirements and are capable of tackling real-world scenarios effectively.

Moving forward, we will examine how to initiate your flows at the right moment, various trigger types, their configuration options, and the best practices to select the appropriate trigger for different business scenarios. This knowledge will complement your conditional logic skills by ensuring your workflows not only make the right decisions, but also start at the right time.

CHAPTER 5
Understanding and Setting Triggers

Part II: The Core of Automation

Introduction

After building a strong foundation in **Part I**, where we explored the basics of Power Automate, including its interface, components, and fundamental concepts, we will now delve into. Part II, which will transform your understanding from basic flow creation to mastering the essential building blocks of sophisticated automation.

Think of Part I as learning the basic vocabulary and grammar of a new language. Now, in Part II, you will learn how to construct complex sentences and tell compelling stories with that language. We will assume you have practiced creating simple flows, experimented with templates, and become comfortable with the Power Automate interface.

Remember, while Part I gave you the ability to create flows, Part II will give you the expertise to craft solutions. Each chapter builds upon the previous ones, gradually increasing in complexity while maintaining practical applicability. By the end of Part II, you will have the skills to tackle complex automation challenges with confidence.

So, whether you are automating business processes, integrating systems, or streamlining workflows, the knowledge gained in these chapters will serve as your foundation for creating robust, efficient, and sophisticated automations. Let us begin this journey into the core of Power Automate, where you will transform from a flow creator into an automation architect.

Structure

Before diving into the specifics, let us outline what we will explore in this comprehensive chapter about *triggers*, which are the essential starting points of any automation in Power Automate. In this chapter, we will cover the following topics:

- Understanding Triggers in Power Automate
- Types of Triggers
- Trigger Configuration Basics
- Working with Core Trigger Components
- Business Scenarios and Implementation
- Advanced Trigger Concepts in Power Automate
- Complex Scenario: Multi-condition Trigger Implementation
- Troubleshooting Common Trigger Issues
- Performance Optimization Strategies

- 10 Essential Power Automate Triggers to Accelerate Your Workflows
- 10 Advanced Power Automate Triggers: Mastering Complex Automation Scenarios

Understanding Triggers in power automate

Just how a car needs a key to start or a domino chain needs that first push, every automated process needs something to initiate it. While we introduced triggers in **Chapter 1: Getting Started with Power Automate**, let us explore their deeper mechanics and sophisticated applications.

The Unique Nature of Triggers

Triggers in Power Automate operate fundamentally differently from actions because they initiate workflow execution rather than performing operations within an already-running flow, and each flow can have only one trigger that defines what event starts the automation. Unlike actions that execute sequentially after a flow begins, triggers continuously monitor external systems—such as SharePoint lists, email inboxes, or Dataverse tables—waiting for specific conditions like new items, modified records, or scheduled times to fire and launch the flow with relevant data passed as trigger outputs for subsequent actions to consume.

Advanced Trigger Mechanics

When implementing triggers, consider these often-overlooked aspects outlined in the following image:

```
# Example: Email Trigger with Advanced Configuration
Trigger: When a new email arrives
Advanced Settings:
    Include Attachments: Yes
    Only with Subject Contains: "Urgent Report"
    From Specific Domain: "@companyname.com"
    Folder Path: "Inbox/Reports"
    Has Attachment: True
```

Figure 5.1: *Advanced Trigger Mechanics*

Note: *Instead of creating multiple flows for similar email triggers, use advanced conditions within a single trigger to handle various scenarios. This reduces resource usage and simplifies maintenance.*

Trigger-Connector Relationship

While connectors provide the bridge to services, triggers determine how we use that bridge. Here is an innovative approach to understanding this relationship:

```
// Advanced SharePoint Trigger Pattern
Trigger: When a file is modified
Connector: SharePoint
Advanced Implementation:
{
    "watchFolder": "/Documents/Active Projects",
    "filePattern": "*.xlsx",
    "trackVersionHistory": true,
    "includeSubfolders": true,
    "monitorMetadataChanges": true
}
```

Figure 5.2: *Trigger-Connector Relationship*

Note: *Create a "trigger mapping document" for your organization that matches business events with appropriate triggers and connectors. This standardizes automation approaches across teams.*

Let me guide you through creating a flow that processes OneDrive files and updates a SharePoint list, which is a common business scenario that demonstrates the Trigger-Connector relationship clearly.

Example: File Processing and Tracking Flow

This practical Power Automate scenario demonstrates how triggers and connectors work together by automatically detecting when files are added to a OneDrive folder (trigger) and then executing a series of connector actions that extract file metadata and log it to a SharePoint tracking list. The flow showcases real-world integration between Microsoft 365 services where the OneDrive trigger captures file properties like name, size, and creation date, then SharePoint connector actions create corresponding tracking records, illustrating how triggers initiate workflows while connectors perform the actual business operations that transform and move data between systems.

Business Scenario

Imagine you need to track when PDFs are added to a specific OneDrive folder and maintain a log in a SharePoint list. This helps teams monitor document submissions and their processing status.

Prerequisites

Before starting, ensure you have:

- Access to OneDrive for Business
- A SharePoint list with these columns:
  - `Title` (default)
  - `FileName` (Single line of text)
  - `FileSize` (Number)
  - `SubmissionDate` (Date and Time)
  - `Status` (Choice: New, Processing, Completed)

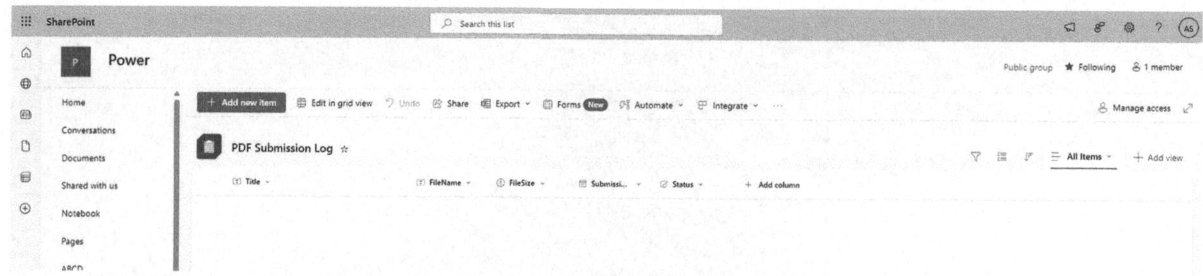

Figure 5.3: *SharePoint List Structure Showing Required Columns*

Step-by-Step Flow Creation

Building this Power Automate flow involves a systematic process where you'll first configure the OneDrive trigger to monitor your target folder, then add SharePoint connector actions that map the trigger's file properties to your list columns. Each step demonstrates core Power Automate development patterns–from selecting triggers and configuring their parameters, to mapping dynamic content between actions, to testing the complete workflow–providing you with a replicable approach for building similar document processing automations across different data sources and destinations.

Step 1: Create the Flow

1. Go to make.powerautomate.com
2. Click "**`Create`**" → "**`Automated cloud flow`**"
3. Name your flow "**`PDF File Tracker`**"
4. Select the trigger "**`When a file is created (OneDrive for Business)`**"

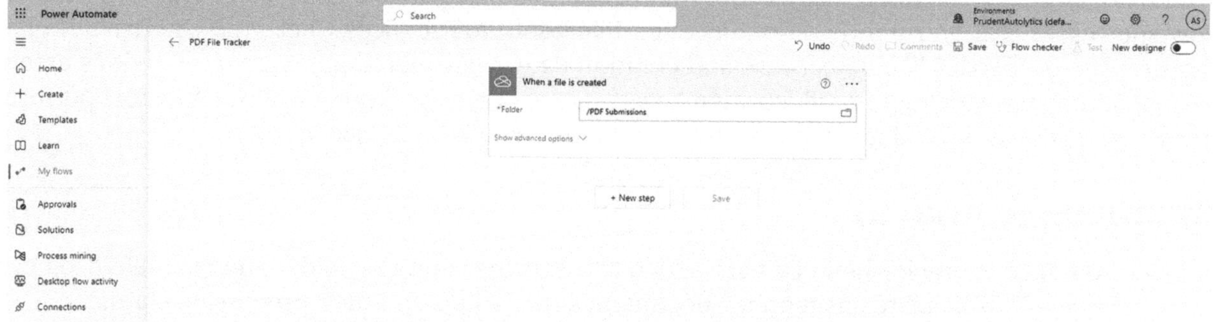

Figure 5.4: *Initial flow creation screen with trigger selection*

Step 2: Configure the Trigger

1. Select the folder you want to monitor
2. Add an advanced trigger condition to filter for PDFs as shown in the following figure:

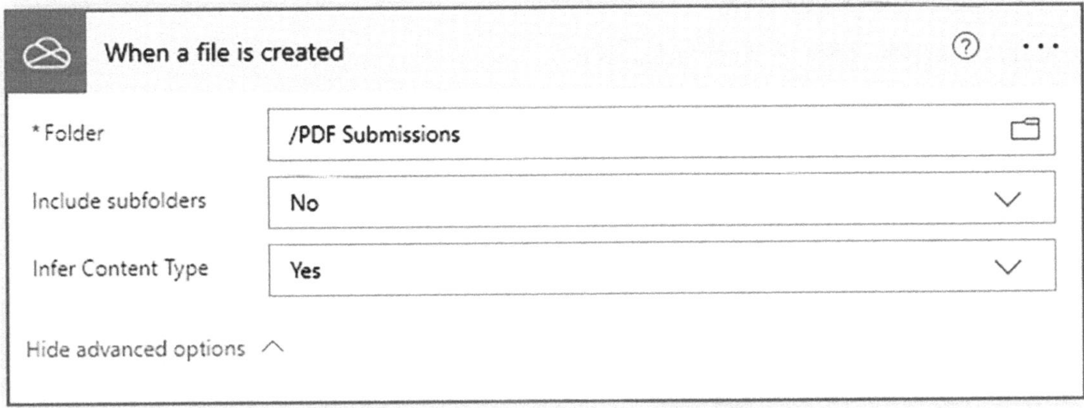

Figure 5.5: *Select Trigger to Kick off the Flow*

Trigger conditions allow you to add specific criteria that must be met before your flow executes, helping you create more precise and efficient automations. By implementing conditions, you can filter events and ensure that your flow only runs when truly necessary.

This configuration screen demonstrates how to set up a condition that only triggers the flow when a file with a PDF extension is detected, showcasing the power of conditional logic in automation workflows.

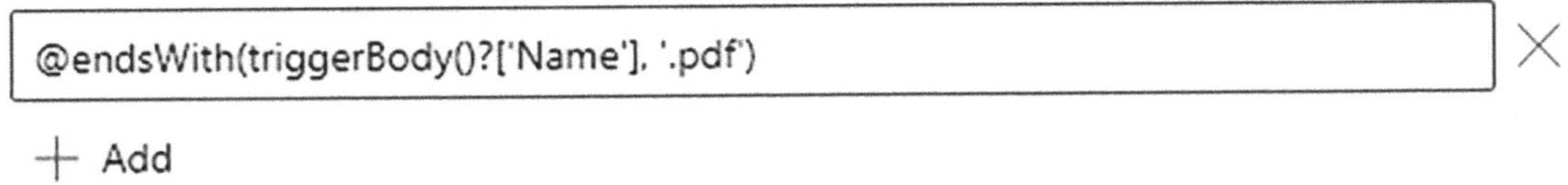

Figure 5.6: *Configure Trigger Condition*

Step 3: Add File Information Action

1. Click "**`New step`**"
2. Search for "**`Get file content`**"
3. Select "**`OneDrive for Business`**" connector
4. Configure to use the ID from the trigger

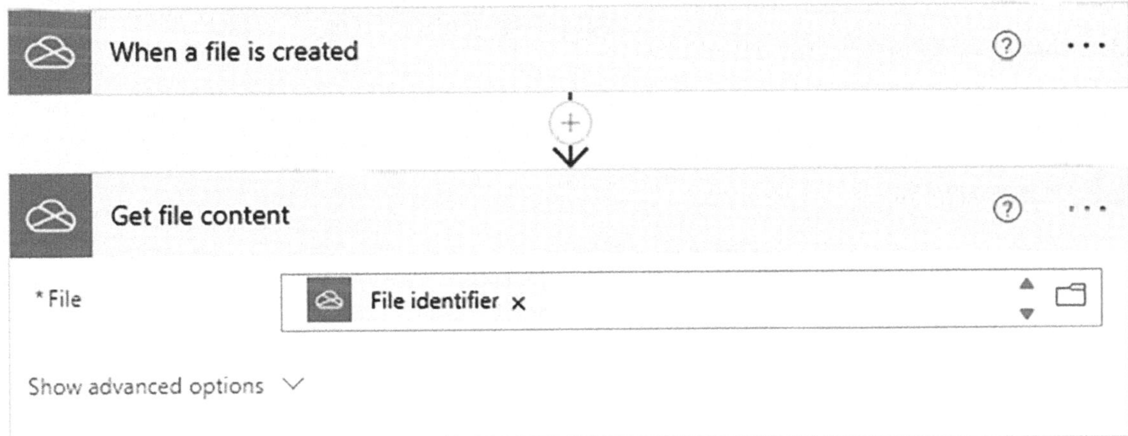

Figure 5.7: *Add File Information*

Step 4: Create SharePoint List Item

1. Add new action "`Create item`" (SharePoint connector)
2. Select your site and list
3. Fill in the fields demonstrated in the figure below:

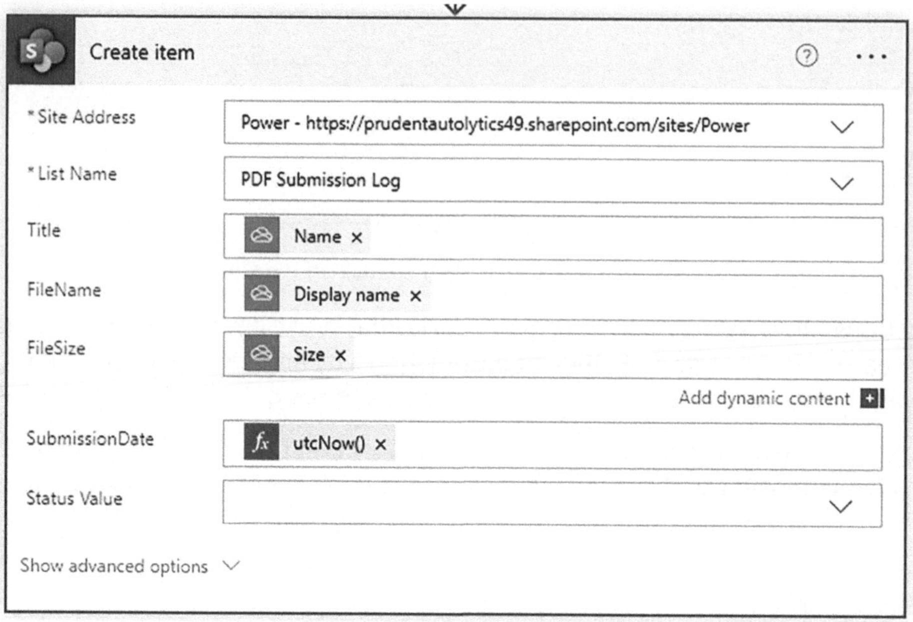

Figure 5.8: *Create SharePoint List Item*

Step 5: Add Error Handling

1. Add a Scope action
2. Within the scope, add your actions
3. Add parallel branch for errors
4. Configure "`Run after`" settings

Testing Your Flow

Test Scenario 1: Upload Valid PDF

1. Upload a PDF to your monitored OneDrive folder
2. Wait for flow to trigger
3. Check SharePoint list for new entry

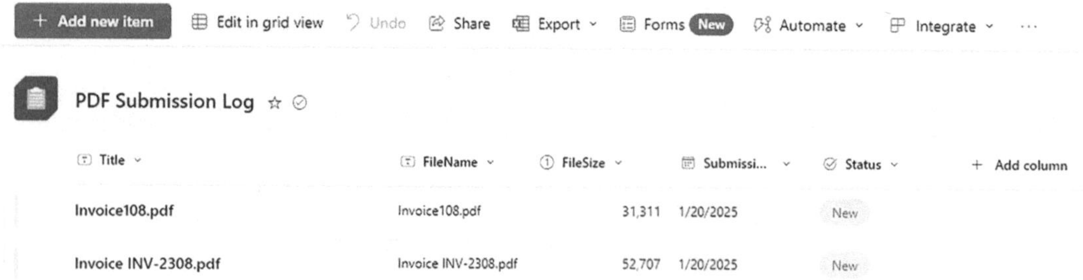

Figure 5.9: *Validating Power Automate for Successful Execution*

Test Scenario 2: Upload Non-PDF

1. Upload a Word document
2. Verify flow does not trigger (due to PDF filter)

Tips and Best Practices

1. File Naming Convention

   Instead of using just the filename, consider this format: `FileName: concat(formatDateTime(utcNow(), 'yyyyMMdd'), '_', triggerOutputs()?['body/Name'])`

2. Dynamic Status Updates

   ```
   // Add a Switch action to determine status based on file size
   Switch(triggerOutputs()?['body/Size']) Case: less than 1MB -> 'Quick Processing'
   Case: 1MB to 5MB -> 'Standard Processing' Default: 'Extended Processing'
   ```

3. Flow Optimization
   - Use trigger conditions instead of flow conditions where possible
   - Initialize variables for frequently used values
   - Add appropriate error handling for each critical action

Types of Triggers in Power Automate

Before diving into specific trigger types, it is essential to understand that triggers are the starting point of any flow in Power Automate. They act as the catalyst that initiates your automation process based on specific conditions or actions.

Automated Triggers (Event-based)

When your flow needs to respond immediately to events happening in your connected services, automated triggers will be your go-to choice. These triggers monitor for specific events and initiate your flow automatically when those events occur.

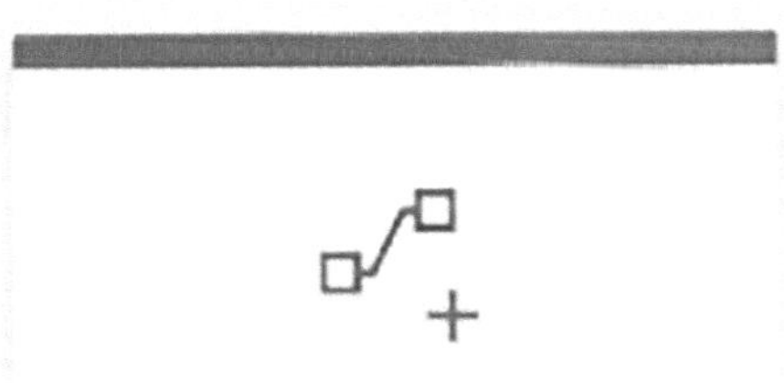

Figure 5.10: *Automated Triggers (Event-Based Trigger)*

Common Use Cases

Power Automate triggers span a wide range of business scenarios, from monitoring communication channels and document libraries to tracking data changes and social media activity. Understanding typical trigger scenarios helps you recognize automation opportunities within your own organization:

- When a new email arrives in Outlook
- When a file is modified in SharePoint
- When a new record is created in Dataverse
- When a new tweet mentions your company
- When a form response is submitted

Real-World Example

Let us say you are managing a customer service team. A case scenario in that event might look like something like this:

```
Trigger: When a new email arrives in shared mailbox
↓
Check if email contains "urgent" in subject
↓
Create high-priority ticket in service desk
↓
Notify team lead via Teams
```

Figure 5.11: *Automated Trigger Use Case Scenario*

Setting Up Email Trigger Configuration

The email trigger is one of the most commonly used automated triggers in Power Automate, allowing your flows to respond immediately when new messages arrive. This trigger provides essential configuration options to specify which folder to monitor and additional advanced settings for precise control.

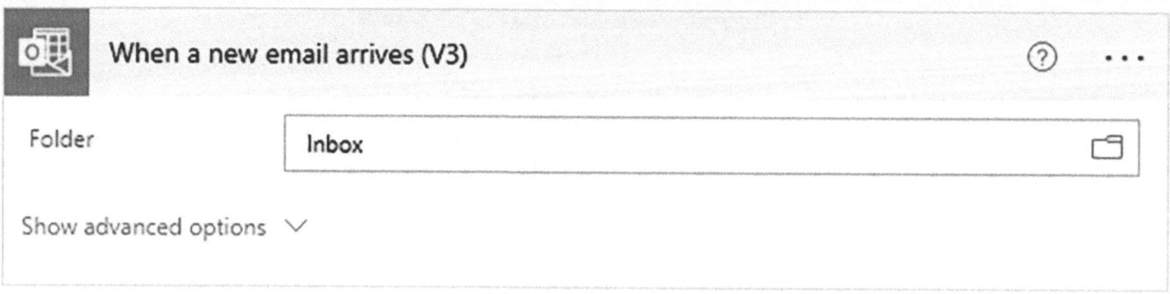

Figure 5.12: *Email Trigger Basic Setup*

This configuration screen shows the fundamental setup for monitoring incoming emails, with options to specify the target folder and access advanced filtering capabilities through the expandable options section.

Best Practices

- Configure trigger conditions carefully to avoid unnecessary flow runs.
- Test thoroughly with different event scenarios.
- Monitor trigger history for unexpected behaviours.

Scheduled Triggers (Time-based)

These triggers run your flows at predetermined intervals and are perfect for routine tasks that need to happen on a schedule.

Common Use Cases

- Daily data backup at midnight
- Weekly report generation every Monday
- Monthly invoice processing on the 1st
- Hourly system health checks
- Seasonal marketing campaign activation

Real-World Example: Inventory Management

A retail business managing their stock levels might use a flow like this one:

```
Trigger: Every day at 6 AM before store opening
↓
Query inventory management system for items below threshold
↓
Generate low stock report categorized by:
    - Critical items (stock < 10%)
    - Warning items (stock < 30%)
    - Review items (stock < 50%)
↓
If critical items exist:
    Send urgent notification to purchasing team
    Create purchase orders automatically
    Update digital signage for out-of-stock items
↓
Send daily inventory summary to store managers
```

Figure 5.13: *Inventory Management Flow*

The automated process shown above prevents stockouts and maintains optimal inventory levels.

Real-World Example

A finance department's monthly reconciliation process might employ a flow that looks like this:

```
Trigger: First day of every month at 9 AM
↓
Export last month's transactions
↓
Generate reconciliation report
↓
Send to finance team
↓
Schedule review meeting
```

Figure 5.14: *Monthly Reconciliation Flow*

Configuration Options

- Recurrence patterns (minutes, hours, days, weeks, months)
- Start time and end time
- Time zone settings
- Advanced scheduling (first Monday, last Friday, and so on.)

Manual Triggers (User-initiated)

When you need human discretion to start a process, manual triggers allow you to initiate flows with or without additional inputs.

Common Use Cases

- Approval request initiation
- Custom report generation
- Document processing on demand
- IT service requests
- Employee onboarding kick-off

Real-World Example: Here is a flow for a marketing content approval process:

```
Trigger: Button click in Power Apps
↓
Input: Content title, type, deadline
↓
Create review task
↓
Notify stakeholders
↓
Track approval status
```

Figure 5.15: *Marketing Content Approval Workflow*

Real-World Example: Employee Expense Processing

An expense reimbursement workflow might look like the following illustration:

```
Trigger: Employee clicks "Submit Expense" button in Teams
↓
Input Required:
    - Expense amount
    - Category (Travel, Supplies, Client Entertainment, etc.)
    - Receipt image
    - Project code
    - Business justification
↓
Validation:
    - Check against expense policy limits
    - Verify receipt image clarity
    - Validate project code
↓
If amount > $500:
    Route to manager AND department head
Else:
    Route to manager only
↓
After approval:
    Create payment request in finance system
    Update expense tracking spreadsheet
    Send confirmation to employee
    Archive documentation
```

***Figure 5.16**: Expense Reimbursement Workflow*

This process streamlines expense submissions while ensuring compliance with company policies.

Custom Triggers

When standard triggers do not meet your needs, custom triggers allow you to create specialized conditions for starting your flows.

Common Use Cases

- Complex business rules
- Multi-condition triggers
- Integration with custom APIs
- Legacy system monitoring
- Industry-specific requirements

Real-World Example

A manufacturing quality control process might have a flow like this:

```
Custom Trigger: Multiple sensor readings exceed thresholds
↓
Evaluate severity level
↓
Alert maintenance team
↓
Log incident details
↓
Schedule inspection
```

Figure 5.17: *Manufacturing Quality Control Process Workflow*

Development Guidelines

1. Document custom trigger logic thoroughly
2. Include error handling
3. Plan for scalability
4. Monitor performance impacts

Choosing the Right Trigger Type

Selecting the appropriate trigger type is a critical decision in automation design, as it fundamentally determines how your workflow responds to business events and directly impacts system performance, reliability, and user experience. Choosing the wrong trigger can lead to delayed responses, resource waste, missed opportunities, or system overload, while the right selection will ensure optimal automation efficiency.

The importance of this decision extends beyond technical considerations to business outcomes. A well-chosen trigger type can mean the difference between real-time customer service responses and delayed reactions that affect satisfaction. It influences operational costs through resource utilization, affects system scalability as your business grows, and determines the overall success of your automation strategy. Understanding the nuances of each trigger type and matching them to your specific business requirements, timing constraints, system capabilities, and resource availability is essential for building robust, efficient automations that deliver measurable value to your organization.

Decision Framework

Consider these factors when selecting a trigger type:

- Timing requirements (immediate vs. scheduled)
- User interaction needs
- System dependencies
- Resource implications

- Maintenance overhead

Trigger Type Selection Guide

To help you make informed decisions about trigger selection, the following comparison matrix provides a clear overview of key characteristics for each trigger type. This matrix serves as a quick reference tool to evaluate which trigger best matches your specific automation requirements.

This comparison matrix allows you to quickly assess the type of trigger that best aligns with your project requirements by comparing response time expectations, user interaction needs, implementation complexity, and typical use case scenarios.

Comparison Matrix

Trigger Type	Response Time	User Input	Complexity	Use Case
Automated	Immediate	No	Low-Medium	Event response
Scheduled	Fixed time	No	Low	Routine tasks
Manual	On-demand	Yes	Low	User discretion
Custom	Varies	Optional	High	Special needs

Table 5.1: *Trigger Type Comparison Matrix*

Tips and Best Practices

Performance Optimization

- Use appropriate polling intervals for automated triggers
- Batch scheduled triggers to prevent system overload
- Implement error handling and retry logic
- Monitor trigger execution history

Security Considerations

- Review trigger permissions regularly
- Implement data access controls
- Audit trigger usage patterns
- Document security configurations

Maintenance Guidelines

- Regular trigger health checks
- Performance monitoring
- Documentation updates
- User training and support

Figure 5.18: *Displaying the Trigger Performance Monitoring Interface*

Common Troubleshooting Scenarios

Automated Triggers

- Connection issues
- Missing permissions
- Event detection delays
- Duplicate triggers

Scheduled Triggers

- Time zone misconfigurations
- Holiday handling
- Daylight saving time issues
- Resource conflicts

Manual Triggers

- Access problems
- Input validation errors
- Response time issues
- User interface problems

Custom Triggers

- Integration failures
- Performance bottlenecks
- Logic errors
- Maintenance challenges

Practical Exercises

To reinforce your understanding, try these hands-on exercises:

- Create an automated trigger for new email monitoring
- Set up a scheduled trigger for weekly reports
- Implement a manual trigger with input parameters
- Design a custom trigger with multiple conditions

Trigger Configuration in Power Automate

Proper trigger configuration is the backbone of successful automation workflows in Power Automate. Simply selecting the right trigger type is not enough; the way you configure these triggers determines their reliability, performance, and effectiveness in meeting your business requirements. Configuration encompasses everything from basic connection settings and timing parameters, to advanced options like error handling, concurrency control, and performance optimization.

Understanding trigger configuration is essential because even the most appropriate trigger type can fail to deliver expected results if not properly configured. Well-configured triggers ensure consistent execution, handle unexpected scenarios gracefully, and scale effectively as your automation needs grow. This section provides comprehensive guidance on configuring triggers at every level, from fundamental settings that get your automation running, to sophisticated options that fine-tune performance and reliability for enterprise-grade implementations.

Basic Trigger Settings

The foundation of any automation starts with properly configured basic trigger settings. These fundamental configurations determine how and when your flow initiates.

Configuration Steps

1. **Trigger Selection**
   a. Navigate to Power Automate portal
   b. Click "`Create New Flow`"
   c. Choose trigger type based on your needs
2. **Connection Configuration**
   a. Set up required connections
   b. Configure authentication
   c. Test connection status
3. **Basic Properties**
   a. Name your trigger
   b. Set description
   c. Configure initial timing settings

Real-World Example: New Customer Order Alert

```
Trigger: When a new order is created in Dynamics 365
Basic Settings:
- Business Unit: Sales
- Record Type: Order
- Scope: Organization
Initial Timing: Instant
Connection: System Admin Account
```

Figure 5.19: *New Customer Order Alert Workflow*

Best Practices

- Use clear, descriptive names for triggers
- Document configuration choices
- Test connection before saving
- Start with broader settings, then refine

Common Pitfalls

- Incorrect connection credentials
- Missing required permissions
- Inappropriate trigger scope
- Incomplete basic settings

Advanced Trigger Options

For complex business scenarios, advanced trigger options provide greater control and flexibility. When basic trigger configurations cannot meet the demands of sophisticated business processes, advanced trigger options become essential for achieving optimal automation performance. These options are designed for complex scenarios that require precise control over timing, resource management, error handling, and system integration.

Advanced trigger options provide greater control and flexibility for organizations dealing with high-volume data processing, multi-system integrations, or mission-critical operations where standard configurations may not suffice. These settings enable you to fine-tune trigger behavior, implement custom logic, manage system resources effectively, and ensure robust performance under varying conditions.

You should consider implementing advanced trigger options when encountering the following scenarios:

- High volume operations requiring batch processing and resource optimization
- Complex business rules that need sophisticated conditional logic
- Mission critical processes demanding enhanced error handling and failover mechanisms
- Multi system integrations requiring precise timing and coordination

- Performance sensitive applications where standard settings create bottlenecks
- Compliance requirements necessitating detailed logging and audit trails
- Scalability concerns where basic configurations cannot handle growing data volumes

Configuration Steps

1. **Polling Settings**
    a. Configure frequency
    b. Set batch size
    c. Define time windows
    d. Configure concurrent runs
2. **State Management**
    a. Set up checkpoints
    b. Configure session handling
    c. Define state persistence

Real-World Example: Invoice Processing System

```
Trigger: Monitor SharePoint folder for new invoices
Advanced Settings:
- Polling Interval: 5 minutes
- Batch Size: 25 invoices
- Concurrent Processing: 3 batches
- Time Window: Business hours (8 AM - 6 PM)
- State Tracking: Enabled
- Checkpoint Interval: Every 50 items
```

Figure 5.20: *Advance Trigger Settings Criteria*

Best Practices

- Optimize polling frequency
- Set appropriate batch sizes
- Monitor system resources
- Implement state tracking

Common Pitfalls

- Too frequent polling
- Excessive concurrent runs
- Missing state management
- Resource exhaustion

Trigger Conditions and Filters

While triggers determine when your automation starts, trigger conditions and filters act as intelligent gatekeepers that ensure your flows execute only when specific criteria are met. These powerful features transform basic triggers into sophisticated decision-making mechanisms that can evaluate data, assess business rules, and filter out irrelevant events before processing begins.

Refining trigger behavior using conditions and filters to process only relevant events significantly improves automation efficiency and reducing unnecessary resource consumption. By implementing proper filtering logic, you can prevent flows from running on every trigger event, instead focusing on processing data that truly requires attention. This targeted approach not only enhances performance but also reduces costs associated with flow executions and API calls.

The strategic use of conditions and filters is particularly valuable in high-volume environments where triggers fire frequently but only a subset of events require processing. Rather than allowing every trigger event to initiate the full workflow, these filters act as an early screening mechanism, ensuring that your automation resources are dedicated to meaningful business scenarios while maintaining responsiveness to critical events.

Configuration Steps

1. **Condition Setup**
    a. Define trigger conditions
    b. Set up dynamic content
    c. Configure expressions
    d. Test condition logic
2. **Filter Implementation**
    a. Configure input filters
    b. Set up output filters
    c. Define validation rules

Real-World Example: High-Priority Email Processing

```
Trigger: When new email arrives
Conditions:
IF @contains(triggerBody()?['subject'], 'Urgent')
   AND @equals(triggerBody()?['importance'], 'high')
   AND @not(contains(triggerBody()?['from'], 'internal.com'))
THEN
   Create high-priority ticket
ELSE
   Add to regular queue
```

Figure 5.21: *Trigger Condition and Filtering*

Best Practices

- Start with simple conditions
- Test edge cases
- Document complex expressions
- Use meaningful names

Common Pitfalls

- Overcomplicated conditions
- Missing error cases
- Incorrect logical operators
- Insufficient testing

Error Handling

In Microsoft Power Automate cloud automation flows, error handling is not just a best practice, it's a fundamental requirement for building enterprise grade automations that can withstand real world operational challenges. Cloud based flows operate in dynamic environments where network connectivity, service availability, data integrity, and external system responses can vary unpredictably, making robust error handling essential for maintaining business continuity.

Implement robust error handling to ensure reliability and resilience in your Power Automate cloud flows. Effective error handling transforms fragile automations into dependable business processes that can gracefully manage exceptions, recover from temporary failures, and maintain operational stability even when unexpected conditions arise. This proactive approach to error management is crucial because cloud automations often operate unattended and must be capable of self-recovery or appropriate escalation without human intervention.

The importance of error handling in Power Automate extends beyond technical stability to business impact. Poorly handled errors can result in lost data, incomplete processes, customer service disruptions, and compliance violations. Conversely, well designed error handling ensures that your automations continue to deliver value even when facing challenges, providing fallback mechanisms, retry logic, and intelligent notifications that keep stakeholders informed while maintaining process integrity across your organization's cloud automation ecosystem.

Configuration Steps

1. **Retry Logic**
    a. Configure retry count
    b. Set retry intervals
    c. Define timeout periods
    d. Set up recovery actions
2. **Error Notification**
    a. Configure alerts
    b. Set up logging
    c. Define escalation paths

Real-World Example: Critical Database Operation

```
Error Handling Configuration:
Retry Settings:
- Count: 3 attempts
- Interval: Exponential backoff
- Initial Delay: 30 seconds
- Maximum Delay: 5 minutes

Notifications:
- Teams alert to IT Support
- Email to System Admin
- Log to Azure Monitor
- Create incident ticket

Recovery Actions:
- Switch to backup system
- Initiate manual intervention
- Log detailed error info
```

Figure 5.22: *Error Handling Configuration*

Best Practices

- Implement comprehensive retry logic
- Set up proper monitoring
- Document error scenarios
- Test failure cases

Common Pitfalls

- Missing retry logic
- Inadequate error logging
- No notification system
- Incomplete error handling

Implementation Examples

Example 1: Customer Data Sync

```
Basic Settings:
- Trigger: SQL Database changes
- Scope: Customer table
- Frequency: Real-time

Advanced Options:
- Batch: 100 records
- Concurrent: 2 processes

Conditions:
- Only active customers
- Changed fields: contact info

Error Handling:
- Retry: 3 times
- Log failures
- Alert support team
```

Figure 5.23: *Customer Data Sync Configuration*

Example 2: Document Approval Flow

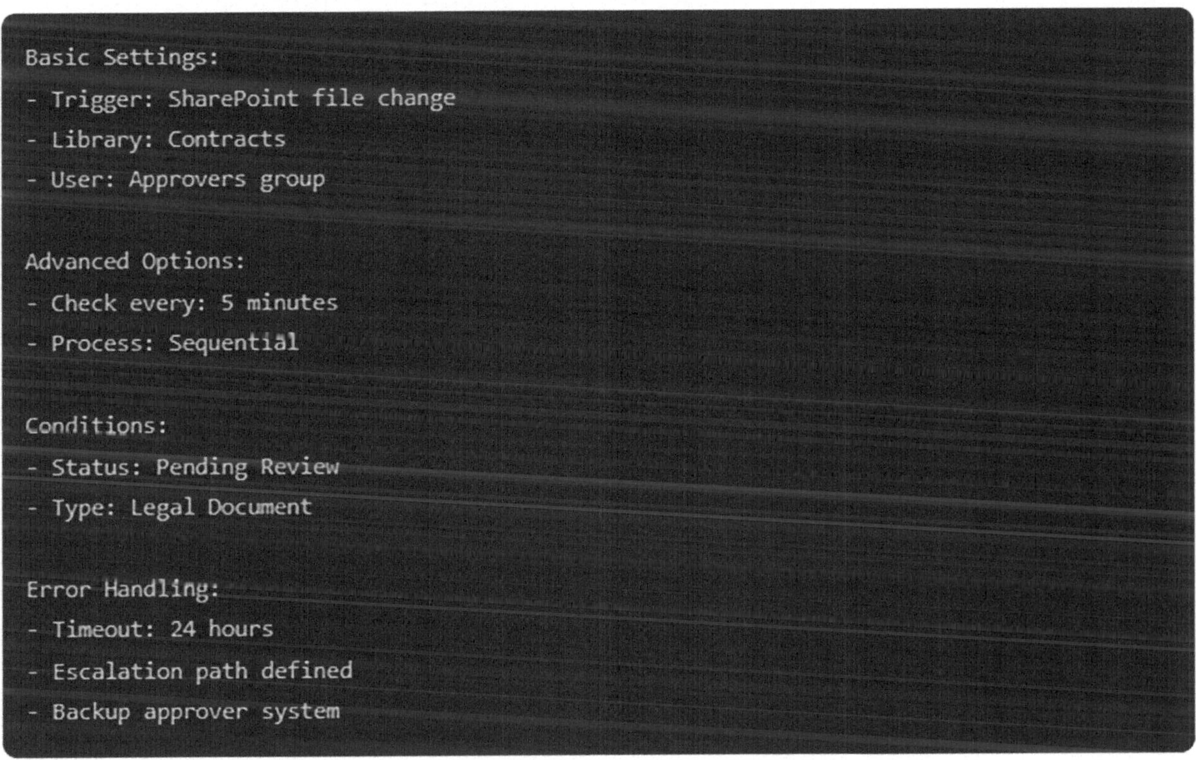

```
Basic Settings:
- Trigger: SharePoint file change
- Library: Contracts
- User: Approvers group

Advanced Options:
- Check every: 5 minutes
- Process: Sequential

Conditions:
- Status: Pending Review
- Type: Legal Document

Error Handling:
- Timeout: 24 hours
- Escalation path defined
- Backup approver system
```

Figure 5.24: *Document Approval Workflow Configuration*

Monitoring and Maintenance

Regular Checks

- Review trigger performance
- Monitor error rates
- Check resource usage
- Update documentation

Optimization Steps

- Analyze trigger patterns
- Adjust configurations
- Update conditions
- Refine error handling

Advanced Trigger Concepts in Power Automate

As organizations scale their automation initiatives and tackle complex business scenarios, basic trigger configurations often reach their limitations. Advanced trigger concepts in Power Automate represent the sophisticated techniques and strategies required to build enterprise-grade automations that can handle high volume operations, complex integrations, and demanding performance requirements while maintaining reliability and cost effectiveness.

Advanced trigger concepts become critical when your automation requirements exceed standard configurations. These concepts address challenges such as managing API rate limits, optimizing resource utilization, handling concurrent processing, and implementing sophisticated debugging strategies. Understanding these advanced techniques is essential for automation architects, developers, and administrators who need to deliver robust solutions that perform consistently under varying load conditions and business demands.

The strategic implementation of advanced trigger concepts directly impacts your organization's automation success by ensuring scalability, reducing operational costs, minimizing downtime, and providing the technical foundation for complex business process automation. These techniques enable organizations to move beyond simple workflow automation to sophisticated, interconnected systems that can adapt to changing business needs while maintaining optimal performance.

Consider implementing advanced trigger concepts when encountering the following scenarios:

- High volume processing requiring optimization of throughput and resource management
- Enterprise scale deployments with multiple interconnected flows and complex dependencies
- Performance critical applications where response times and reliability are paramount
- Complex integration scenarios involving multiple systems with varying service limits
- Regulatory compliance requirements demanding detailed monitoring and audit capabilities
- Cost optimization initiatives focusing on efficient resource utilization and API consumption
- Troubleshooting complex issues that require advanced debugging and monitoring techniques
- Scalability planning for growing automation portfolios and increasing data volumes

Trigger Throttling and Limits

Understanding throttling and limits is crucial for building reliable automations that scale effectively.

Types of Limits

- **API Request Limits**
  - Per-connection limits
  - Per-user limits
  - Per-endpoint limits
- **Time-based Limits**
  - Requests per minute
  - Requests per hour
  - Daily quotas

API Request Limits

API request limits help maintain service quality and prevent system overload. These limits are implemented at different levels:

- **Per-Connection Limits:** These limits apply to each unique connection to a service.
  - Example: SharePoint Connection

```
Standard Limits:
- 2,000 requests per connection per 5 minutes
- 100 concurrent requests per connection
- Maximum payload size: 100MB
```

Figure 5.25: *SharePoint Connection Standard Limits*

  - Real-World Scenario:

```
Business Need: Monitor multiple SharePoint lists
Solution:
1. Create separate connections for different site collections
2. Distribute load across connections
3. Implement connection pooling for high-volume operations
```

Figure 5.26: *SharePoint Connection Limits Monitoring*

- **Per-User Limits:** These limits apply to actions performed by individual users.
  - Example: Microsoft 365 User

```
Standard Limits:
- 2,000 API requests per user per day
- 50 concurrent flow runs per user
- 600 flow creations or modifications per day
```

Figure 5.27: *MicroSoft 365 User Standard Limits*

- Best Practices for User Limits:
  - Use service accounts for high-volume operations
  - Implement user request pooling
  - Monitor individual user consumption
  - Set up alerts for approaching limits
- **Per-Endpoint Limits:** These apply to specific service endpoints or operations.
  - **Example: Dynamics 365 Endpoint**

```
Standard Limits:
- 1,000 requests per endpoint per minute
- Maximum batch size: 1,000 records
- Timeout: 2 minutes per operation
```

Figure 5.28: *Dynamics 365 Endpoint*

  - Implementation Tips:

```
For High-Volume Operations:
1. Batch Processing:
   - Group requests into optimal batch sizes
   - Schedule batches across time windows
   - Monitor batch completion rates

2. Error Handling:
   - Implement retry logic
   - Log failed operations
   - Queue items exceeding limits
```

Figure 5.29: *Important tips to implement for high volume operations*

Time-based Limits

Time-based limits control the rate of operations over different time periods.

- **Requests Per Minute (RPM):** These limits control short-term burst activity.
  - **Common RPM Limits:**

```
SharePoint Online:
- 600 requests/minute per connection
- 1,200 requests/minute per site collection

Microsoft Graph:
- 2,000 requests/minute per tenant
- 400 requests/minute per app/user
```

Figure 5.30: Common RPM Limits

- **Managing RPM Limits:**
  - Implement request throttling
  - Use exponential backoff
  - Schedule non-urgent operations
  - Monitor real-time usage
- **Requests Per Hour:** Medium-term limits help manage sustained load.
  - **Example Hourly Limits:**

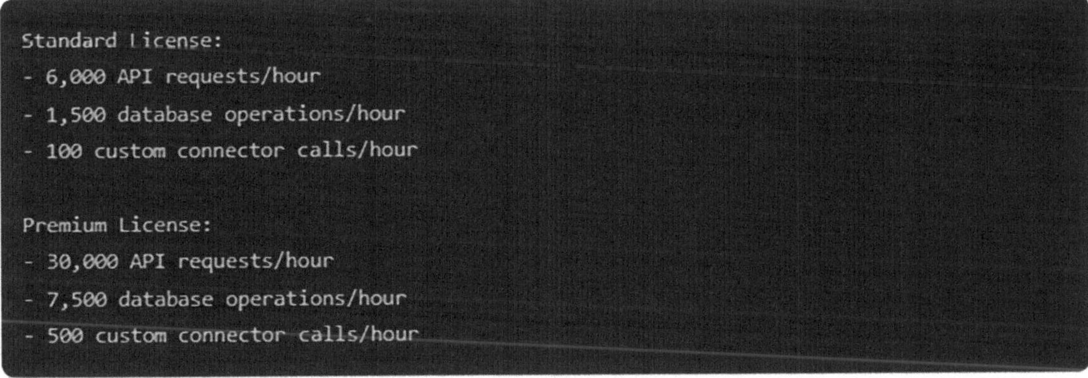

```
Standard License:
- 6,000 API requests/hour
- 1,500 database operations/hour
- 100 custom connector calls/hour

Premium License:
- 30,000 API requests/hour
- 7,500 database operations/hour
- 500 custom connector calls/hour
```

Figure 5.31: *Hourly Limits Example*

- **Optimization Strategies**

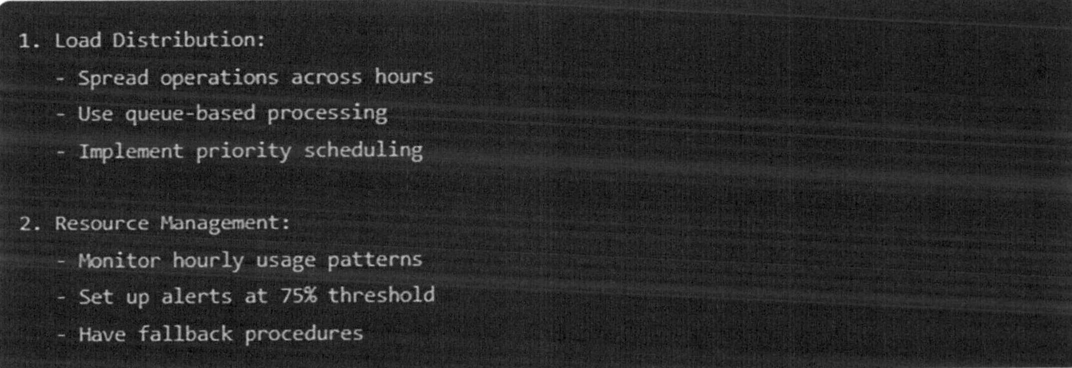

```
1. Load Distribution:
   - Spread operations across hours
   - Use queue-based processing
   - Implement priority scheduling

2. Resource Management:
   - Monitor hourly usage patterns
   - Set up alerts at 75% threshold
   - Have fallback procedures
```

Figure 5.32: *Optimization Strategy*

- **Daily Quotas:** Long-term limits ensure sustainable resource usage.
  - **Standard Daily Quotas:**

```
Per Flow:
- 10,000 actions per day
- 2,000 emails per day
- 100,000 iterations per day

Per User:
- 50 flows created per day
- 15 premium connectors
- 5 custom connectors
```

Figure 5.33: *Standard Daily Quotas*

Monitoring and Managing Limits

Built-in Monitoring Tools

- Automation Center
- Flow analytics
- Usage reports
- Alert configurations

Custom Monitoring Solutions

```
Implementation Example:
1. Create monitoring flow:
   - Track usage metrics
   - Log consumption patterns
   - Generate alerts
   - Archive statistics
```

Figure 5.34: *Custom Monitoring Solutions*

Best Practices for Limit Management

Design Principles

- Plan for scale from start
- Implement rate limiting
- Use batch processing
- Design for failures

Implementation Guidelines

```
1. Resource Planning:
   - Calculate expected usage
   - Add buffer margins
   - Plan for peak loads
   - Document assumptions

2. Error Handling:
   - Detect limit violations
   - Implement retry logic
   - Log and alert
   - Have fallback plans
```

Figure 5.35: *Implementation Guideline*

Official Documentation and Resources

For the most up-to-date information on limits and quotas, refer to the following sources:

Official Microsoft Documentation:

- Power Automate Limits: https://docs.microsoft.com/power-automate/limits-and-config
- ServiceLimits: https://docs.microsoft.com/power-platform/admin/api-request-limits-allocations
- Microsoft Graph Limits: https://docs.microsoft.com/graph/throttling

Common Scenarios and Solutions

Scenario 1: High-Volume Data Processing

```
Problem: Processing 100,000 records daily
Solution:
1. Implement batch processing (1,000 records/batch)
2. Use distributed time windows
3. Monitor batch completion
4. Handle partial failures
```

***Figure 5.36:** High Volume Data Processing Implementation Tip*

Scenario 2: Real-time Monitoring

```
Problem: Continuous SharePoint monitoring
Solution:
1. Use webhook when possible
2. Implement connection pooling
3. Set up retry logic
4. Monitor rate limits
```

***Figure 5.37:** Continuous SharePoint Implementation Tip*

Troubleshooting Guide

Common Issues and Solutions

- Rate limit exceeded
- Quota exhaustion
- Timeout errors
- Concurrent run limits

Recommended Resolution Steps

For each issue:

- Identify limit type
- Check current usage
- Review error logs
- Apply appropriate solution

Trigger Concurrency

Managing multiple trigger instances running simultaneously for optimal performance.

Concurrency Settings

- **Sequential Processing**
  - Configuration:
    - Single instance
    - Ordered execution
    - Queue management
- **Parallel Processing**
  - Configuration:
    - Multiple instances
    - Degree of parallelism
    - Resource allocation

Real-World Examples

Example 1: Invoice Processing System

```
Scenario: Processing multiple invoices
Concurrency Setup:
- Maximum concurrent runs: 5
- Batch size: 100 invoices
- Queue threshold: 1000
- Error queue handling

Implementation:
1. Parallel processing for different vendors
2. Sequential processing within vendor
3. Priority queue for urgent items
```

Figure 5.38: *Invoice Processing System and Workflow Example*

Example 2: Document Approval Flow

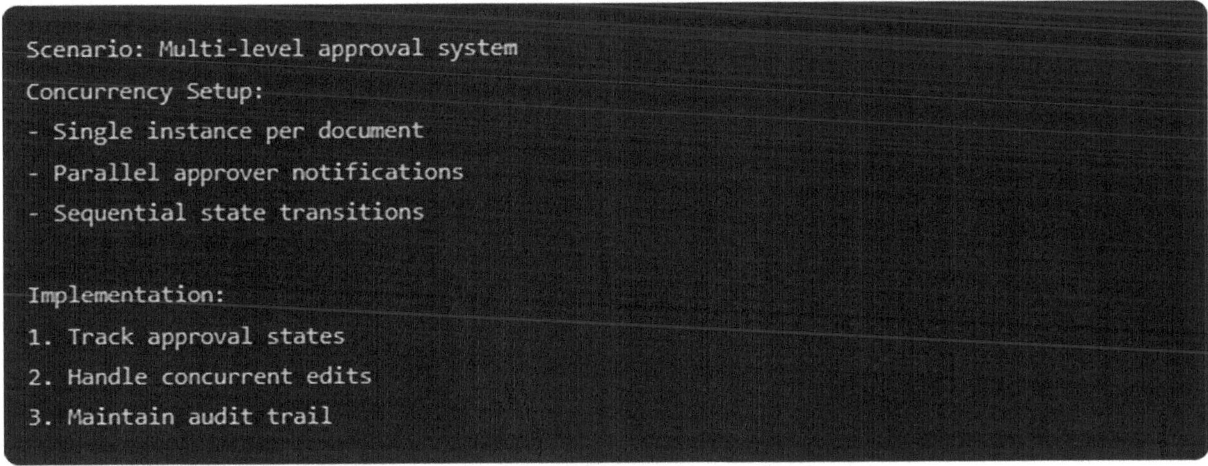
```
Scenario: Multi-level approval system
Concurrency Setup:
- Single instance per document
- Parallel approver notifications
- Sequential state transitions

Implementation:
1. Track approval states
2. Handle concurrent edits
3. Maintain audit trail
```

Figure 5.39: *Document Approval Workflow Example*

Best Practices

- Set appropriate concurrency limits
- Monitor system resources
- Implement queue management
- Handle race conditions

Trigger Debugging

Debugging triggers in Power Automate requires specialized techniques because trigger failures often occur before the flow even starts running, making them invisible in standard run history where you'd normally troubleshoot action-level errors. Mastering trigger debugging strategies–such as examining trigger conditions, reviewing firing history in the flow details page, testing with manual triggers, and understanding polling intervals–is essential for resolving issues where flows don't start when expected or fire on incorrect data, ensuring your automations reliably respond to the business events they're designed to monitor.

Debugging Tools

- **Built-in Tools**
  - Flow checker
  - Run history
  - Expression tester
  - Monitor portal
- **Advanced Debugging**
  - Custom logging
  - Diagnostic settings
  - Alert configuration

Debugging Scenarios

Example 1: Failed Trigger Resolution

```
Problem: Trigger not firing
Debug Steps:
1. Check connection status
2. Verify permissions
3. Review trigger conditions
4. Analyze error logs
5. Test trigger manually
```

Figure 5.40: *Failed Trigger Resolution Example*

Example 2: Performance Investigation

```
Problem: Slow trigger response
Debug Steps:
1. Monitor execution time
2. Check resource usage
3. Analyze data volume
4. Review concurrent runs
5. Test different conditions
```

Figure 5.41: *Performance Investigation Example*

Best Practices

- Implement comprehensive logging
- Use structured error handling
- Monitor trigger metrics
- Document debugging steps

Performance Optimization Strategies and Techniques for Maximizing Trigger Efficiency.

Optimization Areas

Trigger Configuration

- Polling intervals
- Batch processing
- Resource allocation
- Connection management

Data Handling

- Payload optimization
- Response filtering
- Caching strategies
- Compression techniques

Optimization Examples

Example 1: Large Dataset Processing

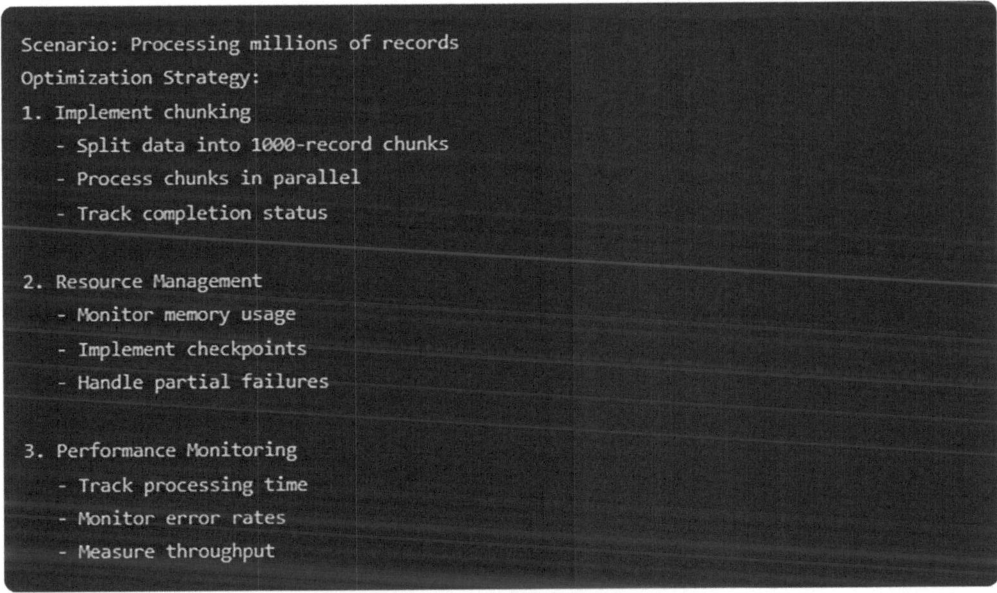

```
Scenario: Processing millions of records
Optimization Strategy:
1. Implement chunking
   - Split data into 1000-record chunks
   - Process chunks in parallel
   - Track completion status

2. Resource Management
   - Monitor memory usage
   - Implement checkpoints
   - Handle partial failures

3. Performance Monitoring
   - Track processing time
   - Monitor error rates
   - Measure throughput
```

Figure 5.42: *Flow Optimization Example*

Example 2: Real-time Notification System

```
Scenario: High-frequency notifications
Optimization Strategy:
1. Message Batching
   - Group similar notifications
   - Implement priority queues
   - Set batch timeouts

2. Delivery Optimization
   - Use webhook when possible
   - Implement deduplication
   - Handle offline scenarios

3. Resource Efficiency
   - Minimize payload size
   - Use connection pooling
   - Implement caching
```

Figure 5.43: *Flow Optimization Example*

Performance Best Practices

Design Principles

- Minimize API calls
- Use efficient data structures
- Implement caching
- Optimize trigger conditions

Monitoring and Maintenance

- Regular performance reviews
- Resource usage tracking
- Optimization cycles
- Documentation updates

Common Performance Issues

Resource Constraints

- Memory limitations
- CPU bottlenecks
- Network latency
- Storage constraints

Design Issues

- Inefficient triggers
- Poor error handling
- Missing optimizations
- Resource leaks

Implementation Guidelines

Initial Setup

- Plan resource requirements
- Configure monitoring
- Set up alerts
- Document baseline metrics

Ongoing Management

- Regular performance reviews
- Optimization cycles
- Capacity planning
- Documentation updates

Monitoring and Analytics

Key Metrics

- Trigger response time
- Success rate
- Resource utilization
- Error frequency
- Processing volume

Analysis Tools

- Power Automate analytics
- Custom dashboards
- Log analytics
- Performance reports

Integration Scenarios in Microsoft Power Automate

Building upon the trigger fundamentals covered in **Chapter 1: Getting Started with Power Automate**, we will now explore how triggers function across different services, platforms, and enterprise environments. Understanding these integration scenarios will help us create robust automation solutions that work seamlessly across an organization's technology landscape.

Triggers Across Different Services

When automating business processes, organizations often need to connect multiple services. Power Automate provides several robust capabilities to create triggers that work across various Microsoft and third-party services explained as follows:

Microsoft Services Integration

Let us explore how triggers work across the Microsoft ecosystem through a practical example of a customer support workflow:

Example: Customer Support Case Management

```
Initial Trigger: Microsoft Forms (Customer Submission)
Connected Services:
- SharePoint (Case Documentation)
- Teams (Support Team Notification)
- Outlook (Customer Communication)
- Dataverse (Case Tracking)
```

Figure 5.44: *Customer Support Case Management*

Implementation Steps:

1. Create a Microsoft Form for customer submissions
2. Configure the "`When a new response is submitted`" trigger
3. Set up SharePoint document library integration
4. Configure Teams channel notifications
5. Establish Outlook email templates
6. Connect to Dataverse for case tracking

Note: *Use environment variables to store service connection details. This makes it easier to move flows between development and production environments while maintaining service connections.*

Third-Party Service Integration

Power Automate can trigger actions based on events in external systems. Here is an example of a sales process integration:

Example: Sales Process Automation

```
Primary Trigger: Salesforce (New Opportunity)
Connected Services:
- DocuSign (Contract Generation)
- SAP (Order Processing)
- Slack (Team Communication)
```

Figure 5.45: *Sales Process Automation*

Best Practices for Service Integration:

- Use OAuth 2.0 authentication when available
- Implement proper error handling for service outages
- Monitor API usage limits
- Document service dependencies

Cross-Platform Trigger Considerations

Creating triggers that work across different platforms requires careful planning and implementation.

Mobile Platform Integration

Example: Field Service App Integration

```
Platforms:
- Power Apps mobile application
- iOS native apps
- Android native apps
```

Figure 5.46: *Field Service App Integration*

Key Considerations:

- Network connectivity handling
- Device-specific limitations
- Authentication persistence
- Data synchronization

Tips and Best Practices

For successful integration scenarios:

- Service Connection Management
    - Regular connection testing
    - Automated notification for expired credentials
    - Connection pooling where applicable
- Error Handling
    - Implement retry logic
    - Clear error messages
    - Fallback mechanisms
- Performance Optimization
    - Batch processing
    - Caching strategies
    - Resource management
- Security Best Practices
    - Least privilege access
    - Regular security audits
    - Encryption in transit and at rest

Common Integration Challenges

Understanding and preparing for common challenges:

- Service Availability
    - Monitor service health
    - Implement circuit breakers
    - Define fallback procedures
- Data Consistency
    - Transaction management
    - Data validation
    - Conflict resolution
- Performance Issues
    - Bottleneck identification
    - Resource optimization
    - Scaling strategies

Conclusion

Throughout this chapter, we have explored the intricate world of triggers in Microsoft Power Automate and examined their purpose in being the foundation for automated workflows that drive modern business processes. We have journeyed from basic trigger concepts to advanced implementation patterns, understanding how triggers can bridge different services, platforms, and enterprise environments.

Building on this foundational understanding, the next chapter will focus on **Actions in Power Automate for Workflows**, where we will explore the execution components that transform triggered events into meaningful business outcomes through data manipulation, system integrations, and automated decision-making processes. We will also learn about how actions work in conjunction with triggers to create comprehensive automation solutions that deliver real business value.

CHAPTER 6

Actions in Power Automate for Workflows

Introduction

In the previous chapters, we explored the fundamentals of Power Automate, its interface, and learned how to create basic flows. We delved into triggers that initiate workflows and learned how to configure various connection settings. Now, we take a deeper dive into actions, which are the building blocks that define the aftermath of a trigger in Power Automate workflows.

Actions in Power Automate are the tasks automatically performed by a flow. They range from sending emails and creating files to updating database records and posting messages to Teams channels. This chapter will guide you through the diverse array of actions, while showing you how to combine them effectively to create powerful automated workflows that solve real business challenges.

By the end of this chapter, you will understand how to select appropriate actions, configure them correctly, and chain them together to create efficient workflows. You will learn practical techniques for handling data between actions, implementing conditional logic, and troubleshooting common issues that arise when working with multiple actions.

Structure

This chapter addresses the following topics:

- Understanding Actions in Power Automate
- Types of Actions
- Action Configuration Basics
- Working with Core Actions
- Business Scenarios and Implementation
- Deep Dive: Types of Actions in Power Automate
- Complex Scenario: Multi-step Approval Process
- Troubleshooting Common Action Issues
- Performance Optimization Tips
- 10 Essential Power Automate Actions to Transform Your Workflows
- 10 Advanced Power Automate Actions: Mastering Complex Workflow Automation

Understanding Actions in Power Automate

Before exploring specific action types, let us understand what actions represent in the context of

Power Automate workflows. Actions are the individual steps executed by a flow to achieve the desired automation outcome.

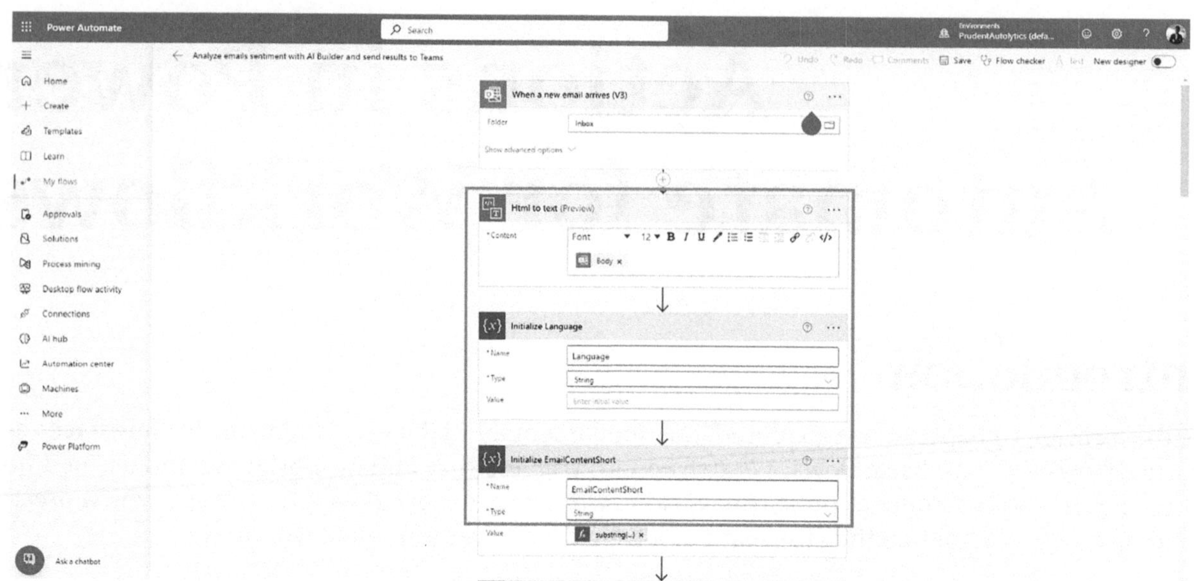

Figure 6.1: *Power Automate Actions Panel showing different categories of actions*

Types of Actions

Power Automate offers several categories of actions to help you build comprehensive workflows:

Core Actions

Core actions handle fundamental operations within your flows. These include:

- Control actions (Condition, Switch, Do until, Apply to each)
- Variable handling (Initialize, Set, Increment)
- Data operations (Compose, Select, Filter array)
- Response handling (Response, Parse JSON)

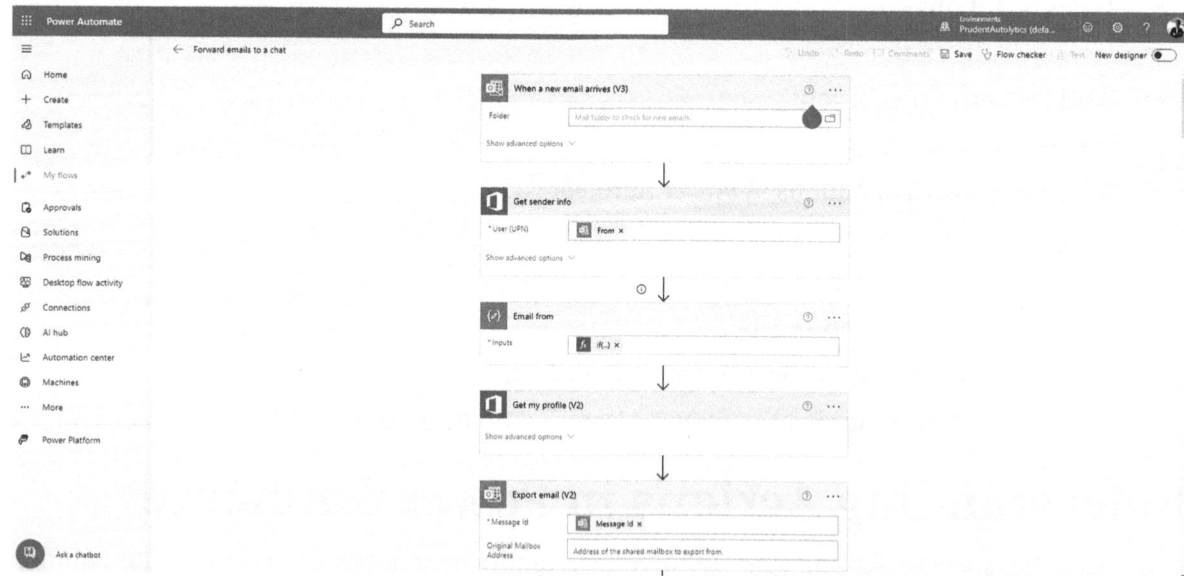

Figure 6.2: *Core Actions available in Power Automate*

Connector Actions

These actions work with specific services and applications:

- Microsoft 365 services (SharePoint, Teams, Outlook)
- Database systems (SQL Server, Dataverse)
- Third-party services (Salesforce, Twitter, DocuSign)

Note: *When selecting connector actions, remember to check if you need additional licensing or permissions before incorporating them into your workflow.*

Action Configuration Basics

Every action in Power Automate requires proper configuration to function effectively. These configuration basics are mentioned as follows:

- Input Parameters
  - Required fields (marked with *)
  - Optional parameters
  - Dynamic content from previous steps
- Output Handling
  - Understanding action outputs
  - Using outputs in subsequent steps

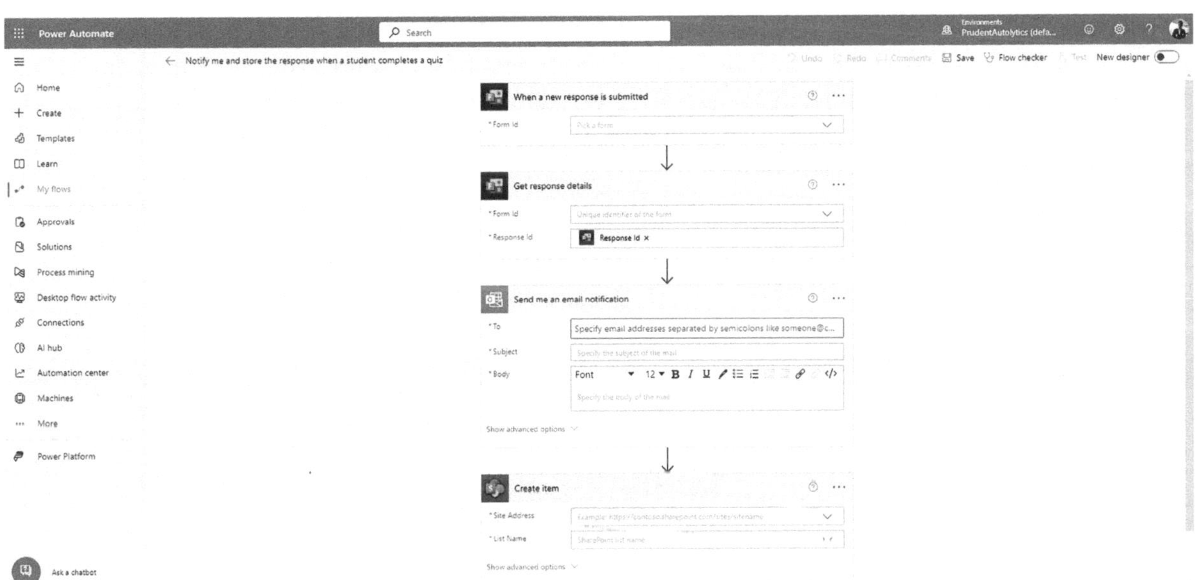

Figure 6.3: *Action Configuration Panel with input parameters*

Working with Core Actions

Core actions in Power Automate represent the fundamental building blocks that every flow developer must master, including control actions for logic and looping, data operations for transforming and manipulating information, and variable actions for maintaining state throughout execution. Understanding how to effectively use these essential actions, such as Condition for branching logic, Apply to each for iteration, Compose for data checkpoints, and Parse JSON for working with complex objects, enables you to build sophisticated workflows that handle real-world business scenarios with efficiency and reliability.

Conditional Actions

Conditional actions in Power Automate including Condition, Switch, and Do until, control your flow's execution path by evaluating data and determining which branches or loops should run based on the results. These decision-making actions form the logical backbone of intelligent workflows, allowing you to route approvals based on request amounts, handle different document types with specific processing rules, repeat operations until success criteria are met, or skip unnecessary steps when certain conditions aren't satisfied. Conditional actions help you create intelligent workflows that make decisions based on data as shown in *Figure 6.4*:

```
if (triggerBody()?['status'] == 'approved') {
    // Perform approval actions
} else {
    // Handle rejection
}
```

Figure 6.4: *SmartWorkflow ConditionalLogic DecisionPaths*

Best Practice: Always include error handling in your conditional logic to manage unexpected scenarios.

Loop Actions

Loop actions in Power Automate enable you to process collections of items, repeat operations until specific conditions are met, or continue executing steps while certain criteria remain true. These iterative controls are essential for handling arrays of data, retrying failed operations, or performing batch processing within your workflows. Power Automate provides three primary loop actions, each designed for different iteration scenarios:

- Apply to each
- Do until
- Do while

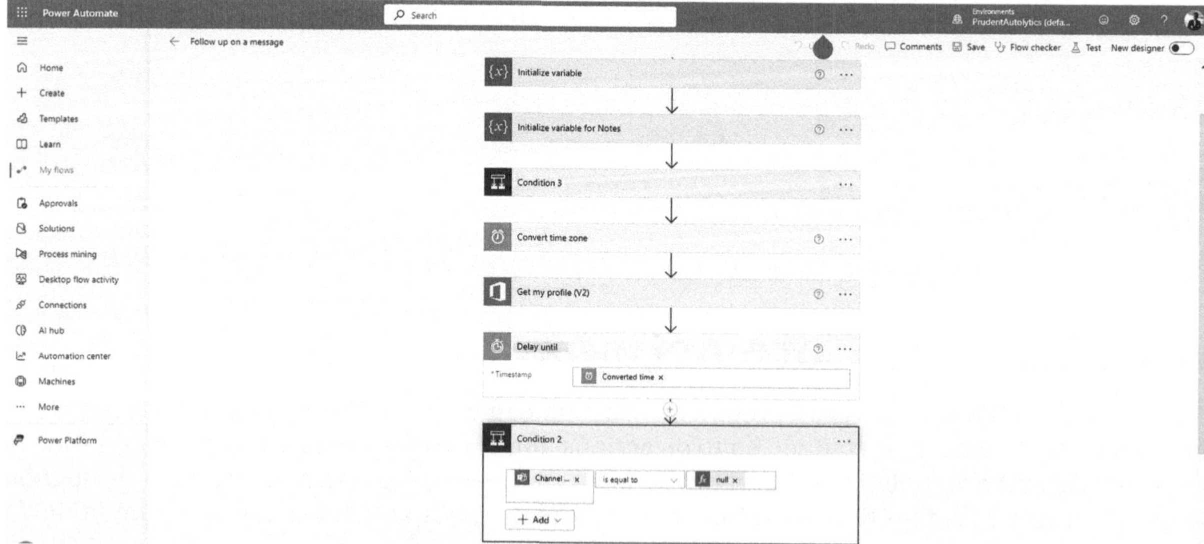

Figure 6.5: *Loop Action Configuration*

Business Scenarios and Implementation

Hands-on Tutorial: Employee Onboarding Workflow

Let us create a comprehensive employee onboarding workflow that demonstrates various action types and best practices. This workflow will automate tasks across multiple departments when a new employee joins the organization.

Business Requirements

- HR needs to create necessary employee accounts
- IT must set up equipment and system access
- Facilities need to prepare workspace
- Training team needs to schedule orientation sessions
- Manager needs to be kept informed of progress

Prerequisites

- Power Automate premium license
- SharePoint list for employee information
- Microsoft 365 admin access
- Teams environment

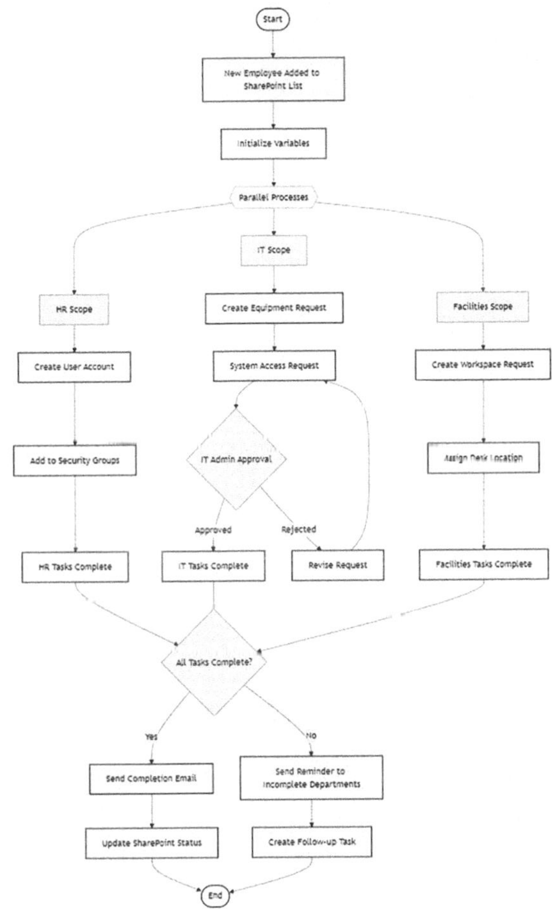

Figure 6.6: *Employee Onboarding Flow Overview*

Step-by-Step Implementation

Step 1: Create the Initial Trigger

1. Open Power Automate and select "**`Create New Flow`**"
2. Choose "**`Automated cloud flow`**"
3. Select "**`When an item is created`**" SharePoint trigger
4. Configure the trigger:
    a. Site Address: [Your SharePoint site]
    b. List Name: "**`New Employees`**"

Step 2: Initialize Variables

We'll create variables to track the onboarding progress:

```
Initialize variable
Name: "onboardingStatus"
Type: String
Value: "Started"

Initialize variable
Name: "employeeEmail"
Type: String
Value: "pending"
```

Figure 6.7: *Onboarding Progress InitializeVariables WorkflowSetup*

Step 3: Set Up Scope Actions

Create three scope actions for different departments:

- HR Scope
- IT Scope
- Facilities Scope

Note: *Scope actions help organize your flow and make troubleshooting easier by grouping related actions together.*

Step 4: Configure HR Scope

Inside the HR scope, add these actions:

1. Create user account:

```
Action: Create user (Microsoft 365 Users)
First Name: [SharePoint Item First Name]
Last Name: [SharePoint Item Last Name]
User Principal Name: [SharePoint Item Email]
```

Figure 6.8: HRScope *Configure* CreateUserAccount *Actions*

2. Add to appropriate security groups:

```
Action: Add user to group
User: [Created User Email]
Group: "New Employees"
```

***Figure 6.9:** HRScope AddToSecurityGroups UserProvisioning*

Step 5: Configure IT Scope (Parallel Branch)

Create a parallel branch for IT tasks that can run simultaneously with HR tasks:

1. Create equipment request:

```
Action: Create item (SharePoint)
List: "IT Equipment Requests"
Title: concat('Equipment for ', triggerBody()?['Title'])
Status: "Pending"
```

***Figure 6.10:** ITScope ParallelBranch CreateEquipmentRequest*

2. Create system access request:

```
Action: Start and wait for an approval
Approvers: "IT Admin Team"
Details: Equipment and access requirements
```

***Figure 6.11:** ITScope ParallelBranch CreateSystemAccessRequest*

Step 6: Configure Facilities Scope

Add actions for workspace preparation:

1. Create workspace request:

```
Action: Create item (SharePoint)
List: "Workspace Requests"
Title: concat('Workspace for ', triggerBody()?['Title'])
Department: [SharePoint Item Department]
```

***Figure 6.12:** FacilitiesScope CreateWorkspaceRequest SetupActions*

Step 7: Add Condition Actions

Add a condition to check if all tasks are completed:

Condition:

```
if(variables('hrTasksComplete') and variables('itTasksComplete') and
variables('facilitiesTasksComplete'))
```

True branch:

- Send completion email to manager
- Update SharePoint status

False branch:

- Send reminder to incomplete departments
- Create follow-up task

Step 8: Implement Error Handling

Add "**Configure run after**" settings for critical actions:

1. In each scope, add error handling:

```
Scope: HR Tasks
Run after: If previous action failed
Action: Send email to HR admin
Action: Log to error tracking list
```

Figure 6.13: *ErrorHandling ConfigureRunAfter Critical Actions*

Testing Your Flow

1. Create a test record in the SharePoint list
2. Monitor the flow run
3. Check each scope's completion
4. Verify all systems are updated

Best Practices During Implementation

1. Name your actions descriptively:
    a. "**Create_HR_Ticket**" instead of "**Create item**"
    b. "**Send_Manager_Notification**" instead of "**Send email**"
2. Add comments to complex logic:
    a. Use notes in parallel branches
    b. Document condition criteria
3. Use expressions effectively:

```
concat('Onboarding for ', triggerBody()?['FirstName'], ' ',
triggerBody()?['LastName'])
```

Troubleshooting Guide

Common issues and solutions

- Parallel Branch Timing:
    - Issue: Branches completing out of order

- Solution: Add wait conditions if sequence is important
- Permission Errors:
  - Issue: Actions failing due to permissions
  - Solution: Verify connection credentials and permissions

Exercise for Readers

Modify the base workflow to include:

- A teams channel notification when each scope completes
- A customized welcome email to the new employee
- An approval step for equipment costs over $1000

Try implementing these modifications and test your flow with sample data.

Deep Dive: Types of Actions in Power Automate

Power Automate offers a comprehensive library of actions that help you build sophisticated automation workflows. These actions are the building blocks for connecting different services, processing data, and implementing business logic within your flows.

- **Connector Actions:** Pre-built actions that integrate with specific services such as SharePoint, Outlook, Teams, and hundreds of third-party applications, allowing seamless data exchange between platforms
- **Built-in Actions:** Core functionality actions such as conditions, loops, variables, and data operations that provide essential logic and control flow capabilities for your automation workflows

Data Operation Actions

These actions help you manipulate and transform data within your flows.

Compose Action Example: Data Formatting

```
Scenario: Format customer information for a report

1. Compose
Input: {
    "customerName": "@triggerBody()?['name']",
    "orderDate": "@formatDateTime(triggerBody()?['date'], 'yyyy-MM-dd')",
    "totalAmount": "@float(triggerBody()?['amount'])"
}
```

Figure 6.14: *Compose Action Configuration*

Select Action Example: Data Transformation

```
Scenario: Extract specific fields from an array of records

1. Select
From: @variables('orderItems')
Map: {
    "productId": "@item()?['id']",
    "quantity": "@item()?['qty']",
    "subtotal": "@multiply(item()?['price'], item()?['qty'])"
}
```

Figure 6.15: *Transforming Data with Compose*

Control Actions

Control actions manage the flow of your automation logic.

Condition Action Example: Order Processing

```
Scenario: Route orders based on amount

1. Condition
    If: @greater(triggerBody()?['orderTotal'], 1000)
    True:
        - Send to manager approval
        - Create high-value order record
    False:
        - Process automatically
        - Send confirmation email
```

Figure 6.16: *Using Condition Action to Manage Order Processing Logic*

Switch Action Example: Multi-path Routing

```
Scenario: Process support tickets by category

1. Switch
    On: @triggerBody()?['category']
    Cases:
        - Technical: Route to IT
        - Billing: Route to Finance
        - Account: Route to Customer Service
        Default: Route to General Support
```

Figure 6.17: *Flow Branching Using Switch Action*

Variable Actions

Actions for managing state within your flows.

Initialize Variable Example: Order Processing

```
Scenario: Track order processing status

1. Initialize variable
    Name: orderStatus
    Type: String
    Value: "Received"

2. Initialize variable
    Name: processingSteps
    Type: Array
    Value: ["Validation", "Inventory", "Payment", "Shipping"]
```

Figure 6.18: *Using Variables to Track State in Order Processing*

Increment Variable Example: Batch Processing

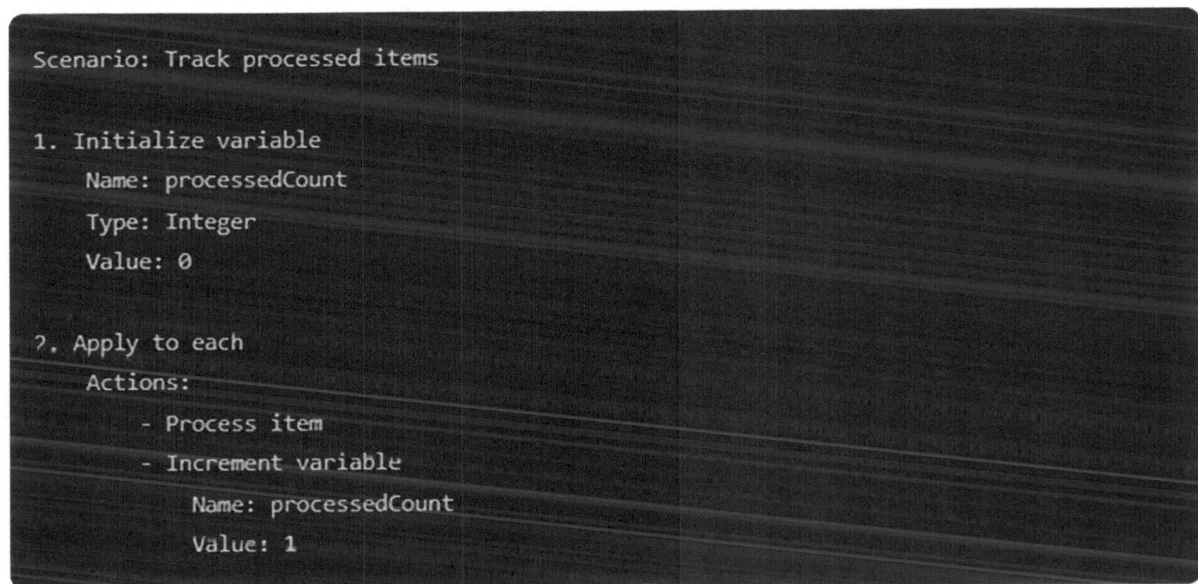

```
Scenario: Track processed items

1. Initialize variable
    Name: processedCount
    Type: Integer
    Value: 0

2. Apply to each
    Actions:
        - Process item
        - Increment variable
            Name: processedCount
            Value: 1
```

Figure 6.19: *Using Increment Variable to Control Batch Flow Logic*

Schedule Actions

Actions for timing and recurring operations.

Delay Action Example: Follow-up Sequence

```
Scenario: Customer engagement sequence

1. Send welcome email
2. Delay
    Units: Days
    Count: 3
3. Send follow-up email
4. Delay
    Units: Hours
    Count: 48
5. Send feedback request
```

Figure 6.20: *Delay Action Configuration*

Document Automation Actions

Actions for handling files and documents.

PDF Actions Example: Invoice Processing

```
Scenario: Create and process invoices

1. Create PDF file
    Template: Invoice template
    Data: @variables('invoiceData')

2. Convert to PDF
    File: @triggerBody()?['documentLink']

3. Merge PDF
    File 1: @variables('invoice')
    File 2: @variables('terms')
```

Figure 6.21: *Automating Invoices with PDF Actions in Power Automate*

Complex Scenario: Multi-step Approval Process

Let us create a flow that handles a complex approval process with multiple stakeholders.

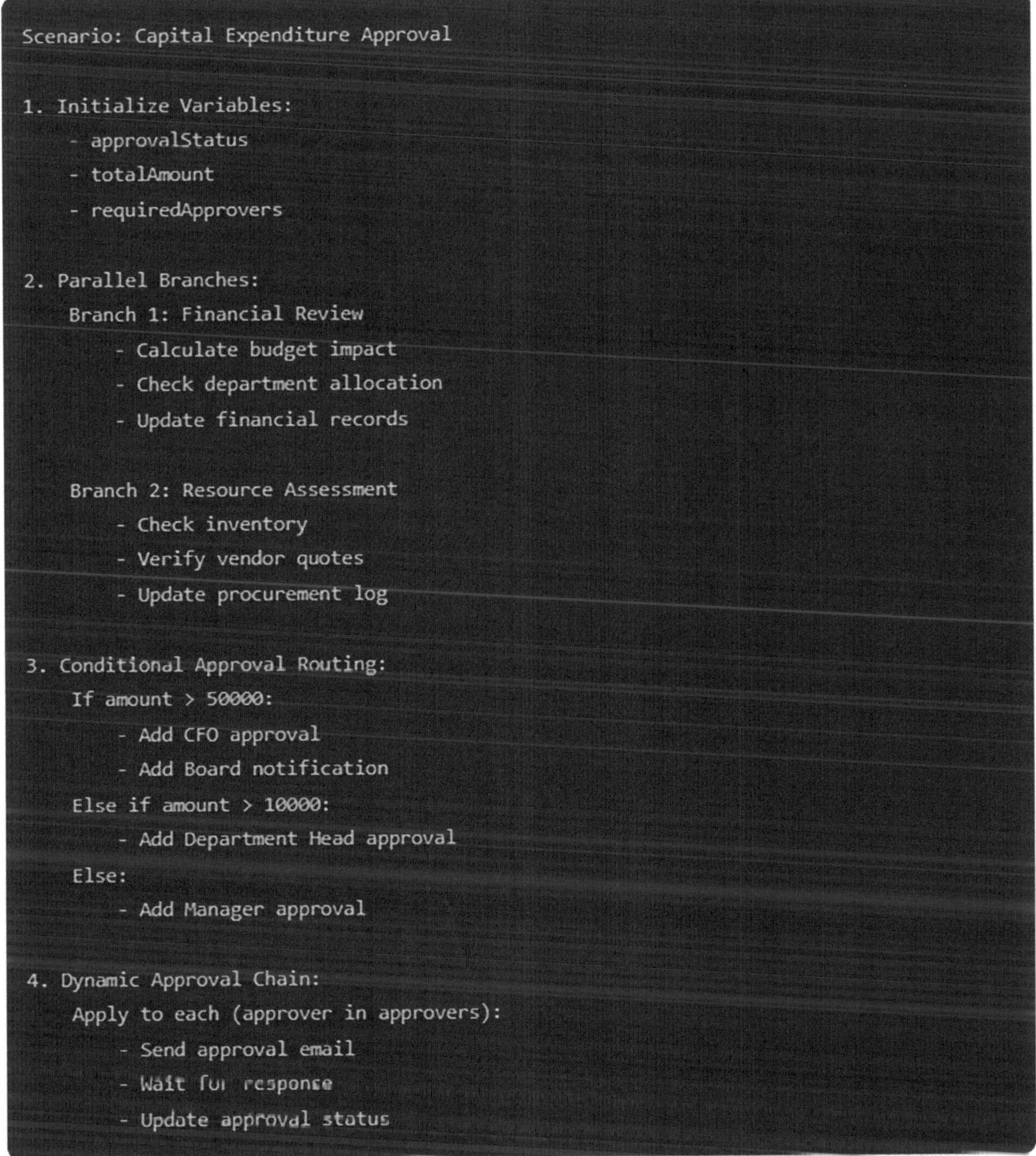

```
Scenario: Capital Expenditure Approval

1. Initialize Variables:
    - approvalStatus
    - totalAmount
    - requiredApprovers

2. Parallel Branches:
    Branch 1: Financial Review
        - Calculate budget impact
        - Check department allocation
        - Update financial records

    Branch 2: Resource Assessment
        - Check inventory
        - Verify vendor quotes
        - Update procurement log

3. Conditional Approval Routing:
    If amount > 50000:
        - Add CFO approval
        - Add Board notification
    Else if amount > 10000:
        - Add Department Head approval
    Else:
        - Add Manager approval

4. Dynamic Approval Chain:
    Apply to each (approver in approvers):
        - Send approval email
        - Wait for response
        - Update approval status
```

Figure 6.22: *Complex Approval Flow*

Troubleshooting Common Action Issues

1. Data Type Mismatches

```
Problem: "Invalid type. Expected: String, Got: Object"
Solution: Add string() or json() conversion:
string(variables('myObject'))
```

Figure 6.23: *Common Error Messages and Solutions*

2. Null Value Handling

```
Problem: Action fails when processing null values
Solution: Add coalesce function:
coalesce(triggerBody()?['field'], 'default value')
```

Figure 6.24: *Common Error Messages and Solutions*

3. Array Processing Errors

```
Problem: "Cannot process null array"
Solution: Add array initialization check:
if(empty(variables('myArray')), createArray(), variables('myArray'))
```

Figure 6.25: *Common Error Messages and Solutions*

Performance Optimization Tips

1. Batch Processing

```
Instead of:
Apply to each (item in items) {
    Create item
}

Use:
Create multiple items
```

Figure 6.26: *Batch Processing*

2. Concurrent Operations

```
Use Parallel Branches for independent operations:
- Data processing
- Notification sending
- Log updates
```

Figure 6.27: *Concurrent operations*

3. Data Minimization

```
Use Select to reduce payload:
Select
From: @variables('largeDataset')
Map: {
    "id": "@item()?['id']",
    "status": "@item()?['status']"
}
```

Figure 6.28: *Data Minimization*

Practice Exercise: Build a Customer Service Workflow

Create a flow that:

- Monitors a shared mailbox for customer inquiries
- Categorizes emails using AI
- Creates appropriate tickets
- Assigns to correct department
- Sends automated responses
- Tracks resolution time

Common Challenges and Solutions

Challenge 1: Handling Timeouts

Solution: Implement pagination and batch processing for large datasets

Challenge 2: Managing Dependencies

Solution: Use clear naming conventions and documentation

Challenge 3: Performance Issues

Solution: Optimize action sequences and reduce unnecessary steps

Practice Questions

1. What would be the most appropriate action sequence for processing a list of 1000 records while staying within API limits?
2. In a document approval workflow, how would you handle scenarios where the approver is out of office?
3. Design a solution using parallel branches to process customer orders while simultaneously updating inventory and sending notifications.

10 Essential Power Automate Actions to Transform Your Workflows

Power Automate offers hundreds of actions, but mastering a few of them can significantly enhance your automation capabilities. These essential actions are instrumental in creating efficient, scalable, and maintainable workflows. Understanding these core actions will help you solve common business challenges and create more sophisticated automations.

Why These Actions Matter

Before diving into specific actions, let us understand why these particular actions are crucial for your automation journey:

- **Foundation for Complex Workflows:** These actions form the backbone of most business processes.
- **Time-Saving Capabilities:** They automate repetitive tasks effectively.
- **Error Reduction:** Properly using these actions reduces manual intervention and potential mistakes.
- **Scalability:** These actions work efficiently with both small and large data sets.

The Essential Actions

Condition Action

Why It is Essential: Decision-making is fundamental to automation

```
Example Use Case:
If invoice amount > $1000
    Route to manager approval
Else
    Process automatically
```

Figure 6.29: *Condition Action Configuration*

Business Impact:

- Automated decision-making
- Reduced manual oversight
- Consistent policy enforcement

Apply to Each

Why It is Essential: Handles bulk operations efficiently

```
Example Use Case:
For each new order in daily orders:
    - Create invoice
    - Send confirmation
    - Update inventory
```

Figure 6.30: *Handling Bulk Data with Apply to Each*

Business Impact:

- Process multiple items automatically
- Maintain data consistency
- Scale operations easily

Initialize Variable

Why It is Essential: Manages workflow state and data

```
Example Use Case:
Initialize variable
Name: "processStatus"
Type: "String"
Value: "Started"
```

Figure 6.31: *Using Initialize Variable to Control Flow State and Data*

Business Impact:

- Track process status
- Store temporary data
- Enable complex logic

Compose

Why It is Essential: Transforms and formats data

```
Example Use Case:
Compose JSON:
{
    "customerName": "@triggerBody()?['name']",
    "orderDate": "@utcNow()",
    "status": "@variables('processStatus')"
}
```

Figure 6.32: *Data Shaping with Compose Action*

Business Impact:

- Format data consistently
- Prepare data for external systems
- Simplify complex data structures

HTTP Action

Why It is Essential: Enables external system integration

```
Example Use Case:
Method: POST
URL: https://api.example.com/orders
Headers: {
    "Content-Type": "application/json"
}
Body: @variables('orderData')
```

Figure 6.33: *External Integration via HTTP Action*

Business Impact:

- Connect with external services
- Enable API integrations
- Build extensible workflows

Parse JSON

Why It is Essential: Handles structured data effectively

```
Example Use Case:
Content: @body('HTTP_Request')
Schema: {
    "type": "object",
    "properties": {
        "orderId": {"type": "string"},
        "amount": {"type": "number"}
    }
}
```

Figure 6.34: *Structured Data Processing with Parse JSON*

Business Impact:

- Process API responses
- Validate data structure
- Enable dynamic workflows

Select

Why It is Essential: Transforms data collections

```
Example Use Case:
From: @variables('orderList')
Map: {
    "id": "@item()?['orderId']",
    "total": "@item()?['amount']"
}
```

Figure 6.35: *Using Select to Refine Data Sets in Flows*

Business Impact:

- Streamline data processing
- Reduce data transfer
- Improve performance

Create HTML Table

Why It is Essential: Formats data for communication

```
Example Use Case:
From: @variables('salesData')
Columns: [
    "Date",
    "Product",
    "Revenue"
]
```

Figure 6.36: *Data Presentation with Create HTML Table*

Business Impact:

- Create readable reports
- Format email content
- Present data effectively

Start and Wait for Approval

Why It is Essential: Manages human interaction in workflows

```
Example Use Case:
Approvers: @triggerBody()?['manager']
Details: "Please approve expense report"
```

Figure 6.37: *Approval Workflows with Start and Wait for Approval*

Business Impact:

- Streamline approvals
- Track decisions
- Maintain audit trails

Join

Why It is Essential: Combines data effectively

```
Example Use Case:
From: @variables('nameList')
Join with: ", "
```

Figure 6.38: *Data Merging with Join Action*

Business Impact:

- Format output strings
- Create reports
- Combine data sets

Practical Implementation Example

Let us combine these actions in a real-world scenario:

Expense Report Processing

- Initialize Variables (Status tracking)
- Parse JSON (Expense data)
- Apply to Each (Process each line item)
- Condition (Check amount thresholds)
- Select (Format for approval)

- Create HTML Table (Summary view)
- Start and Wait for Approval
- HTTP Action (Update accounting system)

Best Practices

- **Error Handling**
  - Add try-catch patterns
  - Include timeout handling
  - Log errors appropriately
- **Performance Optimization**
  - Minimize action usage
  - Batch operations where possible
  - Use variables efficiently
- **Maintenance**
  - Document action usage
  - Use clear naming conventions
  - Structure workflows logically

Common Challenges and Solutions

- **Data Type Mismatches**
  - Use appropriate conversion actions
  - Validate data early
  - Handle null values
- **Performance Issues**
  - Optimize loops
  - Reduce HTTP calls
  - Use batch operations

Mastering these ten essential actions provides a solid foundation for building powerful workflows in Power Automate. They enable you to:

- Automate complex business processes
- Reduce manual work
- Improve accuracy and consistency
- Scale operations efficiently
- Integrate systems seamlessly

Remember that while Power Automate offers many more actions, proficiency with these core actions will help you solve most business automation challenges effectively.

Practice Exercise

Create a workflow that uses at least five of these essential actions to:

- Process incoming data

- Apply business rules
- Get approvals
- Update systems
- Send notifications

This will help you understand how these actions work together in real-world scenarios.

10 Advanced Power Automate Actions: Mastering Complex Workflow Automation

Advanced Power Automate actions can help you create sophisticated, efficient, and scalable automated workflows. The following section explores ten powerful actions that can transform your automation capabilities:

Parallel Branch Action

Purpose

To execute multiple actions simultaneously to reduce workflow execution time

Advanced Implementation

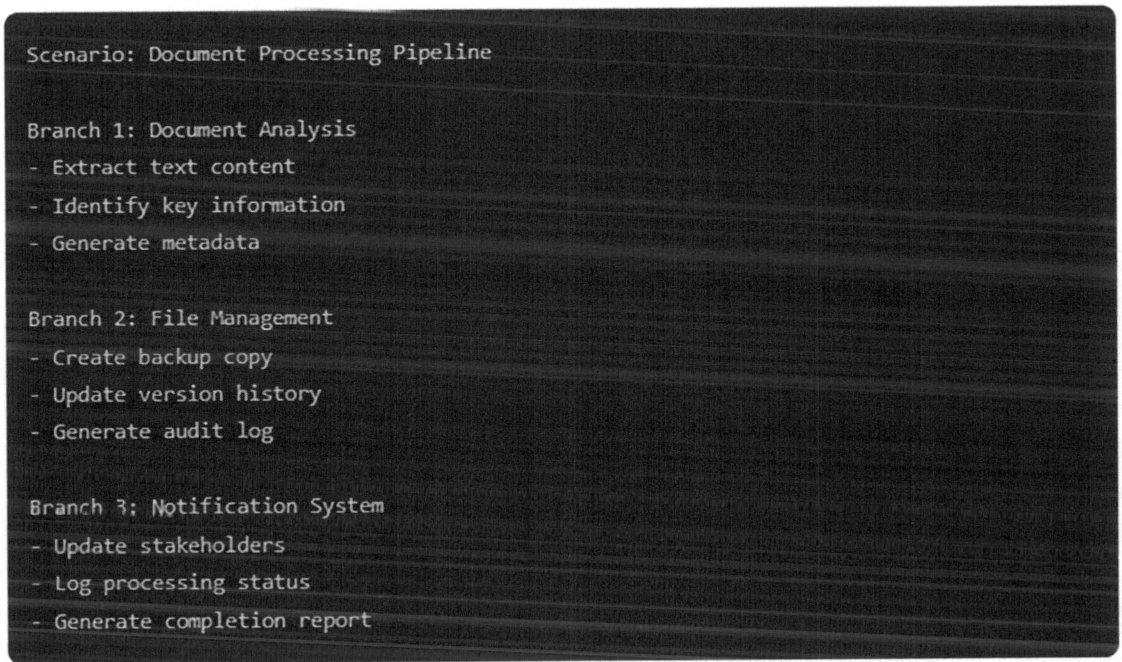

```
Scenario: Document Processing Pipeline

Branch 1: Document Analysis
- Extract text content
- Identify key information
- Generate metadata

Branch 2: File Management
- Create backup copy
- Update version history
- Generate audit log

Branch 3: Notification System
- Update stakeholders
- Log processing status
- Generate completion report
```

Figure 6.39: *Parallel Branch Configuration*

Note: *Use Scope actions within each branch for better error handling and monitoring.*

Complex Condition Action

Purpose

To make sophisticated decisions based on multiple criteria and dynamic content

Advanced Implementation

```
Scenario: Invoice Processing

Conditions:
IF (Amount > 50000 AND Department = "Finance")
    OR
    (Amount > 25000 AND Department = "Marketing")
    OR
    (Amount > 10000 AND RequiresExpedited = true)
THEN
    Route to Senior Management
ELSE IF (Multiple Approvers Required)
    Initialize parallel approval
ELSE
    Standard processing
```

Figure 6.40: *Complex Condition Setup*

Dynamic Content Creator

Purpose

To generate dynamic content based on multiple data sources and conditions

Advanced Implementation

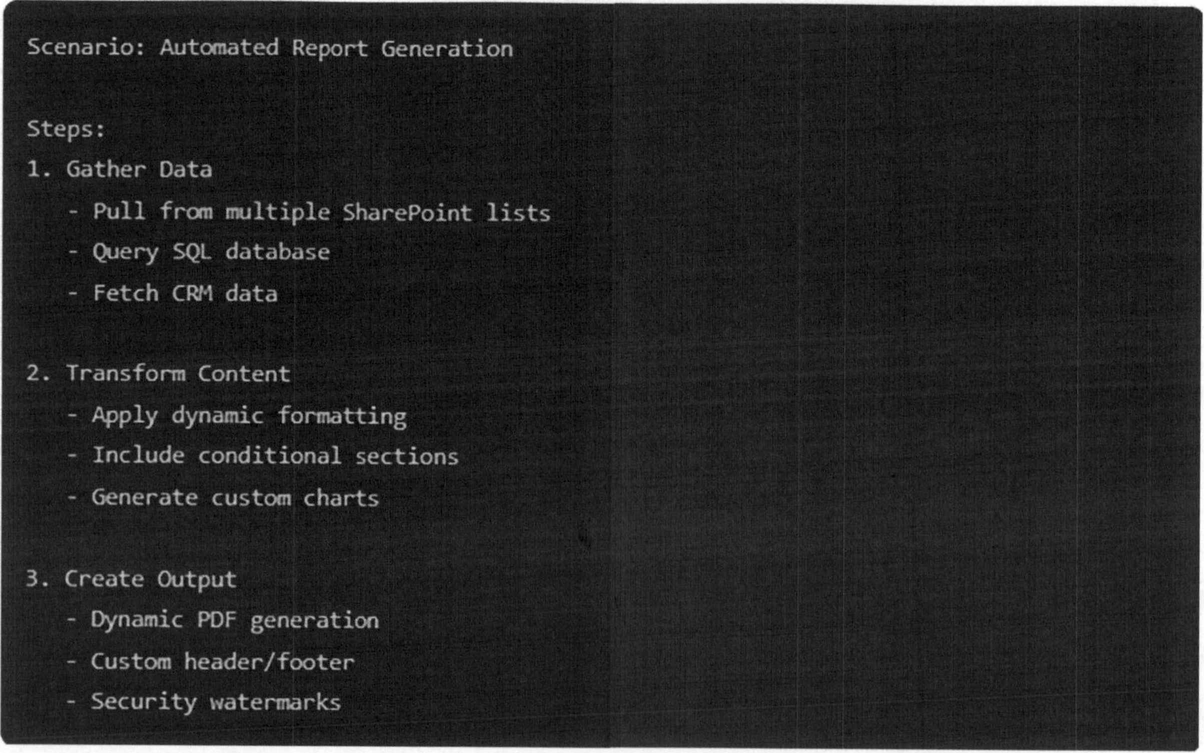

```
Scenario: Automated Report Generation

Steps:
1. Gather Data
   - Pull from multiple SharePoint lists
   - Query SQL database
   - Fetch CRM data

2. Transform Content
   - Apply dynamic formatting
   - Include conditional sections
   - Generate custom charts

3. Create Output
   - Dynamic PDF generation
   - Custom header/footer
   - Security watermarks
```

Figure 6.41: *Advanced Flow Design: Dynamic Content Generation*

Advanced HTTP Request

Purpose

To interact with external systems using complex API calls and authentication

Advanced Implementation

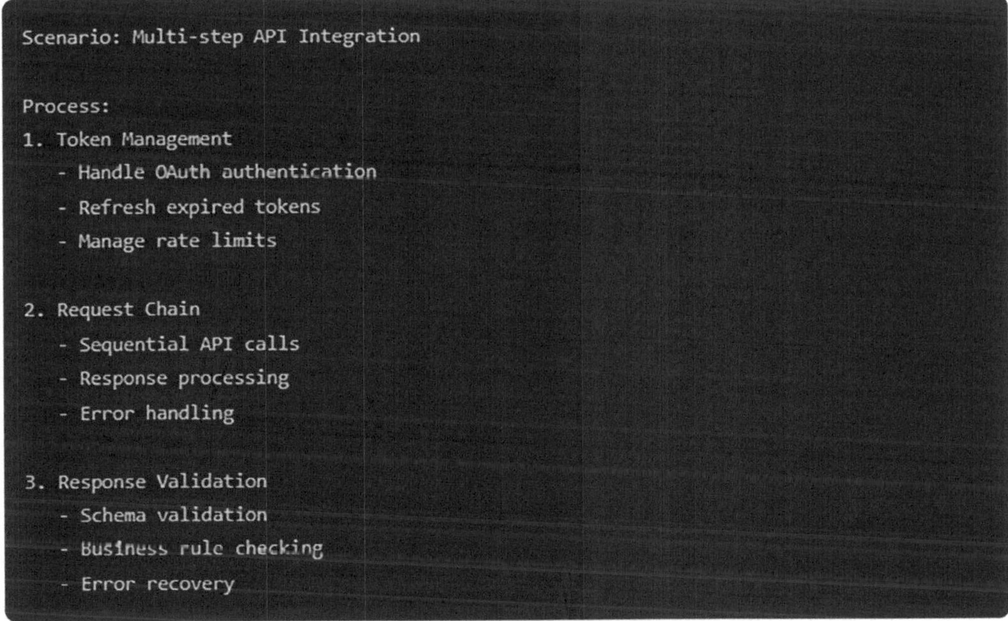

```
Scenario: Multi-step API Integration

Process:
1. Token Management
   - Handle OAuth authentication
   - Refresh expired tokens
   - Manage rate limits

2. Request Chain
   - Sequential API calls
   - Response processing
   - Error handling

3. Response Validation
   - Schema validation
   - Business rule checking
   - Error recovery
```

Figure 6.42: *Advanced HTTP Integration in Flows*

Data Operation Composer

Purpose

To transform and manipulate complex data structures efficiently

Advanced Implementation

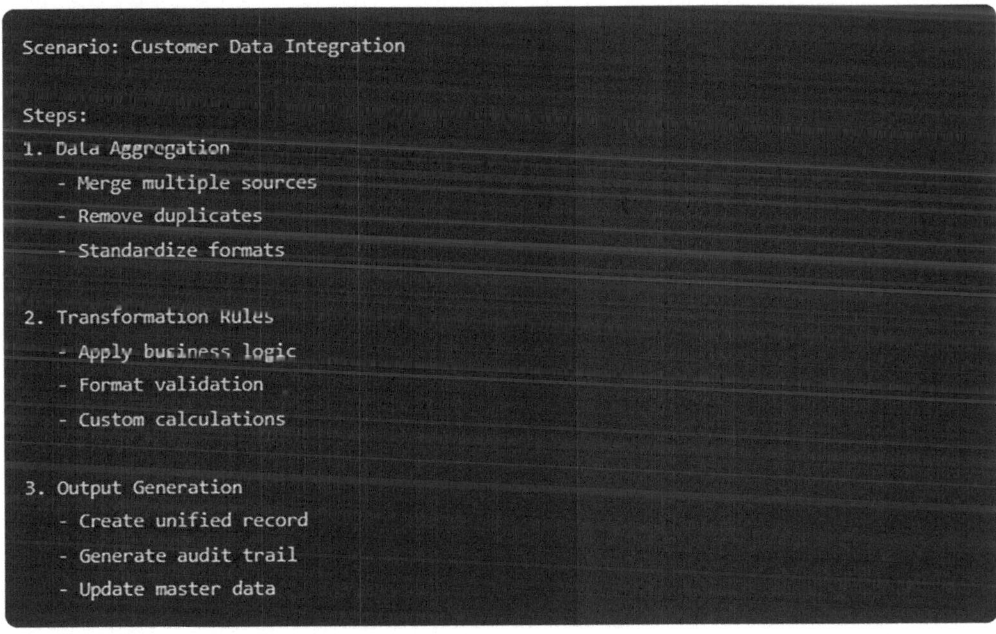

```
Scenario: Customer Data Integration

Steps:
1. Data Aggregation
   - Merge multiple sources
   - Remove duplicates
   - Standardize formats

2. Transformation Rules
   - Apply business logic
   - Format validation
   - Custom calculations

3. Output Generation
   - Create unified record
   - Generate audit trail
   - Update master data
```

Figure 6.43: *Advanced Data Manipulation with Data Operation Composer*

Scoped Error Handler

Purpose

To implement sophisticated error handling and recovery mechanisms

Advanced Implementation

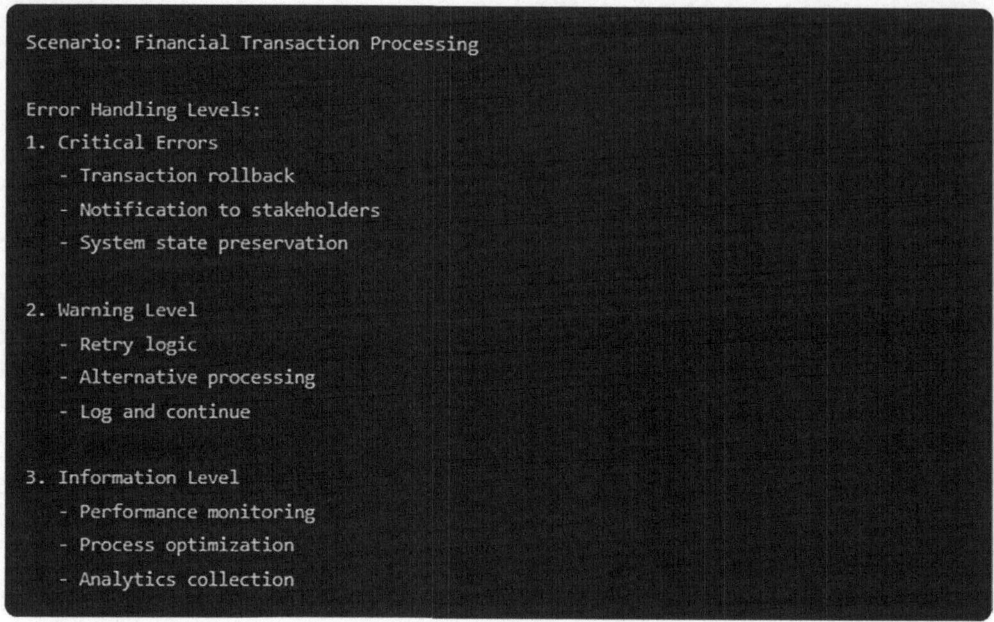

```
Scenario: Financial Transaction Processing

Error Handling Levels:
1. Critical Errors
   - Transaction rollback
   - Notification to stakeholders
   - System state preservation

2. Warning Level
   - Retry logic
   - Alternative processing
   - Log and continue

3. Information Level
   - Performance monitoring
   - Process optimization
   - Analytics collection
```

Figure 6.44: *Implementing Scoped Error Handlers for Reliable Automation*

Dynamic Schema Transformer

Purpose

To handle varying data structures and formats adaptively

Advanced Implementation

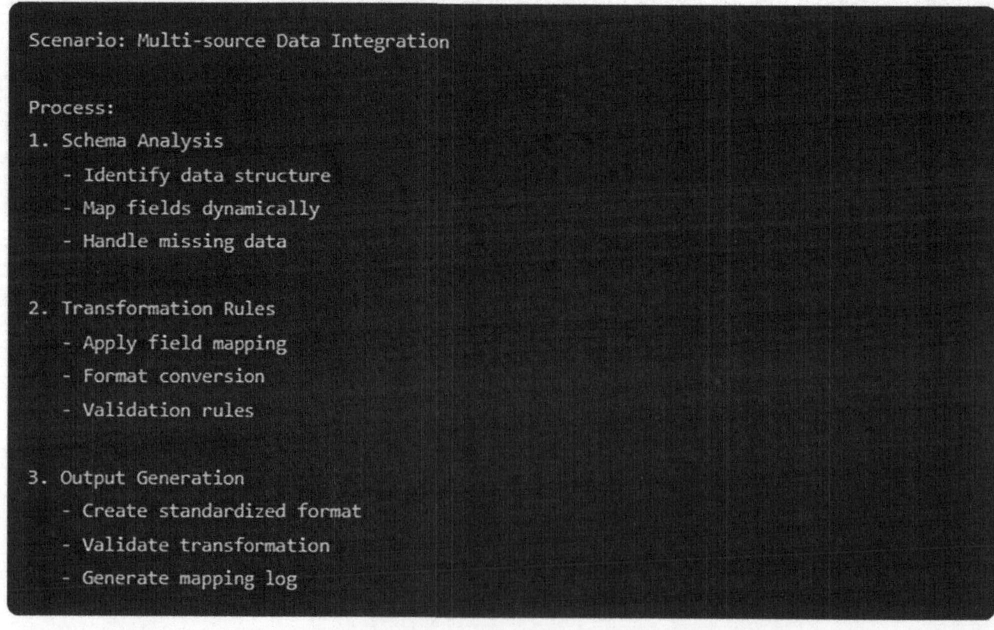

```
Scenario: Multi-source Data Integration

Process:
1. Schema Analysis
   - Identify data structure
   - Map fields dynamically
   - Handle missing data

2. Transformation Rules
   - Apply field mapping
   - Format conversion
   - Validation rules

3. Output Generation
   - Create standardized format
   - Validate transformation
   - Generate mapping log
```

Figure 6.45: *Dynamic Schema Handling in Flows: Advanced Techniques*

Advanced Approval Orchestrator

Purpose

To manage complex approval workflows with multiple stakeholders

Advanced Implementation

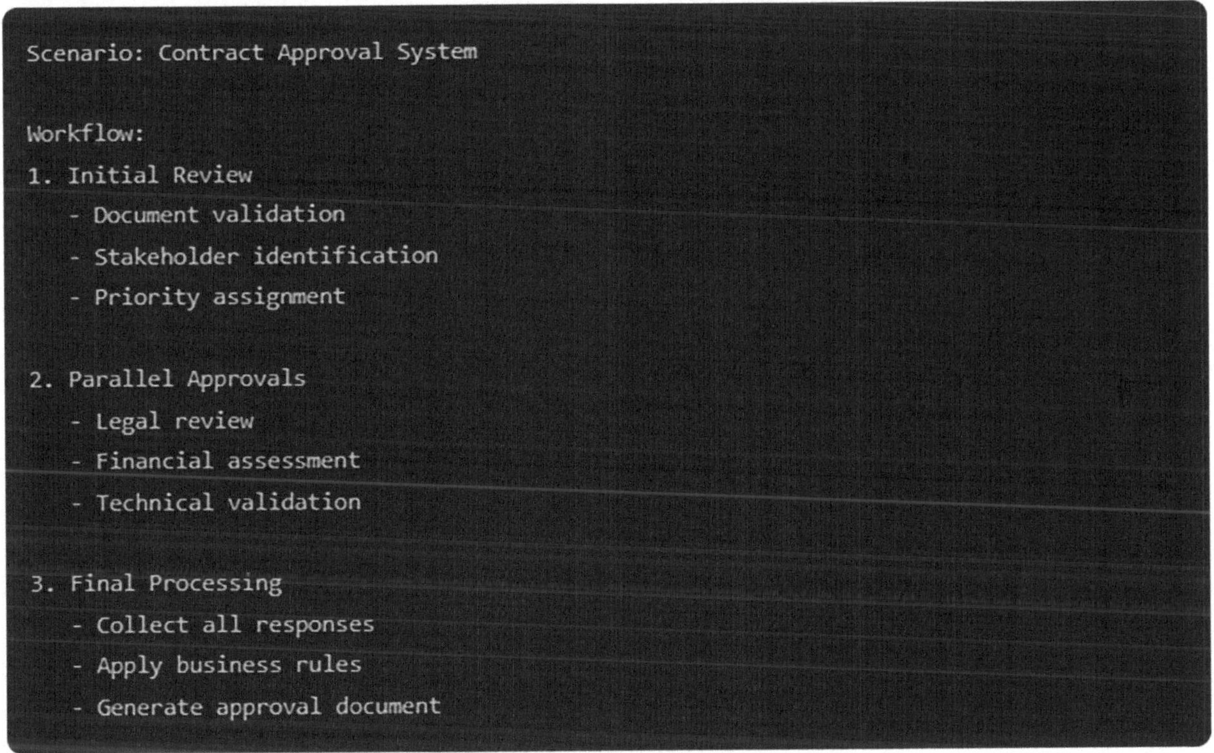

```
Scenario: Contract Approval System

Workflow:
1. Initial Review
   - Document validation
   - Stakeholder identification
   - Priority assignment

2. Parallel Approvals
   - Legal review
   - Financial assessment
   - Technical validation

3. Final Processing
   - Collect all responses
   - Apply business rules
   - Generate approval document
```

Figure 6.46: *Orchestrating Multi-Level Approvals in Flows*

File Operation Manager

Purpose

To handle complex file operations across multiple systems

Advanced Implementation

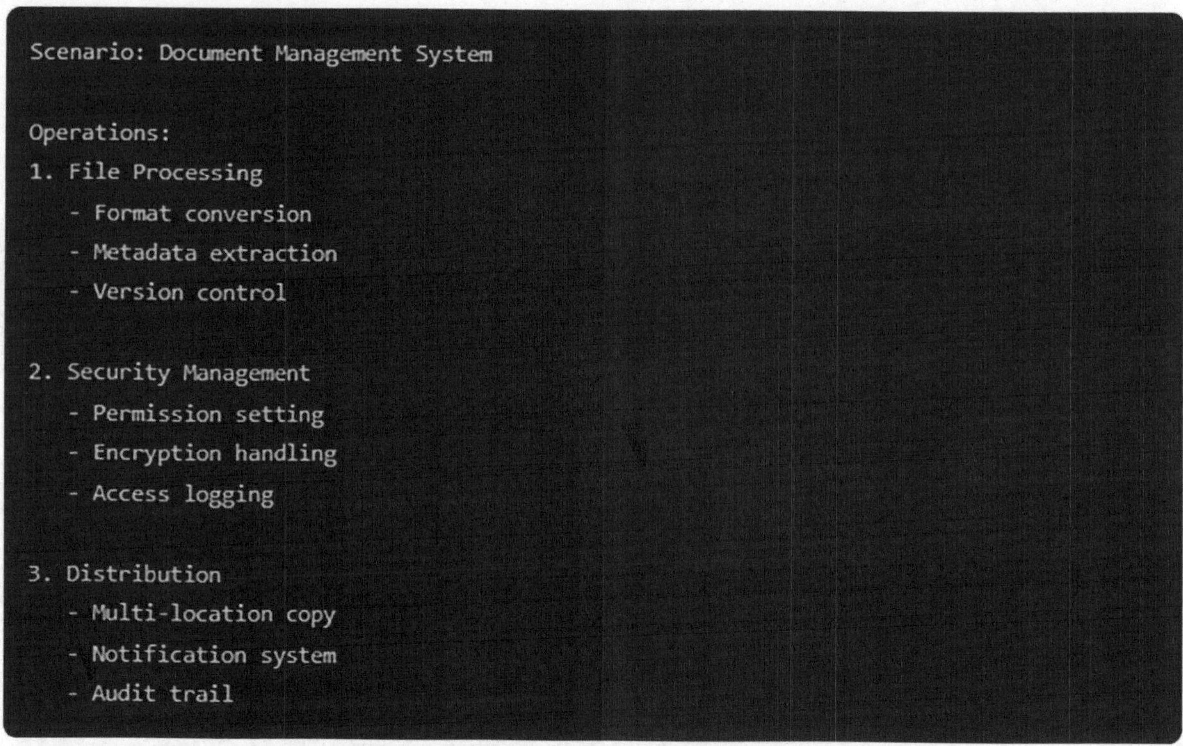

```
Scenario: Document Management System

Operations:
1. File Processing
   - Format conversion
   - Metadata extraction
   - Version control

2. Security Management
   - Permission setting
   - Encryption handling
   - Access logging

3. Distribution
   - Multi-location copy
   - Notification system
   - Audit trail
```

Figure 6.47: *Managing Cross-System File Operations with File Operation Manager*

Advanced Timer Controller

Purpose

To implement sophisticated timing and scheduling mechanisms

Advanced Implementation

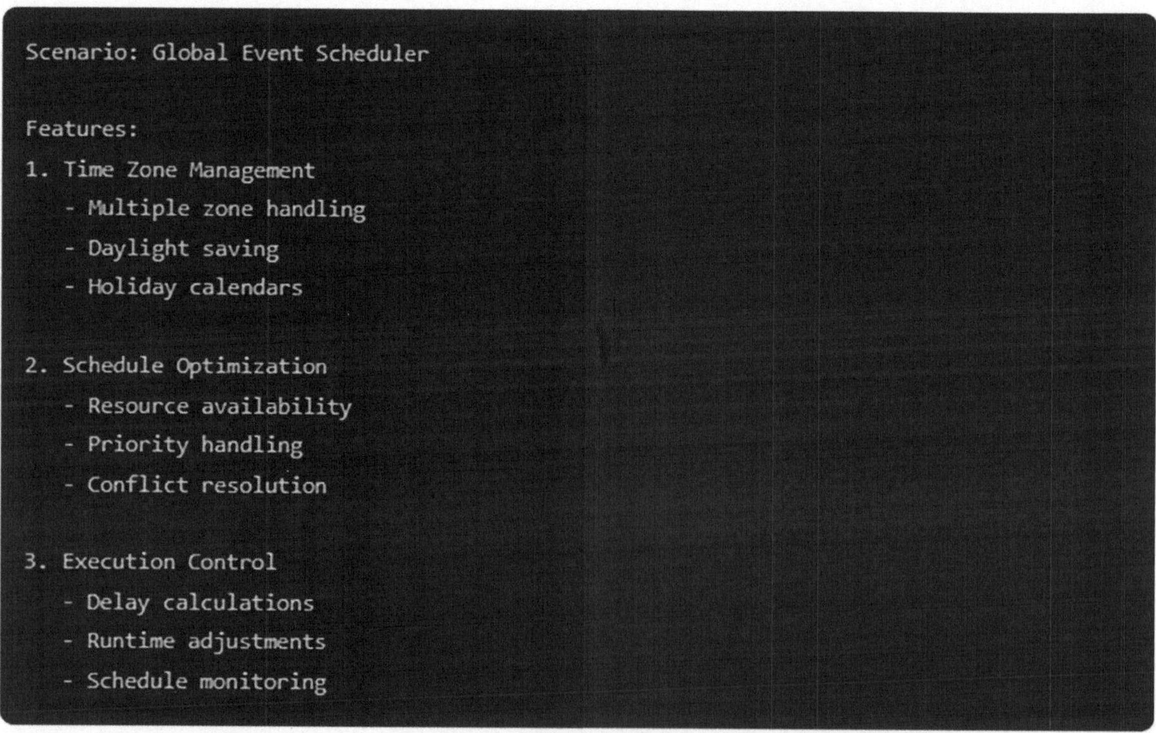

```
Scenario: Global Event Scheduler

Features:
1. Time Zone Management
   - Multiple zone handling
   - Daylight saving
   - Holiday calendars

2. Schedule Optimization
   - Resource availability
   - Priority handling
   - Conflict resolution

3. Execution Control
   - Delay calculations
   - Runtime adjustments
   - Schedule monitoring
```

Figure 6.48: *Time-Based Automation with Advanced Timer Controller*

Implementation Example: End-to-End Solution

Let us combine these actions in a real-world scenario:

Global Invoice Processing System

- Parallel Branch Action
  - Document processing
  - Data validation
  - Notification system
- Complex Condition Action
  - Amount thresholds
  - Regional rules
  - Approval requirements
- Dynamic Content Creator
  - Custom reports
  - Approval documents
  - Audit trails
- Error Handler
  - Process monitoring
  - Recovery procedures
  - Stakeholder notification

Best Practices

- Performance Optimization
  - Use parallel processing effectively
  - Implement batch operations
  - Monitor resource usage
- Error Management
  - Implement comprehensive logging
  - Create recovery procedures
  - Monitor system health
- Maintenance
  - Document complex configurations
  - Create testing procedures
  - Plan for scalability

Practice Exercise

Create a workflow that implements at least five of these advanced actions:

- Set up parallel processing
- Implement complex conditions
- Handle dynamic content
- Manage errors effectively
- Control timing precisely

These advanced Power Automate actions provide the building blocks for creating sophisticated, enterprise-grade automation solutions. By mastering these actions, you can:

- Build more efficient workflows
- Handle complex business processes
- Implement robust error handling
- Create scalable solutions

Conclusion

Actions in Power Automate are powerful tools that enable the creation of sophisticated automated workflows. Through this chapter, we have explored various types of actions, their configuration, and practical implementation in real-world scenarios. Understanding how to effectively combine and configure actions can help you create efficient, scalable, and maintainable workflows.

You can use Power Automate actions successfully by choosing the right actions for your specific needs, implementing proper error handling, and following best practices for performance optimization. As you continue to work with Power Automate, you must experiment with different combinations of actions and learn from the outcomes to build increasingly sophisticated solutions.

Remember that well-designed workflows strike a balance between functionality and maintainability. Keep your flows organized, documented, and optimized for performance while ensuring they meet your business requirements effectively.

In the next chapter, we will dive deep into data operations, exploring how to effectively manipulate, transform, and process data within your Power Automate workflows. You will learn essential techniques for working with arrays, objects, and complex data structures that will enhance your automation capabilities.

CHAPTER 7
Navigating Data Operations

Introduction

In the previous chapters, we have explored the fundamentals of Microsoft Power Automate Cloud Flows, from creating your first flow to understanding triggers and actions. We have already covered the basic building blocks, flow control mechanisms, and connection to various Microsoft services. Now, it is time to dive into one of the most critical aspects of automation: data operations.

Data is the lifeblood of any workflow. Whether you are moving information between systems, transforming content from one format to another, or making decisions based on specific data points, understanding how to effectively manipulate data is essential for creating powerful and efficient flows. This chapter builds upon the foundations we've established and focuses specifically on how to work with, transform, and optimize data within your Power Automate Cloud Flows.

As your automation journey progresses and your flows become more sophisticated, they will inevitably involve increasingly complex data operations. In real-world business scenarios, data rarely arrives in the exact format you need. Consider a common scenario: when a customer submits a Microsoft Form, Power Automate receives the response data, but you need to transform it before creating a record in Dataverse—perhaps splitting a full name into first and last names, converting text responses into choice values, or formatting date fields to match your database requirements. Similarly, when retrieving items from a SharePoint list to send in an email notification, you might need to filter the items based on specific criteria, sort them by priority, and format the data into a readable HTML table. Or when working with external APIs through HTTP actions, you'll receive JSON responses that need to be parsed, validated, and mapped to your internal data structures before being stored in SQL Server or Excel Online.

The skills you'll learn in this chapter will empower you to handle these Power Automate-specific challenges effectively. You'll discover how to use the built-in data operation actions like "Compose", "Parse JSON", "Select", and "Filter array" to manipulate data efficiently within your flows. You'll learn to leverage Power Automate's expression language to transform data on-the-fly, validate information to ensure quality before it reaches your target systems, map fields between different connectors and services, and implement proper error handling using Scope actions and "Configure run after" settings when data doesn't meet expectations. You'll understand when to use variables versus direct references, how to optimize performance by minimizing actions within "Apply to each" loops, and how to structure your flows for maintainability as data operations become more complex.

By mastering these Power Automate data operations, you'll be able to build flows that are not only functional but also resilient, efficient, and capable of handling the complexities of enterprise data environments. These capabilities will transform you from creating simple trigger-action flows to developing robust, production-ready solutions that can intelligently process data from multiple sources, handle exceptions gracefully, and adapt to the unpredictable nature of real-world data. Whether you're building approval workflows that require data aggregation, integration flows that synchronize information across platforms, or scheduled flows that generate reports from multiple data sources, the data operation techniques in this chapter will be your essential toolkit for success.

Structure

This chapter will address the following topics:

- Understanding Data operation fundamentals
- Working with variables and data collection
- Data transformation techniques and expressions
- Parsing and formatting complex data types (JSON, XML, CSV)
- Data mapping strategies between different systems
- Filtering, sorting, and grouping techniques
- Advanced data manipulation with Power Automate expressions
- Error handling for data operations
- Performance optimization for data-intensive flows
- Security considerations when handling sensitive data
- Integration with various data sources (SharePoint, Dataverse, SQL, etc.)
- Best practices for manageable and maintainable data operations

Understanding Data Operations Fundamentals

Data operations in Power Automate encompass all the actions and techniques you can use to work with data within your flows. These operations range from simple variable assignments to complex transformations involving multiple data sources.

Types of Data in Power Automate

Before diving into operations, it is important to understand the types of data you will be working with:

Data Type	Description	Example
String	Text data	"Hello World"
Number	Numeric data	42, 3.14
Boolean	True/false values	true, false
Array	Ordered collection of items	["item1", "item2", "item3"]
Object	Key-value pairs	{"name": "John", "age": 30}
Null	Empty or undefined value	null
DateTime	Date and time values	"2023-09-20T14:30:00Z"

Table 7.1: *Types of Data in Power Automate*

Power Automate primarily deals with JSON data under the hood, even though the interface often shields you from this complexity. Therefore, understanding these data types is crucial for effective data manipulation.

Note: *When troubleshooting data operations, it is helpful to use the "`Peek code`" option in the Flow editor to see the underlying JSON representation of your actions.*

Data Flow in Power Automate

Data in Power Automate flows in a specific way:

1. **Input data** comes from triggers, connections, or manual inputs.
2. **Processing** happens through various actions and expressions.
3. **Output data** is passed to subsequent actions or as the flows final result.

This flow follows a sequential pattern, where each action can use data from previous steps but cannot access data from future steps.

Try It Yourself: Examining Data Types

1. Create a new instant flow with a manual trigger
2. Add an "`Initialize variable`" action
3. Try creating variables with different data types
4. Use "`Compose`" actions to see how Power Automate handles these different types
5. Run the flow and observe the outputs

Working with Variables and Data Collection

Variables are essential tools for storing and manipulating data in your flows. Power Automate provides several actions for working with variables.

Initializing Variables

The "`Initialize variable`" action creates a new variable with a specified name, type, and initial value. This is one of the first steps in your data operation sequence.

```
Action: Initialize variable
Name: customerData
Type: Object
Value: {
    "customerId": "12345",
    "name": "Contoso Corp",
    "status": "Active"
}
```

Figure 7.1: *Initializing Variables in a Workflow*

Manipulating Variables

Once variables are initialized, you can manipulate them using the following actions:

- **Set variable**: Changes the value of an existing variable
- **Increment variable**: Increases a numeric variable by a specified value
- **Decrement variable**: Decreases a numeric variable by a specified value

- **Append to array variable**: Adds an item to an array variable

Common Pitfall: Variables in Power Automate have flow-level scope. This means they cannot be directly accessed across different flows or even across different "`Apply to each`" loops unless you specifically pass them.

Working with Arrays and Collections

Arrays are particularly useful for working with collections of data. Here are some common operations:

Creating an Array:

```
Action: Initialize variable
Name: products
Type: Array
Value: [
    {
        "id": "P001",
        "name": "Laptop",
        "price": 999
    },
    {
        "id": "P002",
        "name": "Mouse",
        "price": 25
    }
]
```

***Figure* 7.2:** *Create an Array*

Processing Arrays: The "`Apply to each`" action is the primary way to iterate through arrays in Power Automate. It allows you to perform actions on each item in the collection.

```
Action: Apply to each
Items: variables('products')
  Action: Compose
  Inputs: @{items('Apply_to_each').name}: @{items('Apply_to_each').price}
```

***Figure* 7.3:** *Common Operations for Arrays and Collections*

Note: *For better performance with large arrays, consider using the "`Filter array`" action before "`Apply to each`" to reduce the number of iterations.*

Try It Yourself: Variable Manipulation

1. Create a flow with an array variable containing product information.
2. Use "`Apply to each`" to process each product.

3. Add a condition to filter products above a certain price.
4. Store the filtered products in a new array variable.
5. Use the Compose action to display the final results.

Data Transformation Techniques

Data rarely comes in exactly the format you need. Transformation techniques allow you to reshape data to meet your requirements.

Using Expressions for Data Transformation

Power Automate provides a rich expression language that allows you to transform data in numerous ways. Some essential expressions include:

Expression	Purpose	Example
concat()	Combine strings	concat('Hello', ' ', 'World')
replace()	Replace text in a string	replace('Hello World', 'World', 'Universe')
split()	Split a string into an array	split('apple,orange,banana', ',')
length()	Get length of string or array	length('Hello') or length(variables('myArray'))
substring()	Extract part of a string	substring('Hello World', 0, 5)
int() / float()	Convert to number	int('42') or float('3.14')
json()	Parse a JSON string	json('{"name": "John"}')
string()	Convert to string	string(42)

Table 7.2: *Key Expressions Used to Transform Data in Power Automate Workflows*

Note: *The expression editor in Power Automate provides auto-completion and documentation for expressions, making them easier to learn and use.*

Complex Data Transformations

For more complex transformations, you may need to combine multiple expressions:

Example: Formatting a Name

Action: Compose

```
Inputs:@{toUpper(substring(variables('fullName'),0, 1))}@{toLower(substring
(variables('fullName'), 1, sub(length(variables('fullName')), 1)))}
```

This expression takes a name and formats it with an uppercase first letter and lowercase remaining letters.

Data Mapping Between Systems

When integrating different systems, you often need to map data from one format to another:

Action: Compose

```
Inputs: {
    "customer": {
        "id": "@{variables('salesforceCustomer').sf_id}",
```

```
        "fullName": "@{concat(variables('salesforceCustomer').first_name, ' ',
variables('salesforceCustomer').last_name)}",
        "emailAddress": "@{variables('salesforceCustomer').email}",
        "accountType": "@{if(equals(variables('salesforceCustomer').
customer_type, 'Premium'), 'Gold', 'Standard')}"
    }
}
```

Common Pitfall: Be careful with null or undefined values when mapping data. Always include appropriate error handling to check if properties exist before trying to access them.

Try It Yourself: Customer Data Transformation

1. Create a flow that initializes a variable with customer data from a CRM system.
2. Transform this data to match the format required by your billing system.
3. Use expressions to handle special cases (for example, formatting phone numbers, capitalizing names).
4. Output the transformed data using a Compose action.

Parsing and Formatting Complex Data Types

Working with complex data formats is a common requirement in enterprise integration scenarios.

JSON Operations

JSON (JavaScript Object Notation) is the native format for Power Automate. Here is how to work with it:

Parsing JSON:

```
Action: Parse JSON
Content: @{body('HTTP_Request')}
Schema: {
    "type": "object",
    "properties": {
        "id": {
            "type": "string"
        },
        "items": {
            "type": "array",
            "items": {
                "type": "object",
                "properties": {
                    "name": { "type": "string" },
                    "quantity": { "type": "integer" }
                }
            }
        }
    }
}
```

Figure 7.4: Parse JSON

Creating JSON:

```
Action: Compose
Inputs: {
    "orderId": "@{variables('orderId')}",
    "customer": "@{variables('customerName')}",
    "items": "@{variables('orderItems')}"
}
```

Figure 7.5: *JSON Schema Creation*

Note: *To generate a JSON schema automatically, use sample data in the "`Parse JSON`" action and click "`Generate from sample`."*

XML Handling

XML is still commonly used in enterprise systems. Power Automate provides actions for working with XML.

Parsing XML:

```
Action: Parse XML
Content: @{body('HTTP_Request')}
Schema: <schema>...</schema>
```

Figure 7.6: *Parsing XML*

Converting between XML and JSON:

```
Action: Compose
Inputs: @{xml(json(variables('xmlContent')))}
```

Figure 7.7: *Converting between XML and JSON*

CSV and Table Data

Working with tabular data is common in reporting and data analysis scenarios:

Parsing CSV:

```
Action: Compose
Inputs: @{split(variables('csvContent'), '\n')}
```

Figure 7.8: *Parsing CSV*

For more complex CSV parsing, you may need to use a combination of expressions or the "**`Table`**" functions in Power Automate.

Try It Yourself: Processing a Product Catalog

1. Create a flow that receives a CSV product catalog.

2. Parse the CSV into an array of products.
3. Transform this into a JSON format.
4. Filter for products meeting specific criteria.
5. Output the filtered product list in a structured format.

Data mapping strategies between different systems

Data mapping is the process of defining how data fields from a source system correspond to fields in a target system. This is essential when integrating different applications in Power Automate Cloud Flows that use varying data structures and formats.

Common Integration Scenarios

Source	Target	Mapping Challenge
Dynamics 365 Sales	SharePoint List	Field name differences (e.g., “fullname” vs “CustomerName”)
Excel Online	SQL Database	Data type conversion (text to numbers)
HTTP Response (JSON)	Email Template	Converting structured data to readable text
Forms	Dataverse	Handling optional fields and validation

Table 7.3: *Common Integration Scenarios*

Basic Mapping Techniques

Direct Field Mapping

When field names and types align between systems

Target Field: Customer Name

```
Expression: @{triggerOutputs()?['body/fullname']}
```

Field Concatenation

Combining multiple source fields into one target field:

Target Field: Full Address

```
Expression:@{concat(triggerOutputs()?['body/address1_line1'],'',
triggerOutputs()?['body/address1_city'],',', triggerOutputs()?['body/address1_
stateorprovince'])}
```

Field Splitting

Breaking one source field into multiple target fields:

```
First Name: @{split(triggerOutputs()?['body/fullname'], ' ')?[0]}
LastName:@{if(greater(length(split(triggerOutputs()?['body/fullname'],'')),1),
split(triggerOutputs()?['body/fullname'], ' ')?[1], '')}
```

Handling Data Type Conversions

Text to Number Conversion

```
Expression:@{if(empty(triggerOutputs()?['body/revenue']),0, int(trigger
Outputs()?['body/revenue']))}
```

Date Format Standardization

```
Expression: @{formatDateTime(triggerOutputs()?['body/createdon'], 'yyyy-MM-dd')}
```

Boolean Value Mapping

```
Expression: @{if(equals(triggerOutputs()?['body/isactive'], 'Yes'), true, false)}
```

Advanced Mapping Patterns

Conditional Value Mapping

Use switch expressions for value translation as demonstrated:

Priority Mapping:

```
@{switch(
    triggerOutputs()?['body/urgency'],
    'Low', 3,
    'Medium', 2,
    'High', 1,
    3
)}
```

Null and Empty Value Handling

```
Expression:@{coalesce(triggerOutputs()?['body/email'], triggerOutputs()?
['body/alternativeemail'], 'no-email@company.com')}
```

Array Transformation

Using Select action to transform collections in the following manner:

Action: Select

```
From: @{triggerOutputs()?['body/orderitems']}
Map:
{
    "ProductID": @{item()?['productid']},
    "Quantity": @{int(item()?['qty'])},
    "UnitPrice": @{float(item()?['price'])}
}
```

Practical Implementation Steps

Step 1: Analyze Source and Target Schemas

Before building your flow, make sure to:

- Document all source fields and their data types
- Identify corresponding target fields

- Note any required transformations

Step 2: Handle Required Fields First

Always map mandatory fields with appropriate validation.

Step 3: Implement Default Values

Provide fallbacks for optional fields.

Note: *Always test your mappings with various data scenarios, including empty values, special characters, and edge cases to ensure robust data transformation.*

Filtering, Sorting, and Grouping Data

Efficiently working with data collections often requires filtering, sorting, or grouping operations.

Filtering Data

The "**`Filter array`**" action allows you to select items from an array based on specific criteria as shown in the following illustration:

```
Action: Filter array
From: variables('customers')
Where: @equals(item()?['status'], 'Active')
```

Figure 7.9: *Filtering Data*

For more complex filtering, you can use expressions such as:

```
Action: Filter array
From: variables('orders')
Where: @and(
    greater(item()?['total'], 1000),
    equals(item()?['status'], 'Pending'),
    contains(item()?['customer'], 'Contoso')
)
```

Figure 7.10: *Complex Data Filtering*

Sorting Data

To sort an array, you can use the "**`Sort`**" expression in the following manner:

```
Action: Compose
Inputs: @{sort(variables('products'), 'price')}
```

Figure 7.11: *Using sort Expression*

For descending order, use the following action:

```
Action: Compose
Inputs: @{reverse(sort(variables('products'), 'price'))}
```

Figure 7.12: *Using reverse sort Expression*

Grouping and Aggregating Data

Grouping data often requires more complex expressions. Here is an example of grouping orders by customer:

```
Action: Compose
Inputs: @{
    union(
        union(
            createArray(),
            variables('customers')?[0]
        ),
        skip(variables('customers'), 1)
    )
}
```

Figure 7.13: *Grouping and Aggregating Data*

Note: *For complex grouping operations, consider using the "`Select`" expression to reshape your data first.*

Try It Yourself: Sales Data Analysis

1. Create a flow with a variable containing sales transaction data.
2. Filter transactions for a specific date range.
3. Group transactions by product category.
4. Calculate total sales for each category.
5. Sort categories by total sales in descending order.

Advanced Data Manipulation with Expressions

Power Automate's expression language provides powerful capabilities that can be harnessed for complex data operations.

Working with Collections

Selecting Properties:

```
Action: Compose
Inputs: @{select(variables('employees'), item() => {
    name: item().displayName,
    email: item().mail,
    department: item().department
})}
```

Figure 7.14: *Select expression for working with collections*

Joining Arrays:

```
Action: Compose
Inputs: @{join(variables('items'), ', ')}
```

Figure 7.15: *Joining arrays for working with collections*

Date and Time Operations

Date manipulation is common in business processes, just like in the following illustration:

```
Action: Compose
Inputs: @{formatDateTime(addDays(utcNow(), 30), 'yyyy-MM-dd')}
```

Figure 7.16: *Date and Time Manipulation Expression*

This creates a date 30 days from now in the format "`YYYY-MM-DD`".

Conditional Data Transformation

Using conditional logic in data operations as stipulated here:

Action: Compose

```
Inputs: @{
    map(variables('orders'), item() => {
        orderId: item().id,
        customer: item().customerName,
        priority: if(greater(item().total, 10000), 'High', if(greater(item().
total, 5000), 'Medium', 'Low'))
    })
}
```

Common Pitfall: Complex expressions can be difficult to debug. Build them incrementally and test each part separately.

Try It Yourself: Dynamic Reporting Data

1. Create a flow with sales data across multiple regions.
2. Use expressions to calculate growth percentages between periods.

3. Categorize results using conditional logic.
4. Format the data for a report with appropriate labels and formatting.
5. Output the processed data in a structured format.

Error Handling in Data Operations

Robust data operations require proper error handling to deal with unexpected situations. No matter how carefully you design your data transformations and validations, real-world scenarios will inevitably present challenges: APIs may be temporarily unavailable, data formats might change unexpectedly, required fields could be missing, or network timeouts may occur during data transfers. To build resilient flows that can gracefully handle these situations rather than simply failing, Power Automate provides several error handling patterns and techniques that you can implement within your data operations.

Try-Catch Pattern

Power Automate supports a pattern similar to try-catch using "**Scope**" and "**Configure run after**":

1. Create a Scope action to contain your data operations.
2. Add your main data processing actions inside this scope.
3. Add a Parallel branch.
4. Configure the Parallel branch to run only when the Scope has failed.
5. Inside this branch, add actions to handle the error (for instance, logging and notification).

Handling Specific Data Errors

For specific data issues, use conditions to check for problematic values just like in the following figure:

```
Action: Condition
Condition: @or(
    equals(variables('customerData'), null),
    equals(length(variables('customerData')), 0)
)
If yes: [Actions to handle missing data]
If no: [Normal processing]
```

Figure 7.17: *How to use conditional logic handling Specific Data Errors*

Implementing Retry Logic

For operations that might fail due to temporary issues, implement retry logic as illustrated here:

```
Action: HTTP
Method: POST
URI: https://api.example.com/data
Headers: {
    "Content-Type": "application/json"
}
Body: @{variables('requestPayload')}
Retry Policy: {
    "count": 3,
    "interval": "PT30S"
}
```

Figure 7.18: *Implementing Retry Logic*

Note: *Add logging throughout your data operations to make troubleshooting easier if issues occur in production.*

Try It Yourself: Robust Data Import

1. Create a flow that imports data from an external API.
2. Implement comprehensive error checking for the data.
3. Add appropriate error handling for API failures.
4. Create a notification mechanism for critical failures.
5. Implement a retry mechanism for transient errors.

Performance Optimization for Data Operations

As your flows handle more data, performance becomes increasingly important. In Power Automate Cloud Flows, performance directly impacts both user experience and operational costs slow flows can delay critical business processes, cause timeouts that result in failed runs, and consume more API calls against your organization's daily limits. Moreover, poorly optimized flows processing large datasets can hit Power Automate's execution time limits (typically 30 days for most plans, but individual actions have timeout thresholds), leading to incomplete data operations and unreliable automation. Understanding performance optimization techniques is essential for building enterprise grade flows that can scale from processing dozens of records during testing to handling thousands of records in production environments without degradation or failure.

Within Power Automate, performance optimization takes on specific dimensions that differ from traditional programming. Each action in your flow consumes execution time and counts toward API call quotas, so minimizing unnecessary actions is crucial. For instance, when working with SharePoint lists containing 5,000 items, retrieving all items and then filtering them within an "Apply to each" loop is significantly slower and more resource-intensive than using OData filter queries in the "Get items" action to retrieve only the records you need. Similarly, processing items one-by-one through individual connector actions (like updating 100 SharePoint items with 100 separate "Update item" actions) not only takes longer but also consumes 100 API calls, whereas batch operations can accomplish the same result with a single HTTP request.

Power Automate's parallel processing capabilities also play a crucial role in performance optimization. When your data operations don't depend on each other for example, retrieving customer data from Dataverse while simultaneously fetching product information from SharePoint–using parallel branches allows both operations to execute concurrently rather than sequentially, effectively cutting your processing time in half. Additionally, the "Concurrency Control" setting in "Apply to each" actions enables you to process multiple items simultaneously (up to 50 items at once), though this must be balanced against rate limiting considerations for the target systems.

Understanding theseperformance factors enables you to design flows that not only work correctly but work efficiently, ensuring your automation solutions remain responsive, reliable, and scalable as your business needs grow.

Minimizing Iterations

Each iteration in an "`Apply to each`" loop takes time. Optimize by:

- Filtering data early to reduce the number of items processed
- Using "`Select`" to extract only needed properties before processing
- Considering batch operations where possible

Batch Processing

For operations against systems that support it, use batch processing as shown in the following figure:

```
Action: HTTP
Method: POST
URI: https://api.example.com/batch
Headers: {
    "Content-Type": "application/json"
}
Body: {
    "requests": @{variables('batchRequests')}
}
```

Figure 7.19: *Batch Processing Logic*

Pagination Strategies

When working with large datasets that are paginated–meaning the data is split across multiple pages or batches by the source system–you need to implement a strategy to retrieve all the data systematically. Many systems, including SharePoint, Dataverse, and external APIs, limit the number of records returned in a single request to prevent performance issues and timeouts. For example, SharePoint's "Get items" action has a threshold of 5,000 items, and many REST APIs return only 100 or 500 records per page. To process the complete dataset, your Power Automate flow must repeatedly request subsequent pages until all data has been retrieved.

Figure 7.20 demonstrates a pagination pattern using Power Automate's "Do until" loop control. The flow continues to execute as long as there are more pages to retrieve (tracked by the `hasMorePages` variable set to `false` when the last page is reached). Within each iteration, the flow performs four key operations: first, it gets the current page of data using the page token from the previous iteration; second, it processes the data from that page (performing transformations, validations, or storing the records); third, it updates the page token to point to the next set of records; and finally, it checks whether additional pages exist by examining the API response for a "next page" indicator or by verifying if the returned record count is less than the page size. This loop continues until the condition evaluates to true (no more pages remain), ensuring your flow retrieves and processes every record in the dataset regardless of how many pages the data spans across.

```
Action: Do until
Condition: @equals(variables('hasMorePages'), false)
Actions:
    [Get data with current page token]
    [Process current page data]
    [Update page token for next iteration]
    [Check if more pages exist]
```

Figure 7.20: *Pagination Strategy*

Common Pitfall: Be careful with memory usage in large data operations. Power Automate often places limits on the size of data that can be processed in a single flow run.

Try It Yourself: Optimizing a Data Export

1. Create a flow that needs to process a large collection of items.
2. Implement pagination to handle the data in manageable chunks.
3. Use filtering to reduce the processing load.
4. Implement batch operations where possible.
5. Measure and compare the performance difference.

Security Considerations for Data Operations

Handling data securely is paramount, especially when dealing with sensitive information. Therefore, factoring in key security considerations becomes an important exercise to safeguard the integrity of data.

Handling Sensitive Data

Avoid exposing sensitive data in:

- Flow names
- Variable names
- Comments
- Outputs (unless necessary)

Use secure handling techniques as demonstrated in the following figure:

```
Action: Initialize variable
Name: secureConnectionString
Type: String
Value: @{decodeBase64(triggerOutputs().headers['X-MS-CLIENT-SECRET'])}
```

Figure 7.21: *Secure Connection String*

Data Encryption and Masking

When storing sensitive data, make sure to:

- Use environment variables for sensitive values
- Consider encrypting sensitive fields
- Implement data masking for logging and debugging

Access Control for Data Flows

Implement proper access controls to:

- Restrict who can edit flows that handle sensitive data
- Use connection references to manage credentials separately
- Audit access to sensitive flows regularly

Note: *Review your flows regularly to ensure they follow security best practices, especially after making changes.*

Try It Yourself: Secure Customer Data Processing

1. Create a flow that processes customer financial information.
2. Implement appropriate security measures for sensitive fields.
3. Set up proper error handling that does not expose sensitive data.
4. Use environment variables for connection strings.
5. Add audit logging for all data access operations.

Integration with Different Data Sources

Throughout this chapter, we have explored various data operation techniques transforming, filtering, mapping, and optimizing data within your flows. However, these operations become truly powerful when applied across the diverse ecosystem of applications and services that Power Automate can connect to. Power Automate can connect to numerous data sources, each with unique considerations, connection requirements, and best practices that influence how you structure your data operations.

Understanding the nuances of each connector from Microsoft's own services like SharePoint and Dataverse to external databases like SQL Server and third-party APIs—enables you to design flows that not only move data between systems but do so efficiently, securely, and reliably. Each data source has its own authentication mechanisms, query languages, rate limits, and data formats, which directly impact how you implement the data transformation and error handling techniques we've covered. Let's explore how to effectively integrate with the most commonly used data sources in Power Automate Cloud Flows.

SharePoint Data Operations

Working with SharePoint lists and libraries might look something like this:

```
Action: Get items
Site Address: https://contoso.sharepoint.com/sites/project
List Name: Projects
Filter Query: Status eq 'Active'
```

Figure 7.22: *SharePoint Data Operations*

Optimizing SharePoint Operations involves:

- Using OData filter queries to reduce data transfer
- Selecting only required columns
- Using batch operations for multiple updates

Dataverse Integration

Working with Dataverse (formerly Common Data Service) might look something like this illustration here:

```
Action: List records
Entity name: contacts
Filter Query: contains(fullname,'Contoso')
```

Figure 7.23: *Contains Filter Query*

Dataverse Best Practices:

- Use FetchXML for complex queries.
- Leverage batch operations for multiple records.
- Consider Dataverse plugins for complex transformations.

SQL Server Operations

Connecting to SQL databases often looks like this:

```
Action: Execute query
Server name: sqlserver.database.windows.net
Database name: customerdb
Query: SELECT * FROM Customers WHERE Region = @{variables('region')}
```

Figure 7.24: *Connecting SQL db*

SQL Integration Tips:

- Use parameterized queries to prevent SQL injection.
- Consider stored procedures for complex operations.
- Use table-valued parameters for batch operations.

Try It Yourself: Multi-source Data Integration

1. Create a flow that retrieves data from SharePoint.
2. Enrich this data with information from Dataverse.
3. Store the combined results in a SQL database.
4. Implement appropriate error handling for each system.
5. Optimize the data operations for performance.

Best Practices for Managing Data Flows

Abiding by the following best practices ensures your data operations remain manageable and maintainable:

Modular Design

As your data operations grow in complexity, maintaining a monolithic flow with hundreds of actions becomes increasingly difficult to debug, update, and manage. Modular design is a best practice approach that involves breaking down complex data operations into smaller, logical, and reusable units within Power Automate. This architectural approach not only improves maintainability but also enhances collaboration among team members and reduces the likelihood of errors.

Using Child Flows for Reusable Data Operations

Child flows (also known as "Call a child flow" action) allow you to create standalone flows that can be invoked from multiple parent flows. This is particularly valuable for data operations that you perform repeatedly across different automation scenarios. For example, if you frequently need to validate and format customer email addresses, you can create a child flow that accepts an email address as input, performs validation checks, standardizes the format (converts to lowercase, trims whitespace), and returns the cleaned email address. This child flow can then be called from any parent flow that processes customer data–whether it's a form submission handler, a data synchronization flow, or a reporting workflow.

To implement this in Power Automate:

- Create a new flow with a "Manual trigger" that includes input parameters for the data you want to process
- Add your data operation actions within this child flow
- Use the "Respond to a Power Automate or Power Apps" action to return the processed data
- In your parent flow, use the "Run a child flow" action and pass the required parameters
- Capture the returned values and continue with your main flow logic

Creating Scopes to Group Related Actions

Scope actions in Power Automate serve as containers that group related actions together, making your flows more organized and easier to understand. When working with complex data operations, scopes provide several benefits. First, they create logical boundaries in your flow–you might have one scope for "Data Retrieval," another for "Data Transformation," and a third for "Data Validation." This visual organization makes it immediately clear what each section of your flow accomplishes.

Second, scopes enable sophisticated error handling through the "Configure run after" feature. You can create a scope for your primary data operations, then add a parallel branch that only runs if the scope fails, times out, or is skipped. This allows you to implement try-catch-like patterns in

Power Automate. For instance, if your data transformation scope encounters an error (perhaps due to unexpected null values or malformed JSON), you can catch this failure and execute alternative actions—logging the error to a SharePoint list, sending a notification to the flow administrator, or attempting a fallback transformation method.

To implement scopes effectively:

- Add a "Scope" action and give it a descriptive name (e.g., "Transform Customer Data")
- Move related actions inside the scope by dragging and dropping
- Add additional scopes for error handling configured to run after failures
- Use the scope status in conditions to determine subsequent flow behavior

Considering Azure Logic Apps for Complex Operations

While Power Automate Cloud Flows excel at citizen developer scenarios and straightforward automations, some data operations may exceed its optimal use cases. Azure Logic Apps, which shares the same underlying technology as Power Automate but is designed for enterprise IT scenarios, should be considered when your data operations involve high-volume processing (processing thousands of records per minute), require advanced enterprise connectors not available in Power Automate, need fine-grained control over retry policies and timeout settings, or demand integration with Azure services like Azure Functions for custom code execution.

For example, if you're building a data integration that processes real-time IoT sensor data from thousands of devices, performs complex transformations requiring custom C# code, and writes results to Azure Cosmos DB with specific consistency requirements, this scenario is better suited for Azure Logic Apps. However, you can still maintain a hybrid approach: use Power Automate for user-facing workflows (like approval processes or form submissions) and call Azure Logic Apps via HTTP actions for the heavy data processing operations.

The decision to move to Logic Apps should be based on:

- Data volume and processing throughput requirements
- Need for advanced enterprise features and connectors
- Requirement for custom code integration through Azure Functions
- Performance and scalability demands beyond Power Automate's service limits
- IT governance and deployment requirements (Logic Apps support Infrastructure as Code)

By implementing modular design principles in your Power Automate flows, you create a more sustainable automation architecture. Your flows become easier to troubleshoot because issues can be isolated to specific modules, simpler to enhance because changes to one module don't affect others, and more efficient because reusable components eliminate duplicate logic across multiple flows. This approach transforms your collection of flows from isolated automations into a cohesive, enterprise-grade automation platform.

Documentation and Naming

Maintain clear documentation by:

- Using descriptive names for actions and variables
- Adding comments for complex expressions
- Documenting the data structure with examples
- Keeping a change log for major updates

Testing and Validation

Implement thorough testing by:

- Creating test cases for different data scenarios
- Validating outputs at key transformation points
- Testing with edge cases (empty data, maximum sizes, special characters)
- Implementing data validation checks

Note: *Create a separate test flow that runs your data operations with sample data to verify they work correctly before deploying to production.*

Try It Yourself: Refactoring a Complex Data Flow

1. Take an existing complex flow with multiple data operations.
2. Refactor it using modular design principles.
3. Add appropriate documentation and naming.
4. Implement validation checks at key points.
5. Create a test harness to verify the operations.

Practical Application

Use Case 1: Customer Data Synchronization

Business Scenario: A company needs to synchronize customer data between their CRM system (Dynamics 365) and their marketing platform (Mailchimp). The synchronization needs to happen daily, ensuring that any new or updated customer information is reflected in both systems.

Implementation:

1. **Trigger:** Recurrence (Daily at 2:00 AM)
2. **Data Retrieval:**
    a. Get updated customers from Dynamics 365 using "`List records`" action.
    b. Filter for records modified in the last 24 hours.
3. **Data Transformation:**
    a. Map Dynamics 365 customer fields to Mailchimp fields.
    b. Format email addresses and names according to Mailchimp requirements.
    c. Categorize customers into appropriate marketing segments.
4. **Data Validation:**
    a. Check for required fields (email, name)
    b. Validate email format
    c. Handle duplicates

5. **Data Upload:**
   a. Batch customer updates to Mailchimp API.
   b. Log results and handle any errors.

Challenges and Solutions:

Challenge	Solution
Different data formats	Create a mapping function using expressions
Large data volumes	Implement pagination and batching
Handling failed updates	Create an error queue for manual review
Preventing duplicates	Implement deduplication logic using "exists" checks

Table 7.4: *Self Solve Data Operation Challenges*

Use Case 2: Sales Report Automation

Business Scenario: A retail company needs to generate daily sales reports from multiple store systems, aggregate the data, and distribute a formatted report to executives.

Implementation:

1. **Trigger:** Recurrence (Daily at 6:00 AM)
2. **Data Collection:**
   a. Retrieve sales data from multiple store databases using parallel HTTP requests.
   b. Extract data from Excel files in SharePoint using Office 365 Excel connector.
3. **Data Processing:**
   a. Normalize data from different sources.
   b. Calculate daily totals, averages, and comparisons to previous periods.
   c. Group sales by product category, region, and store.
4. **Report Generation:**
   a. Create a structured JSON object with the processed data.
   b. Generate an Excel report using Excel Online (Business) connector.
   c. Create a PowerPoint summary using Office 365 PowerPoint connector.
5. **Distribution:**
   a. Save reports to SharePoint.
   b. Send email notification with report links.
   c. Update Power BI dataset for interactive dashboards.

Challenges and Solutions:

Challenge	Solution
Inconsistent data formats	Create a standardization process before aggregation
Time zone differences	Convert all timestamps to a standard time zone

Calculation accuracy	Implement validation checks against control totals
Performance with large datasets	Use filtering and aggregation at the source when possible

Table 7.5: *Self Solve Data Operation Challenges*

Use Case 3: IoT Data Processing Pipeline

Business Scenario: A manufacturing company collects sensor data from IoT devices on their production lines. This data needs to be processed, analyzed for anomalies, and stored for both real-time monitoring and historical analysis.

Implementation:

1. **Trigger:** When an Event Hub message is received
2. **Data Ingestion:**
    a. Parse JSON data from Event Hub.
    b. Validate sensor data structure and values.
3. **Data Processing:**
    a. Convert units as needed.
    b. Calculate derived metrics (efficiency, utilization).
    c. Detect anomalies using threshold rules.
4. **Routing and Storage:**
    a. Store raw data in Azure Data Lake.
    b. Send processed metrics to SQL Database.
    c. Route anomalies to alert system.
5. **Real-time Actions:**
    a. Trigger alerts for critical anomalies.
    b. Update real-time dashboards via Power BI streaming dataset.
    c. Log events for audit purposes.

Challenges and Solutions:

Challenge	**Solution**
High volume of messages	Implement batch processing
Data quality issues	Add validation and error handling for each sensor type
Real-time requirements	Use parallel processing paths for critical vs. historical data
Complex anomaly detection	Implement a scoring system with multiple indicators

Table 7.6: *Self Solve Data Operation Challenges*

Conclusion

In this chapter, we have explored the critical role that data operations play in creating effective Power Automate Cloud Flows, learning how to work with variables, transform data between different formats, filter and sort collections, handle complex data types like JSON and XML, implement error handling, optimize performance, secure sensitive data, and integrate with various data sources. These foundational skills enable you to create flows that handle real-world business scenarios, where data transformation and manipulation are essential for successful automation.

You can now create and manipulate variables, work with arrays and collections, use expressions for data transformation, parse structured data formats, implement filtering operations, handle errors in data operations, optimize flow performance, secure sensitive data, connect to various data sources, and design modular maintainable flows.

In the next chapter, we will master the powerful expression language and function categories that form the backbone of advanced data operations. You will learn to combine functions strategically and implement sophisticated data manipulation patterns for complex automation scenarios.

Additional Resources

- Microsoft Power Automate Data Operations Documentation
- Power Automate Expression Reference
- JSON Schema Documentation
- OData Query Reference for Filtering Data
- Microsoft Power Automate Community Forums

Multiple Choice Questions

1. Which of the following expressions would correctly extract the first 5 characters of a string stored in a variable named 'productCode'?

   a. `first(variables('productCode'), 5)`

   b. `substring(variables('productCode'), 0, 5)`

   c. `extract(variables('productCode'), 0, 5)`

   d. `left(variables('productCode'), 5)`

2. When working with large arrays in Power Automate, which approach would provide the best performance?

   a. Process all items with a single "`Apply to each`" action

   b. Use "`Filter array`" before "`Apply to each`" to reduce iterations

   c. Convert the array to a string and then back to an array

   d. Process each item with individual actions outside of loops

3. Which security practice is recommended when handling sensitive data in Power Automate?

   a. Include the sensitive data in flow names for easy identification

   b. Store connection strings in environment variables

   c. Always output full data sets for debugging

   d. Use hardcoded credentials for reliability

4. Which approach is most efficient for updating multiple items in a SharePoint list?
    a. Use multiple individual "`Update item`" actions
    b. Use the "`Send an HTTP request to SharePoint`" action with a batch request
    c. Create a separate flow for each update
    d. Export to Excel, update, and re-import
5. When implementing error handling for data operations, which pattern is recommended?
    a. Ignore errors and continue processing
    b. Use a Scope action with "`Configure run after`" settings
    c. Terminate the flow immediately on any error
    d. Use only try-catch expressions within formulas

Answers

1. b
2. b
3. b
4. b
5. b

CHAPTER 8
Expressions and Functions in Power Automate

Introduction

In the world of automation, the ability to manipulate data dynamically can transform a simple sequence of steps into intelligent, adaptable workflows. Expressions and functions in Power Automate are the engines that drive this transformation, while enabling your flows to make actionable decisions, transform data, and be responsive to changing conditions.

Think of expressions as the language that allows you to communicate with your data that help you shape, extract, and analyze it precisely. When considered thus, they empower you to create flows that are not just automated but truly intelligent.

As we have seen in previous chapters, creating basic flows with triggers and actions provides valuable automation capabilities. You have already learned how to set up cloud flows, connect to various services, and implement basic workflow logic. However, to unlock the full potential of Power Automate, we will need to dive into the world of expressions and functions that pave the way for dynamic, conditional, and sophisticated data handling.

This chapter serves as a critical juncture in your journey with Power Automate. While earlier chapters focused on the "what" and "where" of automation, this chapter explores the "how" and "why." By mastering expressions and functions, you will elevate your flows from simple process automation to intelligent business solutions that can adapt to changing inputs, make decisions based on conditions, and transform data as needed.

Structure

In this chapter, we will cover the following topics:

- Understanding Expressions in Power Automate
- Mastering the Expression Syntax
- Working with String Functions
- Manipulating Date and Time with Functions
- Collection and Array Operations
- Mathematical and Logical Functions
- Conversion Functions
- Using Variables with Expressions
- Implementing Conditional Logic

- Advanced Expression Techniques
- Expression Debugging and Troubleshooting
- Building Complex Workflows with Expressions
- Integrating Expressions with Connectors

Understanding Expressions in Power Automate

Expressions are powerful formulas that can help you manipulate data, make calculations, and implement business logic within workflows. Unlike static configurations, expressions allow flows to respond dynamically to data and conditions, making them truly intelligent automation solutions.

At their essence, expressions are text strings that are evaluated at runtime when the flow is executing. They provide the computational power that transforms basic automation into sophisticated business processes. Whether you need to format data, perform calculations, make decisions, or transform information between systems, expressions are the key to unlocking these capabilities.

The Business Value of Expressions in Power Automate

Modern business processes require more than simple data transfer between systems. They need intelligent decision-making, data transformation, and adaptive behavior based on changing conditions. Expressions provide this intelligence by allowing you to:

- Transform data formats to match different system requirements
- Implement complex business rules and validation logic
- Perform calculations and mathematical operations
- Make decisions based on multiple conditions and criteria
- Extract and manipulate portions of data from various sources
- Create dynamic content that adapts to specific situations

Expression Fundamentals vs. Static Configuration

The difference between using expressions and static configuration is the difference between building rigid automations and creating adaptive solutions. Static configurations work well for predictable scenarios with fixed requirements, but business reality often demands flexibility.

For example, a static email notification might always send the same message to the same recipients. An expression-driven notification can customize the message content, determine recipients based on data attributes, and adjust timing based on business rules.

Mastering the Expression Syntax

Basic Expression Structure

Every expression in Power Automate follows a consistent structure that makes them both powerful and predictable. Understanding this structure is essential for building reliable workflows.

Expression Syntax Basics

Core Syntax Rules:

- **All expressions start with @:** The **@** symbol tells Power Automate to evaluate what follows as an expression rather than treating it as literal text.

- **Function-based structure:** Most expressions follow the pattern **`@function(parameter1, parameter2, ...)`**.
- **Nested function support**: You can use the output of one function as the input to another, enabling complex operations.
- **Case sensitivity**: Function names are case-sensitive, so **`concat()`** works while **`Concat()`** does not.
- **Parameter requirements**: Every function has specific parameter requirements that must be met.

Here is a basic example of a simple expression:

```
@utcNow()                          // Get current UTC date/time
@concat('Hello', ' ', 'World')     // Combine strings
@length('Power Automate')          // Get string length
@add(5, 3)                        // Perform addition
```

Figure 8.1: *Simple Expression Example*

Expression Editor Interface

Power Automate provides a dedicated expression editor that you access by clicking the "**`fx`**" button in any field that supports expressions. This editor offers several helpful features such as:

- **Syntax highlighting**: Makes it easier to read complex expressions
- **Function suggestions**: Provides autocomplete for available functions
- **Parameter hints**: Shows required parameters for functions
- **Error detection**: Identifies syntax issues before you save

Note: *The expression editor includes a "Dynamic content" tab alongside the "Expression" tab. You can switch between these modes to combine static expressions with dynamic values from previous flow steps.*

Combining Expressions with Static Text

One of the most powerful features of Power Automate expressions is the ability to combine them seamlessly with static text. This allows you to create dynamic content that includes both fixed and calculated elements.

Examples:

```
The current time is: @utcNow()
Order total: $@formatNumber(variables('orderAmount'), 2)
Customer @concat(variables('firstName'), ' ', variables('lastName')) has placed
an order
```

Figure 8.2: *Simple Expression Example*

When combining expressions with text, Power Automate automatically converts expression results to strings, making integration seamless.

Expression Validation and Error Prevention

Power Automate validates expressions when you save them, but understanding common validation rules helps prevent errors:

- **Parentheses must be balanced**: Every opening parenthesis needs a matching closing parenthesis.
- **String literals require quotes**: Text values must be enclosed in single or double quotes.
- **Parameter types must match**: Functions expect specific data types for their parameters.
- **Function names must be exact**: No variations or typos in function names are allowed.

Working with String Functions

String manipulation is a common requirement in business automation. Power Automate provides a comprehensive set of string functions that handle everything from basic text operations to complex pattern matching. These functions are mentioned as follows:

Referencing Dynamic Content

The ability to reference dynamic content is one of the most powerful aspects of expressions. Dynamic content refers to the data that comes from the previous steps in a flow. You can refer to outputs from previous actions using the **`outputs()`** function, or by using the dynamic content picker.

For example, to reference the subject of an email that triggered your flow, you can use:

```
@[triggerOutputs()?['body/subject']]
```

Figure 8.3: *Referencing Dynamic Content*

Note: Testing Expressions

When developing complex expressions, test them incrementally. Start with the innermost function and gradually build outward, while verifying that each layer works as expected before adding more complexity.

Try It Yourself: Basic Expression

1. Create a new instant cloud flow with a manual trigger.
2. Add a "**`Compose`**" action.
3. In the Inputs field, enter the expression: **`@ [concat('Hello, ', 'Power Automate!')]`**.
4. Save and test the flow.
5. Verify that the output is "**`Hello, Power Automate!`**".

Working with String Functions

String functions in Power Automate allow you to manipulate text data, which is essential for many automation scenarios.

Common String Functions

`concat()`

The **concat()** function combines multiple strings into a single string.

```
@[concat('Hello', ' ', 'World')]
```

Figure 8.4: *concat() expression*

Result: **Hello World**

substring()

The **substring()** function extracts a portion of a string, starting from a specified index.

```
@[substring('Power Automate', 6, 8)]
```

Figure 8.5: *substring() expression*

Result: Automate

replace()

The **replace()** function substitutes all occurrences of a specified string with another string.

```
@[replace('Power Platform', 'Platform', 'Automate')]
```

Figure 8.6: *replace() expression*

Result: Power Automate

indexOf()

The **indexOf()** function returns the starting position of the first occurrence of a specified string within another string.

```
@[indexOf('Power Automate', 'Auto')]
```

Figure 8.7: *indexOf() expression*

Result: 6

toLower() and toUpper()

These functions convert a string to lowercase or uppercase.

```
@[toLower('Power Automate')]
```

Figure 8.8: *toLower() expression*

Result: **power automate**

```
@[toUpper('Power Automate')]
```

Figure 8.9: *toUpper() expression*

Result: POWER AUTOMATE

Practical Example: Name Formatting

Let us say you receive user input with names in various formats and need to standardize them.

Here is how you might create a properly capitalized name:

```
@[concat(
    toUpper(substring(triggerBody()?['firstName'], 0, 1)),
    toLower(substring(triggerBody()?['firstName'], 1)),
    ' ',
    toUpper(substring(triggerBody()?['lastName'], 0, 1)),
    toLower(substring(triggerBody()?['lastName'], 1))
)]
```

Figure 8.10: *Name Formatting Expression Example*

This expression takes a first name and last name, capitalizes the first letter of each, and ensures the rest is lowercase.

Common Pitfall: String vs. Number Confusion

Be careful when working with numbers stored as strings. Operations like addition will behave differently depending on whether values are interpreted as strings or numbers. Use the **`int()`**, **`float()`**, or **`string()`** functions to ensure proper type conversion.

Try It Yourself: Email Username Extractor

1. Create a new instant cloud flow with a manual trigger that accepts an email address.
2. Add a "**`Compose`**" action.
3. Use the **`substring()`** and **`indexOf()`** functions to extract the username part (before the **`@`** symbol).
4. Test with different email addresses.

The expression might look like this:

```
@[substring(
    triggerBody()?['text'],
    0,
    indexOf(triggerBody()?['text'], '@')
)]
```

Figure 8.11: *Email Username Extractor expression example*

Think About It

How would you modify the email username extractor to ensure it handles cases where the input is not a valid email address (does not contain an **`@`** symbol)?

Manipulating Date and Time with Functions

Date and time manipulation is crucial for scheduling, calculating durations, and managing time-sensitive workflows.

Current Date and Time

The **utcNow()** function returns the current UTC date and time.

```
@[utcNow()]
```

Figure 8.12: *utcNow() expression example*

Result: 2023-05-15T14:30:45.1234567Z

Date Formatting

The **formatDateTime()** function formats a date according to a specified template.

```
@[formatDateTime(utcNow(), 'yyyy-MM-dd')]
```

Figure 8.13: *formatDateTime() expression example*

Result: 2023-05-15

Common format specifiers include:

- **yyyy**: Four-digit year
- **MM**: Two-digit month
- **dd**: Two-digit day
- **HH**: Hour in 24-hour format
- **mm**: Minutes
- **ss**: Seconds

Date Calculations

You can add or subtract time periods using **addDays()**, **addHours()**, and so on.

```
@[addDays(utcNow(), 7)]
```

Figure 8.14: *Date Calculations expression example*

Result: The date and time 7 days from now

Other similar functions include:

- **addHours()**
- **addMinutes()**
- **addSeconds()**
- **addMonths()**
- **addYears()**

Date Comparisons

You can compare dates using standard comparison operators.

```
@[greater(utcNow(), '2023-01-01T00:00:00Z')]
```

Figure 8.15: *Date Comparisons expression example*

Result: true (assuming the current date is after January 1, 2023)

Extracting Date Components

Extract specific parts of a date using functions like:

- **`dayOfMonth()`**
- **`dayOfWeek()`**
- **`dayOfYear()`**
- **`month()`**
- **`year()`**

For example:

```
@[month(utcNow())]
```

Figure 8.16: *Extracting Date Components expression example*

Result: The current month as a number (1-12)

Practical Example: Business Day Calculation

Let us create an expression that calculates a due date that's 5 business days in the future (excluding weekends):

```
@[
    varDay: dayOfWeek(utcNow());
    varAddDays: if(
        greater(varDay, 5),
        7 - varDay + 5,
        if(
            equals(varDay, 5),
            3,
            5
        )
    );
    addDays(utcNow(), varAddDays)
]
```

Figure 8.17: *Business Day Calculation expression example*

This expression determines how many days to add based on the current day of the week to ensure the result falls on a business day.

Note: Time Zone Handling

Power Automate operates in UTC by default. To work with local time zones, use the **`convertTimeZone()`** *function.*

```
@[convertTimeZone(utcNow(), 'UTC', 'Eastern Standard Time')]
```

Figure 8.18: *`convertTimeZone` expression example*

Common Pitfall: Date String Formats

Different systems might use different date formats. Always ensure you are parsing dates correctly, especially when integrating with external systems.

Try It Yourself: Meeting Scheduler

1. Create a flow that calculates the next three weekly meeting dates.
2. Use a manual trigger that accepts a day of week (1-7) and time.
3. Calculate the dates for the next three occurrences of that day.
4. Format the output in a user-friendly format.

Collection and Array Operations

Power Automate provides powerful functions for working with arrays (collections of items).

Creating Arrays

You can create arrays using the **`createArray()`** function:

```
@[createArray('apple', 'banana', 'orange')]
```

Figure 8.19: *`createArray` expression example*

Result: **`["apple", "banana", "orange"]`**

Array Functions

`length()`

Returns the number of items in an array.

```
@[length(createArray('apple', 'banana', 'orange'))]
```

Figure 8.20: *`Length` expression example*

Result: 3

`first()` and `last()`

Returns the first or last item in an array.

```
@[first(createArray('apple', 'banana', 'orange'))]
```

Figure 8.21: *`first()` and `Last()` expression example*

Result: apple

`union()`

Combines two arrays, removing duplicates.

```
@[union(createArray('apple', 'banana'), createArray('banana', 'orange'))]
```

Figure 8.22: ***union()*** *expression example*

Result: [**"apple", "banana", "orange"**]

`intersection()`

Returns items common to both arrays.

```
@[intersection(createArray('apple', 'banana'), createArray('banana', 'orange'))]
```

Figure 8.23: ***intersection()*** *expression example*

Result: [**"banana"**]

`contains()`

Checks if an array contains a specific value.

```
@[contains(createArray('apple', 'banana', 'orange'), 'banana')]
```

Figure 8.24: ***contains()*** *expression example*

Result: true

Working with JSON Data

When dealing with JSON data, you will often need to access nested properties. Use the **?** operator for safe property access.

```
@[triggerBody()?['data']?['items']]
```

Figure 8.25: *Working with JSON* ***data*** *example*

Filtering and Mapping

The **filter()** function allows you to select items from an array based on a condition.

```
@[filter(triggerBody()?['items'], item => equals(item?['status'], 'completed'))]
```

Figure 8.26: ***filter()*** *function example*

This returns an array containing only the items where the status is "**completed**".

The **map()** function transforms each item in an array.

```
@[map(triggerBody()?['items'], item => item?['name'])]
```

Figure 8.27: ***map()*** *example*

This returns an array containing just the name property of each item.

Practical Example: Processing Approvals

Let us say you have an array of approval responses and want to check if everyone has approved:

```
@[
    varResponses: triggerBody()?['approvalResponses'];
    varApprovalCount: length(filter(varResponses, response => equals
(response?['decision'], 'Approve')));
    equals(varApprovalCount, length(varResponses))
]
```

This expression checks if the number of "**Approve**" responses equals the total number of responses.

Common Pitfall: Arrays vs. Objects

Be careful not to confuse arrays (collections of items) with objects (collections of key-value pairs). Different functions apply to each.

Try It Yourself: Task Prioritization

1. Create a flow that takes an array of tasks with priority levels.
2. Filter out completed tasks.
3. Sort remaining tasks by priority.
4. Return the top three highest-priority tasks.

Mathematical and Logical Functions

Power Automate provides a range of mathematical and logical functions for calculations and decision-making.

Mathematical Operations

Basic arithmetic operations include:

- **add(a, b)**: Addition
- **sub(a, b)**: Subtraction
- **mul(a, b)**: Multiplication
- **div(a, b)**: Division
- **mod(a, b)**: Modulo (remainder)

For example:

```
@[add(5, mul(3, 2))]
```

***Figure 8.28**: Mathematical Operations Example*

Result: 11

Statistical Functions

Power Automate offers functions for statistical calculations:

- **min()**: Returns the minimum value
- **max()**: Returns the maximum value
- **average()**: Calculates the average
- **sum()**: Calculates the sum

For example:

```
@[average(createArray(10, 20, 30))]
```

Figure 8.29: *Statistical Functions Operations Example*

Result: 20

Logical Operations

Logical functions help with decision-making:

- **and()**: Logical AND
- **or()**: Logical OR
- **not()**: Logical NOT
- **if()**: Conditional branching

For example:

```
@[if(
    and(
        greater(triggerBody()?['temperature'], 25),
        less(triggerBody()?['humidity'], 60)
    ),
    'Comfortable',
    'Uncomfortable'
)]
```

Figure 8.30: *Logical Operations Example*

This expression evaluates whether conditions are comfortable based on temperature and humidity.

Comparison Operators

Common comparison functions include:

- **equals()**: Equal to
- **greater()**: Greater than
- **greaterOrEquals()**: Greater than or equal to
- **less()**: Less than
- **lessOrEquals()**: Less than or equal to

Random Number Generation

Generate random numbers using the **rand()** function:

```
@[rand(1, 100)]
```

Figure 8.31: *Random Operations Example*

Result: A random number between 1 and 100

Practical Example: Price Calculator

Let us create an expression that calculates a final price with tax and discounts:

```
@[
    varBasePrice: float(triggerBody()?['price']);
    varDiscountRate: if(
        greater(varBasePrice, 1000),
        0.15,
        if(
            greater(varBasePrice, 500),
            0.1,
            0.05
        )
    );
    varDiscountAmount: mul(varBasePrice, varDiscountRate);
    varPriceAfterDiscount: sub(varBasePrice, varDiscountAmount);
    varTaxAmount: mul(varPriceAfterDiscount, 0.07);
    add(varPriceAfterDiscount, varTaxAmount)
]
```

Figure 8.32: *Price Calculator Expressions Example*

This expression calculates a tiered discount based on the base price, applies the discount, and then adds tax.

Note: Handling Division by Zero

Always check for potential division by zero to avoid errors:

```
@[if(
    equals(triggerBody()?['denominator'], 0),
    'Cannot divide by zero',
    div(triggerBody()?['numerator'], triggerBody()?['denominator'])
)]
```

Figure 8.33: *Handling Division by Zero Example*

Common Pitfall: Type Conversion

Ensure values are of the correct type before performing mathematical operations. Use ***int()***, ***float()***, *or* ***decimal()*** *to convert string values to numbers.*

Try It Yourself: Budget Analyzer

1. Create a flow that takes an array of expenses with categories
2. Calculate the total spent in each category
3. Determine what percentage of the total budget each category represents
4. Identify the category with the highest spending

Conversion Functions

Conversion functions allow you to transform data from one type to another.

String Conversion

- **string()**: Converts a value to a string
- **int()**: Converts a value to an integer
- **float()**: Converts a value to a floating-point number
- **bool()**: Converts a value to a boolean
- **array()**: Converts a value to an array
- **base64ToString()**: Converts base64 encoded data to a string
- **base64ToBinary()**: Converts base64 encoded data to binary
- **dataUriToString()**: Converts a data URI to a string

JSON Handling

- **json()**: Parses a string as JSON
- **xml()**: Parses a string as XML

For example:

```
@[json('{"name":"John","age":30}')]
```

Figure 8.34: *JSON Handling Example*

Result: A JSON object with properties name and age

Binary Data Conversion

- **base64()**: Encodes a string as base64
- **dataUri()**: Creates a data URI from a string

Practical Example: CSV to JSON Conversion

Let us convert a CSV string to a JSON array:

```
@[
    varCsv: triggerBody()?['csvData'];
    varLines: split(varCsv, '\n');
    varHeaders: split(first(varLines), ',');

    skip(varLines, 1) | map(line => {
        varValues: split(line, ',');
        json(range(0, length(varHeaders)) | map(i => {
            formatString('"{0}":"{1}"',
                         varHeaders[i],
                         varValues[i])
        }) | join(',') | formatString('{{{0}}}', @))
    })
]
```

Figure 8.35: *Convert a CSV String to a JSON Array*

This expression splits the CSV into lines, extracts headers, and then creates a JSON object for each data row.

Note: Handling Special Characters

When converting to or from strings, be aware of special characters that might need escaping, especially in JSON and XML conversions.

Common Pitfall: Empty or Null Values

Always handle potential empty or null values when performing conversions to avoid runtime errors.

Try It Yourself: Data Format Transformer

1. Create a flow that accepts data in one format (like JSON).
2. Convert it to another format (such as, a formatted string or XML).
3. Test with different input structures.

Using Variables with Expressions

Variables in Power Automate allow you to store and reuse values throughout your flow.

Creating and Setting Variables

Use the "`Initialize variable`" action to create a variable:

- Name: The variable's identifier
- Type: String, Integer, Float, Boolean, Array, or Object
- Value: The initial value (can be an expression)

Use the "`Set variable`" action to update a variable's value.

Accessing Variables in Expressions

Reference variables in expressions using the **`variables()`** function:

```
@[variables('myVariable')]
```

***Figure 8.36**: Accessing Variables in Expressions*

Incrementing and Decrementing

Use the "**`Increment variable`**" and "**`Decrement variable`**" actions for numerical variables.

Scope of Variables

Variables are scoped to the flow or to a specific "**`Scope`**" action. Use scopes to create temporary variables that are only needed for a portion of your flow.

Practical Example: Incremental Processing

Let us create a flow that processes items in batches:

1. Initialize a counter variable: counter (Integer, value: 0)
2. Initialize a results array: results (Array, value: [])
3. For each item: a. Process the item b. Add the result to the results array c. Increment the counter d. If the counter reaches 100, store the results and reset the counter

The expression for updating the results array might look like:

```
@[concat(variables('results'), createArray(outputs('Process_item')))]
```

***Figure 8.37**: Incremental Processing Using Expressions*

Note: Using Complex Objects

Store complex objects in variables to simplify your flow and reduce the need for repetitive expressions:

```
@[json('{
    "customerInfo": {
        "name": "John Doe",
        "email": "john@example.com"
    },
    "orderDetails": {
        "orderNumber": "ORD-12345",
        "items": [
            {"id": "ITEM-1", "quantity": 2},
            {"id": "ITEM-2", "quantity": 1}
        ]
    }
}')]
```

***Figure 8.38**: Using Complex Objects Expressions*

Common Pitfall: Variable Type Mismatches

Ensure that you are using the correct variable type. For example, trying to increment a string variable will result in an error.

Try It Yourself: Counter with Notification

1. Create a flow that runs on a schedule.
2. Initialize a counter variable.
3. Increment the counter each time the flow runs.
4. When the counter reaches a specified threshold, send a notification and reset the counter.

Implementing Conditional Logic

Conditional logic allows your flows to make decisions based on data and conditions.

Condition Action

The "**`Condition`**" action in Power Automate allows you to create if-then-else branches in your flow:

- **`If`**: The condition to evaluate
- **`Then`**: Actions to perform if the condition is true
- **`Else`**: Actions to perform if the condition is false

Switch Action

The "**`Switch`**" action allows you to handle multiple possible cases:

- On: The value to switch on
- Case 1, Case 2, etc.: Different possible values
- Default: Actions to perform if none of the cases match

Conditional Expressions

Use the **`if()`** function in expressions for inline conditional logic:

```
@[if(
    equals(triggerBody()?['status'], 'urgent'),
    'High',
    if(
        equals(triggerBody()?['status'], 'important'),
        'Medium',
        'Low'
    )
)]
```

Figure 8.39: *`if()` Function in Expressions*

This expression converts a status value to a priority level.

Practical Example: Approval Workflow

Let us create a conditional approval flow:

1. Check the request amount.
2. If the amount is less than $1,000, auto-approve it.
3. If the amount is between $1,000 and $5,000, send it to the manager for approval.
4. If the amount is over $5,000, send it to the director for approval.

The condition expressions might look like:

```
@[less(triggerBody()?['amount'], 1000)]
```

Figure 8.40: *Conditional Approval Flow Less Expression*

and

```
@[and(
    greaterOrEquals(triggerBody()?['amount'], 1000),
    less(triggerBody()?['amount'], 5000)
)]
```

Figure 8.41: *Conditional Approval Flow Greater Expression*

Note: Nested Conditions

For complex decision trees, consider using nested "Apply to each" and "Condition" actions rather than creating a single complex expression. This makes your flow easier to read and maintain.

Common Pitfall: Boolean Conversion

Be careful when evaluating string values as booleans. The string "false" will evaluate to true when converted to a boolean, unless you explicitly check for equality:

```
@[equals(toLower(triggerBody()?['isActive']), 'true')]
```

Figure 8.42: *Boolean conversion expression*

Try It Yourself: Document Routing

1. Create a flow that processes incoming documents.
2. Route documents to different departments based on document type.
3. Apply different processing rules based on document priority and size.

Advanced Expression Techniques

Let us explore some advanced techniques that combine multiple functions for powerful results:

Building Expressions Step by Step

Complex expressions can be difficult to create and debug. Build them incrementally by:

1. Starting with the innermost logic
2. Testing and verify each layer
3. Adding complexity gradually
4. Using variables to store intermediate results

Composition of Functions

Compose multiple functions to create powerful transformations:

```
@[
    varInput: triggerBody()?['comments'];
    varWords: split(toLower(varInput), ' ');
    varFiltered: filter(varWords, word => greater(length(word), 3));
    varCounted: reduce(varFiltered, {}, (result, word) => {
        varCount: if(
            contains(keys(result), word),
            add(result[word], 1),
            1
        );
        setProperty(result, word, varCount)
    })
]
```

Figure 8.43: *Composition of Functions Example*

This expression counts the frequency of words longer than 3 characters in a comment.

Working with Dynamic Arrays

When the structure of your data is unknown or varies, use dynamic approaches:

```
@[
    varData: triggerBody()?['data'];
    varFields: triggerBody()?['fields'];

    map(varData, item => {
        reduce(varFields, {}, (result, field) => {
            setProperty(result, field, item[field])
        })
    })
]
```

Figure 8.44: *Working with Dynamic Arrays*

This expression extracts specified fields from each item in an array.

Note: Expression Libraries

*Create a "**Compose**" action at the beginning of your flow to define reusable expression fragments:*

```
@[json('{
    "formatCurrency": "@formatNumber(parameters(''amount''), 2, ''en-us'')",
    "formatPhoneNumber": "@concat(''('', substring(parameters(''phone''), 0,
3), '') '', substring(parameters(''phone''), 3, 3), ''-'', substring
(parameters(''phone''), 6))",
    "calculateTax": "@mul(parameters(''amount''), 0.0725)"
}')]
```

Common Pitfall: Expression Complexity

*Highly complex expressions can be difficult to maintain. Consider breaking complex logic into multiple steps using intermediate variables or "**Compose**" actions.*

Try It Yourself: Advanced Data Transformation

1. Create a flow that takes a complex data structure.
2. Transform it into a different structure with calculated fields.
3. Handle edge cases like missing data and formatting requirements.

Expression Debugging and Troubleshooting

Debugging expressions can be challenging. Here are some useful techniques to help identify and resolve issues:

Common Expression Errors

- **Syntax errors**: Missing brackets, parentheses, or quotation marks
- **Type errors**: Attempting operations on incompatible data types
- **Null reference errors**: Trying to access properties of null objects
- **Index out of bounds**: Accessing array elements that don't exist
- **Parsing errors**: Incorrectly formatted data

Debugging Techniques

Use Compose Actions

Insert "**Compose**" actions with partial expressions to see intermediate results.

Add Safe Navigation

Use the **?** operator for safe property access:

```
@[triggerBody()?['data']?['items']?[0]?['name']]
```

Figure 8.45: *how to use '?' operator*

This prevents errors if any part of the path is null or undefined.

Test with Sample Data

Use the "`Test`" feature with sample data to verify expressions work as expected.

Check Run History

Examine the run history to see the actual input and output values.

Handling Errors Gracefully

Use the `coalesce()` function to provide fallback values:

```
@[coalesce(triggerBody()?['name'], 'Anonymous')]
```

Figure 8.46: *`coalesce()` function*

This uses '`Anonymous`' if the name property is null or undefined.

Note: Logging and Monitoring

Add "`Compose`" actions with descriptive names to log important values and decision points. This creates a trail that's invaluable for troubleshooting.

Common Pitfall: Confusing Error Messages

Error messages in Power Automate can sometimes be cryptic. Focus on the specific expression mentioned in the error and check for syntax issues first.

Try It Yourself: Error-Resistant Flow

1. Create a flow that processes potentially inconsistent data.
2. Add error handling for missing or invalid fields.
3. Implement logging to track the flow's decision path.
4. Test with various edge cases.

Building Complex Workflows with Expressions

Let us apply what we have learned to build sophisticated workflows.

Case Study: Invoice Processing System

Let us create a flow that processes invoices:

1. When a new invoice arrives (email or form submission)
2. Extract key information using expressions
3. Validate the data (check for required fields)
4. Calculate totals and tax
5. Compare against purchase orders
6. Route for approval based on amount and department
7. Send notifications with dynamic content
8. Update records in a database

Key expressions include:

```
// Extract invoice number using regex
```

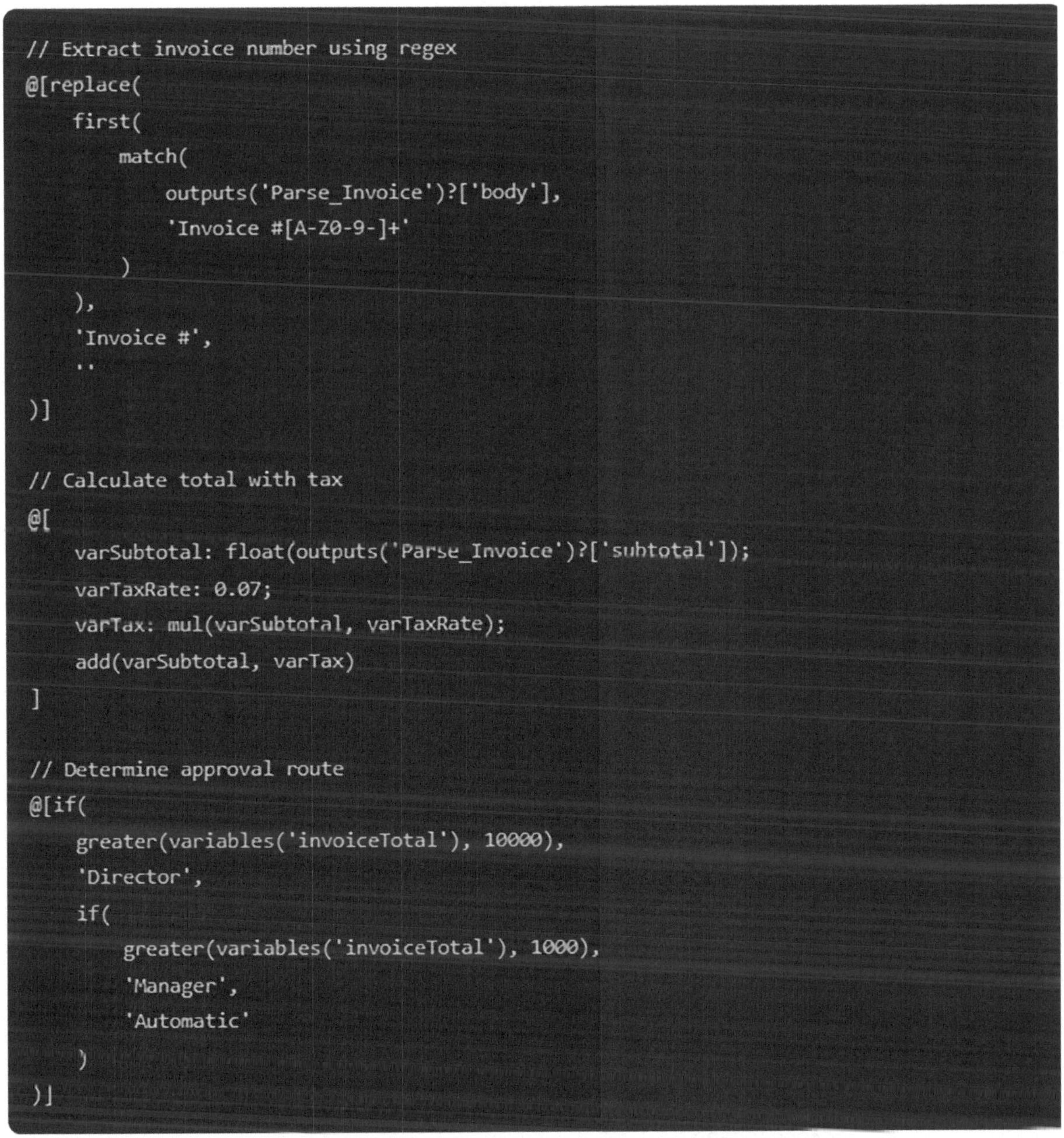

```
// Extract invoice number using regex
@[replace(
    first(
        match(
            outputs('Parse_Invoice')?['body'],
            'Invoice #[A-Z0-9-]+'
        )
    ),
    'Invoice #',
    ''
)]

// Calculate total with tax
@[
    varSubtotal: float(outputs('Parse_Invoice')?['subtotal']);
    varTaxRate: 0.07;
    varTax: mul(varSubtotal, varTaxRate);
    add(varSubtotal, varTax)
]

// Determine approval route
@[if(
    greater(variables('invoiceTotal'), 10000),
    'Director',
    if(
        greater(variables('invoiceTotal'), 1000),
        'Manager',
        'Automatic'
    )
)]
```

Figure 8.47: `Extract invoice number using regex`

```
// Calculate total with tax
@[
    varSubtotal: float(outputs('Parse_Invoice')?['subtotal']);
    varTaxRate: 0.07;
    varTax: mul(varSubtotal, varTaxRate);
    add(varSubtotal, varTax)
]
// Determine approval route
@[if(
    greater(variables('invoiceTotal'), 10000),
    'Director',
    if(
```

```
            greater(variables('invoiceTotal'), 1000),
            'Manager',
            'Automatic'
        )
    )]
```

Case Study: Customer Journey Orchestration

Let us create a flow that manages a customer onboarding journey:

1. When a new customer signs up
2. Send a welcome email with personalized content
3. Wait for specific actions (for example, profile completion)
4. Send reminders if actions are not completed within timeframes
5. Adapt the journey based on customer behavior

Key expressions include:

```
// Personalized greeting based on time of day
@[
    varHour: int(formatDateTime(utcNow(), 'HH'));
    if(
        less(varHour, 12),
        'Good morning',
        if(
            less(varHour, 18),
            'Good afternoon',
            'Good evening'
        )
    )
]

// Calculate days since signup
@[
    varSignupDate: triggerBody()?['signupDate'];
    int(
        div(
            sub(
                ticks(utcNow()),
                ticks(varSignupDate)
            ),
            864000000000
        )
    )
]

// Determine next best action
@[
    varCompletedSteps: length(
        filter(
            triggerBody()?['onboardingSteps'],
            step => equals(step?['status'], 'completed')
        )
    );
    varTotalSteps: length(triggerBody()?['onboardingSteps']);
    varCompletionRate: div(varCompletedSteps, varTotalSteps);
```

```
        if(
            less(varCompletionRate, 0.3),
            'Send Helper Email',
            if(
                less(varCompletionRate, 0.7),
                'Send Progress Encouragement',
                if(
                    less(varCompletionRate, 1),
                    'Send Almost There Reminder',
                    'Send Completion Congratulations'
                )
            )
        )
    ]
```

Note: Modular Design

Break complex flows into child flows that can be reused. Use expressions to pass parameters between parent and child flows.

Common Pitfall: Flow Limits

Be aware of limits you might confront in Power Automate, such as expression complexity, action count, and timeout periods. Test thoroughly with realistic data volumes.

Try It Yourself: Comprehensive Business Process

1. Design a flow for a complete business process (such as, expense reporting, order processing)
2. Implement data validation, calculations, and routing logic
3. Add personalization and dynamic content
4. Include error handling and logging

Integrating Expressions with Connectors

Power Automate's connectors become even more powerful when combined with expressions.

Expression Security and Best Practices

As expressions often process sensitive business data, the following security considerations are paramount:

Security Considerations

- **Data exposure:** Avoid logging sensitive data in debugging steps.
- **Injection prevention:** Sanitize inputs before using in dynamic SQL or API calls.
- **Access control**: Consider who can view flow run histories with expression values.
- **Secrets handling**: Never hardcode credentials in expressions; use secure references.

Optimizing Expression Performance

- **Minimize repetitive calculations:** Store repeated intermediate results in variables.
- **Batch operations:** Process arrays with single operations rather than loops.

- **Limit collection sizes:** Use **`take()`** to limit items when working with large arrays.
- **Use appropriate data types:** Convert early to the most efficient type for your operation.

Maintainability Best Practices

- **Document complex expressions:** Add comments explaining the purpose and logic.
- **Use meaningful variable names:** Clear naming reduces the need for documentation.
- **Test boundary conditions:** Verify behavior with empty, null, or extreme values.
- **Establish naming conventions:** Consistent patterns make flows easier to maintain.
- **Create reusable expression components:** Store common expression patterns in a reference document.

Note: *Create a personal "**expression cookbook**" where you save useful expression patterns for reuse across projects.*

Practical Application

Let us explore some real-world scenarios where expressions and functions transform basic flows into sophisticated business solutions.

Use Case 1: Dynamic Approval Routing

Business Scenario: A purchase requisition system needs to dynamically route approval requests based on request amount, department, and item category.

Implementation:

Request categorization expression:

```
@if(
    greater(variables('requestAmount'), 10000),
    'High Value',
    if(
        and(
            greater(variables('requestAmount'), 1000),
            equals(variables('itemCategory'), 'IT Equipment')
        ),
        'IT Review',
        'Standard'
    )
)
```

Approver determination expression:

```
@switch(
    variables('requestCategory'),
    'High Value', first(filter(variables('seniorApprovers'), (a) => equals(a.
department, variables('requestDepartment')))),
    'IT Review', variables('ITApprover'),
    first(filter(variables(')))
```

Conclusion

In this chapter, we unlocked the true potential of Power Automate by mastering expressions and functions, which are the core tools that enable intelligent automation. From understanding expression syntax to applying advanced functions for string manipulation, date handling, and logical operations, we have built the skills to create dynamic, responsive flows. These techniques empower us to implement complex business logic directly within our workflows, making them smarter and more efficient.

You can now write and debug expressions, manipulate various data types, and optimize flows for performance and reliability. In the next chapter, we will build on this foundation by exploring robust error-handling techniques, input validation, and self-healing flows to ensure that your automations are not only powerful, but also resilient and enterprise-ready.

Additional Resources for Further Learning

Microsoft Documentation

- Power Automate Expressions Reference
- Power Automate Formula Reference
- Working with Date and Time Functions

Advanced Learning

- Microsoft Learn Path: Advanced Power Automate Techniques

Expression Testing Tools

- Power Automate Expression Tester
- Power Fx Playground

Expression Collections

- Power Automate Expressions Collection
- GitHub: Common Power Automate Expression Patterns

CHAPTER 9
Error-Free Power Automate Workflows

Introduction

In the fast-paced world of business process automation, a failed workflow can be more than an inconvenience–it represents lost revenue, damaged customer relationships, or compromised data integrity. As organizations increasingly rely on Microsoft Power Automate to drive mission-critical business processes, the importance of building error-free workflows cannot be undermined. These workflows don't happen by accident; they are the result of deliberate planning, comprehensive testing, robust error handling, and continuous monitoring.

The journey toward error-free workflows is not about eliminating all possibility of errors–which is impossible in any complex system–but rather about creating systems that can anticipate, detect, manage, and recover from errors when they inevitably occur. In this chapter, we'll explore proven techniques for error handling, validation strategies, monitoring practices, and testing methodologies that dramatically reduce workflow failures and minimize their impact. Whether you're building personal productivity flows or enterprise-scale automation solutions, these strategies will help you create more reliable, maintainable, and trusted Power Automate workflows.

Building upon the foundations established in previous chapters–from creating cloud flows and understanding triggers to mastering data operations, expressions, and integrations–we now focus on what separates amateur automation developers from professionals: error prevention, handling, and recovery. The expressions and functions you've learned will now be applied to create validation routines and error handling mechanisms, while the connectors and integrations you've explored will be enhanced with retry policies and fallback options. This chapter represents a shift from simply building workflows that can run to creating workflows that run reliably, consistently, and with minimal manual intervention, even when faced with unexpected conditions or external system failures.

Structure

In this chapter, we will cover the following topics:

- Understanding Error Types in Power Automate
- Implementing Comprehensive Error Handling
- Creating Resilient Workflows with Retry Patterns
- Implementing Data Validation Techniques
- Implementing Monitoring and Alert Systems
- Developing Testing Methodologies for Cloud Flows
- Establishing Workflow Governance and Best Practices
- Optimizing Performance to Prevent Timeout Errors
- Creating Custom Error Logging Systems

- Documenting Flows for Maintainability and Troubleshooting
- Implementing Security Practices to Prevent Unauthorized Access Errors
- Developing Automated Recovery Mechanisms

Understanding Error Types in Power Automate

Before we can effectively handle and prevent errors, we need to understand the common types of errors in Power Automate flows and their root causes.

Types of Errors

Understanding the various types of errors that can occur in Power Automate is the foundation for implementing effective error handling strategies. Each error type requires different prevention and recovery approaches. Some of them are mentioned as follows:

Trigger Errors

Trigger errors occur when a flow fails to start correctly. These can happen due to:

- Connection issues with the trigger service
- Invalid trigger conditions
- Rate limiting by the connected service
- Authentication expiration

Action Errors

Action errors occur when individual actions within a flow fail to execute properly and can happen due to the following reasons:

- Connection failures to external services
- Invalid inputs or parameters
- Timeout errors when actions take too long
- Permission issues when accessing resources

Expression Errors

Expression errors happen when there are issues with the formulas and expressions used in your flow. The following are the possible scenarios for these errors to occur:

- Syntax errors in expressions
- Referencing properties that do not exist
- Type mismatches (trying to use a string as a number, and so on.)
- Null reference errors

Data Handling Errors

Data handling errors occur when there are issues with the data being processed and can be traced to the following reasons:

- Invalid data formats
- Missing required fields

- Data type inconsistencies
- Exceeded size limits

Concurrency and Throttling Errors

These errors happen when your flows hit service limits when the following scenarios take place:

- Too many flows running simultaneously
- Connector throttling limits reached
- API rate limiting from external services

Authentication and Authorization Errors

These errors occur when there are issues with credentials or permissions and because of the following factors:

- Expired connections
- Insufficient permissions
- Changed credentials
- Account lockouts

Common Failure Points

Let us examine some of the most common points where flows tend to fail:

- **External Service Dependencies**: Flows that rely on multiple external services are more prone to failure as any service outage affects the entire workflow.
- **Complex Expressions**: The more complex your expressions, the higher the likelihood of errors, especially when dealing with dynamic data.
- **Large Data Volumes**: Processing large amounts of data can lead to timeout errors or exceed service limits.
- **Conditional Logic Gaps**: Missing edge cases in conditional logic can give rise to unexpected behavior and errors.
- **Authentication Management**: Connections that require regular re-authentication can cause flows to fail if not properly maintained.

Implementing Comprehensive Error Handling

Now that we understand the types of errors, let us explore strategies to handle them effectively.

Using Configure Run after Settings

One of the most powerful error handling features in Power Automate is the "`Configure run after`" setting, which allows you to specify the next course of action when the preceding one succeeds, fails, is skipped, or times out.

Step-by-Step Implementation

1. In the flow editor, select the action that should run after a potential error.
2. Click the ellipsis (`...`) and select "`Configure run after`."
3. Choose the appropriate conditions. Options include:

a. is successful
b. has failed
c. is skipped
d. has timed out

Real-World Example: Order Processing with Error Handling

Consider a flow that processes customer orders. If the primary shipping service fails, you might want to use a backup service as illustrated in the following figure:

```
Trigger: When a new order is received
↓
Action 1: Process payment
↓
Action 2: Submit order to primary shipping service
↓
Action 3 (runs if Action 2 fails): Submit order to backup shipping service
↓
Action 4 (runs after either Action 2 or Action 3): Send confirmation email
```

Figure 9.1: *Order Processing with Error Handling*

Using Scope Actions for Organized Error Handling

Scope actions allow you to group multiple actions together and apply error handling to the entire group, thereby making your flows more organized and easier to manage.

Step-by-Step Implementation

1. Add a "`Scope`" action to your flow.
2. Place related actions inside the scope.
3. Add actions after the scope that will run based on the scope's outcome using "`Configure run after`."

Real-World Example: Customer Data Processing

```
Trigger: When a new customer signs up
↓
Scope: Customer Validation
  ├ Action: Validate email format
  ├ Action: Check for duplicate customers
  │ Action: Validate address information
↓
Action (runs if Scope succeeds): Add customer to CRM
↓
Action (runs if Scope fails): Send alert to support team
```

Figure 9.2: *Customer Data Processing Workflow*

Note: Error Handling with Parallel Branches

For critical workflows, implement parallel processing branches with different approaches to achieve the same outcome. If one branch fails, the others may still succeed.

```
Trigger: Critical data needs processing
↓
Parallel Branch 1: Process using Service A
Parallel Branch 2: Process using Service B
↓
Condition: Check which branch succeeded
```

Figure 9.3: *Error Handling with Parallel Branches in Workflow Execution*

Try-Catch-Finally Pattern Implementation

Borrowing from traditional programming concepts, you can implement a try-catch-finally pattern in Power Automate using scopes and run-after configurations.

Step-by-Step Implementation

1. Create a "`Try`" scope containing your main logic.
2. Add a "`Catch`" scope configured to run after the "`Try`" scope has failed.
3. Add a "`Finally`" scope configured to run after both "`Try`" and "`Catch`" scopes, regardless of outcome.

```
Scope: Try
  └ [Main workflow actions]
↓
Scope: Catch (runs if Try fails)
  └ [Error handling actions]
↓
Scope: Finally (runs after Try and/or Catch)
  └ [Cleanup actions that should always run]
```

Figure 9.4: *Try-Catch-Finally Pattern Using Scopes in Power Automate*

Real-World Example: Document Processing

```
Trigger: When a new document is uploaded
↓
Scope: Try
  ├ Action: Extract text from document
  └ Action: Analyze content
↓
Scope: Catch (runs if Try fails)
  ├ Action: Log error details
  └ Action: Send notification to admin
↓
Scope: Finally (runs after Try and/or Catch)
  └ Action: Move document to processed folder
```

Figure 9.5: *Document Processing in a Real-World Workflow*

Try It Yourself: Implementing Basic Error Handling

Let us practice implementing basic error handling in a flow:

1. Create a new instant flow triggered by a button.
2. Add an HTTP action that calls an external API.
3. Add a scope action named "`Error Handler`" configured to run if the HTTP action fails.
4. Inside the Error Handler scope, add actions to:
   a. Send an email notification about the failure.
   b. Log the error details to a SharePoint list.
5. Test the flow by intentionally causing the HTTP action to fail (use an invalid URL).

Creating Resilient Workflows with Retry Patterns

In a world of unreliable networks and occasionally unavailable services, implementing retry mechanisms can improve workflow reliability by a significant extent.

Built-in Retry Policies

Many connectors in Power Automate have built in retry policies that automatically attempt to retry failed actions.

How to Configure Retry Policies:

1. Select an action in your flow.
2. In the settings pane, look for "`Retry Policy`" (not available for all connectors).
3. Configure the following settings:
   a. **Count**: Number of retry attempts
   b. **Interval**: Time between retries
   c. **Type**: Fixed (same interval) or Exponential (increasing intervals)

Custom Retry Implementation with Do Until

For connectors that do not support built-in retry policies, you can implement custom retry logic using "`Do Until`" loops.

Step-by-Step Implementation

1. Add a "`Do Until`" action to your flow.
2. Inside the loop, add the action you want to retry.
3. Add a "`Condition`" action to check if the action succeeded.
4. Configure the "`Do Until`" loop to exit when the condition is met or after a certain number of iterations.

Real-World Example: File Processing with Retries

```
Trigger: When a file is added to OneDrive
↓
Initialize variable: retryCount = 0
↓
Do Until: success = true OR retryCount > 5
  ├ Try to process file (in a Try scope)
  ├ If successful, set success = true
  ├ If failed, increment retryCount and wait 30 seconds
  └ Log retry attempt
↓
Condition: Was processing successful?
  ├ Yes: Send success notification
  └ No: Send failure notification
```

Figure 9.6: *File Processing with Retry Logic*

Note: Exponential Backoff

When implementing custom retry logic, use exponential backoff to increase the time between retries. This reduces load on external services and increases the chance of success.

```
First retry: Wait 10 seconds
Second retry: Wait 20 seconds
Third retry: Wait 40 seconds
Fourth retry: Wait 80 seconds
```

Figure 9.7: *Implementing Exponential Backoff for Retry Logic*

Common Pitfall Warning: Infinite Loops

When implementing retry logic, always include a maximum number of retry attempts to prevent infinite loops that can consume your flow, run quota and potentially incur additional costs.

Think About It: Retry Strategy Design

Consider these questions when designing your retry strategy:

1. Is the operation idempotent (can be repeated without side effects)?
2. What is an appropriate maximum number of retries?
3. Should you notify someone after a certain number of failed attempts?
4. Are there specific error types that should not trigger retries?

Implementing Data Validation Techniques

One of the most effective ways to prevent errors is to validate data before processing it. Let us explore some robust validation techniques:

Input Validation Strategies

Schema Validation with Conditions

Use condition actions to verify that incoming data meets expected format and requirements.

```
Trigger: Form submission
↓
Condition: All required fields present?
  ├ Yes: Continue processing
  └ No: Terminate flow with error message
```

Figure 9.8: *Input Validation Using Schema and Conditional Logic*

Advanced Schema Validation with Expressions

For complex validation requirements, use expressions to check data integrity.

```
Condition: length(triggerBody()?['email']) > 0 and contains(triggerBody()?['email'], '@')
```

Figure 9.9: *Advanced Schema Validation Using Expressions*

Real-World Example: Customer Registration Validation

```
Trigger: Customer registration form submission
↓
Scope: Validation
  ├ Condition: Email format is valid
  ├ Condition: Phone number matches pattern
  ├ Condition: Required fields are not empty
  └ Condition: Customer doesn't already exist
↓
Condition: All validations passed?
  ├ Yes: Process registration
  └ No: Send back for correction
```

Figure 9.10: *Customer Registration Validation Workflow*

Note: Create Reusable Validation Child Flows

If you use a certain validation logic frequently, it is wise to create child flows that handle specific validation tasks. This promotes reusability and makes your flows easy to maintain.

Try It Yourself: Implementing Data Validation

Create a flow that validates form input data:

1. Create an instant flow triggered by a button with input parameters (email, phone, name).
2. Implement validation checks for each field:
    a. Email must contain '@' and have a valid domain
    b. Phone must match a specific format

c. Name must not be empty

3. If validation fails, send a response with error details.
4. If validation passes, proceed with processing.

Implementing Monitoring and Alert Systems

Even with the best error handling, you need to know when issues occur. Let us explore some monitoring strategies to do so:

Building a Flow Monitoring Dashboard

Step-by-Step Implementation

1. Create a SharePoint list or Azure SQL database to store flow run information.
2. Modify all your important flows to log their status to this central location.
3. Create a Power BI dashboard that visualizes flow health.

Essential Metrics to Track

- Success/failure rate
- Average duration
- Error frequency by type
- Error frequency by flow
- Trends over time

Real-World Example: Enterprise Flow Monitoring

```
For each business-critical flow:
↓
Add to Start: Log flow start (timestamp, flow name, inputs)
↓
Add to End: Log flow completion (duration, outcome)
↓
Add to Error Handler: Log detailed error information
↓
Weekly: Generate flow health report for stakeholders
```

Figure 9.11: *Enterprise Flow Monitoring Workflow*

Automated Alert System

Implement an automated alert system that notifies administrators of critical flow failures or patterns of failures.

Step-by-Step Implementation

1. Create a centralized error logging flow that receives error notifications.
2. Implement logic to determine alert severity based on:
    a. Flow importance
    b. Error type

   c. Frequency of occurrence

3. Set up appropriate notification channels:
   a. Email for non-urgent issues
   b. SMS for urgent issues
   c. Teams notifications for team awareness
   d. Create incidents in IT service management tools

Note: Proactive Monitoring with Heartbeat Flows

Create "heartbeat" flows that run periodically and verify that critical systems and connections are functioning properly. These flows can detect issues before they affect your business processes.

Scenario-based Challenge: Building a Comprehensive Monitoring System

Design a monitoring system for an organization with 50+ production flows across different departments. Your system should:

1. Centralize error logging
2. Provide real-time alerts for critical failures
3. Generate daily and weekly health reports
4. Track error trends
5. Suggest potential improvements based on error patterns

Developing Testing Methodologies for Cloud Flows

Comprehensive testing is crucial for building reliable flows. Let us explore effective testing approaches to do so:

Types of Flow Tests

A comprehensive testing strategy requires different types of tests to validate various aspects of your flows. Each test type serves a specific purpose in ensuring overall flow reliability and functionality.

Unit Testing

Tests individual actions or small groups of actions in isolation

Implementation

- Create test flows that focus on specific functionality.
- Use static test data.
- Verify outputs match expected results.

Integration Testing

Tests how different actions work together, particularly those that interact with external services

Implementation

- Test complete end-to-end processes.
- Use realistic test data.
- Verify that data flows correctly between actions.

Error Simulation Testing

Intentionally causes errors to verify that error handling works as expected

Implementation

- Create test cases that trigger specific error conditions.
- Verify that error handlers respond appropriately.
- Test retry mechanisms under controlled conditions.

Test Environment Strategy

For robust testing, implement separate environments such as:

- **Development**: Where flows are initially built and tested
- **Testing/QA**: Where flows are tested against realistic data
- **Production**: Where flows handle real business processes

Real-World Example: Order Processing Test Strategy

```
Test Case 1: Happy Path
- Submit valid order
- Verify order is processed correctly
- Verify confirmation email is sent

Test Case 2: Invalid Payment
- Submit order with invalid payment details
- Verify error is handled correctly
- Verify customer receives appropriate notification

Test Case 3: Service Outage
- Simulate primary shipping service outage
- Verify order routes to backup service
- Verify order is completed successfully
```

Figure 9.12: *Testing Strategy for Order Processing Workflow*

Note: Create Automated Test Flows

Build automated test flows that run regularly to verify that production flows are functioning correctly. These can serve as an early warning system for potential issues.

Try It Yourself: Creating a Test Harness

Let us create a simple test harness for a flow:

1. Create a test flow that triggers your target flow with various test cases.

2. Include test cases for:
    a. Normal operation
    b. Missing data
    c. Invalid data
    d. Service unavailability
3. Log test results to a central location for analysis.

Establishing Workflow Governance and Best Practices

With your organization's increasing use of Power Automate, establishing governance becomes essential to maintain reliable, secure, and manageable workflows.

Governance Framework Components

Naming Conventions

Establish consistent naming conventions for:

- Flow names
- Connection references
- Variables and parameters
- Error handling components

Example Naming Convention:

```
[Department]-[Process]-[Trigger Type]-[Version]
HR-EmployeeOnboarding-Form-v2
```

Figure 9.13: *Example of a Naming Convention in Workflow Design*

Documentation Requirements

Require documentation for each flow, including:

- Purpose and business process
- Trigger conditions
- Data flows and transformations
- Error handling approach
- Dependencies and connections
- Testing methodology
- Contact information for flow owner

Development Standards

Establish standards for:

- Error-handling requirements
- Logging requirements
- Performance expectations
- Security practices
- Testing requirements
- Code review process

Change Management Process

Implement a formal change management process to:

- Version control for flow definitions
- Approval requirements for production changes
- Rollback procedures
- Testing requirements before deployment

Real-World Example: Enterprise Flow Governance

```
New Flow Request
↓
Review by Center of Excellence
↓
Development in Dev Environment
↓
Peer Review
↓
Testing in QA Environment
↓
Approval for Production
↓
Deployment to Production
↓
Monitoring and Maintenance
```

Figure 9.14: *Example of a Naming Convention in Workflow Design*

Note: Create a Flow Template Library

Develop a library of pre-approved flow templates that include best practices for error-handling, logging, and security. This ensures consistency and reduces development time.

Common Pitfall Warning: Shadow IT

Without proper governance, individual departments may create critical business flows without appropriate oversight, leading to security risks, unreliable processes, and maintenance challenges.

Optimizing Performance to Prevent Timeout Errors

Performance optimization is an important aspect of error prevention, particularly for complex flows processing large datasets.

Common Performance Issues

Performance bottlenecks in Power Automate flows can lead to timeouts, errors, and unreliable execution. Understanding these common issues will help you design more efficient and reliable workflows from the beginning.

Timeout Errors

Power Automate has the following execution time limits:

- **Standard flows:** 30-day timeout
- **Express flows:** 5-minute timeout
- **Scheduled flows:** 7-day timeout

Connector Limitations

Each connector has its own rate limits and timeout settings.

Large Data Processing

Processing large datasets can lead to timeout errors and performance degradation.

Performance Optimization Strategies

Once you understand the common performance issues, you will be able to implement targeted strategies to optimize your flows. These proven techniques will help you build faster, more reliable workflows that stay within service limits.

Batch Processing

For large datasets, process data in smaller batches instead of all at once.

Implementation

- Use "`Apply to each`" with concurrency control
- Split large arrays into smaller chunks
- Process batches in parallel when possible

Minimize External Service Calls

Each external service call introduces potential points of failure and performance delays.

Implementation

- Combine multiple related operations in a single call
- Cache results when appropriate
- Use batch operations when available

Optimize Expressions

Complex expressions can impact performance and reliability.

Implementation

- Break down complex expressions into smaller steps
- Use variables to store intermediate results
- Avoid unnecessary recalculations

Real-World Example: Processing Customer Orders in Batches

```
Trigger: When new orders need processing
↓
Get orders from database
↓
Initialize batch size = 100
↓
Calculate number of batches
↓
For each batch:
  ├ Get batch of orders
  ├ Process each order (with concurrency = 10)
  └ Log batch completion
↓
Send processing summary
```

Figure 9.15: *Batch Processing of Customer Orders in a Real-World Workflow*

Note: Use Concurrent Processing Wisely

While concurrent processing can improve performance, excessive concurrency can lead to throttling errors. Test different concurrency settings to find the optimal balance.

Try It Yourself: Optimizing a Data Processing Flow

Optimize a flow that processes a large dataset:

1. Start with a flow that processes items one by one.
2. Modify it to process items in batches of 50.
3. Implement parallel processing with a concurrency of 5.
4. Compare the performance and reliability of each approach.

Creating Custom Error Logging Systems

A robust error logging system is essential for troubleshooting and continuous improvement of your flows.

Components of an Effective Error Logging System

Error Log Structure

Create a structured format for error logs that includes:

- Timestamp
- Flow name
- Action name
- Error type
- Error message
- Trigger information
- Context data
- Correlation ID (for tracking related errors)

Centralized Logging Repository

Implement a central location for all error logs, such as:

- SharePoint list
- Azure SQL Database
- Log Analytics workspace
- Dynamics 365 entity

Error Categorization and Severity Levels

Categorize errors by:

- Severity (Critical, High, Medium, Low)
- Type (Connection, Expression, Data, etc.)
- Source (Internal, External service)
- Impact (User-facing, Background process)

Step-by-Step Implementation

1. Create a centralized error log repository.
2. Create a child flow for standardized error logging.
3. Modify all production flows to call this error logging flow when errors occur.
4. Implement reporting and alerting based on logged errors.

Real-World Example: Enterprise Error Logging System

```
In each production flow:
↓
When an error occurs:
  ├ Capture error details
  ├ Capture flow context
  ├ Call centralized error logging flow
  └ Determine if immediate alert is needed
↓
In the centralized logging flow:
  ├ Standardize error format
  ├ Categorize error
  ├ Store in repository
  ├ Trigger alerts if needed
  └ Update error dashboard
```

***Figure* 9.16:** *Enterprise Error Logging System*

Note: Correlation IDs for Complex Processes

For processes that span multiple flows, implement a correlation ID system that allows you to trace related errors across different flows and systems.

Developing Automated Recovery Mechanisms

The pinnacle of error-free workflows is the ability to automatically recover from errors without human intervention.

Types of Recovery Mechanisms

Automated recovery mechanisms represent the pinnacle of workflow reliability in Power Automate. These mechanisms enable your flows to detect problems and take corrective action without human intervention, significantly reducing downtime and manual troubleshooting efforts. Let's explore three powerful recovery patterns that can be implemented in your Power Automate workflows.

1. **Self-Healing Flows**

Self-healing flows in Power Automate are designed to detect and automatically fix common issues without requiring manual intervention. This approach transforms reactive error handling into proactive problem resolution, where your flows can identify specific error conditions and implement corrective actions before the issue impacts your business process.

Design flows that can detect and fix common issues automatically.

Implementation:

- Detect specific error conditions using conditional logic and error detection patterns
- Implement automated corrective actions such as data cleanup, reconnection attempts, or format conversions
- Log recovery attempts and results to track self-healing effectiveness and identify recurring issues

2. **Fallback Systems**

Fallback systems provide alternative execution paths in Power Automate when primary services or connectors fail. This redundancy approach ensures business continuity by automatically switching to backup resources when the primary option becomes unavailable, a critical capability for mission-critical workflows.

Implement alternative paths when primary systems fail.

Implementation:

- Detect service unavailability through connection failures or timeout errors
- Switch to backup services or data sources using parallel branches or conditional routing
- Return to primary service when available by implementing health check mechanisms

3. **Circuit Breaker Pattern**

The circuit breaker pattern in Power Automate prevents cascading failures by temporarily disabling calls to problematic external services or connectors. This pattern protects your workflow from repeatedly attempting to connect to failing services, which can exhaust retry limits and cause broader system issues.

Prevent cascading failures by temporarily disabling problematic services.

Implementation:

- Track failure rates for external services using variables or a centralized monitoring system
- Temporarily disable calls to services with high failure rates by routing flows around problematic connectors
- Periodically test disabled services to see if they've recovered using scheduled health check flows.

Real-World Example: Self-Healing Document Processing System

```
Trigger: New document uploaded
↓
Try to process with primary OCR service
↓
If primary service fails:
  ├ Switch to backup OCR service
  ├ Process document
  └ Log service failure
↓
If document format is invalid:
  ├ Attempt automatic format conversion
  ├ Reprocess document
  └ Log conversion attempt
↓
If all automatic recovery fails:
  └ Route to manual processing queue
```

Figure 9.17: *Self-Healing Document Processing System*

Note: Progressive Recovery

Implement progressive recovery steps from least to most disruptive. Try simple fixes first before resorting to more complex or resource-intensive recovery mechanisms.

Scenario-based Challenge: Building a Resilient Order Processing System

Design an order processing system that can handle various failure scenarios such as:

- Primary database unavailability
- Payment processing service outages
- Inventory system failures
- Email notification service issues
- Data validation failures

Your solution should include the following:

- Appropriate error handling for each component
- Retry strategies for transient errors
- Fallback systems for critical components
- Logging and monitoring
- Automated recovery where possible
- Graceful degradation when full recovery is not possible

Real-World Use Cases

Let us explore three detailed, real-world use cases that demonstrate comprehensive error handling and reliability strategies.

Use Case 1: Enterprise Invoice Processing System

Business Context: A large manufacturing company processes thousands of supplier invoices monthly. Any errors or delays can impact supplier relationships and financial reporting.

Flow Architecture:

1. **Trigger**: Email with invoice attachment arrives in shared mailbox
2. **Document Processing**:
    a. Extract invoice data using AI Builder.
    b. Validate against expected format.
3. **Business Validation**:
    a. Match invoice to purchase order.
    b. Validate line items and amounts.
4. **Approval Workflow**:
    a. Route to appropriate approvers.
    b. Track approval status.
5. **Financial System Integration**:
    a. Create invoice record in ERP system.
    b. Schedule payment.

6. **Notification and Documentation**:
    a. Notify stakeholders.
    b. Archive invoice and processing details.

Error Handling Strategies Implemented:

- **Document Processing Errors:**
    - AI Builder confidence score threshold
    - Fallback to secondary OCR service
    - Routing to manual processing for low-confidence extractions
- **Validation Errors:**
    - Structured validation with detailed error messages
    - Automatic correction of common formatting issues
    - Notification to supplier for significant discrepancies
- **Integration Errors:**
    - Queued retry mechanism for ERP system
    - Transaction logging for reconciliation
    - Circuit breaker pattern for system outages
- **Performance Optimization:**
    - Batch processing of invoices
    - Scheduled processing during off-peak hours
    - Priority routing for high-value invoices

Monitoring and Maintenance:

- Daily summary of processed invoices
- Alert system for processing backlogs
- Weekly performance metrics review
- Monthly error pattern analysis

Results:

- 95% reduction in manual processing
- 99.8% invoice processing reliability
- Average processing time reduced from 5 days to 4 hours

Use Case 2: Customer Support Ticket Management System

Business Context: A software-as-a-service company manages customer support tickets across multiple channels (email, web form, social media).

Flow Architecture:

1. **Multiple Triggers**:
    a. Email arrival
    b. Web form submission
    c. Social media mention

2. **Ticket Creation and Categorization**:
    a. Extract customer information
    b. AI-based categorization
    c. Priority assignment
3. **Routing and Assignment**:
    a. Match to appropriate support team
    b. Load balancing among agents
4. **SLA Management**:
    a. Track response times
    b. Escalate approaching deadlines
5. **Resolution and Feedback**:
    a. Capture resolution details
    b. Request customer feedback
    c. Update knowledge base

Error Handling Strategies Implemented:

- **Channel-Specific Error Handling:**
    - Email service connectivity monitoring
    - Web form input validation
    - Social media API throttling management
- **Data Extraction Resilience:**
    - Progressive customer identification (try email, then name, then company)
    - Fallback to manual lookup for unidentified customers
    - Contextual default values for missing data
- **Assignment Failures:**
    - Automatic reassignment for unavailable agents
    - Escalation path for unassignable tickets
    - Alert system for routing bottlenecks
- **SLA Protection:**
    - Proactive monitoring of at-risk tickets
    - Automatic escalation of breached SLAs
    - Recovery actions for delayed responses

Monitoring and Maintenance:

- Real-time dashboard of ticket status
- Agent availability tracking
- Channel health monitoring
- Integration point performance metrics

Results:

- 99.9% ticket capture reliability
- Average response time reduced by 68%
- SLA compliance improved from 82% to 97%

Use Case 3: Retail Inventory Management System

Business Context: A retail chain with 500+ stores needs to maintain accurate inventory across physical locations and e-commerce platforms.

Flow Architecture:

1. **Inventory Update Sources**:
   a. Point-of-sale transactions
   b. Warehouse receipts
   c. Returns processing
   d. Manual adjustments
2. **Central Inventory Processing**:
   a. Consolidate updates from all sources
   b. Apply business rules and validations
   c. Calculate inventory positions
3. **Distribution to Consumers**:
   a. Update store inventory systems
   b. Update e-commerce platforms
   c. Update inventory planning systems
4. **Analysis and Alerting**:
   a. Low stock alerts
   b. Anomaly detection
   c. Reconciliation reporting

Error Handling Strategies Implemented:

- **Data Collection Resilience:**
  - Store-level buffering for connectivity issues
  - Offline operation capability with synchronization
  - Transaction log for audit and recovery
- **Processing Reliability:**
  - Idempotent processing design
  - Transaction integrity validation
  - Duplicate detection and handling
- **Distribution Assurance:**
  - Prioritized update queuing

    - Confirmation and verification of updates
    - Reconciliation workflows for discrepancies
- **System Health Management**:
    - Component health monitoring
    - Automatic failover for critical components
    - Degraded operation modes during partial outages

Monitoring and Maintenance:

- Real-time inventory accuracy metrics
- System component health dashboard
- Transaction volume and performance tracking
- Error trend analysis

Results:

- Inventory accuracy improved from 92% to 99.5%
- Out-of-stock situations reduced by 73%
- System availability increased to 99.99%

Conclusion

In this chapter, we have explored comprehensive strategies for building error-free workflows in Microsoft Power Automate, discovering that truly reliable workflows do not simply avoid errors they anticipate, detect, handle, and recover from them gracefully. We have also covered essential topics including understanding error types and their root causes to implement structured error handling with scopes and run-after configurations, create resilient workflows with retry patterns and fallback systems, validate data proactively, building monitoring and alert systems, develop comprehensive testing methodologies, establish governance practices, optimize performance, create custom error logging systems, and develop automated recovery mechanisms.

When implemented together as a cohesive strategy, these techniques can transform brittle, error prone flows into robust, self-healing automation systems that can withstand the unpredictable nature of real-world business environments. The investment in building these reliability practices pays dividends through reduced maintenance overhead, increased user confidence, and the ability to scale automation initiatives across your organization with confidence. As you surge ahead in your journey with Power Automate, remember that error-free workflows are carefully constructed from deliberate planning, systematic implementation of best practices, and continuous improvement based on monitoring and feedback.

CHAPTER 10
Debugging Your Automations

Introduction

In the journey of mastering Microsoft Power Automate Cloud Flows so far, we have explored various aspects of building automated workflows. We also learned how to create basic flows, work with triggers and actions, incorporate conditions and loops, handle variables, and integrate with different Microsoft services. We examined data operations, expressions, and complex flow patterns and now, we have arrived at a critical skill that separates novice automation builders from experts: debugging.

Debugging is the art and science of finding and fixing issues in your flows. No matter how carefully you plan and build your automations, you will inevitably encounter situations where things do not work as expected. The ability to systematically identify, diagnose, and resolve these issues is essential for creating robust, reliable automations that deliver business value consistently.

In previous chapters, you learned about the building blocks of Power Automate, how to design flows, work with data, and implement logic. This chapter builds upon that foundation by teaching you how to ensure your flows run correctly and handle exceptions gracefully. By mastering debugging techniques, you can confidently deploy your automations to production environments and support them effectively over time.

Structure

In this chapter, we will cover the following topics:

- Understanding the Power Automate Debugging Lifecycle
  - The Debugging Mindset
  - Types of Errors in Power Automate
  - The Debugging Lifecycle
- Using Built-in Debugging Tools
  - Flow Run History and Analytics
  - Run Details and Execution Logs
  - Understanding JSON Outputs
  - Tracking Execution Context
- Implementing Debugging Techniques
  - Incremental Development and Testing
  - Isolating Problem Areas
  - Data Inspection Methods
  - Testing with Sample Data

- Handling Errors Proactively
    - Configuring Error Handling
    - Try-Catch Patterns in Power Automate
    - Creating Custom Error Messages
    - Implementing Retry Policies
- Working with Complex Data Operations
    - Debugging Data Transformations
    - Troubleshooting Data Mapping Issues
    - Validating Data Filters and Conditions
    - Managing Data Type Conversions
- Monitoring and Maintaining Flows
    - Performance Analysis and Optimization
    - Setting Up Alerts and Notifications
    - Implementing Logging Mechanisms
    - Documentation Best Practices
- Advanced Debugging Scenarios
    - Debugging Parallel Branches
    - Troubleshooting Integrations with External Systems
    - Addressing Concurrency and Race Conditions
    - Debugging Secure and Encrypted Connections

Understanding the Power Automate Debugging Lifecycle

Debugging is not a one-time activity, but a lifecycle that spans the entire development process of your automations. Understanding this lifecycle helps you approach debugging systematically rather than reactively.

The Debugging Mindset

Effective debugging begins with the right mindset. Instead of viewing errors as frustrating obstacles, it is more productive to see them as valuable feedback that guides you toward a more robust solution. Every error message, unexpected result, or performance issue is an opportunity to improve the automation's quality.

Successful Power Automate developers embrace these principles:

- **Be methodical:** Follow a consistent process rather than making random changes.
- **Think like a detective:** Gather evidence, formulate hypotheses, and test them systematically.
- **Document your findings:** Keep track of what you have tried and what youve learned.
- **Learn from patterns:** Recognize recurring issues to prevent them in future flows.

Types of Errors in Power Automate

Before diving into specific debugging techniques, it is important to understand the different types of errors you might encounter:

- **Design-time errors:** These occur during flow creation and prevent saving or publishing. Power Automate typically identifies these immediately with red warning indicators.
- **Runtime errors:** These occur when executing your flow and can be further categorized into:
    - **Syntax errors:** Incorrect expressions, function usage, or formatting
    - **Logic errors:** The flow runs but produces incorrect results
    - **Data errors:** Issues with data formats, transformations, or mapping
    - **Connection errors:** Problems with authenticating or communicating with services
    - **Permission errors:** Insufficient access rights to resources
    - **Timeout errors:** Operations taking too long to complete
- **Intermittent errors**: These appear sporadically and may be related to system load, network conditions, or timing issues.
- **Silent failures**: The most challenging type is when flows appear to succeed but do not produce the expected outcomes.

The Debugging Lifecycle

The debugging process in Power Automate typically follows these stages:

1. **Prevention:** Build flows with debugging in mind from the start
2. **Detection:** Recognize when something is not working correctly
3. **Diagnosis:** Determine the root cause of the issue
4. **Resolution:** Implement and verify the fix
5. **Learning:** Apply insights to improve future automations

Note: *Begin with a preventive mindset by building small, testable components and validating each step before moving to the next. This "shift-left" approach catches issues early when they are easier to fix.*

Try It Yourself: Adopt the Debugging Mindset

Before proceeding further, take a moment to reflect on your current approach to troubleshooting:

- Think about a recent flow that did not work as expected. How did you approach diagnosing the issue?
- Did you follow a systematic process or make random changes hoping to fix the problem?
- How did you document what you learned?
- What could you have done differently to make debugging easier?

Using Built-in Debugging Tools

Power Automate provides several built-in tools to help you understand what is happening inside your flows. Mastering these tools is essential for efficient debugging.

Flow Run History and Analytics

The run history is your first stop when investigating issues. To access it:

1. Navigate to "`My Flows`" or the solution containing your flow.
2. Select the flow you want to examine.
3. Click "`Run History`".

Here, you will see a list of recent executions with their status (succeeded, failed, or cancelled) and duration. This overview helps users identify patterns like:

- Are failures consistent or intermittent?
- Did issues start after a specific change or date?
- Are there performance trends over time?

The analytics view provides aggregated statistics about your flow's performance and reliability. Use these metrics to identify flows that need attention before they cause significant problems.

Run Details and Execution Logs

When you select a specific run, Power Automate shows a detailed view of each step in the flow, including:

- The status of each action (Succeeded, Failed, Skipped)
- The time taken for each action to complete
- Input and output data for each step
- Error messages for failed actions

This visual representation helps you:

1. Identify exactly which step failed
2. See the data flowing between steps
3. Understand the execution path through conditions and switches
4. Measure performance bottlenecks

Note: *While examining run details, always expand the failed action first and then work backward to understand what led to the failure. The error message often contains valuable clues about what went wrong.*

Understanding JSON Outputs

Power Automate displays data in JSON format in the run details. Being comfortable reading JSON is crucial for effective debugging. Here is what to look for:

- **Structure:** Objects (enclosed in { }) contain related properties, while arrays (enclosed in [ ]) hold collections of items.
- **Data types:** Pay attention to whether values are strings (in quotes), numbers, booleans, or nested objects.
- **Null values:** Properties with null values might indicate missing data.
- **Special characters:** Watch for escaping issues with quotes, backslashes, and other special characters.

When comparing expected versus actual outputs, check for subtle differences like:

- Extra or missing properties
- Different data types (like string vs. number)
- Differences in casing (Power Automate is often case-sensitive.)
- Trailing spaces or invisible characters

Common Pitfall: *Do not assume that similar-looking values are identical. A string "123" is not the same as the number 123, and this distinction can cause unexpected behavior.*

Tracking Execution Context

As flows become more complex, tracking the execution context–the current values of variables, outputs from previous actions, and the state of your flow–becomes increasingly important. This is especially critical in Power Automate because, unlike traditional development environments where you can pause execution and inspect variables in real-time, cloud flows run asynchronously in the background without direct developer intervention during execution.

The Challenge of Debugging in Cloud-Based Automation

Power Automate operates fundamentally differently from traditional programming environments. When you build applications in languages like Python, C#, or JavaScript, you typically have access to debuggers that let you set breakpoints, step through code line by line, and inspect variable values at any moment during execution. You can literally pause a running program, examine its state, modify values, and continue execution.

In Power Automate, however, once you trigger a flow, it executes in Microsoft's cloud infrastructure completely independently of your interaction. You cannot pause a running flow to inspect its state. By the time you review the run history, the flow has already completed (successfully or with errors), and you're looking at historical data rather than live execution. This asynchronous, cloud-based nature means you must build debugging capabilities directly into your flow design.

Recent Platform Enhancements:

It's worth noting that Microsoft continuously improves Power Automate's debugging capabilities. Recent and upcoming platform enhancements include:

- **Enhanced variable visibility:** Newer versions of Power Automate provide improved visibility into variable values at different execution stages within the run history interface.
- **Improved run details interface:** Microsoft has introduced more intuitive navigation and data visualization in the run details panel, making it easier to trace execution flow and inspect outputs.
- **Real-time monitoring capabilities:** Enhanced monitoring features allow for better tracking of long-running flows and provide more granular insights into execution progress.
- **Advanced analytics and telemetry:** Newer versions include improved analytics dashboards that aggregate execution patterns and highlight anomalies across multiple runs.
- **Step-by-step execution preview:** Microsoft is working on features that provide better pre-execution validation and testing capabilities within the designer itself.

As you upgrade to newer versions of Power Automate, you will notice these improvements in the debugging experience. However, the fundamental principles and techniques covered in this chapter remain relevant, as proactive context tracking within your flow design continues to provide the most detailed and actionable debugging information. Think of platform enhancements as complementing and not replacing the strategic debugging practices you build into your flows.

Pro Tip: Regularly check the Microsoft Power Automate release notes and update announcements to stay informed about new debugging features and capabilities. Enable preview features in your development environment to test and familiarize yourself with upcoming enhancements before they reach general availability.

The Challenge of Variable State Management:

Variables in Power Automate maintain state throughout a single flow execution, but this state is invisible during runtime. Consider a scenario where you have a loop that processes 100 customer records, incrementing a counter and accumulating values. If record 47 causes an unexpected issue, you need to know:

- What was the counter value when the error occurred?
- What were the accumulated values up to that point?
- What specific data from record 47 triggered the problem?
- How did previous iterations affect the current state?

Without explicit tracking mechanisms, answering these questions becomes guesswork. The run history shows you that an error occurred, but it doesn't necessarily show you the progression of variable states that led to that error.

Creating Your Own Contextual Tracking:

Since Power Automate doesn't provide a dedicated "watch" feature like Visual Studio's debugger or browser developer tools (though Microsoft continues to enhance these capabilities with each platform update), you must proactively build visibility into your flows:

1. Compose actions for variable snapshots: Insert Compose actions at strategic points in your flow to capture the current value of variables or expressions. Think of these as manual "print statements" that create checkpoints in your execution history. For example, place a Compose action before and after a complex calculation to see how the values changed.

2. Append to array for execution trails: Build an array of diagnostic information throughout the flow execution. This creates a chronological log of what happened, similar to application logging in traditional software. Each array entry can contain a timestamp, action name, and relevant data values. This is particularly valuable in loops where you need to trace the progression across iterations.

3. Condition-based logging: Use conditions to selectively log information when specific situations occur. This prevents your run history from being cluttered with debugging information for normal executions while capturing detailed context when anomalies are detected. For instance, log detailed information only when a calculation exceeds a threshold or when processing records that match certain criteria.

4. Correlation identifiers: In complex flows with parallel branches or child flows, include correlation identifiers (like GUIDs or timestamps) in your context tracking. This helps you trace how different parts of your automation relate to each other across multiple flow executions.

Pro Tip: Create a dedicated "Debug Mode" variable at the beginning of your flow. Use conditions to only execute these debugging actions when this variable is set to true, allowing you to enable or disable detailed logging without modifying the flow structure. This approach gives you the flexibility to run flows in production with minimal overhead, then enable verbose logging when troubleshooting specific issues similar to changing log levels in traditional applications.

Try It Yourself: Explore Run Details

1. Select a flow you have created previously.
2. Examine its run history and identify a failed execution.
3. Open the run details and expand the failed action.
4. Answer these questions:
    a. What was the specific error message?
    b. What inputs were provided to the failed action?
    c. Were there any warning signs in previous steps?
    d. How could you modify the flow to handle this error gracefully?

Implementing Debugging Techniques

Beyond the built-in tools, successful debugging requires strategic approaches to isolate and resolve issues efficiently. In Power Automate, where flows execute asynchronously in the cloud without real-time interaction, implementing systematic debugging techniques during the design and development phase is essential for creating maintainable, production-ready automations. These proactive strategies help you identify root causes faster, reduce troubleshooting time, and build flows that are inherently easier to diagnose when issues arise.

Incremental Development and Testing

One of the most effective debugging strategies is to prevent complex issues by developing incrementally:

- **Start small:** Begin with the simplest version of your flow that does something meaningful.
- **Test frequently:** Validate each component before adding more complexity.
- **Add gradually:** Introduce new actions, conditions, or data operations one at a time.
- **Verify continuously:** Confirm that each addition works as expected before proceeding.

This approach creates natural checkpoints about the instances when the flow was working correctly, thereby making it easier to identify which changes introduced problems.

Isolating Problem Areas

When troubleshooting existing flows, isolation helps narrow down the source of issues:

- **Divide and conquer:** Temporarily disable branches or sections of the flow to determine if they contribute to the problem.
- **Simplify data:** Replace complex dynamic data with simple static values to eliminate data-related variables.
- **Remove conditions:** Temporarily modify conditions to always evaluate as true or false to test specific paths.
- **Break connections:** Isolate external system dependencies by using mock data instead of live connections.

Note: *Create a copy of your production flow specifically for debugging. This allows you to make temporary modifications for troubleshooting without risking the original implementation.*

Data Inspection Methods

Most debugging challenges involve understanding what data is flowing through your automation. These techniques help make data visible:

- **Strategic Compose actions:** Place Compose actions before and after critical operations to capture input and output data.
- **Data visualization:** Use the Parse JSON action to convert complex data structures into a more readable format.
- **Logging to external systems:** For complex scenarios, log debugging information to SharePoint lists, Excel files, or databases.
- **Conditional email alerts:** Configure email notifications with diagnostic information when specific conditions occur.

Testing with Sample Data

Creating reliable test cases accelerates the debugging process and can be achieved through:

- **Create a test data library:** Maintain a collection of sample inputs covering various scenarios.
- **Design for testability:** Structure flows to allow injection of test data.
- **Develop expected outputs:** Define what success looks like for each test case.
- **Build regression tests:** As you fix issues, add test cases that would detect if the same problem reoccurs.

Common Pitfall: Avoid testing only the "happy path", where everything works perfectly. Deliberately include edge cases, invalid inputs, and error conditions in your test scenarios.

Think About It: Developing a Testing Strategy

Consider a flow that processes customer orders from a form and updates inventory in a database:

- What test cases would you create to validate this flow?
- How would you test error conditions like insufficient inventory?
- What debugging actions would you add to make troubleshooting easier?
- How could you design the flow to simplify testing with sample data?

Handling Errors Proactively

Rather than just reacting to errors, Power Automate allows you to anticipate and handle exceptions gracefully. In production environments where automations support critical business processes, the difference between a flow that crashes on errors versus one that handles them intelligently can mean the difference between minor disruptions and significant operational issues. Power Automate provides multiple mechanisms from configure run after settings to scope-based error handling that enable you to design resilient flows that gracefully degrade rather than fail completely.

Configuring Error Handling

Power Automate offers several options for controlling how your flows respond to errors:

- **Configure run after settings**: For each action, you can specify what should happen if previous actions succeed, fail, are skipped, or time out.
- **Parallel branches**: Run operations in parallel branches to prevent one failure from stopping the entire flow.

- **Timeout settings**: Configure appropriate timeouts to prevent flows from hanging indefinitely.
- **Retry policies**: Specify automatic retry attempts for actions that might fail due to transient issues.

Note: *Review the "`Configure run after`" settings for each action by clicking the ellipsis menu. The default is to run only after the previous action succeeds, but you can configure actions to run even when previous steps fail.*

Try-Catch Patterns in Power Automate

Though Power Automate does not have explicit try-catch blocks like traditional programming languages, you can implement similar patterns:

- **Scope + Configure run after:** Place potentially problematic actions in a Scope, then add error-handling actions configured to run after the Scope fails.
- **Parallel branches:** Create parallel branches where one manages the main logic and another captures and processes any errors.
- **Result checking:** Verify operation results explicitly and implement different paths for success and failure.

Here is a simple try-catch pattern you can initiate:

1. Create a Scope action named "`Try Block`".
2. Add the actions that might fail inside this scope.
3. Add another Scope named "`Catch Block`".
4. Configure the "`Catch Block`" to run only when the "`Try Block`" fails.
5. Inside the "`Catch Block`," add actions to handle the error appropriately.

Creating Custom Error Messages

Generic error messages rarely provide enough context for troubleshooting. You may customize error-handling with the following steps:

- **Contextual information:** Include relevant variable values, record IDs, and operation details.
- **User-friendly explanations:** Translate technical errors into business terms.
- **Actionable guidance:** Suggest possible resolutions or next steps.
- **Support references:** Include links to documentation or contact information for assistance.

Example: Instead of just reporting "`Record not found`," create a message like: "`Customer record #12345 could not be found in the CRM system`." Please verify the customer ID and ensure the customer exists in the system. If the problem persists, contact support at support@example.com with reference code FL-404."

Implementing Retry Policies

Not all errors require immediate failure. For operations susceptible to transient issues (like network timeouts), configure retry policies:

- In the advanced options of applicable actions, locate the retry policy settings.
- Specify the number of retry attempts (typically 2-5 is reasonable).
- Set appropriate intervals between retries (increasing intervals often work best).

- Consider the maximum duration before giving up.

Common Pitfall: *Be cautious with retry policies for operations that have side effects. For example, retrying a "`create record`" operation might generate duplicate records, if the original action actually succeeded but failed to return a response.*

Scenario-based Challenge: Implement Error Handling

Design error handling for a flow that:

- Retrieves customer data from Dynamics 365
- Calls an external API to check credit status
- Updates a SharePoint list with approval decisions
- Sends email notifications to stakeholders

For each step, consider the following questions:

- What could go wrong?
- How should the flow respond to errors?
- What information should be captured for troubleshooting?
- Should any actions be retried automatically?

Working with Complex Data Operations

Data operations are a common source of debugging challenges in Power Automate. Let us explore techniques for troubleshooting these scenarios.

Debugging Data Transformations

When data is not being transformed correctly, follow these steps:

1. **Visualize the input:** Use Compose actions to capture the exact input to your transformation.
2. **Break down complex transformations:** Split multi-step transformations into smaller pieces with intermediate Compose actions.
3. **Test expressions separately:** Use individual Compose actions to test each part of a complex expression.
4. **Compare with expected output:** Create a Compose action with your expected result to easily compare with actual results.

Note: *For complex expressions, build them incrementally. Start with a basic version that works, then add complexity one step at a time, testing after each addition.*

Troubleshooting Data Mapping Issues

When mapping data between systems, watch for these common issues:

- **Schema mismatches:** Differences in field names, data types, or structures between source and destination
- **Required fields:** Missing required fields in the target system
- **Data type conversions:** Implicit conversions that change data (like numbers to strings)
- **Array handling:** Incorrect iteration or selection from arrays

- **Null value handling:** Different systems may handle null values differently

Example: When mapping from a form to a database, the form might submit dates as strings in "`MM/DD/YYYY`" format, while the database expects ISO format or a date object. Use the `formatDateTime()` function to ensure proper conversion.

Validating Data Filters and Conditions

Filters and conditions silently affect which data is processed. You can debug them by:

1. **Making conditions visible:** Add Compose actions that show the evaluation result of your condition.
2. **Checking filter inputs:** Verify that filter expressions receive the expected data.
3. **Testing boundary cases:** Confirm behavior with values at the edges of your conditions.
4. **Counting results:** Add actions to count items before and after filtering to verify expected reduction.

Common Pitfall: Watch out for type-sensitive comparisons. The condition `@equals(variables('Counter'), '3')` will fail if Counter is a number (`3`) rather than a string (`'3'`).

Managing Data Type Conversions

Power Automate often performs implicit type conversions that can lead to subtle bugs, such as:

- **String vs. number issues:** Use explicit conversion functions like `int()`, `float()`, or `string()` when type matters.
- **Date handling:** Always use appropriate date functions rather than string manipulation for dates.
- **Boolean conversions:** Be explicit about boolean conditions; "`false`" (string) is different from false (boolean).
- **Null vs. empty:** Distinguish between null values, empty strings, and empty arrays

Note: *When troubleshooting potential type issues, use the* `dataType()` *function in a Compose action to determine the actual type of a value:* `@dataType(variables('myVariable'))`.

Try It Yourself: Debug a Data Transformation

Consider this scenario: You have a flow that processes a list of orders, calculates total revenue, and groups results by customer. However, the totals are incorrect.

- What Compose actions would you add to diagnose the issue?
- How would you validate the calculation logic?
- What data type issues might be causing incorrect totals?
- How could you isolate whether the problem is in the calculation or the grouping?

Monitoring and Maintaining Flows

Effective debugging extends beyond fixing immediate issues to implementing robust monitoring and maintenance practices.

Performance Analysis and Optimization

Identifying and resolving performance bottlenecks:

- **Timing analysis:** Use the run details to identify which actions take the longest.
- **Batch operations:** Look for opportunities to replace loops with batch operations.
- **Reduce API calls:** Consolidate multiple calls to the same service.
- **Optimize data retrieval:** Only request the fields and records you need.
- **Caching strategies:** Use variables to store frequently accessed data.

Note: *For flows that process large data sets, consider implementing pagination or windowing techniques that process data in manageable chunks rather than all at once.*

Setting Up Alerts and Notifications

Proactive monitoring helps you catch issues before users report them:

- **Flow failure alerts:** Configure notifications for when flows fail or exceed duration thresholds.
- **Business metric monitoring:** Set up alerts based on business metrics (for instance, orders processed) rather than just technical success.
- **Trend analysis:** Monitor for changes in success rates or performance over time.
- **Custom health checks:** Create dedicated flows that validate critical business processes end-to-end.

Example: Create a daily health check flow that tests each critical business process with sample data and reports a comprehensive status to the operations team.

Implementing Logging Mechanisms

Systematic logging facilitates troubleshooting and pattern recognition via the following:

- **Centralized log repository**: Create a SharePoint list, database table, or Azure Log Analytics workspace for storing log entries.
- **Structured logging**: Include consistent fields such as timestamp, flow name, action name, user ID, and correlation IDs.
- **Contextual data:** Log relevant business context with technical details.
- **Severity levels:** Distinguish between informational, warning, and error entries.
- **Retention policy:** Define how long logs should be kept and implement cleanup processes.

Common Pitfall: *Avoid excessive logging that creates performance overhead or storage issues. Log strategically at key points in the flow rather than at every step.*

Documentation - The Best Practice

Clear documentation accelerates debugging and knowledge transfer in the following ways:

- **Flow documentation:** Use comments and notes within the flow to explain complex logic.
- **Data dictionaries:** Document the structure and meaning of key data objects.
- **Dependency maps:** Record integrations with other systems and flows.
- **Troubleshooting guides:** Create specific guidance for common issues.
- **Change logs:** Maintain a history of significant changes to the flow.

Note: *Create a "**README**" document for complex flows that explains their purpose, main components, configuration requirements, and known limitations. Store this in a location accessible to all support personnel.*

Knowledge Check: Monitoring and Maintenance

- What metrics would you monitor to ensure your flows are healthy?
- How would you implement a logging system that balances detail with performance?
- What information should be included in flow documentation to facilitate troubleshooting?
- How often should you review flow performance and error patterns?

Advanced Debugging Scenarios

As your flows become more sophisticated, you will encounter complex debugging challenges that require advanced techniques.

Debugging Parallel Branches

Parallel branches introduce timing and state-sharing complexities such as:

- **Branch isolation:** Test each branch individually before combining them.
- **Race conditions:** Watch for dependencies between branches that might cause timing issues.
- **Variable access patterns:** Be aware that parallel branches might update the same variables.
- **Join conditions:** Verify that join conditions correctly manage all possible branch outcomes.

Note: *When debugging parallel branches, temporarily convert them to sequential actions to eliminate timing variables from your troubleshooting.*

Troubleshooting Integrations with External Systems

External integrations add layers of complexity like:

- **Authentication issues:** Verify credentials, token expiration, and permission levels
- **API contract validation**: Confirm your requests match the expected format
- **Response handling:** Implement robust parsing and error handling for responses
- **Timeout configurations:** Set appropriate timeouts based on typical response times
- **Throttling awareness:** Design for API rate limits and implement backoff strategies

Common Pitfall: *Do not assume external systems are always available or consistent. Implement circuit breaker patterns for critical integrations to prevent cascading failures when external systems have issues.*

Addressing Concurrency and Race Conditions

When multiple flow instances run simultaneously or interact with shared resources such as:

- **Locking mechanisms:** Implement record or resource locking to prevent conflicts.
- **Idempotent operations:** Design actions to be safely repeatable without side effects.
- **Version checking:** Verify resource versions before updates to detect concurrent modifications.
- **Transaction boundaries:** Define clear transaction boundaries to maintain data consistency.

Example: When updating the inventory, first read the current value, then check if it is still the same before applying your update. If not, either retry or implement conflict resolution logic.

Debugging Secure and Encrypted Connections

Security measures can complicate debugging through:

- **Connection validation:** Verify connection credentials and certificates.
- **Permission auditing:** Confirm service principals have required permissions.
- **Secure variable handling:** Use secure outputs for sensitive data.
- **Gateway configuration:** For on-premises connections, validate gateway setup and network rules.
- **Certificate validation:** Check for expired or invalid certificates.

Note: *Create a secure debugging environment that mirrors production security settings but provides additional visibility into encrypted connections and protected data.*

Scenario-based Challenge: Debug a Complex Integration

You have a flow that synchronizes inventory between an e-commerce platform and an ERP system. Users report that sometimes inventory updates do not appear in the e-commerce system, but no errors are logged.

Design a debugging approach that addresses:

- How to reproduce the issue reliably
- Techniques to identify if the problem is in the flow, the e-commerce platform, or the ERP
- Methods to detect and resolve potential race conditions
- Monitoring improvements to catch similar issues proactively

Practical Application: Real-World Use Cases

Let us apply debugging techniques to three realistic scenarios.

Use Case 1: Customer Onboarding Workflow

Scenario: A financial services company uses Power Automate to process new customer applications. The flow retrieves form submissions, performs credit checks via an external API, updates CRM records, and generates welcome packets. Recently, some applications have been stuck in processing without clear errors.

Debugging Approach:

- **Symptom Analysis**:
  - Review flow run history to identify patterns in stuck applications.
  - Examine characteristics of affected customers (location, credit score range, and so on.).
  - Check for correlation with specific times or system maintenance windows.
- **Diagnostic Implementation:**
  - Add timeout handling for the external credit check API.
  - Implement status tracking with timestamps at each major processing stage.
  - Create a parallel monitoring flow that identifies and alerts on stalled applications.

- **Root Cause Resolution:**
    - Discovered that credit check API occasionally returns a 202 (Accepted) status but never completes.
    - Implemented a maximum wait time with fallback to manual review process.
    - Added circuit breaker to detect API health issues and route applications accordingly.
- **Preventive Measures:**
    - Created health check probe that validates API responsiveness every 15 minutes.
    - Implemented comprehensive logging of all API interactions.
    - Developed dashboard showing application processing metrics and exception rates.

Lessons Learned: *External dependencies require robust timeout handling and fallback mechanisms. Never assume third-party services will always return a definitive success or failure response.*

Use Case 2: Inventory Management System

Scenario: A retail company uses Power Automate to sync inventory levels between stores and their online platform. Some products show incorrect inventory levels online despite the flow reporting successful execution.

Debugging Approach:

- **Data Flow Analysis:**
    - Added Compose actions to capture inventory data at each processing stage
    - Implemented detailed logging of before/after values for each product update
    - Created data comparison routines to identify discrepancies
- **Concurrency Investigation:**
    - Discovered multiple update sources modifying the same products
    - Implemented version checking to detect concurrent modifications
    - Added timestamp logging to identify precise timing of conflicting updates
- **Root Cause Resolution:**
    - Found race conditions between periodic inventory sync and real-time purchase processes
    - Implemented optimistic concurrency control with retry logic
    - Created a transaction log to reconcile conflicts automatically
- **Monitoring Improvements:**
    - Developed inventory discrepancy detection flow that runs hourly
    - Implemented alerts for products with unusual update patterns
    - Created audit reports showing update history for troubleshooting

Lessons Learned: *When multiple processes update shared resources, explicit concurrency control is essential. Time-based synchronization alone is insufficient for high-volume transaction systems.*

Use Case 3: Approval Workflow with Document Generation

Scenario: A manufacturing company uses Power Automate for their capital expenditure approval process. The flow routes approval requests, collects signatures, and generates final documentation.

Users report that sometimes approvals appear to complete but documents are missing attachments or contain incorrect information.

Debugging Approach:

- **Process Validation:**
  - Created detailed process map showing all approval paths and document generation points
  - Implemented state tracking with validation at each transition
  - Added verification steps comparing inputs to outputs at key transformation points
- **Document Generation Analysis:**
  - Added detailed logging of template selection logic and data mapping
  - Implemented document validation steps to verify structure and completeness
  - Created separate test flow to verify document generation with standardized inputs
- **Root Cause Resolution:**
  - Discovered timing issue where approval status updated before document generation completed
  - Found data mapping errors for specific approval scenarios
  - Identified permission issues when handling large attachments
- **Solution Implementation:**
  - Restructured flow to ensure document completion before status updates
  - Improved error handling with specific recovery paths for each potential failure
  - Added data validation before template processing to catch formatting issues early

Lessons Learned: *Multi-stage processes need transaction-like guarantees to prevent incomplete states. Document generation requires robust validation to ensure completeness and accuracy.*

Conclusion

Mastering the art of debugging Power Automate flows is a transformative skill that elevates you from a casual flow builder to a professional automation developer. Through this comprehensive exploration, we have journeyed from understanding the fundamental debugging mindset to implementing sophisticated error handling strategies for complex enterprise scenarios.

The debugging process is far more than just fixing broken flows it is a systematic discipline that encompasses prevention, detection, diagnosis, resolution, and continuous learning. By embracing this lifecycle approach, you transform potential failures into opportunities for building more robust, resilient automations that deliver consistent business value.

Power Automate's built-in debugging arsenal from detailed run histories to granular execution logs provides unprecedented visibility into your automation's inner workings. When combined with strategic techniques like incremental development, proactive error handling, and comprehensive monitoring, these tools empower you to create flows that work correctly and gracefully handle unexpected situations, while providing clear diagnostic information when issues arise.

The real-world scenarios we have examined demonstrate that effective debugging extends beyond technical proficiency to include business acumen, understanding how automations fit into larger organizational processes, and anticipating the various ways users might interact with your systems. Whether you are troubleshooting a customer onboarding workflow, resolving inventory synchronization conflicts, or ensuring document generation accuracy, the principles and techniques in this chapter provide a solid foundation for tackling any debugging challenge.

Remember that debugging is both an art and a science it requires technical knowledge, creative problem-solving, and persistence. By applying the techniques in this chapter consistently, you will be able to develop an intuition for quickly identifying and resolving issues, which will eventually make you a more effective and confident automation developer.

Additional Resources

- Official Microsoft Documentation: Monitor and troubleshoot flows
- Power Automate Community: Debugging Techniques
- Blog: Advanced Error Handling in Power Automate
- Microsoft Learn: Troubleshooting module for Power Automate
- Power CAT Team: Best Practices for Production Flows

CHAPTER 11

Using Copilot to Develop Power Automate Flows

Introduction

In the previous chapters of this book, we have explored the fundamentals of Microsoft Power Automate Cloud Flows and have learned about creating your first flow, implementing complex business logic, and integrating the flow with various data sources. You have also explored how to build flows manually, configure triggers and actions, handle conditions and loops, and implement error handling. This knowledge will form a solid foundation for understanding automation concepts within Power Platform.

Now, we face a new era in flow development, where artificial intelligence becomes your collaborative partner in creating, optimizing, and troubleshooting Power Automate flows. Microsoft Copilot for Power Automate transforms how to approach automation, thus enabling you to describe your business process in plain English and watch as a complete flow materializes before your eyes. In this chapter, we will explore how Copilot revolutionizes the flow development process through natural language generation, AI-assisted optimization, and practical examples across various business scenarios. By the end of this chapter, you will understand how to leverage Copilot's capabilities to streamline the flow development process and achieve more with less effort.

Structure

This chapter will cover the following topics:

- Understanding Copilot in the Power Automate Ecosystem
- Copilot's Capabilities in Power Automate
- Getting Started with Copilot in Power Automate
- Practical Examples of Using Copilot for Different Flow Types
- Best Practices for Working with Copilot

Understanding Copilot in the Power Automate Ecosystem

Before diving into the specifics of using Copilot for flow development, it is important to understand how it fits within the broader Power Automate ecosystem and builds upon the concepts we have explored previously.

Copilot's Role in the Power Platform

Microsoft Copilot is an evolutionary step in the Power Platform's mission to democratize app development and process automation. While the platform has always aimed to make automation accessible for users with varying technical backgrounds, Copilot takes this to a new level by introducing natural language understanding and generation capabilities.

Copilot acts as an intelligent layer that sits on top of the existing Power Automate infrastructure. It does not replace the underlying flow engine, connectors, or actions that we have discussed already. Instead, it provides an alternative interface for interacting with these components and is based on natural language rather than point-and-click operations.

Copilot operates as an intelligent translation layer between natural language and Power Automate's technical components. When you describe "send an approval request when a new item is added to SharePoint," Copilot translates this into the specific triggers, actions, and configurations you learned in earlier chapters such as the "When an item is created" trigger, the "Start and wait for an approval" action, and the "Update item" action to record the decision. Your understanding of how these components work, what parameters they require, and how they connect together becomes essential when reviewing and refining what Copilot generates.

For instance, if Copilot creates an approval flow, your knowledge from **Chapter 7: Navigating Data Operations** helps you verify that the approval action is correctly configured with the right approvers, that dynamic content is properly referenced from the SharePoint trigger, and that the conditional logic accurately reflects your business rules. Similarly, when Copilot suggests using expressions to format dates or manipulate text, your familiarity with Power Automate's expression language from **Chapter 4: Working with Conditional Logic** enables you to assess whether the generated formula is optimal or needs adjustment. This synergy between your foundational knowledge and Copilot's generation capabilities creates a more powerful development experience than either approach alone.

Building on Previous Knowledge

Your understanding of Power Automate fundamentals is the foundation for effective use of Copilot. Here is how your existing knowledge connects to this new capability:

- **Flow Triggers and Actions** (Chapters 2-3): Copilot needs to select appropriate triggers and actions for your flows. Your familiarity with these components helps you verify that Copilot has chosen the right building blocks for your solution.
- **Expressions and Variables** (Chapter 4): Copilot can generate complex expressions and variable manipulations. Your understanding of these concepts allows you to review and refine Copilot's suggestions.
- **Conditions and Loops** (Chapter 5): When you describe business logic to Copilot, it translates your requirements into conditions and loops. Knowing how these control structures work helps you validate Copilot's implementation.
- **Error Handling** (Chapter 6): Copilot can recommend error-handling approaches, but your knowledge of best practices in this area enables you to oversee robust error management in AI-generated flows.
- **Connectors and Data Operations** (Chapters 7-8): Copilot suggests appropriate connectors and data manipulation techniques based on your descriptions. Your familiarity with these components helps you assess the effectiveness of these suggestions.
- **Flow Solutions for Business Scenarios** (Chapters 9-10): Your exposure to various business solutions provides context for evaluating whether Copilot's recommendations align with established patterns and practices.

Transforming Flow Creation with Copilot

Copilot fundamentally changes how you build Power Automate flows by allowing you to describe your automation requirements in natural language rather than manually selecting and configuring each trigger, action, and connector. This transformation shifts your focus from technical implementation details to business process outcomes, while Copilot handles the translation into working flow components.

From Technical to Conceptual Thinking

Traditional flow development requires you to think in terms of technical components such as triggers, actions, and their configurations. With Copilot, you can focus on describing the business process and outcomes you want to achieve. The AI handles the translation from business concepts to technical implementation.

Accelerated Development

Creating flows manually involves multiple steps, such as selecting triggers and actions, configuring their properties, establishing connections between components, and testing the result. Copilot can generate a complete flow draft in seconds, allowing you to spend more time refining and testing, rather than building from scratch.

Knowledge Augmentation

Even experienced flow developers cannot memorize all available connectors, actions, and their parameters. Copilot acts as a knowledge extension, suggesting relevant components that might not have occurred to you before and providing configurations that follow best practices.

Reduced Learning Barrier

For newcomers to Power Automate, the platform's extensive capabilities can be overwhelming. Copilot reduces this cognitive load by allowing users to describe what they want in familiar terms, making automation accessible to a broader audience.

Iterative Refinement

Rather than building flows incrementally, Copilot enables a different workflow, where you start with a complete draft and then refine it through further natural language instructions or manual adjustments.

In the following sections, we will explore these enhancements in detail, while providing practical examples and guidance on how to maximize the benefits of Copilot in your flow development process.

Copilot's Capabilities in Power Automate

Microsoft Copilot brings a suite of AI-powered capabilities to Power Automate, fundamentally changing how users approach flow development. Let us explore these capabilities in detail.

Natural Language Flow Generation

Copilot's core functionality is its ability to interpret natural language descriptions and generate corresponding flows. This eliminates the need to manually select and configure each component of your flow.

Working

When you describe a process to Copilot, it:

- Analyzes your description to identify the core automation objective
- Determines the appropriate trigger for initiating the flow
- Identifies the required actions to fulfill the objective
- Establishes logical connections between these components
- Configures parameters and properties for each element
- Implements appropriate control flow (conditions, loops) as needed
- Generates a complete, functional flow draft

Example

Consider this prompt to Copilot:

`"I need a flow that monitors my Outlook inbox for emails with attachments from my manager. When such an email arrives, save the attachments to a specific SharePoint document library and send me a mobile notification with the email subject and attachment names."`

From this description, Copilot can generate a complete flow that:

- Uses the "**`When a new email arrives (V3)`**" Outlook trigger with conditions for attachments and sender
- Implements a "**`Get attachments`**" action to retrieve the files
- Creates a "**`Create file`**" action for each attachment to save it to SharePoint
- Configures a "**`Send a push notification`**" action with the requested information
- Includes appropriate dynamic content references between these steps

All of this happens without you having to select a single action or configure any properties manually. The resulting flow appears as a complete draft that you can then review, test, and refine.

AI Assisted Flow Optimization

Beyond creating new flows, Copilot can analyze existing flows and suggest optimizations to improve their performance, reliability, and maintainability.

Performance Optimization

Copilot can identify opportunities to reduce execution time and resource consumption:

- Replacing multiple sequential actions with more efficient batch operations
- Suggesting parallel branches for independent operations
- Identifying redundant data retrievals that can be consolidated
- Recommending appropriate timeout and retry configurations

Structural Improvements

Copilot can suggest the following architectural changes to make flows more maintainable and robust:

- Breaking complex flows into parent-child flow structures
- Suggesting the use of child flows for repeatable processes
- Recommending scope changes to better organize related actions

- Proposing the use of environment variables for configuration values

Logic Enhancements

Copilot can identify potential logical improvements by:

- Detecting missing error-handling paths
- Suggesting more efficient condition structures
- Identifying opportunities to use switch statements instead of multiple conditions
- Recommending data operation optimizations

Connector Suggestions and Configurations

Copilot excels at recommending appropriate connectors and configuring them correctly based on your described needs.

Connector Discovery

With hundreds of connectors available in Power Automate, it is challenging to know which one best suits your needs. Copilot can:

- Suggest relevant connectors based on your process description
- Recommend alternatives when primary connectors have limitations
- Identify opportunities for custom connectors when standard options are insufficient
- Suggest premium connectors when they offer significant advantages

Intelligent Configuration

Configuring connectors often requires understanding numerous parameters and options. To do so, it can:

- Pre-populate connector parameters based on context
- Set appropriate authentication methods
- Configure pagination settings for data retrieval actions
- Suggest optimal retry policies for unreliable services
- Set up appropriate headers for HTTP requests

Template Recommendations

Copilot can leverage the vast library of existing flow templates to recommend starting points for your automation needs.

Contextual Template Suggestions

Based on your description, Copilot can:

- Identify relevant existing templates
- Suggest modifications to adapt templates to your specific requirements
- Combine elements from multiple templates to create custom solutions
- Recommend industry-specific templates when appropriate

Learning from Templates

Copilot can explain the rationale behind template designs, helping you understand:

- Why certain triggers and actions were chosen
- How the control flow is structured
- What error-handling approaches are implemented
- How dynamic content is utilized throughout the flow

Error Detection and Resolution

Identifying and resolving errors in flows is a critical skill. Copilot provides valuable assistance in this area.

Proactive Error Detection

Copilot can analyze your flow drafts to identify potential issues before you even run them:

- Missing required parameters
- Incompatible data types between connected actions
- Potential null reference points
- Infinite loop risks
- Missing error handling for critical operations

Resolution Suggestions

When errors are detected (either proactively or after a flow run fails), Copilot can:

- Explain the error in plain language
- Suggest specific changes to resolve the issue
- Provide code snippets for complex expressions
- Recommend structural changes to avoid the problem
- Offer alternative approaches when a particular solution path is prone to errors

In the next section, we will explore practical examples of using these capabilities across different flow types and business scenarios.

Getting Started with Copilot in Power Automate

Now that you understand Copilot's capabilities, let us explore how to access and begin using this powerful tool in your Power Automate environment.

Accessing and Enabling Copilot

Copilot integration in Power Automate is available through multiple entry points, ensuring that you can leverage AI assistance throughout your flow development journey.

Prerequisites

Before using Copilot for Power Automate, ensure that you have:

- An appropriate Power Platform license that includes Copilot capabilities

- Administrator-enabled Copilot features for your organization
- Permission to create and modify flows in your environment

Access Points in the Power Automate Portal

Copilot is accessible from several locations in the Power Automate web portal:

- **Home Dashboard:** A dedicated Copilot section appears on the dashboard, allowing you to describe flows you want to create.
- **Flow Creation Screen:** When creating a new flow, you will see a Copilot option that enables you to start with a natural language description rather than selecting a template or blank flow.
- **Flow Editor:** Within the flow editor, a Copilot icon in the command bar provides access to AI assistance for the current flow.
- **Flow Details Page:** When viewing an existing flow, you can access Copilot to get optimization suggestions or modification recommendations.

Copilot Chat Interface

The primary interaction method with Copilot is through a chat-like interface that appears as a panel within the Power Automate portal. This interface allows you to:

- Type natural language descriptions and questions
- View Copilot's responses and suggestions
- See flow previews generated by Copilot
- Apply Copilot's recommendations directly to your flows
- Refine your requests through follow-up prompts

Writing Effective Prompts for Flow Generation

The quality of flows generated by Copilot depends on how you describe your requirements. Effective prompt engineering is the key to getting the results you want.

Prompt Structure Best Practices

For optimal results, structure your prompts to include:

- **Automation Objective:** Clearly state what you're trying to accomplish.
- **Trigger Event:** Describe what should initiate the flow.
- **Data Sources and Destinations:** Specify where data comes from and goes.
- **Process Logic:** Outline the decision points and business rules.
- **Output or Notification:** Describe what should happen when the flow completes.

Example of a Well-Structured Prompt

Poor prompt: "Make a flow for approvals."

Improved prompt: "Create a flow that sends approval requests to my manager when new items are added to a SharePoint list called 'Purchase Requests.' The flow should include the item title, requested amount, and justification in the approval request. If approved, update the SharePoint item status to 'Approved' and notify the requester via email. If rejected, update the status to 'Rejected' and notify the requester with the rejection comments."

Specifying Technical Details

While Copilot excels at interpreting general descriptions, you can enhance its accuracy by including technical details when relevant:

- **Connector names:** Use the Office 365 Outlook connector
- **Action names:** Use the '`Send an email (V2)`' action
- **Environment variables:** The SharePoint site URL is stored in an environment variable named '`HR_SharePoint_URL`'
- **Expression requirements:** Calculate the approval deadline as 3 business days from the request date

Iterative Refinement

Remember that you can refine Copilot's output through follow-up prompts. If the initial flow does not meet all your requirements, you can provide additional guidance through prompts such as:

- "Add error handling if the SharePoint update fails"
- "Modify the flow to also send a weekly summary of all approvals"
- "Change the notification to use Microsoft Teams instead of email"

Step-by-Step Tutorial: Creating Your First Flow with Copilot

Let us walk through the process of creating a flow using Copilot from start to finish:

Step 1: Access Copilot from the Power Automate Home Page

1. Navigate to **https://make.powerautomate.com**.
2. Sign in with your organizational account.
3. Locate the Copilot section on the home dashboard (typically near the top).
4. Click the Copilot chat icon to open the interface.

Step 2: Describe Your Flow Requirements

1. In the Copilot chat panel, type a description of the flow you want to create, like the following:

   ```
   "Create a flow that monitors a specific SharePoint document library for new Word
   documents. When a new document is added, convert it to PDF format and save the
   PDF version in another document library called 'PDF Archives' with the same file-
   name but a .pdf extension. Then send an email notification to the document creator
   with links to both the original and PDF versions."
   ```
2. Press **`Enter`** or click **`Send`** to submit your description.

Step 3: Review Copilot's Response

1. Copilot will analyze your request and generate a response containing:
   a. A summary of its understanding of your requirements
   b. A preview of the flow it plans to create
   c. Clarifying questions if any aspects of your description were ambiguous
2. Review this response carefully to ensure Copilot has correctly interpreted your needs

Step 4: Provide Additional Details if Requested

If Copilot asks for clarification, provide the requested information:

1. For example, Copilot might ask: "Which SharePoint site contains these document libraries?"
2. Respond with the necessary details: "Both document libraries are in the 'Marketing' SharePoint site."

Step 5: Generate and Review the Flow Draft

1. Once Copilot has sufficient information, it will offer to create the flow.
2. Click the "`Create flow`" or similar button in the Copilot interface.
3. Copilot will generate the complete flow and open it in the flow editor.
4. Review each step of the generated flow:
   - Verify the trigger is configured correctly to monitor the specified document library.
   - Check that the PDF conversion action is properly set up.
   - Ensure the "`Create file`" action targets the correct destination library.
   - Confirm the email notification contains all required information.

Step 6: Modify the Flow as Needed

1. Make any necessary adjustments to the generated flow:
   a. Rename steps for clarity
   b. Add or modify conditions
   c. Adjust action parameters
   d. Add error handling if not included by Copilot
2. You can also return to the Copilot chat and request specific modifications like: "Please add error handling to retry the PDF conversion if it fails initially."

Step 7: Save and Test the Flow

1. Save your flow with a descriptive name.
2. Use the "`Test`" button to run a manual test:
   a. Choose the "`Manually`" trigger option.
   b. Add a test document to the source library.
   c. Monitor the test run to ensure each step executes correctly.
3. Review the results and make additional adjustments if needed.

Step 8: Turn on the Flow

Once you are satisfied with the testing results:

1. Return to the flow details page.
2. Toggle the flow from "`Off`" to "`On`".
3. Your Copilot-generated flow is now active and will run automatically based on the specified trigger.

This step-by-step process demonstrates the efficiency of using Copilot for flow creation. What might have taken 30+ minutes of manual configuration was accomplished in a fraction of the time, with Copilot handling the technical implementation details while you focus on the business requirements.

Practical Examples of Using Copilot for Different Flow Types

To illustrate Copilot's versatility, let us explore several practical examples across different flow categories. These examples demonstrate how Copilot handles various complexity levels and business scenarios.

Automated Data Processing Flows

Data processing is one of the most common automation scenarios. Let us see how Copilot can assist with these flows.

Example: Scheduled Data Consolidation

Prompt to Copilot: `"Create a flow that runs every Monday at 8 AM, exports data from three different SharePoint lists ('Sales-North,' 'Sales-South,' and 'Sales-West'), combines the data into a single Excel file with separate worksheets for each region, and saves it to a SharePoint document library called 'Weekly Reports.' Then send the Excel file to the sales management team via email."`

Copilot-Generated Solution: Copilot will create a flow with:

1. A "**`Recurrence`**" trigger configured for Mondays at 8 AM
2. Three "**`Get items`**" actions (one for each SharePoint list)
3. An "**`Initialize variable`**" action to create an array variable for storing the combined data
4. "**`Apply to each`**" loops to process items from each list
5. "**`Append to array variable`**" actions to store the processed data
6. A "**`Create Excel file`**" action with dynamic worksheet creation
7. A "**`Create file`**" action to save the Excel file to the specified library
8. A "**`Send an email`**" action with the Excel file as an attachment

Analysis of Copilot's Approach: Notice how Copilot:

- Selected appropriate connectors for SharePoint and Outlook
- Implemented a data structure for combining multiple data sources
- Created the necessary control flow with loops and arrays
- Generated a complete end-to-end solution from a single description

Example: Data Transformation and Validation

Prompt to Copilot: `"I need a flow that triggers when a new item is added to a SharePoint list called 'Customer Submissions.' The flow should validate that required fields (Name, Email, Phone) are not empty, format the phone number to a standard format (XXX-XXX-XXXX), check if the email domain is from an approved list stored in another SharePoint list called 'Approved Domains,' and then create a new record in Dataverse if all` validations pass. If any validation fails, send an email to the submission reviewer with details of the issues."

Copilot-Generated Solution: For this more complex scenario, Copilot will generate a flow with:

1. A "**`When an item is created`**" SharePoint trigger
2. A series of "**`Condition`**" actions to check for empty required fields
3. A "**`Compose`**" action with an expression to format the phone number
4. A "**`Get items`**" action to retrieve the approved domains list
5. A "**`Filter array`**" action to check if the submitted email domain is approved
6. A condition to check if the email domain validation passed
7. A "**`Create a new row`**" Dataverse action for valid submissions
8. "**`Compose`**" actions to build error messages for failed validations
9. A "**`Send an email`**" action with dynamic content showing validation errors

Analysis of Copilot's Approach: In this example, Copilot demonstrates its ability to:

- Implement complex business logic with multiple validation rules
- Use expressions for data transformation (phone formatting)
- Create conditional paths based on validation results
- Generate appropriate error messages and notifications
- Connect multiple systems (SharePoint and Dataverse)

Approval Workflow Flows

Approval workflows are essential for many business processes. Let us examine how Copilot handles these scenarios.

Example: Multi-level Expense Approval

Prompt to Copilot: "Create an expense approval flow that triggers when a new item is added to an 'Expense Claims' SharePoint list. If the amount is less than $100, automatically approve it. If it is between $100 and $1,000, send an approval request to the employee's direct manager (stored in the 'Manager' field). If it is over $1,000, first send an approval to the direct manager, and if it is approved, send a second approval to the finance director. Update the SharePoint item status after each approval or rejection and notify the employee about the final decision."

Copilot-Generated Solution: Copilot will create a flow with:

1. A "**`When an item is created`**" SharePoint trigger
2. A "**`Condition`**" action to check if the amount is less than $100
3. In the "**`Yes`**" path: An "**`Update item`**" action to set status to "**`Approved`**"
4. In the "**`No`**" path: Another condition to check if the amount is between $100 and $1,000
5. For $100-$1,000: A "**`Start and wait for an approval`**" action assigned to the manager
6. For >$1,000: A sequence of two approval actions (manager then finance director)
7. Condition actions to check approval results

8. "`Update item`" actions to update the status in SharePoint
9. "`Send an email`" actions to notify the employee of the outcome

Analysis of Copilot's Approach: This example showcases Copilot's ability to:

- Implement complex conditional logic with nested conditions
- Create multi-stage approval processes
- Use dynamic assignments based on SharePoint metadata
- Track and update status throughout the process
- Generate appropriate notifications at different stages

Integration Flows between Systems

Integration flows connect different systems to create unified processes. Here is how Copilot handles these scenarios.

Example: CRM to Marketing Automation Integration

Prompt to Copilot: "`Create a flow that monitors new qualified leads in Dynamics 365 Sales. When a lead's status changes to 'Qualified,' check if they've already been added to our marketing campaign in Mailchimp by looking up their email in a list called 'Active Campaigns.' If they are not found, add them to the Mailchimp audience called 'Product Interest' and tag them based on their product interest field from Dynamics. Then update a custom field in Dynamics called 'Marketing_Status' to 'Added to Campaign' with today's date.`"

Copilot-Generated Solution: Copilot will generate a flow with:

1. A "`When a record is updated`" Dynamics 365 trigger with filter for status = "`Qualified`"
2. A "`List records`" action to check if the email exists in Mailchimp
3. A "`Condition`" action to check if the contact was found
4. In the "`No`" path: A "`Create list member`" Mailchimp action
5. A "`Add member tag`" Mailchimp action with dynamic tag based on product interest
6. An "`Update a record`" Dynamics action to set the `Marketing_Status` field
7. Error handling for potential API failures

Analysis of Copilot's Approach: This example demonstrates Copilot's ability to:

- Work with specialized connectors (Dynamics 365 and Mailchimp)
- Implement lookups to prevent duplicate entries
- Use dynamic values from one system as inputs to another
- Handle data mapping between different platforms
- Include status tracking for cross-system operations

Document Processing Flows

Document automation is a powerful use case for Power Automate. Let us see how Copilot handles document-centric flows:

Example: Contract Review Process

Prompt to Copilot: "`Create a flow for our contract review process. When a new contract document is uploaded to our 'Contracts Pending Review' SharePoint library, use AI Builder to extract the contract value, effective date, and client name. Create an approval task in Planner assigned to our legal team with the extracted information and a link to the document. After approval, move the document to either 'Approved Contracts' or 'Rejected Contracts' library based on the decision, and send a notification to the sales representative (stored in a column called 'Account Manager') with the approval status and any comments.`"

Copilot-Generated Solution: Copilot will create a flow with:

1. A "**`When a file is created`**" SharePoint trigger
2. An "**`AI Builder - Extract information from documents`**" action
3. "**`Compose`**" actions to format the extracted information
4. A "**`Create a task`**" Planner action with dynamic content
5. A "**`Start and wait for an approval`**" action
6. Conditions to check the approval result
7. "**`Copy file`**" and "**`Delete file`**" actions to move the document to the appropriate library
8. A "**`Get user profile`**" action to retrieve the account manager's email
9. A "**`Send an email`**" action with the notification details

Analysis of Copilot's Approach: This example showcases Copilot's ability to:

- Integrate with AI services for document processing
- Coordinate across multiple systems (SharePoint, Planner, Outlook)
- Implement document management operations
- Use dynamic assignments based on metadata
- Create contextual notifications with relevant information

These examples demonstrate the breadth and depth of flows that Copilot can generate across different scenarios. From simple data processing to complex multi-system integrations, Copilot provides substantial assistance in translating business requirements into functional flows.

Best Practices for Working with Copilot

To maximize the benefits of using Copilot for Power Automate flow development, follow these best practices that balance AI assistance with human oversight and refinement.

Effective Prompt Engineering

The way you communicate with Copilot significantly impacts the quality of its output. Here are some strategies for crafting effective prompts:

Be Specific and Comprehensive

Include all relevant details in your initial prompt:

- Specify the exact names of SharePoint lists, document libraries, or Dataverse tables.
- Mention field names for data mapping.

- Describe conditions with specific thresholds.
- Include notification recipients and content requirements.
- Specify any timing or scheduling parameters.

Note: *Rather than asking Copilot to "create an approval flow," describe the complete process: "Create a flow that sends vacation requests from a SharePoint list called 'Time Off Requests' to the requester's manager for approval, updates the status field after approval or rejection, and notifies the requester via email."*

Start with the Outcome, Then Provide Details

Structure your prompts to first state the overall objective before diving into implementation details:

1. **Begin with the business goal:** "I need a flow that consolidates weekly sales data".
2. **Then describe the trigger:** "It should run every Monday morning".
3. **Follow with data sources:** "It needs to gather data from our Dataverse 'Sales' table".
4. **Specify processing requirements:** "Group the data by region and calculate totals".
5. **End with output/notification needs:** "Create a Power BI-ready CSV file and email it to the sales team".

Use Technical Terminology When Appropriate

While Copilot understands plain language, using Power Automate terminology can improve precision through the following prompts:

- "Initialize a variable" instead of "create a counter"
- "Apply to each" instead of "loop through"
- "Send an HTTP request" instead of "connect to the API"
- "Parse JSON" instead of "interpret the data"

Describe Business Rules Clearly

For complex logic, clearly articulate the business rules in the following way:

- "If the order total exceeds $1,000, require director approval; otherwise, manager approval is sufficient."
- "Only process invoices that are less than 30 days old and have a status of 'Unpaid'."
- "Check if the customer exists in Dataverse before creating a new record; if they exist, update their information instead."

Reviewing and Modifying Copilot-Generated Flows

While Copilot produces impressive results, it does not undermine the importance of human review. Follow these practices when reviewing AI-generated flows:

Systematic Review Process

Develop a checklist for reviewing Copilot-generated flows:

- **Verify the trigger configuration:**
  - Is it watching the correct data source?
  - Are trigger conditions appropriate?
  - Is the recurrence schedule correct (if applicable)?

- **Check data operations:**
  - Are "`Get items/rows`" actions retrieving the right data?
  - Are filters configured correctly?
  - Are all necessary fields being processed?
- **Validate business logic:**
  - Do conditions accurately reflect business rules?
  - Are expressions correctly formulated?
  - Is the flow handling all possible scenarios?
- **Examine error handling:**
  - Are critical actions protected with error handling?
  - Is appropriate logging in place?
  - Are fallback paths implemented for service disruptions?
- **Review security and compliance:**
  - Are connections using appropriate authentication?
  - Is sensitive data handled securely?
  - Does the flow comply with organizational policies?

Common Adjustment Areas

Based on experience, these areas often require adjustment in Copilot-generated flows:

- **Dynamic content references:** Copilot may not always select the optimal source for dynamic values
- **Expression complexity:** Simplifying complex expressions for maintainability
- **Error handling coverage:** Adding comprehensive error handling for mission-critical flows
- **Connection configurations:** Adjusting connection references to use shared connections
- **Flow naming conventions:** Updating action names to follow organizational standards

Iterative Refinement Strategy

Rather than extensively modifying a flow manually, consider using Copilot iteratively:

1. Generate an initial flow with a comprehensive prompt.
2. Review the result and identify gaps or issues.
3. Return to Copilot with a follow-up prompt like: "The flow looks good, but please add error handling for the HTTP request and send a notification if it fails".
4. Review the updated flow and repeat if necessary.

This approach leverages Copilot's strengths while incorporating your domain knowledge and requirements.

Finding the Right Balance between AI and Manual Development

Copilot is a powerful tool, but it is important to understand when to rely on it and when to take manual control.

When to Fully Leverage Copilot

Copilot excels in these scenarios:

- **Creating initial flow drafts:** Let Copilot generate the basic structure and components.
- **Standard business processes:** Copilot handles common patterns like approvals effectively.
- **Learning new connector capabilities:** Copilot can demonstrate how to use unfamiliar connectors.
- **Rapid prototyping:** Quickly generate and test different approaches to a problem.
- **Converting process descriptions:** Translating business requirements into technical implementations.

When to Take Manual Control

Consider a more hands-on approach in these situations:

- **Highly customized processes:** Unique business logic might require manual implementation.
- **Performance-critical flows:** Fine-tuning for optimal performance often requires manual optimization.
- **Complex data transformations:** Advanced data manipulation might needs custom expressions occasionally.
- **Security-sensitive operations:** Flows handling highly sensitive data might warrant manual review of each step.
- **Enterprise-scale solutions:** Flows that will be widely deployed or affect critical systems benefit from detailed manual configuration.

Hybrid Approach for Optimal Results

A balanced strategy often yields the best outcomes:

1. Use Copilot to generate the initial flow structure.
2. Manually review and adjust critical components.
3. Return to Copilot for assistance with specific challenging sections.
4. Manually implement organization-specific best practices.
5. Use Copilot to suggest optimizations for the refined flow.

Note: *Even experienced developers can benefit from Copilot's suggestions. Consider generating a Copilot version of a flow you would normally build manually and compare the approaches, you might discover new techniques or more efficient implementation patterns.*

Conclusion

Throughout this chapter, we have explored how Microsoft Copilot transforms the Power Automate experience, making flow development more accessible, efficient, and powerful. By leveraging AI assistance, you can accelerate your automation journey while focusing more on business outcomes than on technical implementation details. The integration of natural language processing with Power Automate's robust automation capabilities creates unprecedented opportunities for both novice and experienced developers to create sophisticated solutions with great ease and speed.

As we conclude our exploration of Copilot-assisted flow development, we turn our attention to an equally critical aspect of Power Automate: Security. In the next chapter, we will explore how to protect your flows, data, and connections from potential vulnerabilities and ensure compliance with organizational policies and regulatory requirements.

Points to Remember

By working through this chapter, you have developed the following skills:

- **Accessing Copilot in Power Automate:** You can locate and engage with Copilot through various entry points in the Power Automate portal.
- **Crafting Effective Prompts:** You understand how to structure natural language descriptions that clearly communicate your automation requirements to Copilot.
- **Reviewing AI-Generated Flows:** You can systematically evaluate Copilot-generated flows, identifying areas that require adjustment or enhancement.
- **Iterative Refinement:** You know how to use follow-up prompts to refine and enhance initial flow drafts generated by Copilot.
- **Natural Language Flow Generation:** You can create complete flows using natural language descriptions rather than manual component selection.
- **AI-Assisted Optimization:** You understand how to leverage Copilot's suggestions to improve flow performance, structure, and reliability.
- **Enhanced Connector Utilization:** You can discover and configure appropriate connectors based on Copilot's recommendations.
- **Template Discovery and Adaptation:** You know how to use Copilot to identify relevant templates and adapt them to your specific requirements.
- **Error Detection and Resolution:** You can employ Copilot to identify potential issues in your flows and implement appropriate solutions.
- **Making Strategic AI/Manual Decisions:** You understand when to fully leverage Copilot and when to take manual control over flow development.
- **Cross-System Integration:** You can create flows that connect multiple systems and services through Copilot-assisted development.
- **Complex Logic Implementation:** You know how to describe complex business logic in natural language and validate Copilot's implementation.

Additional Resources

To further enhance your skills with Copilot for Power Automate, consider exploring these additional resources:

Official Microsoft Documentation

- **Power Automate Copilot Overview:** Comprehensive documentation covering all aspects of Copilot functionality
- **Advanced Prompt Techniques for Power Automate:** Guidance on crafting effective prompts for specific scenarios

Learning Paths

- **Microsoft Learn: AI-Assisted Development in Power Platform:** Structured learning path covering Copilot across the Power Platform
- **Power Automate Community Webinars: Copilot Series:** Regular webinars featuring Copilot techniques and use cases

Community Resources

- **Power Automate Community Forum: Copilot Discussion:** Active community forum for sharing experiences and solving challenges
- **Power Automate Blog: Copilot Updates:** Regular updates on new Copilot features and capabilities

Practical Learning

- **Microsoft Power Up Program: Copilot Challenges:** Hands-on challenges designed to build practical Copilot skills

Advanced Topics

- **Enterprise Copilot Strategy Whitepaper:** Guidance for organizations implementing Copilot at scale
- **Power Platform AI Integration Guide:** Broader context of AI capabilities within the Power Platform

By leveraging these resources alongside the knowledge gained in this chapter, you will be well-equipped to harness the full potential of Copilot for Power Automate, creating sophisticated automation solutions with unprecedented efficiency and accessibility.

As we move forward, remember that Copilot represents just one aspect of the evolving Power Automate landscape. By combining AI-assisted development with sound security practices, effective governance, and continuous learning, you will be able to create flows that are not only powerful and efficient but also secure, compliant, and aligned with your organization's broader automation strategy.

CHAPTER 12
Security Measures in Power Automate

Introduction

In today's digital landscape, automation has become the backbone of organizational efficiency. As we have explored throughout this book, Microsoft Power Automate provides powerful capabilities to streamline processes, integrate systems, and reduce manual workloads. However, with great power comes great responsibility, particularly when it comes to security.

The very attributes that make Power Automate so valuable—connecting disparate systems, processing sensitive data, and operating with elevated permissions—can also create significant security considerations. A single misconfigured flow can expose confidential information, violate compliance requirements, or create vulnerabilities in your organization's digital infrastructure.

In the previous chapter, we explored how Copilot enhances your flow development capabilities, allowing you to create more sophisticated automation solutions with less effort. Now, we must ensure these powerful automation tools are deployed within a comprehensive security framework. Every connector we have discussed so far, from SharePoint and Dynamics 365 to custom APIs and third-party services, represents both an opportunity for integration and a potential security boundary to manage.

Security is not a standalone concept in Power Automate—it permeates every aspect of flow development, from initial planning through deployment and ongoing governance. The patterns and practices we have covered for business processes, data integration, and administrative automation, all require appropriate security controls to be truly effective.

In this chapter, we will comprehensively explore the security landscape of Power Automate, covering everything from fundamental concepts like Data Loss Prevention policies and authentication to advanced topics like security monitoring and incident response. By the end of this chapter, you will have a robust understanding of how to implement security measures that protect your organization, while enabling the full potential of automated workflows.

Structure

This chapter addresses the following key security areas:

- Power Automate Security Architecture
- Identity and Access Management
- Data Loss Prevention (DLP) Policies
- Data Protection Mechanisms
- Environmental Security Controls
- Connection Security

- Runtime Security
- Encryption and Data Protection
- Security Monitoring and Auditing
- Compliance and Governance Frameworks
- Security Best Practices
- Incident Response Procedures

Let us begin by understanding the fundamental security architecture of Power Automate and how it fits within the broader Microsoft security ecosystem.

Power Automate Security Architecture

The Power Automate security framework is built on multiple layers, where each provides distinct protection while working together to create a defense-in-depth approach.

Understanding the Security Layers

Power Automate security operates across four primary layers:

- **Identity and Authentication Layer**: Controls who can access Power Automate and with what level of permissions
- **Service Layer**: Manages the security of the Power Automate service itself
- **Connection Layer**: Secures the connections to data sources and service endpoints
- **Data Layer**: Protects data as it flows through automated processes

These layers align with Microsoft's broader security framework while providing specialized control specific to automation scenarios.

Integration with Microsoft Security Ecosystem

Power Automate inherits and integrates with several Microsoft security frameworks such as:

- **Microsoft Entra ID** (formerly Azure Active Directory): Provides identity services, authentication, and authorization
- **Microsoft Purview**: Offers data governance, risk management, and compliance capabilities
- **Microsoft Defender for Cloud**: Delivers threat protection for cloud resources
- **Microsoft 365 Security Center**: Centralizes security management across Microsoft services

This integration creates a cohesive security environment where Power Automate benefits from enterprise-grade security controls while contributing to the overall security posture.

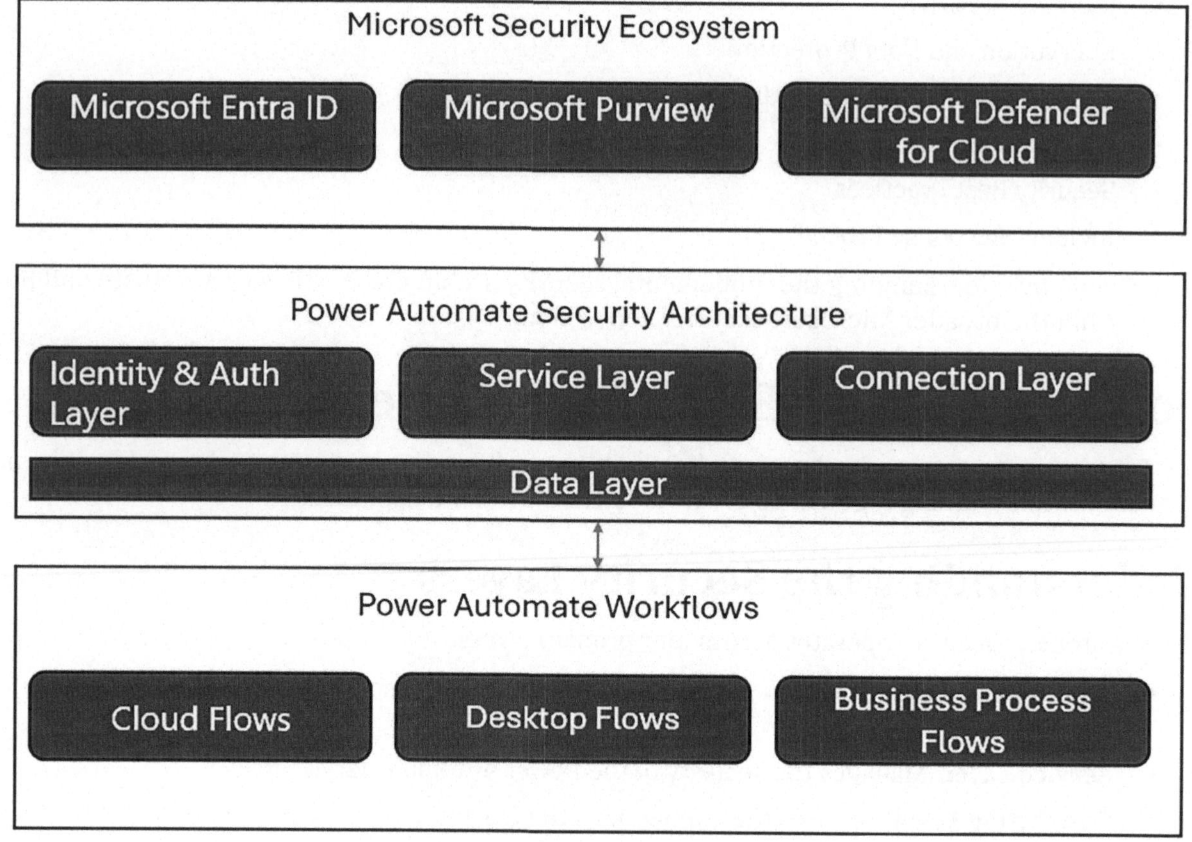

Figure 12.1: *Security Architecture Diagram*

Security Alert: *Never assume that Microsoft's security controls eliminate the need for your own security oversight. While Power Automate benefits from Microsoft's security investments, proper configuration and governance remain your responsibility.*

Now that we understand the architectural foundation, let us explore each security domain in detail.

Identity and Access Management

Identity and Access Management (IAM) forms the first and most critical security boundary in Power Automate. It determines who can create, modify, or use flows and with what level of permissions.

Authentication Methods

Power Automate supports multiple authentication methods, each with different security characteristics:

Authentication Method	**Security Level**	**Use Cases**	**Considerations**
Microsoft Entra ID	High	Enterprise environments, Microsoft 365 integration	Requires Microsoft Entra ID implementation
Microsoft Account	Medium	Personal use, smaller organizations	Limited enterprise management capabilities
Service Principals	High	Automated processes, service-to-service	Requires careful credential management

Managed Identities	Very High	Azure-hosted flows, service connections	Limited to Azure resources

Table 12.1: *Supported Authentication Methods in Power Automate*

Authorization Models

Once authenticated, authorization determines what actions users can perform the following actions:

- **Role-Based Access Control (RBAC)**: Assigns permissions based on roles such as:
  - Environment Admin
  - Environment Maker
  - Flow Owner
  - Flow Co-owner
  - Flow Run-only User
- **Resource-Based Authorization**: Controls access to specific resources like:
  - Individual flows
  - Connection references
  - Custom connectors
  - Environments

Implementing Secure IAM Practices

To establish robust identity security:

- **Configure Microsoft Entra Conditional Access policies** to control Power Automate access based on:
  - User identity
  - Device state
  - Location
  - Risk signals
- **Implement Least Privilege Principle**
  - Grant only necessary permissions.
  - Regularly review and adjust access rights.
  - Use environment-scoped roles.
  - Avoid over-privileged service accounts.
- **Manage Flow Ownership**
  - Establish ownership policies.
  - Create procedures for flow transfers when employees leave.
  - Implement shared responsibility models for critical flows.
  - Document ownership of all production flows.

Note: *Create dedicated service accounts for critical production flows rather than using individual user accounts. This prevents disruption when employees change roles or leave the organization.*

Security Assessment Exercise: Identity and Access

Take a moment to assess your current identity and access controls by answering these questions:

- Do you have a documented process for granting and revoking Power Automate access?
- Are you using conditional access policies to control Power Automate access?
- Have you implemented least privilege principles for Power Automate roles?
- Do you have a process for transferring flow ownership when employees leave?
- Are you using service accounts for critical flows?

If you answered "no" to any of these questions, consider implementing those controls before proceeding.

Data Loss Prevention (DLP) Policies

Data Loss Prevention (DLP) policies are specialized controls that govern how data can move between connectors in Power Automate. They serve as security boundaries that prevent sensitive data from flowing to unauthorized or less secure destinations.

Understanding DLP Policy Fundamentals

DLP policies operate by categorizing connectors into groups and controlling data flow between these groups:

- **Business Data Only**: High-trust connectors for organizational data
- **No Business Data Allowed**: Lower-trust connectors that may pose data leakage risks
- **Blocked**: Connectors that cannot be used at all

When properly configured, these policies can prevent sensitive data from flowing from high-trust to lower-trust connectors, thus reducing the risk of data leakage.

Step-by-Step Tutorial: Implementing DLP Policies

Follow these steps to configure effective DLP policies:

1. **Access the Power Platform Admin Center**
    a. Navigate to https://admin.powerplatform.microsoft.com.
    b. Log in with administrator credentials.
    c. Select "`Policies`" from the left navigation, then "`Data policies`".
2. **Create a New Policy**
    a. Click "`New policy`".
    b. Name the policy (for example, "`Finance Data Protection Policy`").
    c. Select the environments where the policy will apply.
    d. Click "`Next`".
3. **Configure Connector Groups**
    a. Review the default connector classifications.
    b. Move connectors between groups based on your security requirements.

c. Consider your data sensitivity and compliance needs.

d. Click "**`Next`**" when finished.

4. **Review and Create**

a. Review your policy settings.

b. Click "**`Create policy`**" to implement.

5. **Validate Policy Effectiveness**

a. Attempt to create a flow that would violate the policy.

b. Verify that the system prevents the connection.

c. Test boundary cases.

DLP Policy Best Practices

To maximize the effectiveness of your DLP policies, make sure you follow these best practices:

1. **Take an Environment-Specific Approach**
   - Create stricter policies for environments with sensitive data.
   - Consider less restrictive policies for development environments.
   - Align policies with data classification schemes.
2. **Regularly Review and Update**
   - Schedule quarterly reviews of DLP configurations.
   - Adjust as new connectors are added to Power Automate.
   - Update when organizational data handling requirements change.
3. **Document Policy Decisions**
   - Maintain records of why connectors are placed in specific groups.
   - Document exceptions and their justifications.
   - Create a connector classification framework.

Security Alert: *DLP policies are powerful but not full proof. They should be one component of a comprehensive security strategy, not the sole control that protects sensitive data.*

Aspect	**Basic Approach**	**Advanced Approach**	**Enterprise Approach**
Policy Scope	Single policy for all environments	Environment-specific policies	Granular policies with exception handling
Connector Classification	Default groupings	Custom classification	Risk-based assessment for each connector
Review Frequency	Annual	Quarterly	Monthly plus change-triggered reviews
Exceptions	Ad-hoc	Documented process	Formal governance with approval workflows
Integration	Standalone	Aligned with Microsoft 365 DLP	Integrated with enterprise data governance

***Table 12.2:** DLP Policy Comparison Table*

Think about It: DLP Strategy Scenarios

Consider these scenarios to test your understanding of DLP policy implementation:

- Your organization processes healthcare data through Power Automate. How would you configure DLP policies to ensure HIPAA compliance?
- Your marketing team needs to connect to social media platforms, but you are concerned about data leakage. What DLP approach would balance functionality with security?
- You have contractors who need to use Power Automate for specific projects. How would you use DLP policies to restrict their data access?

Connection Security

Connections in Power Automate represent the authentication credentials and configurations used to access data sources and services. Securing these connections is crucial to maintaining the overall security of your automation environment.

Connection Types and Their Security Implications

Power Automate supports the following connection types, where each has different security characteristics:

Connection Type	Security Level	Key Considerations
OAuth 2.0	High	Token-based, limited lifetime, scope-restricted
API Key	Medium	Long-lived, potential for leakage if not protected
Basic Authentication	Low	Password-based, susceptible to brute force attacks
Windows Authentication	Medium-High	Domain credential-based, familiar enterprise model
Certificate-based	Very High	Strong cryptographic protection, complex management

Table 12.3: *Connection Type and Their Security Implications Table*

Connection Credentials Management

Securing the credentials used for connections requires special attention:

- **Understanding Credential Storage**
  - Connection credentials are encrypted at rest.
  - They are stored in the Microsoft Power Platform service.
  - Access to these credentials is controlled by the connection owner.
- **Managing Connection Ownership**
  - Connections are owned by the user who created them.
  - Flows using these connections operate with the owner's permissions.
  - When users leave, connections must be recreated or transferred.
- **Using Connection References**
  - Create connection references to centralize management.
  - Share connections across multiple flows.
  - Simplify credential rotation.

Step-by-Step: Implementing Secure Connection Practices

Follow these steps to secure your Power Automate connections:

1. **Audit Existing Connections**
   a. Navigate to make.powerautomate.com.
   b. Select "`Data`" > "`Connections`".
   c. Document all connections, their types, and owners.
2. **Implement Connection References**
   a. In Solution Explorer, create a new connection reference.
   b. Select the appropriate connector.
   c. Configure the connection settings.
   d. Share with appropriate users or teams.
3. **Establish Connection Rotation Procedures**
   a. Create a schedule for credential rotation.
   b. Document the process for updating connections.
   c. Test the impact on existing flows.
   d. Implement with minimal disruption.
4. **Monitor Connection Usage**
   a. Regularly review connection usage.
   b. Identify and remove unused connections.
   c. Verify appropriate access levels.

Note: *For highly sensitive systems, consider creating dedicated service accounts with restricted permissions specifically for Power Automate connections. This allows you to define permission control more precisely and simplify monitoring.*

Security Assessment Exercise: Connection Inventory

Create an inventory of your existing connections by documenting:

- Connection name and type
- Owner and last used date
- Services or data sources accessed
- Sensitivity level of accessed data
- Whether the connection uses a personal or service account
- Credential rotation schedule

This inventory will serve as a foundation for your connection security strategy.

Environmental Security Controls

Environments in Power Automate act as containers for your flows and related resources. They provide security boundaries and enable different governance models for different business needs.

Environment Types and Security Characteristics

Power Automate supports several environment types, each with different security implications:

Environment Type	Security Level	Use Cases	Considerations
Default Environment	Basic	Personal productivity, learning	Limited governance controls
Production Environment	High	Business-critical workflows	Full governance capabilities
Sandbox Environment	Medium	Development, testing	Isolated from production data
Developer Environment	Medium-Low	Individual development	Limited lifetime, personal use
Trial Environment	Low	Evaluation, proof of concept	Limited lifetime, basic controls

Table 12.4: *Environment Types and Security Characteristics Table*

Environment Security Controls

To secure your Power Automate environments, you must follow the mentioned steps:

1. **Environment Creation and Access Policies**
    a. Restrict who can create environments.
    b. Implement naming conventions.
    c. Define lifetime management policies.
    d. Configure data residency settings.
2. **Environment-Specific Settings**
    a. Enable or disable specific features.
    b. Control sharing capabilities.
    c. Manage connector availability.
    d. Configure environment-specific DLP policies.
3. **Resource Governance**
    a. Implement solution management practices.
    b. Control flow creation and modification.
    c. Manage connection references.
    d. Configure custom connector controls.

Step-by-Step: Configuring Environment Security

Follow these steps to implement robust environmental security:

1. **Create a Security-Focused Environment Strategy**
    a. Define environment types for different purposes.
    b. Establish naming conventions.
    c. Document governance requirements.
    d. Create lifetime management policies.
2. **Configure Environment-Specific Settings**
    a. Access the Power Platform Admin Center.
    b. Select the target environment.
    c. Configure settings based on security requirements.
    d. Document configuration decisions.
3. **Implement Access Controls**
    a. Assign appropriate security roles.
    b. Configure Microsoft Entra groups for access management.
    c. Establish request and approval processes.
    d. Document access control matrices.
4. **Set Up Monitoring and Compliance**
    a. Configure audit logging.
    b. Establish environment review processes.
    c. Create compliance validation procedures.
    d. Schedule regular security assessments.

Security Alert: *The default environment has limited security controls and should never be used for sensitive or production workflows. Create dedicated environments with appropriate security configurations for all business-critical processes.*

Security Breach Analysis: Environment Separation

Consider this scenario:

A marketing employee creates a flow in the default environment that extracts customer data from your CRM, processes it, and shares it with a third-party analytics service. The flow runs with the employee's credentials, which have broad access to customer records. When the employee leaves the company, the flow continues to run, now processing data they should no longer have access to.

Questions to consider:

- What environmental security controls could have prevented this situation?
- How would proper environment separation have mitigated the risk?
- What process changes would help identify and remediate this issue?

Gateway Security

On-premises data gateways enable Power Automate to securely connect to on-premises data sources. Properly securing these gateways is critical for protecting your internal systems.

Gateway Architecture and Security Model

The on-premises data gateway consists of several components:

- **Gateway Cloud Service**: Manages gateway registration and configuration
- **Gateway Management Service**: Handles administration and updates
- **Gateway Runtime**: Executes data source connections and queries

The security model includes:

- **Encrypted Communications**: All traffic is encrypted using TLS 1.2+
- **No Inbound Ports**: The gateway initiates all communications
- **Azure Service Bus Relay**: Mediates communication between cloud and on-premises
- **Local Windows Service**: Runs under a service account with controlled permissions

Gateway Security Best Practices

To implement secure gateway configurations, follow these steps:

1. **Installation and Network Configuration**
    a. Install on a dedicated server, not a domain controller.
    b. Place in a controlled network segment.
    c. Configure firewall rules for outbound connections only.
    d. Use a reliable, secured power source.
2. **Authentication and Authorization**
    a. Use a dedicated service account with minimal permissions.
    b. Implement regular password rotation.
    c. Configure gateway administrators carefully.
    d. Document access control procedures.
3. **Recovery and Business Continuity**
    a. Document the recovery key in a secure location.
    b. Configure high availability for critical gateways.
    c. Implement monitoring and alerting.
    d. Create a recovery plan.

Step-by-Step: Securing Your Data Gateway

Follow these steps to implement a secure gateway:

1. **Prepare the Gateway Environment**
    a. Select a dedicated server meeting minimum requirements.

   b. Ensure the operating system is fully patched.
   c. Configure antivirus exclusions for gateway components.
   d. Document network configuration.

2. **Secure Gateway Installation**
   a. Download from official Microsoft source.
   b. Use a dedicated service account.
   c. Document the recovery key securely.
   d. Configure gateway service for automatic updates.

3. **Configure Gateway Security**
   a. Set up gateway administrators.
   b. Configure data source credentials securely.
   c. Implement monitoring.
   d. Test connectivity securely.

4. **Ongoing Maintenance**
   a. Monitor gateway health and performance.
   b. Regularly review security configurations.
   c. Update the gateway software.
   d. Audit gateway usage

Note: *For maximum security, consider implementing a gateway farm with load balancing rather than a single gateway. This improves both security and reliability by removing single points of failure.*

Security Knowledge Check: Gateway Security

Test your understanding of gateway security by answering these questions:

- What security protocol does the gateway use to encrypt communications?
- What is the purpose of the Azure Service Bus Relay in the gateway architecture?
- Why should gateways be installed on dedicated servers rather than domain controllers?
- What security information must be securely stored after gateway installation?
- How does the gateway establish connections to cloud services?

Encryption and Data Protection

Encryption is a fundamental security control that protects data both in transit and at rest within Power Automate.

Encryption in Transit

All data traveling to, from, and within Power Automate is protected:

- **External Communications**
  - TLS 1.2+ encryption for all external connections

- Certificate validation to prevent man-in-the-middle attacks
- Secure cipher suites following industry best practices
- **Internal Service Communications**
  - Service-to-service encryption within Microsoft data centers
  - Mutual TLS authentication between services
  - Network security controls at multiple levels

Encryption at Rest

Data stored within Power Automate receives strong protection:

- **Flow Definitions**
  - Encrypted in Microsoft Dataverse or SharePoint
  - Protected by platform-level encryption
  - Access controlled by authorization systems
- **Connection Credentials**
  - Encrypted using service-managed keys
  - Stored in secured credential vaults
  - Protected by multiple security layers
- **Run History and Inputs/Outputs**
  - Encrypted within the service database
  - Retained according to data retention policies
  - Protected by access controls

Data Protection Strategies

Beyond encryption, consider these additional data protection measures:

- **Data Minimization**
  - Process only essential data inflows.
  - Implement filtering at the source.
  - Avoid storing sensitive data when not required.
  - Use expressions to redact sensitive information.
- **Secure Inputs and Outputs**
  - Validate all inputs to prevent injection attacks.
  - Sanitize outputs to prevent data leakage.
  - Implement proper error handling to avoid information disclosure.
  - Use secure input and output parameters.
- **Sensitive Information Types**
  - Identify and classify sensitive data.
  - Implement special handling for regulated information.
  - Configure additional controls for high-risk data.
  - Monitor for unintended exposure.

Security Alert: *Even with encryption, it's best practice to avoid processing highly sensitive data like credit card numbers, social security numbers, or personal health information in Power Automate when possible. If such processing is necessary, implement additional security controls and compliance measures.*

Practical Example: Implementing Secure Data Handling

Consider a flow that processes employee information from HR systems. Here's how to implement secure data handling:

- **Source Connection Security**
  - Use OAuth with least privilege access.
  - Implement connection reference with service account.
  - Configure secure gateway for on-premises HR system.
- **Data Processing Security**
  - Filter only required fields at source.
  - Use expressions to mask sensitive fields (such as, the last 4 digits only).
  - Process data in memory without intermediate storage when possible.
  - Implement error handling that doesn't expose sensitive data.
- **Output Security**
  - Validate destination security before sending data.
  - Log actions without including sensitive data.
  - Verify successful processing and secure disposal.
  - Implement secure error handling.

```
# Example: Securely handling sensitive data

# 1. Filter at source to minimize data exposure
triggerBody()?['employees']?['value']?[select('id', 'name', 'department', 'title')]

# 2. Mask sensitive information like employee ID
concat(
    substring(item()?['employeeId'], 0, 2),
    '******',
    substring(item()?['employeeId'], length(item()?['employeeId']) - 2, 2)
)

# 3. Secure logging without exposing data
{
    "operation": "Employee record processed",
    "timestamp": utcNow(),
    "status": "Success",
    "recordCount": length(variables('processedRecords'))
}
```

Figure 12.2: *Practical Implementation of Secure Data Handling in a Power Automate Flow*

Security Assessment Exercise: Data Protection Review

Review your existing flows to identify data protection opportunities by:

- Identifying flows processing sensitive or regulated data
- Evaluating current encryption and data protection measures
- Looking for opportunities to implement data minimization
- Reviewing error handling for potential information disclosure
- Assessing compliance with regulatory requirements

Compliance and Governance

Compliance and governance frameworks provide the structure and oversight necessary to maintain security in Power Automate environments. As Power Automate becomes increasingly central to business operations automating critical processes, handling sensitive data, and integrating with essential systems the need for formal governance becomes paramount. Without proper governance, organizations risk creating a sprawling landscape of unmanaged flows that may violate regulatory requirements, create security vulnerabilities, or fail during critical business operations. For developers, understanding compliance and governance isn't just about following rules, it's about building sustainable automation solutions that can be audited, maintained, and trusted by your organization. The governance framework you establish today determines whether your Power Automate implementation becomes a strategic asset or a compliance liability. Moreover, many industries face strict regulatory oversight where non-compliant automation can result in significant fines, legal consequences, or loss of business licenses making governance knowledge essential for any developer working with sensitive data or regulated processes.

Compliance Frameworks and Power Automate

Microsoft Power Automate supports various compliance frameworks such as:

Compliance Framework	Relevance to Power Automate	Key Considerations
ISO 27001	Information security management	Control implementation, risk assessment
SOC 1 and SOC 2	Service organization controls	Process documentation, control testing
GDPR	Personal data protection	Data handling, subject rights, breach notification
HIPAA	Healthcare information protection	PHI handling, BAAs, access controls
FedRAMP	US government data security	Control implementation, continuous monitoring

Table 12.5: *Compliance Frameworks Supported by Power Automate*

Governance Model for Power Automate

Effective governance requires a structured approach as defined in the following steps:

1. **Center of Excellence (CoE) Implementation**
   a. Establish a cross-functional governance team.
   b. Define roles and responsibilities.

   c. Create governance policies and procedures.
   d. Implement the Microsoft CoE Starter Kit.
2. **Policy Development and Management**
   a. Create comprehensive governance policies.
   b. Establish policy enforcement mechanisms.
   c. Implement change management procedures.
   d. Conduct regular policy reviews.
3. **Compliance Monitoring and Reporting**
   a. Configure compliance monitoring tools.
   b. Establish regular compliance reviews.
   c. Implement remediation processes.
   d. Maintain compliance documentation.

Step-by-Step:Establishing Power Automate Governance

Follow these steps to implement effective governance:

1. **Form a Governance Team**
   a. Identify key stakeholders from IT, security, compliance, and business.
   b. Define governance objectives and scope.
   c. Establish meeting cadence and decision-making processes.
   d. Document team charter and responsibilities.
2. **Develop Governance Policies**
   a. Create policies for environment management.
   b. Establish flow development standards.
   c. Define connection management requirements.
   d. Document compliance requirements.
   e. Establish monitoring and enforcement procedures.
3. **Implement CoE Starter Kit**
   a. Deploy the Microsoft CoE Starter Kit.
   b. Configure environment variables.
   c. Customize to organizational requirements.
   d. Implement governance flows.
4. **Establish Ongoing Governance Processes**
   a. Conduct regular governance reviews.
   b. Maintain documentation.

c. Update policies as requirements change.

d. Provide governance training and awareness.

Note: *Use Power Automate itself to automate governance processes. Create flows that audit environments, check for compliance issues, and generate governance reports to minimize manual oversight.*

Think About It: Governance Strategy Scenarios

Consider these scenarios to test your understanding of governance implementation:

- Your organization has recently acquired another company with its own Power Automate environment. How would you approach governance integration?
- Your regulated industry requires strict controls on all automation. How would you implement governance to ensure compliance while enabling innovation?
- Your organization has grown from a small team to an enterprise with hundreds of Power Automate users. How would you scale your governance approach?

Security Monitoring and Auditing

Continuous monitoring and auditing are essential for maintaining security in Power Automate environments. They help you detect potential issues, track user activities, and provide evidence for compliance requirements.

Available Monitoring and Auditing Tools

Power Automate provides several tools for security monitoring such as:

- **Microsoft Purview Audit Log**
  - Records user and administrator activities
  - Provides searchable audit records
  - Offers exportable logs for further analysis
  - Maintains retention based on license level
- **Power Platform Admin Center**
  - Provides environment-level monitoring
  - Offers analytics on usage patterns
  - Enables capacity and license monitoring
  - Supports API access for custom reporting
- **Flow Run History**
  - Records detailed execution information
  - Captures input and output data
  - Provides error and performance metrics
  - Supports troubleshooting and optimization
- **Azure Monitor Integration**
  - Enables advanced monitoring scenarios
  - Supports custom dashboards and alerts
  - Provides long-term storage options

- Integrates with broader monitoring strategies

Implementing Effective Monitoring

To establish comprehensive security monitoring:

- **Configure Audit Logging**
  - Enables comprehensive audit logging
  - Defines retention periods based on requirements
  - Configures access to audit information
  - Establishes regular log review procedures
- **Implement Security Monitoring**
  - Configures alerts for suspicious activities
  - Monitors for unusual access patterns
  - Tracks administrative actions
  - Establishes escalation procedures
- **Create Custom Monitoring Solutions**
  - Develop Power BI dashboards for security metrics
  - Implement custom reporting flows
  - Configure automated alerting
  - Integrate with enterprise security monitoring

Step-by-Step: Setting Up Security Monitoring

Follow these steps to implement security monitoring:

1. **Configure Audit Logging**
   a. Access the Microsoft Purview compliance portal.
   b. Navigate to "`Audit`".
   c. Enable audit logging for Power Automate.
   d. Configure retention settings.
   e. Set up access controls for audit information.
2. **Create Monitoring Dashboards**
   a. Develop Power BI reports for security metrics.
   b. Configure automatic refresh schedules.
   c. Distribute to security and governance teams.
   d. Establish regular review procedures.
3. **Configure Security Alerts**
   a. Identify key security events to monitor.
   b. Create alert rules in Microsoft Purview.
   c. Configure notification destinations.

   d. Test alert functionality.
   e. Document alert response procedures.

4. **Implement Regular Security Reviews**
   a. Schedule weekly or monthly security reviews.
   b. Document review findings and actions.
   c. Track remediation activities.
   d. Update monitoring based on findings.

Security Alert: *Since audit logs have limited retention periods based on your license level, make sure to export and archive critical audit information for compliance and long-term security analysis.*

Security Knowledge Check: Monitoring Capabilities

Test your understanding of monitoring capabilities by answering these questions:

- What types of activities are captured in the Microsoft Purview audit log for Power Automate?
- How can you export audit log data for long-term retention?
- What security information is available in the flow run history?
- How can you create custom security dashboards for Power Automate?
- What automated alerts can be configured for security monitoring?

Despite strong preventive controls, security incidents may still occur. Having a structured approach to incident response ensures that you will be able to handle security breaches effectively in a time-bound fashion.

Power Automate Security Incident Types

Be prepared to handle various security incident types such as:

- **Unauthorized Access**
  - Compromised user accounts
  - Privilege escalation
  - Unauthorized flow creation or modification
  - Connection credential exposure
- **Data Exposure**
  - Sensitive data in flow history
  - Inappropriate data sharing
  - DLP policy bypasses
  - Unencrypted sensitive data
- **Compliance Violations**
  - Regulatory requirement breaches
  - Policy violations
  - Unauthorized data processing
  - Documentation deficiencies

- **Service Vulnerabilities**
  - Zero-day exploits
  - Configuration weaknesses
  - Integration vulnerabilities
  - Third-party connector issues

Incident Response Process

Implement a structured incident response process via the following steps:

1. **Preparation**
   a. Develop incident response plans.
   b. Establish response team roles.
   c. Create communication templates
   d. Conduct regular training and simulations
2. **Detection and Analysis**
   a. Implement monitoring for early detection.
   b. Create incident classification scheme.
   c. Establish analysis procedures.
   d. Document evidence collection methods.
3. **Containment and Eradication**
   a. Define containment strategies.
   b. Create eradication procedures.
   c. Document recovery processes.
   d. Establish verification methods.
4. **Recovery and Follow-up**
   a. Implement recovery procedures.
   b. Conduct post-incident analysis.
   c. Document lessons learned.
   d. Update security controls based on findings.

Step-by-Step: Handling a Power Automate Security Incident

Follow these steps when responding to a security incident:

1. **Initial Response**
   a. Document incident details.
   b. Classify severity and impact.

   c. Notify appropriate stakeholders.
   d. Initiate response team actions.
2. **Containment Actions**
   a. Disable affected flows.
   b. Suspend compromised connections.
   c. Revoke exposed credentials.
   d. Isolate affected environments.
   e. Block external access, if necessary.
3. **Investigation and Remediation**
   a. Identify root cause using audit logs.
   b. Determine exposure scope.
   c. Document affected systems and data.
   d. Implement immediate fixes.
   e. Develop a long-term remediation plan.
4. **Recovery and Reporting**
   a. Restore secure operations.
   b. Implement improved controls.
   c. Document incident details.
   d. Create an incident report.
   e. Communicate with affected parties.
   f. Update security documentation.

Note: *Create a dedicated incident response flow that automates routine aspects of security incident handling, such as disabling affected flows, notifying security personnel, and collecting initial diagnostic information.*

Security Breach Analysis: Incident Response Scenario

Consider this scenario:

An employee's account is compromised, and the attacker uses their Power Automate access to create a flow that extracts customer data from your CRM system and forwards it to an external email address. The flow is discovered during a routine security review two weeks after creation.

Questions

- What monitoring could have detected this incident earlier?
- What immediate containment actions should be taken?
- How would you investigate the scope of the data breach?
- What remediation steps would prevent similar incidents?
- What reporting obligations might this trigger under regulations like GDPR?

Industry-Specific Security Implementations

Different industries face unique security challenges and regulatory requirements. Let us explore how to implement Power Automate security measures in specific sectors.

Financial Services Automation

Financial institutions must implement stringent security controls such as:

- **Regulatory Compliance**
    - Implement controls for regulations like SOX, PCI-DSS, and GLBA.
    - Configure DLP policies to identify and protect financial data.
    - Establish enhanced audit trails for financial transactions.
    - Create documentation for regulatory examinations.
- **Transaction Security**
    - Implement multi-stage approval flows.
    - Configure secure connection handling.
    - Establish transaction limits and monitoring.
    - Create fraud detection mechanisms.
- **Customer Data Protection**
    - Configure enhanced data encryption.
    - Implement strict access controls.
    - Establish data masking for sensitive information.
    - Create comprehensive audit trails.

Implementation Example: Secure Payment Processing Flow

For a payment processing flow in a financial organization:

- Use dedicated service accounts with least privilege.
- Implement connection references with secure credential management.
- Configure approval steps for transactions over thresholds.
- Implement comprehensive logging and monitoring.
- Use secure error handling to prevent information disclosure.
- Configure DLP policies to prevent payment data exfiltration.

Healthcare Data Processing

Healthcare organizations must protect sensitive patient information:

- **HIPAA Compliance**
    - Configure environments for PHI handling.
    - Implement BAA-compliant connections.
    - Establish enhanced audit logging.
    - Create privacy controls for patient data.
- **Patient Data Security**
    - Implement data minimization practices.

    - Configure enhanced encryption.
    - Establish strict access controls.
    - Create data masking for patient identifiers.
- **Clinical Workflow Security**
    - Implement secure authentication.
    - Configure role-based access.
    - Establish workflow validation procedures.
    - Create audit trails for clinical decisions.

Implementation Example: Secure Patient Records Flow

For a patient records processing flow:

- Use healthcare-specific connectors with HIPAA compliance.
- Implement data filtering to process only essential information.
- Configure enhanced logging without PHI in logs.
- Implement encryption for all data stages.
- Use secure error handling to prevent PHI exposure.
- Configure DLP policies to prevent PHI exfiltration.

Multi-National Compliance

Organizations operating globally must address varied regulatory requirements such as:

- **Regional Data Protection**
    - Configure environments for regional data residency.
    - Implement controls for GDPR, CCPA, and other regulations.
    - Establish data transfer mechanisms.
    - Create region-specific security controls.
- **Cross-Border Data Flows**
    - Implement data transfer impact assessments.
    - Configure appropriate safeguards.
    - Establish documentation for cross-border transfers.
    - Create monitoring for international data movements.
- **Global Security Standards**
    - Implement consistent global security baseline.
    - Configure region-specific enhancements.
    - Establish global security monitoring.
    - Create unified incident response capabilities.

Implementation Example: GDPR-Compliant Customer Flow

For a customer data processing flow subject to GDPR:

- Configure EU-based environment for data processing.
- Implement data minimization and purpose limitation.
- Configure consent tracking mechanisms.

- Implement data subject rights handling.
- Establish comprehensive audit logging.
- Create data retention controls.
- Configure breach notification capabilities

Security Best Practices Summary

To conclude our exploration of Power Automate security, let us summarize the key best practices that apply across all implementations:

Technical Security Best Practices

- **Identity and Access Management**
  - Implement least privilege principle.
  - Use conditional access policies.
  - Configure MFA for all Power Automate users.
  - Establish service accounts for critical flows.
  - Review access regularly.
- **Data Protection**
  - Configure comprehensive DLP policies.
  - Implement data minimization.
  - Establish secure connection handling.
  - Configure encryption for sensitive data.
  - Create secure error handling.
- **Infrastructure Security**
  - Secure on-premises data gateways.
  - Implement network security controls.
  - Establish secure environment configuration.
  - Configure connection security.
  - Create backup and recovery capabilities.
- **Monitoring and Auditing**
  - Enable comprehensive audit logging.
  - Implement security monitoring.
  - Establish alerting for security events.
  - Configure custom security dashboards.
  - Create regular security review processes

Administrative Security Best Practices

- **Governance Implementation**
  - Establish a Center of Excellence.
  - Implement comprehensive policies.
  - Configure policy enforcement mechanisms.

  - Create regular governance reviews.
  - Establish clear roles and responsibilities.
- **Documentation**
  - Maintain security architecture documentation.
  - Implement configuration documentation.
  - Establish incident response procedures.
  - Create compliance evidence.
  - Maintain policy documentation.
- **Training and Awareness**
  - Provide security training for developers.
  - Implement awareness programs.
  - Establish secure development guidelines.
  - Create security champions network.
  - Maintain knowledge sharing mechanisms.
- **Continuous Improvement**
  - Conduct regular security assessments.
  - Implement security testing.
  - Establish remediation processes.
  - Create feedback mechanisms.
  - Maintain threat intelligence integration.

Security Implementation Checklist

Use this checklist to ensure comprehensive security implementation:

- Configure Microsoft Entra Conditional Access policies.
- Implement DLP policies appropriate for data sensitivity.
- Configure environment security settings.
- Secure on-premises data gateways.
- Implement connection security best practices.
- Configure comprehensive audit logging.
- Establish security monitoring and alerting.
- Implement incident response procedures.
- Configure compliance controls for regulated data.
- Establish governance framework and policies.
- Create security training and awareness programs.
- Document security controls and configurations.
- Implement regular security reviews and assessments.
- Configure backup and recovery mechanisms.
- Establish continuous improvement processes.

Security Alert: *Security is not a one-time implementation but an ongoing process. Regular reviews, updates, and improvements are essential to maintain an effective security posture.*

Conclusion

Security in Microsoft Power Automate is multifaceted and requires you to pay attention to identity, data, connections, environments, and governance. By implementing the security measures discussed in this chapter, you can create a robust security framework to protect your organization while gaining the benefits of automation.

Remember that security is a balance; controls that are too restrictive may drive users to find workarounds, potentially creating greater security risks. Effective security enables appropriate use while preventing harmful actions. Strive to implement security measures that are both strong and usable.

As we move forward in the next chapter, we will explore how to scale your Power Automate implementations across the enterprise, building on the security foundation we have established here.

Additional Resources

For further reading on Power Automate security, consider these resources:

- **Microsoft Documentation:**
  - Power Automate Security Documentation
  - Data Loss Prevention Policies
  - On-premises Data Gateway Security
- **Microsoft Security Resources**:
  - Microsoft Security Best Practices
  - Microsoft Entra Documentation
  - Microsoft Purview Information Protection
- **Compliance Resources**:
  - Microsoft Trust Center
  - Microsoft Compliance Offerings
  - GDPR Compliance in Power Platform
- **Community Resources**:
  - Power Automate Community
  - Power Platform Center of Excellence Starter Kit
  - Microsoft Power Platform Guidance

CHAPTER 13
AI builder in Power Automate

Introduction

Welcome to Chapter 13, where we will explore one of the most powerful capabilities within the Microsoft Power Platform ecosystem: AI Builder in Power Automate. In today's rapidly evolving business landscape, artificial intelligence has evolved from being a futuristic concept to becoming an essential tool for organizations that seek to gain competitive advantages through automation and intelligent decision-making.

AI Builder represents Microsoft's commitment to democratizing artificial intelligence, making advanced AI capabilities accessible to business users with minimal or no coding experience. By integrating AI Builder with Power Automate cloud workflows, you can now infuse your business processes with intelligent automation that can analyze text, recognize images, process forms, predict outcomes, and much more, without requiring data science expertise.

In this chapter, we will dive deep into how AI Builder can transform your Power Automate flows from simple automation tools into intelligent systems capable of making decisions, extracting insights, and taking actions based on various types of data. Whether you are looking to automate document processing, enhance customer service workflows, or predict business outcomes, AI Builder provides the tools you need to elevate your automation strategies.

Structure

In this chapter, we will cover the following topics:

- AI Builder Fundamentals
    - What is AI Builder and its role in Power Platform
    - Components and capabilities of AI Builder
    - How AI Builder integrates with Power Automate
- AI Builder Models Overview
    - Prebuilt AI models for immediate use
    - Custom AI models that you build and train
    - Model types and use cases
- Prebuilt AI Models in Power Automate
    - Text recognition and analysis
    - Image analysis and object detection
    - Form processing

    - Language detection and sentiment analysis
    - Key phrase extraction
- Custom AI Models in Power Automate
    - Building custom prediction models
    - Creating custom form processing models
    - Training and improving your models
    - Managing model versions
- Implementing AI Builder in Your Flows
    - Adding AI Builder actions to your flows
    - Configuring AI Builder actions
    - Processing AI Builder outputs
    - Error handling and fallback mechanisms
- Advanced AI Builder Usage
    - Combining multiple AI models in a flow
    - Sequential and parallel AI processing
    - Building complex decision trees with AI insights
    - Performance optimization techniques
- Licensing and Credit Management
    - Understanding AI Builder licensing options
    - Managing AI Builder credits effectively
    - Monitoring usage and optimization strategies
    - Cost-benefit analysis for AI implementations
- Real-World Use Cases and Implementation
    - Document processing automation
    - Predictive maintenance workflows
    - Customer sentiment analysis and routing
    - Inventory management with object detection

Understanding AI Builder Fundamentals

AI Builder is a Power Platform capability that allows you to bring AI into your business processes. It provides a point-and-click interface for building, training, and publishing AI models that can be integrated directly into your Power Automate flows, Power Apps, and other Power Platform solutions.

AI Builder: Turning Business Users into AI Innovators

What makes AI Builder particularly powerful is its ability to abstract away the complexity typically associated with AI implementation. Instead of requiring data science expertise, coding skills, or understanding of machine learning algorithms, AI Builder presents a simplified interface that focuses on business outcomes rather than technical implementation.

Note: *AI Builder is designed for citizen developers and business analysts, not data scientists. Focus on the business problem you are trying to solve rather than getting occupied with AI technicalities.*

AI Builder operates on two fundamental principles:

- **Model-Based Architecture:** All AI capabilities in AI Builder are packaged as models that are either prebuilt by Microsoft or custom-built by users. These models encapsulate the AI functionality and can be used as actions within Power Automate flows.
- **Train Once, Use Anywhere:** Models created in AI Builder can be used across the Power Platform, not just in Power Automate. This means you can build a model once and leverage it in your flows, apps, and even Power BI reports.

The AI Builder Workflow

Working with AI Builder involves a general workflow that applies whether you are using prebuilt models or creating your own custom models via the following steps:

1. **Select the AI model type** that addresses your business need (like form processing, prediction, object detection).
2. **Configure the model** with your specific requirements.
3. **Train the model** if it is a custom model that requires training.
4. **Test and publish the model** to make it available for use.
5. **Integrate the model** into your Power Automate flows.

Let us look at how AI Builder models can be integrated into your Power Automate flows:

Example flow structure using AI Builder

Trigger (such as, When a new email arrives) →

AI Builder Action (like Extract information from attached form) →

Condition (Based on extracted data) →

Conditional Actions (for instance, Route to appropriate department)

AI Builder Components in Power Automate

When working with AI Builder in Power Automate, you will interact with the following components:

- **AI Builder Actions**: These are the Power Automate actions that encapsulate AI functionality and can be added to your flows.
- **AI Model Connections**: These connections link your flows to specific AI models that you have created or that are available as prebuilt options.
- **Model Inputs and Outputs**: Each AI Builder action expects specific inputs (like an image file, text content) and produces structured outputs that your flow can process.
- **Run History and Performance Metrics**: AI Builder provides insights into how your models are performing, which can help you optimize and improve your AI implementations.

Common Pitfall: *Not all AI Builder models are available across all Power Platform licenses. Always check the licensing requirements before designing solutions that depend on specific AI capabilities.*

AI Builder Models Overview

AI Builder offers two categories of models:

- **Prebuilt Models**: Ready-to-use AI capabilities that require no training or configuration, built and maintained by Microsoft.

- **Custom Models**: AI models that you create and train with your own data to address specific business needs.

Let us explore both categories in detail:

Prebuilt AI Models

Prebuilt models provide immediate AI capabilities without any training or AI expertise. These models are maintained by Microsoft and are continually improved based on extensive datasets and the latest AI research.

Available Prebuilt Models for Power Automate:

Model Type	Description	Common Use Cases
Text Recognition (OCR)	Extracts text from images and documents	Digitizing printed documents, reading signage in photos
Form Processing	Extracts key-value pairs from forms	Invoice processing, receipt analysis
Language Detection	Identifies the language of text content	Multilingual content routing, translation workflows
Sentiment Analysis	Determines the sentiment (positive, negative, neutral) of text	Customer feedback analysis, social media monitoring
Key Phrase Extraction	Identifies important phrases in text	Document summarization, content categorization
Entity Extraction	Recognizes names, dates, addresses, etc. in text	Contact information extraction, appointment scheduling
Business Card Reader	Extracts contact information from business cards	Networking event follow-ups, contact database maintenance
ID Document Processing	Extracts information from ID cards and passports	Customer onboarding, visitor management
Receipt Processing	Extracts line items and totals from receipts	Expense reporting, purchase reconciliation
Object Detection	Identifies objects within images	Inventory checks, safety compliance monitoring

Table 13.1: *Overview of Prebuilt AI Models Integrated with Power Automate*

Note: *Prebuilt models are great for getting started with AI Builder. They require zero training and often perform exceptionally well for common scenarios, before you invest time in building custom models.*

Custom AI Models

Custom models allow you to train AI capabilities on your specific business data, providing more tailored results for your unique needs. These models learn from examples you provide and improve over time with additional training data.

Available Custom Model Types:

Model Type	Description	Data Requirements	Common Use Cases
Form Processing	Extracts specific information from your form layouts	5+ examples of the same form type with labeled fields	Processing company-specific documents, extracting data from proprietary forms

Object Detection	Identifies and counts specific objects in images	15+ images with labeled objects	Product identification on shelves, manufacturing quality control
Text Classification	Categorizes text into custom categories	50+ text examples per category	Support ticket routing, content moderation
Prediction	Forecasts outcomes based on historical data	Historical data with outcome column	Customer churn prediction, inventory forecasting
Category Classification	Organizes content into custom categories	5+ examples per category	Document categorization, product classification

Table 13.2: *Classification of Custom AI Model Types Supported in Power Platform*

Common Pitfall: *Many users provide too few examples when training custom models, resulting in poor performance. Always aim to exceed the minimum requirements—more quality training data almost always leads to better model performance.*

The choice between prebuilt and custom models depends on your specific needs:

- **Use prebuilt models when:**
  - Your scenario aligns with common use cases.
  - You need immediate implementation.
  - You have limited training data.
  - The general AI capabilities match your requirements.
- **Use custom models when:**
  - You need to process specific document formats unique to your business.
  - You need to identify specialized objects or categories.
  - You have sufficient training data available.
  - Prebuilt models don't deliver the accuracy you need.

Prebuilt AI Models in Power Automate

Let us explore how to implement some of the most commonly used prebuilt AI models in your Power Automate flows.

Text Recognition (OCR) in Power Automate

Text Recognition, also known as Optical Character Recognition (OCR), allows your flows to extract text from images and documents. This capability is invaluable for digitizing paper-based processes and working with image-based content.

Step-by-Step Implementation:

1. **Create a new flow** or open an existing one in Power Automate.
2. **Add a trigger** that provides the image source (such as, "When a new email arrives with attachment").
3. **Add the "`AI Builder - Read text from image`" action.**
4. **Configure the action** by selecting the image source (such as, the email attachment).
5. **Process the extracted text** using subsequent flow actions.

Here is an example flow that processes incoming email attachments with OCR:

Trigger: When a new email arrives with attachments

Action 1: Get attachment content

Action 2: AI Builder - Read text from image

Input: Attachment content

Action 3: Condition (If text contains specific keywords)

True path: Create SharePoint item with extracted text

False path: Send notification email

The output from the OCR action includes:

- The full extracted text
- The confidence score for the extraction
- The position of text elements in the image

Note: *OCR works best with clear, high-resolution images. Consider adding a condition to check the confidence score and implement alternative processing for low-confidence results.*

Form Processing with Prebuilt Models

The prebuilt form processing model can extract information from common business documents like invoices and receipts without requiring you to train a custom model.

Implementation Example for Invoice Processing:

1. **Create a flow** that triggers when a new invoice is uploaded to SharePoint.
2. **Add the** "`AI Builder - Process and save information from invoices`" **action.**
3. **Configure the action** by specifying the invoice document location.
4. **Add actions to process the extracted data** (such as, create records in a database).

The prebuilt invoice processor can extract fields such as:

- Invoice number and date
- Due date
- Vendor information
- Line items and quantities
- Subtotal, tax, and total amounts

Common Pitfall: *The prebuilt form processor works with common invoice layouts but may not recognize highly customized or unusual invoice formats. For those cases, you will need to build a custom form processing model.*

Sentiment Analysis for Customer Feedback

Sentiment analysis helps you automatically determine whether text expresses positive, negative, or neutral sentiment. This is particularly useful for processing customer feedback, social media mentions, or support tickets.

Implementation Steps:

1. **Create a flow** triggered by new feedback (such as, a survey response, social media mention).
2. **Add the "`AI Builder - Analyze sentiment`" action.**
3. **Configure the action** by providing the text to analyze.
4. **Add conditional logic** based on the sentiment score.
5. **Implement appropriate responses** for different sentiment levels.

Example flow for routing customer feedback:

Trigger: When a new survey response is submitted

Action 1: AI Builder - Analyze sentiment

  Input: Survey comments

Action 2: Condition (Check sentiment score)

  If score < 0.4: Create high-priority ticket and alert manager

  If score 0.4-0.7: Create normal priority ticket

  If score > 0.7: Send thank you email and log positive feedback

Note: *You must also examine the confidence level instead of just looking at the overall sentiment score. Low confidence may indicate ambiguous or complex feedback that warrants human review regardless of the sentiment classification.*

Language Detection for Multilingual Support

If your organization deals with content in multiple languages, the language detection model can automatically identify the language of incoming text and route it appropriately.

Implementation Example:

1. **Create a flow** triggered by incoming content (like emails, form submissions)
2. **Add the "`AI Builder - Detect language`" action**
3. **Configure the action** by providing the text to analyze
4. **Add conditional logic** based on the detected language
5. **Implement language-specific processing** (like translation, routing to appropriate teams)

Example flow for multilingual support requests:

Trigger: When a new support request is submitted

Action 1: AI Builder - Detect language

  Input: Support request text

Action 2: Switch (Based on detected language)

  Case “en”: Route to English-speaking support team

  Case “es”: Route to Spanish-speaking support team

  Case “fr”: Route to French-speaking support team

  Default: Translate to English and route to general support

Object Detection for Image Analysis

Object detection allows your flows to identify and count specific objects within images. This capability can be applied in spheres like inventory management, safety compliance, retail analytics, and more.

Implementation Steps:

1. **Create a flow** that processes images (such as, from email attachments, mobile app submissions)
2. **Add the "`AI Builder - Detect and count objects in images`" action.**
3. **Configure the action** by specifying the image source and the objects to detect.
4. **Process the detection results** in subsequent flow actions.

Example application for retail shelf monitoring:

Trigger: When a store employee uploads a shelf photo

Action 1: AI Builder - Detect and count objects in images

Input: Uploaded image

Objects to detect: Product SKUs

Action 2: Compare detected count with expected inventory

Action 3: If discrepancy detected, create restocking task

Note: *The prebuilt object detection model can identify common objects like people, cars, and animals. For specific products or custom objects, you will need to create a custom object detection model.*

Try It Yourself: Implementing Prebuilt AI Models

Exercise 1: Sentiment Analysis for Customer Emails

In this exercise, you will create a flow that analyses the sentiment of incoming customer emails and routes them based on the detected sentiment.

Requirements:

- Access to Power Automate with AI Builder capabilities
- Office 365 email account
- SharePoint list or Microsoft Dataverse table for logging feedback

Steps:

1. Create a new flow with the trigger "`When a new email arrives (V3)`".
2. Configure the trigger to monitor a specific folder (like "`Customer Feedback`").
3. Add the "`AI Builder - Analyse sentiment`" action.
4. Set the input text to the email body.
5. Add a condition to check the sentiment score.
6. Create branches for positive, neutral, and negative sentiment.
7. Implement appropriate actions for each branch (for instance, create items in different lists).

Test the flow by sending test emails with clearly positive and negative content.

Think about It:

- How will you handle emails that contain both positive and negative sentiments in different sections?
- What are the additional AI Builder actions that can complement sentiment analysis to provide more context?
- How can you implement a feedback loop to improve the accuracy of your sentiment routing over time?

Custom AI Models in Power Automate

While prebuilt models offer immediate value, custom AI models allow you to address specific business scenarios with tailored AI capabilities. Let us explore how to create and implement custom AI models in your Power Automate flows.

Building Custom Prediction Models

Prediction models allow you to forecast outcomes based on historical data. For example, you might predict customer churn, inventory needs, or maintenance requirements.

Creating a Custom Prediction Model involves the following steps:

1. Access AI Builder from the Power Automate maker portal.
2. Select "`Predict`" model type.
3. Define what you want to predict (the outcome).
4. Select your data source (Excel, SharePoint, Dataverse).
5. Select the fields (features) that will help predict the outcome.
6. Train the model using your historical data.
7. Review the model performance.
8. Publish the model when satisfied with its accuracy.

Example: Customer Churn Prediction

Let us walk through an example of creating a churn prediction model:

- Start with historical customer data that includes:
    - Customer demographics (age, location, and so on.)
    - Product usage statistics
    - Support interaction history
    - Whether the customer churned (the outcome we want to predict)
- Create and train the model in AI Builder:
- Name: Customer Churn Predictor
- Data source: Customer History (Dataverse table)
- Outcome field: Churned (Yes/No)
- Features: Select relevant customer attributes

Training: Allow AI Builder to analyze and build the prediction model

- Review the model insights like:
  - Key influencing factors
  - Accuracy metrics
  - Feature importance
- Implement the model in Power Automate:
- Trigger: Scheduled (daily)
- Action 1: Get active customers from Dataverse
- Action 2: Apply to each (For each customer)
- Action 2.1: AI Builder - Predict (Customer Churn Predictor)
- Action 2.2: Condition (If churn probability > 70%)
- True path: Add to high-risk segment and trigger engagement campaign

False path: Continue normal customer journey

Note: *After implementing a prediction model, track the actual outcomes against the predictions to measure the model's real-world performance. Use this data to refine your model regularly.*

Custom Form Processing Models

Custom form processing models allow you to extract specific information from forms that are unique to your business, such as purchase orders, registration forms, applications, or any other document with a consistent structure.

Creating a Custom Form Processing Model involves these steps:

1. Access AI Builder from the Power Automate maker portal.
2. Select "`Extract information from forms`" model type.
3. Upload sample forms (at least 5 examples of the same form type).
4. Define the fields you want to extract from the forms.
5. Label your sample forms by identifying where each field appears.
6. Train the model using your labeled examples.
7. Test the model with new form examples.
8. Publish the model when satisfied with its accuracy.

Example: Processing Company-Specific Purchase Orders

Here is an example of creating a custom form processor for internal purchase orders:

1. Collect at least 5 examples of your company's purchase order form.
2. Create a new form processing model in AI Builder: .
3. Name: Internal PO Processor.
4. Collection: Upload your PO examples.

Fields to extract: PO Number, Requestor, Department, Items, Quantities, Prices, Total, Approval Status

5. Label the fields on each example form.

6. Train and publish the model.
7. Implement in Power Automate: .
8. Trigger: When a file is added to SharePoint "Incoming POs" folder
9. Action 1: AI Builder - Extract information from forms
10. Input: File content
11. Model: Internal PO Processor
12. Action 2: Create record in "Purchase Orders" table with extracted fields

Action 3: Start approval process based on extracted department and total

Common Pitfall: *Form recognition works best when your training examples represent the variation you will see in real-world usage. Include examples with different handwriting styles, slightly different alignments, or minor formatting differences to build a more robust model.*

Custom Object Detection Models

Custom object detection allows you to train models to identify specific objects that matter to your business, like your products, equipment, assets, or other visual elements.

Creating a Custom Object Detection Model involves the following steps:

1. Access AI Builder from the Power Automate maker portal.
2. Select "`Object detection`" model type.
3. Upload training images (at least 15 images containing your objects).
4. Label the objects in each image by drawing bounding boxes.
5. Train the model using your labeled images.
6. Test the model with new images.
7. Publish the model when satisfied with its accuracy.

Example: Product Compliance Verification

Here is an example of creating a custom object detection model for product compliance verification:

1. Collect at least 15 images of compliant and non-compliant product packaging.
2. Create a new object detection model in AI Builder:
3. Name: Compliance Verification

Objects to detect: `Compliant_Label`, `Missing_Label`, `Incorrect_Label`

4. Label each object instance in your training images.
5. Train and publish the model.
6. Implement in Power Automate:
7. Trigger: When a photo is uploaded to "Quality Assurance" folder
8. Action 1: AI Builder - Detect objects
9. Input: Uploaded image
10. Model: Compliance Verification

11. Action 2: Condition (Check for non-compliant objects)
12. True path: Create quality incident and notify production manager

False path: Log compliant product and proceed with shipment

Note: *The quality of your training images significantly impacts model performance. Use clear, well-lit images from multiple angles, and ensure your labelled bounding boxes are tight and accurate around the objects.*

Try It Yourself: Building a Custom AI Model

Exercise 2: Creating a Custom Form Processor

In this exercise, you will create a custom form processing model for a specific document type and implement it in a Power Automate flow.

Requirements:

- Access to Power Automate with AI Builder capabilities
- At least 5 examples of a specific form type (such as, expense reports, registration forms)
- SharePoint library or other storage location for processed forms

Steps:

1. Collect 5+ examples of your chosen form type.
2. Access AI Builder from the Power Platform maker portal.
3. Create a new "`Extract information from forms`" model.
4. Upload your form examples.
5. Define the fields you want to extract.
6. Label each field on your example forms.
7. Train and publish your model.
8. Create a Power Automate flow that:
   a. Triggers when a new form is uploaded
   b. Uses your custom form processing model to extract information
   c. Creates a record in a database or list with the extracted information
   d. Notifies relevant stakeholders

Think About It:

- How will you handle variations in form layout or formatting?
- What measures can you implement to handle extraction errors or low-confidence results?
- How will you continuously improve your form processing model over time?

Implementing AI Builder in Your Flows

Now that we have explored both prebuilt and custom AI models, let us dive deeper into how to effectively implement AI Builder actions in your Power Automate flows.

Adding AI Builder Actions to Your Flows

AI Builder actions can be found in the "AI Builder" category when adding a new action to your flow. Each action corresponds to a specific AI capability and may require different inputs and configuration.

General Steps for Adding AI Builder Actions:

1. Create or edit a flow in Power Automate.
2. Add a new step where you want to incorporate AI capabilities.
3. Search for "`AI Builder`" in the actions search box.
4. Select the appropriate AI Builder action based on your needs.
5. Configure the action with required inputs and settings.
6. Process the AI outputs in subsequent flow steps.

Configuring Common AI Builder Actions

Let us look at the configuration details for some common AI Builder actions:

- **Text Recognition (Read text from image)**
  - **Input type**: Image content (file content) or image URL
  - **Settings**: None additional
  - **Outputs**: Extracted text, confidence score, text positions
- **Sentiment Analysis**
  - **Input**: Text to analyze
  - **Settings**: None additional
  - **Outputs**: Sentiment score (0-1), sentiment label, confidence score
- **Form Processing**
  - **Input**: Form document (file content) or document URL
  - **Settings**: Select the appropriate form processing model
  - **Outputs**: Extracted fields as key-value pairs, confidence scores per field
- **Prediction**
  - **Input**: Record with features required by the prediction model
  - **Settings**: Select the appropriate prediction model
  - **Outputs**: Prediction result, confidence score, influencing factors

Note: *While configuring AI Builder actions, use dynamic content from previous steps whenever possible. This allows your flow to process dynamic inputs rather than being limited to static values.*

Processing AI Builder Outputs

AI Builder actions produce structured outputs that can be used in subsequent flow steps. Understanding these output schemas is crucial for effectively leveraging AI insights in your automation.

Example: Processing Sentiment Analysis Output

The "**`Analyze sentiment`**" action produces an output with this structure:

```
json
{
  "sentiment": "positive",
  "confidenceScore": 0.92,
  "sentences": [
    {
      "sentiment": "positive",
      "confidenceScore": 0.95,
      "text": "Your product is amazing!"
    },
    {
      "sentiment": "neutral",
      "confidenceScore": 0.68,
      "text": "I've been using it for two weeks."
    }
  ]
}
```

You can refer to these outputs in subsequent actions:

Condition: confidenceScore is greater than 0.7

Create SharePoint Item:

Title: New Feedback

Sentiment: sentiment

Score: confidenceScore

Example: Processing Form Extraction Output

Form processing models produce outputs with extracted fields:

```
json
{
  "fields": {
    "InvoiceNumber": {
      "value": "INV-2023-1234",
      "confidence": 0.98
    },
    "Date": {
      "value": "2023-09-15",
      "confidence": 0.95
    },
    "Total": {
      "value": 1250.00,
      "confidence": 0.96
    }
  }
}
```

You can reference these fields in subsequent actions:

Create Record:

InvoiceNumber: `outputs('Extract_invoice_information')?['fields']?['InvoiceNumber']?['value']`

Invoice Date: `outputs('Extract_invoice_information')?['fields']?['Date']?['value']`

Total Amount: `outputs('Extract_invoice_information')?['fields']?['Total']?['value']`

Common Pitfall: *AI Builder outputs may contain null values or missing fields if the AI could not detect certain information with sufficient confidence. Always implement error handling to manage these scenarios gracefully.*

Error Handling and Fallback Mechanisms

AI is probabilistic by nature, which means it will not always produce correct or high-confidence results. Implementing proper error handling and fallback mechanisms is essential for building robust AI-powered flows.

Best Practices for AI Error Handling

- **Check confidence scores** and implement conditional processing based on confidence thresholds.
- **Provide fallback paths** for low-confidence results or processing failures.
- **Implement human review** for borderline cases.
- **Log AI performance metrics** to identify improvement opportunities.
- **Use "`Configure run after`" settings** to handle potential AI action failures.

Example: Robust Invoice Processing with Fallbacks

Trigger: When a new file is added to "Invoices" folder

Action 1: AI Builder - Process invoice

Action 2: Condition (Check if confidence scores > 0.7 for critical fields)

  True path: Proceed with automated processing

  False path: Route for manual review

Action 3 (Configure to run after Action 1 fails): Notify accounting team of processing failure

Note: Implement a continuous improvement process for your AI models. Regularly review cases where the AI produced low-confidence results or errors, and use these examples to retrain and improve your models.

Try It Yourself: Implementing AI Builder Actions

Exercise 3: Building a Sentiment-Based Customer Support Flow

In this exercise, you will create a flow that analyzes incoming customer support requests and routes them based on sentiment and content.

Requirements

- Access to Power Automate with AI Builder capabilities
- Customer support request source (like, email, form submissions, SharePoint list)
- Support ticket system or destination for routed requests

Steps

1. Create a new flow with an appropriate trigger for your support requests.
2. Add the "**`AI Builder - Analyze sentiment`**" action.

3. Add the "`AI Builder - Extract key phrases`" action.
4. Create a condition based on sentiment score:
    a. High priority: Negative sentiment (score < 0.4)
    b. Medium priority: Neutral sentiment (score between 0.4 and 0.7)
    c. Low priority: Positive sentiment (score > 0.7)
5. Within each branch, implement additional logic based on extracted key phrases.
6. Create appropriate support tickets with priority, sentiment, and key phrases included.
7. Implement notifications for high-priority tickets.
8. Test your flow with various support request scenarios.

Think About It:

- How will you combine sentiment analysis with other AI capabilities like language detection or entity extraction?
- What kind of metrics can help you evaluate the effectiveness of your sentiment-based routing?
- How can you implement a feedback loop to measure whether the assigned priorities matched the actual urgency of the issues?

Advanced AI Builder Usage in Power Automate

As you become more comfortable with basic AI Builder implementations, you can move on to tackle more sophisticated scenarios that leverage multiple AI models, complex decision trees, and advanced flow patterns.

Combining Multiple AI Models in a Flow

Some business scenarios benefit from applying multiple AI capabilities in sequence or parallel. By combining different AI models, you can extract richer insights and enable more intelligent automation.

Example: Comprehensive Document Processing

Trigger: When a new document is uploaded

Action 1: AI Builder - Read text from image (Convert document to text)

Action 2: AI Builder - Detect language (Identify document language)

Action 3: Condition (Check language)

English path:

Action 3.1: AI Builder - Extract key phrases

Action 3.2: AI Builder - Analyze sentiment

Action 3.3: Process results directly

Non-English path:

Action 3.1: Translate document to English

Action 3.2: AI Builder - Extract key phrases

Action 3.3: AI Builder - Analyze sentiment

Action 3.4: Process translated results

This multi-model approach allows you to:

1. First extract all text from a document image.
2. Determine the document's language.
3. Extract key insights like important phrases and sentiment.
4. Process the document differently based on language and content.

Note: *When combining multiple AI models, consider using parallel branches for independent AI processing tasks to improve flow performance. Use "Compose" actions to collect and organize the outputs before proceeding to decision-making steps.*

Sequential vs. Parallel AI Processing

Depending on your scenario, you may need to process AI tasks sequentially (one after another) or in parallel (simultaneously).

Sequential Processing is appropriate when:

- Successive AI tasks depend on the outputs of preceding ones.
- You need to make decisions between AI processing steps.
- Resources are limited, and you want to avoid concurrent processing.

Parallel Processing is beneficial when:

- AI tasks are independent of each other.
- You want to reduce overall processing time.
- You are working with the same input for multiple AI analyses.

Example: Parallel Customer Feedback Analysis

Trigger: When new customer feedback is submitted

Parallel Branch 1:

Action 1.1: AI Builder - Analyze sentiment

Parallel Branch 2:

Action 2.1: AI Builder - Extract key phrases

Parallel Branch 3:

Action 3.1: AI Builder - Category classification

Join: Wait for all branches to complete

Building Complex Decision Trees with AI Insights

Complex decision trees leverage multiple AI outputs to create sophisticated business logic that can handle nuanced scenarios requiring multiple factors for decision-making. By combining AI insights from different models, you can build flows that make intelligent decisions based on comprehensive analysis, rather than simple rule-based logic.

Business Case Example: Intelligent Customer Support Ticket Routing

Let us examine a real-world scenario where a telecommunications company needs to route customer support tickets based on multiple AI-driven factors:

Business Challenge: TechCorp receives 15,000+ customer support requests daily through email, chat, and phone transcripts. The company needs to route these requests to the appropriate specialist teams while prioritizing urgent issues and identifying potential escalation risks.

AI-Driven Decision Tree Implementation:

Trigger: When new support request is received

Action 1: AI Builder - Analyze sentiment (Get emotional tone)

Action 2: AI Builder - Extract key phrases (Identify topic areas)

Action 3: AI Builder - Extract entities (Find product names, account numbers)

Action 4: AI Builder - Language detection (Identify customer language)

Action 5: AI Builder - Text classification (Categorize request type)

Decision Tree Implementation:

Condition 1: Check sentiment score

    If sentiment < 0.3 (Very Negative):

        Condition 1.1: Check for extracted entities containing "cancel", "refund", "billing"

            True path: High Priority + Retention Team + Immediate escalation

            False path: Continue to technical severity assessment

    If sentiment 0.3-0.6 (Neutral/Slightly Negative):

        Condition 1.2: Check extracted key phrases for urgency indicators

            Contains "outage", "down", "emergency": Priority routing based on service type

            Contains "setup", "install", "activate": Route to provisioning team

            Default: Continue to standard classification

    If sentiment > 0.6 (Positive):

        Condition 1.3: Check text classification result

            "Compliment" or "Praise": Route to customer success team for follow-up

            "Question" or "Information": Route to general support with normal priority

            Default: Standard processing

Condition 2: Check detected language

    If language != "en":

        Route to multilingual support team with detected language flag

    Else: Continue with English-speaking teams

Condition 3: Check extracted entities for VIP customer indicators

If entities contain VIP account numbers or premium service identifiers:

Increase priority level and route to dedicated VIP support team

Else: Continue with standard priority assignment

Final Action: Create support ticket with:

- Calculated priority (1-5 scale based on AI insights)

- Assigned team (based on decision tree outcomes)

- AI-extracted metadata (sentiment, key phrases, entities)

- Escalation flags (if multiple negative indicators detected)

Decision Tree Logic Breakdown:

- **Primary Decision Factor**: Sentiment analysis determines the initial routing path.
- **Secondary Factors**: Key phrases and entities refine the routing decision.
- **Tertiary Factors**: Language and customer tier influence final assignment.
- **Compound Scoring**: Multiple AI outputs contribute to a final priority score.

Note: *When building complex decision trees, use "Compose" actions to calculate aggregate scores from multiple AI outputs. This allows you to create weighted scoring systems that consider multiple factors simultaneously.*

Performance Optimization Techniques

As your AI Builder implementations scale, optimizing performance becomes crucial for maintaining efficient operations and managing credit consumption effectively. Here are some key optimization strategies with practical examples:

- **Batch Processing Optimization:** Instead of processing items individually, batch multiple operations together to reduce the number of API calls and improve throughput.
- **Conditional AI Processing:** Implement logic to only invoke AI operations when they add value, avoiding unnecessary credit consumption.
- **Caching and Result Reuse:** Store AI results to avoid reprocessing identical content.
- **Confidence-Based Processing Chains:** Optimize AI model selection based on confidence requirements and credit costs.
- **Parallel Processing with Resource Management:** Balance parallel processing benefits with system resource limitations.
- **Error Handling and Retry Optimization:** Implement smart retry logic to handle temporary failures without excessive credit consumption.

Performance Monitoring Best Practices:

- **Track Key Metrics:**
  - Average processing time per document type
  - Credit consumption patterns by model and volume
  - Success rates and confidence score distributions
  - Error rates and failure patterns

- **Implement Performance Dashboards:**
    - Create Power BI reports showing AI Builder usage trends.
    - Monitor flow performance metrics in Power Automate analytics.
    - Track business outcomes (processing time, accuracy improvements).
- **Regular Optimization Reviews:**
    - Monthly analysis of credit consumption vs. business value
    - Quarterly review of model performance and potential improvements
    - Annual assessment of AI strategy and technology updates

Common Pitfall: *Over-optimizing for credit consumption at the expense of accuracy can lead to poor business outcomes. Always balance performance optimization with the quality requirements of your business processes.*

By implementing these performance optimization techniques, organizations typically see:

- 40-60% reduction in AI Builder credit consumption
- 50-80% improvement in overall processing throughput
- 90%+ reduction in processing errors and failures
- Significant improvement in user experience and business outcomes

These optimization strategies ensure that your AI Builder implementations scale effectively, while maintaining cost efficiency and delivering consistent business value.

Licensing and Credit Management

Licensing and Credit Management for AI Builder involves understanding how AI operations consume credits from your monthly allocation and implementing strategies to monitor, allocate, and optimize credit usage across your organization's Power Automate flows.

Understanding AI Builder Licensing Options in Power Automate

AI Builder in Power Automate follows a capacity-based licensing model that's different from standard Power Automate licensing. There are two primary ways to access AI Builder capabilities:

- **Per-user add-on**: This option provides individual users with a monthly allocation of AI Builder credits, that can be used across any AI models. This is ideal for scenarios where you have a limited number of users who need AI capabilities.
- **Capacity add-on**: This enterprise-focused option provides your organization with a pool of AI Builder credits that can be shared across users. This is more cost-effective for widespread AI implementation across the organization.

Additionally, there are:

- **Trial allocations**: Every Power Platform environment receives a free allocation of AI Builder credits that can be used for testing and proof-of-concept development.
- **Bundled credits** with certain license types: Some premium Power Platform licenses (like Power Apps Premium and Power Automate Premium) include a limited allocation of AI Builder credits.

Note: *The licensing landscape for AI Builder evolves frequently. Always check the official Microsoft documentation for the most current pricing and licensing structure before planning large-scale implementations.*

Managing AI Builder Credits Effectively

AI Builder credits are consumed based on the type and volume of AI operations you perform. Understanding how credits are consumed is essential for effective management:

- **Credit consumption patterns:**
  - Prebuilt models generally consume fewer credits than custom models.
  - Training custom models consumes credits separate from using them.
  - Different model types have varying credit consumption rates.
  - Credit consumption occurs per operation (such as, per image analyzed, per form processed)
- **Credit management strategies:**
  - Allocate credits strategically across high-value business processes.
  - Implement quotas for different departments or processes.
  - Reserve a portion of credits for development and testing.
  - Create usage policies to prevent unexpected credit depletion.
- **Credit efficiency tactics:**
  - Batch processing to reduce the number of API calls.
  - Implementing caching mechanisms for repeated analyses.
  - Using conditional logic to only invoke AI when necessary.
  - Choosing the right model type for each scenario.

Monitoring Usage and Optimization Strategies

Microsoft provides several tools to monitor and optimize your AI Builder credit usage:

- **Power Platform Admin Center**: Provides organization-wide visibility into AI Builder credit usage, allowing administrators to track consumption patterns and allocate resources effectively.
- **AI Builder usage metrics**: Within the AI Builder portal, you can view detailed metrics on model usage, performance, and credit consumption.
- **Usage alerts**: Configure alerts to notify administrators when credit usage reaches certain thresholds, helping prevent unexpected depletion.

Optimization strategies include:

- **Regular model reviews**: Periodically review model performance and usage to identify optimization opportunities.
- **Scheduled retraining**: For custom models, schedule regular retraining with improved data to enhance accuracy and potentially reduce the need for human review.
- **Flow optimization**: Analyze your flows to ensure AI actions are only invoked when necessary, using conditions to bypass AI processing for scenarios where it adds little value.
- **Load balancing**: Distribute AI workloads across time periods to avoid consumption spikes and ensure credit availability for critical processes.

Common Pitfall: *Many organizations implement AI Builder without proper monitoring, only to discover mid-month that they've depleted their credit allocation. Always implement proactive monitoring from the start.*

Cost-Benefit Analysis for AI Implementations

Before implementing AI Builder in production workflows, conduct a thorough cost-benefit analysis:

- **Quantifying benefits**
    - Time saved through automation
    - Error reduction and accuracy improvements
    - Staff reallocation to higher-value tasks
    - Faster processing and reduced cycle times
    - Enhanced customer experience metrics
- **Calculating costs**
    - AI Builder licensing costs
    - Implementation and maintenance effort
    - Training requirements for staff
    - Integration with existing systems
    - Ongoing monitoring and optimization
- **ROI calculation framework**
    - Document baseline metrics before implementation
    - Calculate expected yearly savings from AI implementation
    - Determine total cost of ownership including licenses and maintenance
    - Calculate payback period and ROI percentage
    - Establish measurement parameters for ongoing ROI tracking

AI Builder Licensing and Credit Management Example

Let us work through a practical example for a mid-sized organization implementing AI Builder for multiple processes:

Scenario: PrudentCorp Industries wants to implement AI Builder for invoice processing, customer support routing, and product quality inspection.

Credit Allocation Analysis:

Process	AI Model Type	Est. Monthly Volume	Credits per Operation	Monthly Credits
Invoice Processing	Custom Form Processing	5,000 invoices	0.5 credits/invoice	2,500
Support Request Routing	Sentiment Analysis & Key Phrase Extraction	8,000 requests	0.25 credits/request	2,000
Quality Inspection	Custom Object Detection	3,000 inspections	1 credit/inspection	3,000
Total				7,500

Table 13.3: *Breakdown of Credit Distribution across Entities or Activities*

Licensing Decision:

- Option 1: 10 individual add-ons (1,000 credits each) = $400/month
- Option 2: Capacity add-on for 10,000 credits = $375/month

Implementation Strategy:

1. Start with capacity add-on for 10,000 credits/month.
2. Allocate credits with buffers:
    a. Invoice Processing: 3,000 credits (40%)
    b. Support Routing: 2,500 credits (33%)
    c. Quality Inspection: 3,500 credits (27%)
    d. Reserve 1,000 credits for unexpected needs and testing.

Monitoring Plan:

- Weekly usage reports to department heads
- Alerts at 50%, 75%, and 90% utilization thresholds
- Monthly optimization review meetings
- Quarterly ROI assessment and license adjustment

Cost-Benefit Result:

- Annual licensing cost: $4,500
- Estimated annual savings:
    - Reduced manual invoice processing: $45,000
    - Improved support request handling time: $30,000
    - Reduced quality issues and returns: $65,000
- Total estimated annual savings: $140,000
- ROI: 3,111% (savings minus costs : costs × 100%)
- Payback period: Less than 2 weeks

Note: *Start with a conservative AI Builder implementation focused on high-ROI processes. Use the demonstrated success and savings from these initial implementations to justify expanding to additional processes.*

Let us work through a practical example for invoice processing automation:

Scenario: Your company needs to process 5,000 invoices monthly using a custom form processing model in Power Automate.

Credit Calculation:

- Custom form processing: 0.5 credits per document
- Monthly volume: 5,000 invoices
- Total monthly credits needed: 5,000 × 0.5 = 2,500 credits

Licensing Options:

- Use existing premium licenses:
    - If you have 1 Power Automate Premium license = 5,000 credits
    - This provides sufficient credits for your invoice processing needs.

- Or purchase specific AI Builder add-on:
  - One add-on provides 1,000,000 credits, far exceeding your needs
  - This option makes sense if you plan to implement multiple AI processes.

Monitoring Approach:

1. Check the AI Builder consumption report weekly.
2. Identify any unusual spikes in usage.
3. If consumption approaches allocation, consider:
   a. Allocating additional credits to the environment
   b. Optimizing flows to reduce unnecessary AI operations
   c. Implementing batching to process multiple documents per operation

Cost-Benefit Result:

- Annual cost: Covered by existing Power Automate Premium license
- Estimated annual savings:
  - 5,000 invoices × 12 months = 60,000 invoices annually
  - 10 minutes saved per invoice = 10,000 hours annually
  - At $25/hour labor cost = $250,000 annual savings
- ROI: Substantial positive return, especially when using existing licensing

Note: *For testing and development, you can use the free trial allocation of AI Builder credits. Note that while testing trained models is free, testing prebuilt models consumes credits at the standard rate.*

Real-World Use Cases and Implementation

Real-world use cases demonstrate how AI Builder transforms theoretical AI capabilities into practical business solutions that solve actual challenges across different industries. These implementations showcase the tangible benefits and measurable outcomes that organizations achieve when they successfully integrate AI Builder into their Power Automate workflows.

Document Processing Automation

Document processing represents one of the most impactful applications of AI Builder, allowing organizations to automate the extraction and processing of information from various document types.

Use Case: Automated Invoice Processing System

Business Challenge: A manufacturing company processes 8,000+ supplier invoices monthly and requires 4 full time employees to manually extract data and enter it into their ERP system, leading to delays and errors.

AI Builder Solution:

- **Implementation approach**:
  - Custom form processing model trained on the company's top 20 supplier invoice formats
  - Prebuilt invoice processing model for less common suppliers
  - Power Automate flow orchestrating the end-to-end process

- **Flow architecture**:
  - Trigger: When email arrives in Accounts Payable inbox with attachment.
  - Action 1: Get attachment content.
  - Action 2: Condition (Check file type)
  - Action 3: AI Builder - Process invoice (Custom model or prebuilt model based on supplier)
  - Action 4: Check confidence scores for critical fields.
  - Action 5: Create record in ERP system for high-confidence extractions.
  - Action 6: Route low-confidence extractions for human review.
  - Action 7: Send notification of processing completion.
- **Results achieved:**
  - 85% reduction in manual data entry
  - Processing time reduced from 15 minutes to 45 seconds per invoice
  - Data entry error rate reduced by 93%
  - Staff reallocated to supplier relationship management and cash flow optimization

Implementation Detail: The solution included a continuous improvement loop where human-reviewed invoices were added to the training dataset monthly, gradually improving the model's accuracy from 76% to 94% over six months.

Predictive Maintenance Workflows

Predictive maintenance uses AI to forecast when equipment might fail, allowing for scheduled maintenance before costly breakdowns occur. This approach significantly reduces downtime and maintenance costs.

Use Case: Manufacturing Equipment Predictive Maintenance

Business Challenge: A food processing plant experienced unplanned equipment downtime costing $35,000 per hour, with conventional scheduled maintenance missing emerging issues.

AI Builder Solution:

- **Implementation approach**:
  - Custom prediction model trained on historical equipment data
  - IoT sensors transmitting real-time equipment telemetry
  - Power Automate flows processing sensor data and triggering maintenance actions
- **Flow architecture:**
  - Trigger: Scheduled (hourly)
  - Action 1: Get equipment telemetry data from IoT Hub.
  - Action 2: Apply to each (For each equipment unit).
    - Action 2.1: Prepare data for prediction model.
    - Action 2.2: AI Builder - Predict (Failure prediction model)
    - Action 2.3: Condition (If failure probability > 60%)
    - True path: Create high-priority maintenance ticket.
    - False path: Condition (If failure probability > 30%)
    - True path: Create advisory notification for next maintenance window.

- False path: Log normal operation status.

- **Results achieved:**
  - 78% reduction in unplanned downtime
  - 42% decrease in overall maintenance costs
  - Extended equipment lifespan by 15-20%
  - Improved production scheduling with predictable maintenance windows

Note: *For predictive maintenance, the quality of your historical data is crucial. Include both successful and failure cases in your training data, and ensure you capture all relevant sensor metrics that might indicate impending failures.*

Customer Sentiment Analysis and Routing

Understanding customer sentiment allows organizations to identify issues, prioritize responses, and improve customer experience. AI Builder makes this accessible without requiring data science expertise.

Use Case: Intelligent Customer Support Triage

Business Challenge: An e-commerce company struggled with a 48-hour response time for customer inquiries, resulting in poor satisfaction scores and lost sales opportunities.

AI Builder Solution:

- **Implementation approach**
  - Sentiment analysis for incoming support requests
  - Key phrase extraction to identify specific product issues
  - Entity extraction to identify product mentions and order numbers
  - Automated routing based on sentiment, urgency, and topic
- **Flow architecture**
  - Trigger: When new support request is submitted
  - Action 1: AI Builder - Analyze sentiment
  - Action 2: AI Builder - Extract key phrases
  - Action 3: AI Builder - Extract entities
  - Action 4: Calculate priority score (Algorithm combining sentiment, key phrases, and customer tier).
  - Action 5: Condition (Check priority score)
    - High priority path: Create urgent ticket and notify support manager.
    - Medium priority path: Create normal ticket and assign to appropriate team.
    - Low priority path: Create ticket in general queue.
  - Action 6: Apply automated response template based on detected issues.
- **Results achieved:**
  - Average response time was reduced from 48 hours to 3.5 hours.
  - Customer satisfaction scores increased by 42%.
  - Support team capacity increased by 35% without adding staff.
  - Emerging product issues were identified proactively.

Implementation Detail: The solution incorporated a feedback loop where support agents could flag incorrect AI classifications, with these examples added to a retraining dataset to continually improve model accuracy.

Inventory Management with Object Detection

Object detection allows organizations to automate visual inspection tasks, count items, verify compliance, and monitor inventory levels through image analysis.

Use Case: Retail Shelf Monitoring System

Business Challenge: A retail chain struggled with maintaining optimal shelf stock levels, leading to out-of-stock situations and lost sales estimated at $2.3 million annually.

AI Builder Solution:

- **Implementation approach**
  - Custom object detection model trained to recognize specific products
  - Mobile app for store associates to capture shelf images
  - Power Automate flow processing images and updating inventory systems
- **Flow architecture**
  - Trigger: When new image is uploaded to "Shelf Monitoring" folder
  - Action 1: Get image metadata (Store, Aisle, Section).
  - Action 2: AI Builder - Detect objects
  - Action 3: Process detection results (Count products, identify gaps).
  - Action 4: Compare detected inventory with expected planogram.
  - Action 5: Condition (If restocking needed)
    - True path: Create restocking task with specific products and quantities.
    - False path: Log compliance with expected inventory levels.
  - Action 6: Generate weekly compliance report per store.
- **Results achieved**
  - Out-of-stock incidents reduced by 78%
  - Planogram compliance improved from 61% to 94%
  - Sales increase of 8.3% due to improved product availability
  - Saved 15 hours of labour per store per week from automated inventory checks

Note: *For optimal object detection performance in retail environments, train your model with images taken under various lighting conditions and angles that represent real-world scenarios. Include images with partial occlusion and varying product arrangements to build model resilience.*

AI Builder vs. Azure Document Intelligence: When to Use Each

Both AI Builder and Azure Document Intelligence (formerly Form Recognizer) provide document processing capabilities, but serve different use cases and audiences. Understanding when to use each will help you make the most effective choice in terms of technology.

AI Builder in Power Automate is best for:

- **Citizen developers and business analysts** who need AI capabilities without coding
- **Power Platform-centric implementations** that need to integrate with Power Apps, Power BI, and other Microsoft business applications
- **End-to-end business process automation** where document processing is one component of a larger workflow
- **Organizations standardized on Power Platform** with existing licenses and skills
- **Implementations requiring rapid development** with minimal technical overhead
- **Scenarios requiring a diverse range of AI capabilities** beyond just document processing

Azure Document Intelligence is best for:

- **Developer-led implementations** requiring precise control and customization
- **Enterprise-scale document processing** with high-volume requirements
- **Complex scenarios requiring advanced document understanding** capabilities
- **Integration with custom applications** outside the Power Platform ecosystem
- **Multi-stage document processing pipelines** with specialized pre and post-processing
- **Organizations with existing Azure investments** and DevOps practices

Comparison Table

Factor	AI Builder	Azure Document Intelligence
Target Users	*Business analysts, citizen developers*	*Developers, data scientists*
Integration	*Native with Power Platform*	*Requires custom API integration*
Development Speed	*Rapid with low-code approach*	*More time-intensive but highly customizable*
Scalability	*Good for departmental to medium-sized implementations*	*Excellent for enterprise-scale implementations*
Customization	*Limited to platform capabilities*	*Extensive through API and SDK options*
Cost Structure	*Credit-based consumption*	*Pay-per-page processing*
UI/UX	*Guided, intuitive interface*	*Developer-focused, code-based approach*
Document Complexity	*Best for common document types with moderate complexity*	*Superior for highly complex or specialized documents*
Maintenance	*Low maintenance overhead*	*Requires traditional application maintenance*

Table 13.4: *Best-Suited Scenarios for Azure Document Intelligence Capabilities*

Decision Framework

Consider these questions when choosing between AI Builder and Azure Document Intelligence:

- **Who will build and maintain the solution?**
  - Business teams → AI Builder
  - IT/development teams → Consider Azure Document Intelligence
- **What is your integration landscape?**
  - Primarily Microsoft 365 and Power Platform → AI Builder
  - Custom applications or non-Microsoft systems → Consider Azure Document Intelligence

- **What is your volume of documents?**
  - Hundreds to thousands per month → Either solution works
  - Millions of pages → Azure Document Intelligence provides better scaling
- **How complex are your documents?**
  - Standard business documents → AI Builder is sufficient
  - Highly specialized or variable documents → Azure Document Intelligence provides better results
- **What is your timeline for implementation?**
  - Days to weeks → AI Builder offers faster time-to-value
  - Can accommodate longer development cycles → Azure Document Intelligence may provide more robust results

Note: *Many organizations implement a hybrid approach, using AI Builder for business-user accessible scenarios while leveraging Azure Document Intelligence for complex, high-volume document processing needs. The two technologies can complement each other in a well-designed enterprise architecture.*

Here is an example of a hybrid scenario:

- Use Azure Document Intelligence for initial bulk processing of historical documents.
- Use AI Builder in Power Automate for day-to-day document workflows integrated with business processes.
- Share model improvements and training data between both systems.

This approach allows organizations to leverage the strengths of both platforms, while mitigating their respective limitations.

Conclusion

As we conclude our journey through AI Builder in Power Automate, it is clear that this powerful capability represents a significant leap forward in the evolution of business process automation. By combining the accessibility of Power Automate with the intelligence of AI Builder, Microsoft has democratized artificial intelligence, making it available to business users without requiring extensive technical expertise or data science knowledge.

Throughout this chapter, we have explored how AI Builder transforms ordinary flows into intelligent processes capable of understanding documents, interpreting text, analyzing sentiment, detecting objects, and predicting outcomes. We have seen how both prebuilt and custom AI models can be integrated seamlessly into your automation workflows, bringing nw intelligence to previously manual tasks.

The real power of AI Builder lies in its practical applications. Whether you are automating invoice processing to free up your finance team, implementing predictive maintenance to reduce costly equipment failures, analyzing customer sentiment to improve service quality, or using object detection to streamline inventory management, AI Builder provides the tools you need to solve real business challenges.

We have also gained a clear understanding of AI Builder's licensing model and credit management system. With the knowledge of how to effectively allocate, monitor, and optimize your AI Builder credits, you can implement intelligent automation in a cost-effective manner and deliver substantial return on investment. In the next chapter, we will explore how to extend Power Automate's connectivity beyond its extensive library of built-in connectors by creating custom connectors that integrate with proprietary systems, specialized APIs, and unique business applications. You will learn to build connectors that bridge the gap between Power Automate and any REST-based service, enabling truly comprehensive automation solutions.

Key Takeaways

- AI Builder democratizes artificial intelligence by making it accessible through the familiar Power Automate interface.
- Both prebuilt models and custom models offer valuable capabilities for different business scenarios.
- Effective implementation requires thoughtful planning around model selection, flow design, and error handling.
- AI Builder licensing works on a credit-based consumption model that requires strategic management.
- Real-world applications span document processing, predictive analytics, sentiment analysis, and object detection.
- When properly implemented, AI Builder can deliver substantial ROI through time savings, error reduction, and process improvement.

Additional Resources

Refer to these resources to build your AI Builder expertise further:

- Microsoft Power Platform Licensing Guide: For detailed information on AI Builder credit consumption rates
- AI Builder documentation: https://learn.microsoft.com/en-us/ai-builder/
- Microsoft Power Automate Community: Connect with others implementing AI Builder
- AI Builder samples and templates in the Microsoft Power Platform Center of Excellence
- Microsoft Learn paths for AI Builder certification preparation

The journey to intelligent automation is continuous. With the foundation you have built in this chapter, you are now well-equipped to leverage AI capabilities in your Power Automate solutions. As you go on to explore custom connectors in the next chapter, remember how these capabilities can work together to create comprehensive, connected, and intelligent business solutions.

CHAPTER 14
Building Custom Connectors

Introduction

In a rapidly evolving digital landscape, organizations frequently encounter scenarios where standard connectors fall short of meeting their unique integration requirements. Perhaps you need to connect to an internal line-of-business application, integrate with a niche third-party service, or establish communication with a legacy system that does not offer a pre-built connector. This is where custom connectors in Microsoft Power Automate come in and become a powerful bridge between your cloud workflows and virtually any system with an accessible API.

Throughout our journey so far, we have explored how to leverage the extensive library of standard connectors in Power Automate to create robust workflow solutions. In Chapter 12, we delved into the critical security considerations that protect your automated processes. We have also touched upon fundamental API integration concepts that are the building blocks for more advanced integration scenarios. Now, we are ready to take a significant step forward by creating custom connectors that extend Power Automate's capabilities to match your exact requirements.

Custom connectors represent one of the most powerful features in the Power Automate ecosystem, acting as the gateway between your flows and external systems. They enable you to wrap your API in a Power Automate-friendly interface, making it accessible to both technical and non-technical users across your organization. By the end of this chapter, you will have possessed the knowledge and skills to design, build, implement, and manage custom connectors that seamlessly integrate with your cloud workflows.

Structure

In this chapter, we will explore:

- The Architecture and Fundamental Concepts of Custom Connectors
- OpenAPI (Swagger) Specifications and Their Role in Connector Development
- Authentication Methods and Security Implementations
- Defining and Implementing Actions and Triggers
- Request and Response Handling with Data Transformations
- Testing, Debugging, and Troubleshooting Approaches
- Deployment, Sharing, and Governance Practices
- Integration with Enterprise Systems and Services
- Performance Optimization and Monitoring Strategies

The Architecture and Fundamental Concepts of Custom Connectors

Custom connectors in Power Automate serve as a translation layer between your flows and external APIs. Before diving into the development process, it is essential to understand the architectural components that make up a custom connector and how they interact within the broader Power Automate framework.

The Anatomy of a Custom Connector

A custom connector consists of several key components:

- **OpenAPI Definition:** The foundation of your connector which describes the API's operations, parameters, and responses using the OpenAPI (formerly Swagger) specification
- **Connection Configuration:** Defines how users authenticate with the API, including authentication type, credentials management, and connection parameters
- **Actions and Triggers:** The operations that can be performed, or events that can be monitored through the connector
- **Policies:** Optional rules that modify the behavior of the connector, such as request transformation, response manipulation, or error handling
- **Visibility and Access Controls:** Determine who can use the connector and how it is shared within your organization

These components work together to create a seamless experience for flow creators, abstracting the complexities of direct API integration.

Custom Connectors in the Power Automate Ecosystem

Custom connectors in Power Automate act as a bridge layer that translates API operations into user-friendly actions and triggers within cloud flows, allowing flow creators to interact with external systems without needing to understand the underlying API complexities. This architecture enables organizations to extend Power Automate's native capabilities by wrapping any REST or SOAP API in a reusable connector that can be shared across multiple flows and users within the organization. Custom connectors occupy a unique position in the Power Automate architecture:

```
[Power Automate Cloud Flows] ↔ [Custom Connector] ↔ [External API/Service]
```

Figure 14.1: *Extending Power Automate with Custom Connectors*

The connector acts as a mediator, translating Power Automate's operations into API calls and transforming API responses into a format that Power Automate can process. This architectural approach provides several advantages:

- **Abstraction**: It shields flow creators from the complexities of direct API interaction.
- **Reusability**: Once created, a connector can be used across multiple flows.
- **Governance**: It provides a centralized point for managing API access and security.
- **Discoverability**: It makes your APIs discoverable through the Power Automate connector interface.

Unlocking Integration Possibilities with Custom Connectors

While standard connectors cover a wide range of services, custom connectors become necessary in several scenarios:

- When connecting to internal or proprietary systems
- When integrating with third-party services that don't have standard connectors
- When you need more control over the connection parameters or authentication
- When you want to simplify complex API interactions for non-technical users
- When you need to implement custom business logic at the connector level

Note: *Before building a custom connector, check if your needs can be met using the* HTTP *connector with custom headers and authentication. For simple, one-off* API *calls, this approach might be more efficient than developing a full custom connector.*

Now that we understand the architectural foundations, let us explore the building blocks of custom connectors, starting with the OpenAPI specification.

OpenAPI (Swagger) Specifications and Their Role in Connector Development

The OpenAPI specification (formerly known as Swagger) forms the foundation of custom connector development in Power Automate. This specification provides a standardized way to describe RESTful APIs, making them discoverable and understandable for both humans and machines.

Understanding OpenAPI Basics

OpenAPI is a language-agnostic specification for describing REST APIs. It allows you to define:

- Available endpoints and operations (`GET, POST, PUT, DELETE`, and so on.)
- Operation parameters and their validation rules
- Authentication methods
- Contact information, license, terms of use, and other metadata

An OpenAPI definition can be written in either YAML or JSON format. Here is a simplified example of an OpenAPI specification in JSON:

```
{
  "swagger": "2.0",
  "info": {
    "title": "My Custom API",
    "description": "A custom API for demonstration purposes",
    "version": "1.0"
  },
  "host": "api.example.com",
  "basePath": "/v1",
  "schemes": ["https"],
  "produces": ["application/json"],
  "paths": {
    "/customers": {
      "get": {
        "summary": "Retrieves all customers",
```

```
          "description": "Returns a list of all customers in the system",
          "responses": {
            "200": {
              "description": "Successful operation",
              "schema": {
                "type": "array",
                "items": {
                  "$ref": "#/definitions/Customer"
                }
              }
            }
          }
        }
      }
    },
    "definitions": {
      "Customer": {
        "type": "object",
        "properties": {
          "id": {
            "type": "string"
          },
          "name": {
            "type": "string"
          },
          "email": {
            "type": "string"
          }
        }
      }
    }
  }
```

Creating an OpenAPI Definition for Your Connector

There are several approaches to creating an OpenAPI definition for your custom connector like the following:

- **Generate from an existing API:** If your API already has documentation in a compatible format, you might be able to generate the OpenAPI definition automatically.
- **Create from scratch:** Use tools like the Swagger Editor (https://editor.swagger.io/) to create your definition manually.
- **Import from Power Automate:** Power Automate offers an import wizard that can help you create a connector from an existing OpenAPI definition.
- **Start from a template:** Begin with a template for common API types and customize it for your specific needs.

When creating your OpenAPI definition, consider these best practices:

- **Be thorough in your descriptions:** Clear documentation allows users to understand how to use a connector.
- **Use meaningful operation IDs:** In Power Automate, actions are named as operation IDs, which are clear labels meant for better organization.
- **Define schemas for all request and response objects:** This helps Power Automate understand the data structure.

- **Include examples:** Provide example requests and responses to aid understanding.

OpenAPI Extensions for Power Automate

Power Automate extends the standard OpenAPI specification with additional properties that enhance the connector experience. These extensions, prefixed with x-ms, allow you to customize how your connector appears and behaves within Power Automate.

Key extensions include:

- **`x-ms-summary`:** Provides a user-friendly name for operations, parameters, and properties
- **`x-ms-visibility`:** Controls when and where elements appear in the Power Automate designer
- **`x-ms-dynamicValues`:** Enables dynamic dropdown lists populated by API calls
- **`x-ms-dynamic-schema`:** Defines dynamic schemas based on runtime information

Here is an example of how these extensions might be used:

```
{
  "get": {
    "summary": "Get customer",
    "operationId": "GetCustomer",
    "x-ms-summary": "Get a customer by ID",
    "parameters": [
      {
        "name": "customerId",
        "in": "path",
        "required": true,
        "type": "string",
        "x-ms-summary": "Customer ID",
        "x-ms-visibility": "important",
        "description": "The unique identifier of the customer"
      }
    ]
  }
}
```

Figure 14.2: *OpenAPI Extensions for Custom Connectors in Power Automate*

Note: *Invest time in properly configuring these extensions. They significantly impact the usability of your connector by determining how it appears to end users in the Power Automate designer.*

With the OpenAPI foundation in place, let us explore how to implement authentication for your custom connector.

Authentication Methods and Security Implementations

Authentication is a critical component of any API integration, ensuring that only authorized users can access your services. Power Automate custom connectors support various authentication methods, each with its respective implementation requirements and security implications.

Supported Authentication Types

Power Automate custom connectors support the following authentication types:

- **No Authentication:** The API is publicly accessible without credentials.
- **Basic Authentication:** Uses username and password credentials.
- **API Key:** Requires an API key in the header, query parameter, or body.
- **OAuth 2.0:** Uses token-based authentication with various grant types.
- **OAuth 1.0:** An older token-based authentication protocol.
- **Windows Authentication:** For on-premises data gateway connections.
- **Custom Authentication:** For specialized authentication scenarios.

Let us compare these authentication methods:

Comparison of Authentication Methods by Security, Complexity, and Use Case

Understanding the trade-offs between different authentication methods is essential when designing custom connectors in Power Automate, as your choice directly impacts both the security of your integrations and the ease with which users can create connections to your API. The following comparison helps you select the most appropriate authentication approach based on your specific security requirements, technical capabilities, and the intended use case within your organization's Power Automate environment.

Authentication Type	**Security Level**	**Implementation Complexity**	**Best Used For**
No Authentication	Low	Simple	Public APIs, testing
Basic Authentication	Medium	Simple	Internal APIs with limited exposure
API Key	Medium	Simple	Partner APIs, controlled access
OAuth 2.0	High	Complex	Enterprise applications, third-party services
OAuth 1.0	High	Complex	Legacy systems requiring secure authentication
Windows Authentication	High	Complex	On-premises systems in Active Directory environments
Custom Authentication	Varies	Complex	Specialized security requirements

Table 14.1: *Authentication Methods Comparison*

Implementing OAuth 2.0 Authentication

OAuth 2.0 is the most common authentication protocol for modern APIs, offering a secure way to grant limited access to user accounts on third-party services. Implementing OAuth 2.0 in your custom connector involves several steps such as:

1. **Register your application** with the OAuth provider to obtain client credentials.
2. **Configure authentication settings** in the OpenAPI definition as shown in the figure:

```
{
  "securityDefinitions": {
    "oauth2_auth": {
      "type": "oauth2",
      "flow": "accessCode",
      "authorizationUrl": "https://auth.example.com/oauth2/authorize",
      "tokenUrl": "https://auth.example.com/oauth2/token",
      "scopes": {
        "read": "Read access to the API",
        "write": "Write access to the API"
      }
    }
  }
}
```

Figure 14.3: *Configuring Authentication Settings in the OpenAPI Specification*

3. **Apply security requirements** to operations:

```
{
  "paths": {
    "/resource": {
      "get": {
        "security": [
          {
            "oauth2_auth": ["read"]
          }
        ],
        "responses": {
          "200": {
            "description": "Success"
          }
        }
      }
    }
  }
}
```

Figure 14.4: *Applying Security Requirements to OpenAPI Operations*

4. **Configure OAuth settings** in the Power Automate custom connector wizard:
   a. Client ID and Secret
   b. Authorization and Token URLs
   c. Scope requirements

d. Identity provider settings

API Key Authentication Implementation

API key authentication is simpler to implement and commonly used for service-to-service communication. Here is how to configure it:

1. **Define security scheme** in the OpenAPI specification:

```
{
  "securityDefinitions": {
    "api_key": {
      "type": "apiKey",
      "name": "X-API-Key",
      "in": "header"
    }
  }
}
```

Figure 14.5: *Defining Security Schemes in the OpenAPI Specification*

2. **Apply security requirements** to operations:

```
{
  "paths": {
    "/resource": {
      "get": {
        "security": [
          {
            "api_key": []
          }
        ],
        "responses": {
          "200": {
            "description": "Success"
          }
        }
      }
    }
  }
}
```

Figure 14.6: *Applying Security Requirements to Individual Operations in OpenAPI*

3. **Configure in Power Automate** by specifying:

   a. Parameter name (for instance, "X-API-Key")

b. Parameter location (header, query, or body)

Security Best Practices for Custom Connectors

When implementing authentication for your custom connectors, follow these security best practices:

- **Use HTTPS exclusively** for all API communication.
- **Implement proper scope restrictions** for OAuth to limit access to necessary resources.
- **Rotate credentials regularly**, especially for API keys.
- **Store sensitive values as parameters** rather than hardcoding them.
- **Implement IP restrictions** where appropriate to limit access to trusted networks.
- **Monitor authentication failures** to detect potential security incidents.
- **Apply the principle of least privilege** when defining connector permissions.

Note: *Avoid using Basic Authentication for public-facing* APIs, *as it transmits credentials that could be intercepted. Always prefer token-based authentication methods like* OAuth 2.0 *for external access.*

With authentication in place, let us move on to defining the operations that users can perform through your custom connector.

Defining and Implementing Actions and Triggers

Actions and triggers form the interactive interface of your custom connector, allowing users to interact with your API through Power Automate flows. Well-designed actions and triggers can significantly enhance the usability of your connector.

Understanding Actions vs. Triggers

Before diving into implementation, it is important to understand the distinction between actions and triggers:

- **Actions** are operations that a flow can perform, such as retrieving data, creating records, or updating information. They are executed when the flow reaches that step.
- **Triggers** initiate a flow when a specific event occurs. They can be:
  - **Polling triggers**: Periodically check for new data or events
  - **Webhook triggers**: Receive push notifications when events occur
  - **Push triggers**: Similar to webhooks but specifically for Power Automate

Defining Actions in OpenAPI

Actions are defined as operations within the paths section of your OpenAPI specification. Each HTTP method (GET, POST, PUT, DELETE, and so on.) represents a potential action:

```
{
  "paths": {
    "/customers": {
      "get": {
        "summary": "Get all customers",
        "operationId": "Gand so onustomers",
        "x-ms-summary": "Get all customers",
        "responses": {
```

```
            "200": {
              "description": "OK",
              "schema": {
                "type": "array",
                "items": {
                  "$ref": "#/definitions/Customer"
                }
              }
            }
          }
        },
        "post": {
          "summary": "Create a customer",
          "operationId": "CreateCustomer",
          "x-ms-summary": "Create a new customer",
          "parameters": [
            {
              "name": "customer",
              "in": "body",
              "required": true,
              "schema": {
                "$ref": "#/definitions/CustomerCreate"
              },
              "x-ms-summary": "Customer information"
            }
          ],
          "responses": {
            "201": {
              "description": "Created",
              "schema": {
                "$ref": "#/definitions/Customer"
              }
            }
          }
        }
      }
    }
  }
```

Here are the key elements to consider when defining actions:

- **operationId:** Becomes the action name in Power Automate
- **x-ms-summary:** Provides a user-friendly description
- **parameters:** Define the inputs required for the action
- **responses:** Specify the expected output structure

Implementing Triggers

Implementing triggers requires additional configuration beyond standard OpenAPI operations. Power Automate supports two main types of triggers in custom connectors:

Polling Triggers

Polling triggers periodically check for new data. They are defined using the x-ms-trigger extension with the type set to polling:

```
{
  "paths": {
    "/customers/recent": {
      "get": {
        "summary": "When a new customer is added",
        "operationId": "OnNewCustomer",
        "x-ms-summary": "When a new customer is added",
        "x-ms-trigger": {
          "type": "polling",
          "kind": "internal"
        },
        "parameters": [
          {
            "name": "since",
            "in": "query",
            "required": true,
            "type": "string",
            "x-ms-summary": "Since",
            "x-ms-trigger-metadata": "timestamp"
          }
        ],
        "responses": {
          "200": {
            "schema": {
              "type": "array",
              "items": {
                "$ref": "#/definitions/Customer"
              }
            }
          }
        }
      }
    }
  }
}
```

The x-ms-trigger-metadata extension with a value of "**timestamp**" indicates that this parameter will be automatically managed by Power Automate to track the last poll time.

Webhook Triggers

Webhook triggers receive push notifications when events occur. They require registration and callback endpoints:

```
{
  "paths": {
    "/webhooks/register": {
      "post": {
        "summary": "When a customer is updated",
        "operationId": "OnCustomerUpdated",
        "x-ms-summary": "When a customer is updated",
        "x-ms-trigger": {
          "type": "webhook",
          "kind": "internal"
        },
        "parameters": [
          {
            "name": "callbackUrl",
```

```
        "in": "body",
        "required": true,
        "schema": {
          "type": "object",
          "properties": {
            "callbackUrl": {
              "type": "string",
              "title": "Callback URL"
            }
          },
          "required": ["callbackUrl"]
        },
        "x-ms-visibility": "internal",
        "x-ms-summary": "Callback URL"
      }
    ],
    "responses": {
      "200": {
        "schema": {
          "type": "object",
          "properties": {
            "subscriptionId": {
              "type": "string"
            }
          }
        }
      }
    }
  }
},
"/webhooks/unregister": {
  "post": {
    "summary": "Unregister webhook",
    "operationId": "UnregisterWebhook",
    "x-ms-visibility": "internal",
    "parameters": [
      {
        "name": "subscription",
        "in": "body",
        "required": true,
        "schema": {
          "type": "object",
          "properties": {
            "subscriptionId": {
              "type": "string"
            }
          ],
          "required": ["subscriptionId"]
        }
      }
    ],
    "responses": {
      "200": {
        "description": "Webhook unregistered"
      }
    }
  }
```

```
    }
  }
}
```

Best Practices for Action and Trigger Design

When designing actions and triggers for your custom connector, consider these best practices:

- **Use descriptive names** that clearly indicate the purpose of each action or trigger.
- **Group related operations** logically to create a natural navigation flow.
- **Provide comprehensive parameter descriptions** to guide users.
- **Use appropriate visibility settings** to hide complex or rarely used parameters.
- **Implement paging for large result sets** to improve performance.
- **Include error handling** with meaningful error messages.
- **Use dynamic content** where appropriate to enhance the user experience.

Note: *Design your connector's actions and triggers from the perspective of a Power Automate user who may not understand the underlying API. Focus on creating intuitive, self-explanatory operations.*

Now that we have defined the operations of our custom connector, let us explore how to handle the data flowing through these operations.

Request and Response Handling with Data Transformations

Effective request and response handling is crucial for ensuring smooth data flow between Power Automate and your API. This section covers request formatting, response parsing, data transformations, and error handling.

Request Formatting and Validation

When a user triggers an action in Power Automate, the connector needs to format the request correctly for your API. This involves:

- **Parameter Mapping:** Translating user inputs to API parameters
- **Data Type Conversion:** Ensuring data types match what the API expects
- **Request Validation:** Checking that all required fields are provided and valid

In your OpenAPI definition, you can specify validation rules using JSON Schema:

```
{
  "parameters": [
    {
      "name": "customer",
      "in": "body",
      "required": true,
      "schema": {
        "type": "object",
        "properties": {
          "name": {
            "type": "string",
            "minLength": 1,
            "maxLength": 100
          },
```

```
          "email": {
            "type": "string",
            "format": "email"
          },
          "age": {
            "type": "integer",
            "minimum": 18
          }
        },
        "required": ["name", "email"]
      }
    }
  ]
}
```

For complex validation scenarios, you can implement custom policies (which are discussed later in this chapter) to perform additional validation logic.

Response Parsing and Transformation

After your API processes a request, the connector needs to parse the response and present it in a format that Power Automate can understand. This typically involves:

- **Status Code Handling:** Interpreting different HTTP status codes
- **Response Structure Parsing:** Extracting relevant data from the response
- **Data Transformation:** Converting API-specific formats to Power Automate formats

In your OpenAPI definition, define the expected response structure:

```
{
  "responses": {
    "200": {
      "description": "Success",
      "schema": {
        "type": "object",
        "properties": {
          "id": {
            "type": "string",
            "x-ms-summary": "Customer ID"
          },
          "name": {
            "type": "string",
            "x-ms-summary": "Name"
          },
          "registrationDate": {
            "type": "string",
            "format": "date-time",
            "x-ms-summary": "Registration Date"
          }
        }
      }
    },
    "404": {
      "description": "Customer not found"
    }
  }
}
```

Data Transformation Techniques

Sometimes, your API's data format does not match what is expected in Power Automate. In these cases, you can use several transformation techniques:

- **Template Parameters**: Use template expressions to format string parameters:

```
{
  "parameters": [
    {
      "name": "formattedDate",
      "in": "query",
      "required": true,
      "type": "string",
      "x-ms-summary": "Date",
      "description": "Format: YYYY-MM-DD",
      "x-ms-template-parameter": {
        "template": "{{timestamp:yyyy-MM-dd}}"
      }
    }
  ]
}
```

- **Response Transform Policies**: Implement policies that transform the response before it reaches Power Automate.
- **Custom Code in Flows**: For complex transformations, you can use Power Automate's built-in data operations or Azure Functions.

Error Handling and Retry Logic

Robust error handling is essential for creating reliable connectors. Power Automate custom connectors should handle errors gracefully by:

- **Providing meaningful error messages** that help users understand and resolve issues.
- **Implementing retry logic** for transient errors.
- **Differentiating between client errors (4xx) and server errors (5xx)**.

In your OpenAPI definition, define common error responses:

```
{
  "responses": {
    "400": {
      "description": "Bad request",
      "schema": {
        "type": "object",
        "properties": {
          "errorCode": {
            "type": "string"
          },
          "message": {
            "type": "string"
          },
          "details": {
            "type": "array",
            "items": {
              "type": "string"
            }
          }
```

```
            }
          }
        },
        "401": {
          "description": "Unauthorized"
        },
        "429": {
          "description": "Too many requests"
        },
        "500": {
          "description": "Internal server error"
        }
      }
    }
```

For advanced error handling, you can implement custom policies that:

- Detect specific error conditions
- Transform error responses into a consistent format
- Implement retry strategies for transient errors
- Log detailed error information for troubleshooting

Note: *Avoid exposing sensitive information in error messages. Ensure that error responses contain enough information to be helpful without revealing implementation details or security vulnerabilities.*

Now that we understand how to handle data flow in custom connectors, let us explore how to implement custom behaviors through policies.

Advanced Features: Policies and Templates

Policies allow you to extend and customize the behavior of your connector beyond what is possible with the standard OpenAPI definition. They enable you to implement advanced features such as request transformation, response manipulation, and complex business logic.

Understanding Connector Policies

Policies in Power Automate custom connectors are XML snippets that modify the behavior of your connector at runtime. They can be applied at different scopes such as:

- **Global:** Applied to all operations
- **Operation:** Applied to a specific operation
- **Request:** Applied to the outgoing request
- **Response:** Applied to the incoming response

Common policy use cases include:

- Transforming request formats
- Modifying response structures
- Implementing rate limiting
- Adding or removing headers
- Implementing caching
- Custom authentication logic
- Error handling and retry logic

Implementing Common Policy Templates

Power Automate provides several policy templates that you can customize for your connector:

Request Transformation Policy

This policy transforms the structure of the request before it reaches your API:

```
<policies>
  <inbound>
    <base />
    <set-body template="liquid">
      {
        "customerData": {
          "fullName": "{{body.firstName}} {{body.lastName}}",
          "contactInfo": {
            "emailAddress": "{{body.email}}",
            "phoneNumber": "{{body.phone}}"
          }
        }
      }
    </set-body>
  </inbound>
</policies>
```

Response Transformation Policy

This policy transforms the API response before it returns to Power Automate:

```
<policies>
  <outbound>
    <base />
    <json-to-xml apply="always" consider-accept-header="false" />
  </outbound>
</policies>
```

Caching Policy

This policy implements response caching to improve performance:

```
<policies>
  <inbound>
    <base />
    <cache-lookup vary-by-developer="false" vary-by-developer-groups="false">
      <vary-by-header>Accept</vary-by-header>
      <vary-by-header>Accept-Charset</vary-by-header>
    </cache-lookup>
  </inbound>
  <outbound>
    <base />
    <cache-store duration="3600" />
  </outbound>
</policies>
```

Creating Custom Policy Templates

For advanced scenarios, you can create custom policy templates tailored to your specific requirements via the following steps:

1. **Identify the requirement** that cannot be addressed through the OpenAPI definition.
2. **Determine the appropriate policy scope** (global, operation, request, or response).
3. **Create the policy XML** using available policy expressions and functions.
4. **Test the policy** thoroughly to ensure it behaves as expected.

Here is an example of a custom policy that implements token refresh logic:

```
<policies>
  <inbound>
    <base />
    <choose>
      <when condition="@(context.Variables.GetValueOrDefault<string>
("tokenExpired") == "true")">
        <send-request mode="new" response-variable-name="tokenResponse"
timeout="30" ignore-error="false">
          <set-url>https://auth.example.com/token/refresh</set-url>
          <set-method>POST</set-method>
          <set-body>@{
            return $"refresh_token={(string)context.Variables
["refreshToken"]}";
          }</set-body>
        </send-request>
        <set-variable name="newToken" value="@{
          var response = ((IResponse)context.Variables["tokenResponse"]).Body.
As<JObject>();
          return response.Value<string>("access_token");
        }" />
        <set-header name="Authorization" exists-action="override">
          <value>Bearer @((string)context.Variables["newToken"])</value>
        </set-header>
      </when>
    </choose>
  </inbound>
</policies>
```

Policy Testing and Debugging

Testing policies can be challenging due to their runtime nature. Here are some approaches for effective policy testing:

- **Incremental Testing**: Implement and test one policy at a time.
- **Diagnostic Logging**: Use trace policies to log diagnostic information:

```
<policies>
  <inbound>
    <base />
    <trace source="Custom Connector" severity="information">
      <message>@{
        return $"Processing request for operation: {context.Operation.Name}";
      }</message>
      <metadata name="Request Body" value="@(context.Request.Body.
```

```
As<string>())" />
    </trace>
  </inbound>
</policies>
```

- **Mock Responses:** Use mock responses for testing complex logic just like in the following example:

```
<policies>
  <inbound>
    <base />
    <mock-response status-code="200" content-type="application/json">
      {
        "id": "test-id",
        "name": "Test Customer",
        "status": "Active"
      }
    </mock-response>
  </inbound>
</policies>
```

Note: *When developing complex policies, start with a simplified version and gradually add functionality. This incremental approach makes it easier to identify and fix issues.*

With advanced features implemented through policies, let us now focus on testing and debugging your custom connector.

Testing, debugging, and troubleshooting approaches

Thorough testing is essential for ensuring that your custom connector functions correctly and provides a good user experience. This section covers testing approaches, debugging techniques, and tools for verifying connector behavior.

Testing Approaches

Effective testing of custom connectors involves multiple approaches:

Manual Testing in the Custom Connector Designer

The Power Automate custom connector designer provides a built-in test console that allows you to:

- **Test individual operations** with sample input values.
- **Verify authentication** is working correctly.
- **Inspect request and response details** including headers, body, and status code.
- **Identify and diagnose errors** in real-time.

Steps for using the test console:

1. Open your custom connector in edit mode.
2. Navigate to the "`Test`" tab.
3. Create a new connection or select an existing one.
4. Select the operation you want to test.

5. Provide sample values for all required parameters.
6. Click "`Test operation`" and review the results.

Integration Testing with Test Flows

While the test console is useful for individual operations, it is also important to test your connector in the context of actual flows:

- **Create a dedicated test flow** that uses your custom connector.
- **Include typical usage patterns** that represent real-world scenarios.
- **Test with various inputs**, including edge cases and potential error conditions.
- **Verify the flow results** match your expectations.
- **Monitor run history** to identify any issues or unexpected behavior.

Automated Testing

For enterprise-grade connectors, consider implementing automated testing:

- **Create a test suite** using tools such as Postman or Microsoft's PowerApps CLI.
- **Automate test execution** as part of your development pipeline.
- **Implement regression tests** to ensure changes don't break existing functionality.
- **Generate test coverage reports** to identify untested operations or scenarios.

Debugging Techniques

When issues arise, several debugging techniques can help identify and resolve them:

Connector Request/Response Inspection

The most basic debugging approach is to inspect the raw request and response:

1. Use the test console to capture request and response details.
2. Examine request headers, URL, and body to ensure they're formatted correctly.
3. Check response status codes, headers, and body for error information.
4. Compare the actual request with the expected API format.

Flow Run History Analysis

Flow run history provides valuable debugging information:

1. Navigate to the flow containing your custom connector action.
2. Open the run history and select a specific run.
3. Expand the connector action to view inputs, outputs, and duration.
4. Look for error messages or unexpected values.

Diagnostic Logging

Implement diagnostic logging in your API to capture detailed information:

1. Add correlation IDs to track requests across systems.
2. Log request details, including headers and parameters.

3. Record processing steps and intermediate states.
4. Capture detailed error information, including stack traces.

Using API Monitoring Tools

External API monitoring tools can provide additional insights such as:

- **API Gateways**: Tools such as Azure API Management offer detailed monitoring.
- **Network Analyzers**: Tools such as Fiddler or Wireshark can capture network traffic.
- **Log Analytics**: Platforms such as Azure Monitor or Application Insights provide advanced log analysis.

Note: *When troubleshooting connector issues, start by verifying that the API works correctly outside of Power Automate. Use tools like Postman or curl to send requests directly to the API, then compare these results with what you see in the connector.*

Common Issues and Solutions

Several common issues can arise when developing custom connectors:

Authentication Problems

Symptoms:

- "Unauthorized" or "Forbidden" responses
- Authentication tokens not being accepted
- Credentials being rejected

Solutions:

- Verify client ID, client secret, and other credentials.
- Check token expiration and refresh mechanics.
- Ensure correct scopes are requested.
- Confirm redirect URLs match the registered values.

Schema Mismatches

Symptoms:

- "Bad Request" responses
- Missing or incorrect data in responses
- Type conversion errors

Solutions:

- Compare API documentation with your OpenAPI definition.
- Validate request and response examples against schemas.
- Use policies to transform incompatible formats.
- Implement proper type conversions.

Performance Issues

Symptoms:

- Slow connector response times
- Timeouts during operation execution

- High resource utilization

Solutions:

- Implement caching for frequently accessed data.
- Optimize API performance.
- Use batch operations where appropriate.
- Monitor and tune connector behavior.

Visibility and Organization Issues

Symptoms:

- Cluttered connector interface
- Difficulty finding or using operations
- Confusing parameter names or descriptions

Solutions:

- Use descriptive operation and parameter names.
- Organize operations logically.
- Apply appropriate visibility settings.
- Provide clear documentation and examples.

Hands-on Exercise: Debugging a Custom Connector

1. Create a simple custom connector for a test API (or use a public API like JSONPlaceholder).
2. Deliberately introduce an error in the OpenAPI definition (for instance, incorrect parameter name).
3. Test the connector and observe the error behavior.
4. Use the debugging techniques discussed above to identify the issue.
5. Fix the problem and verify that the connector now works correctly.

With testing and debugging covered, let us now explore how to deploy and share your custom connector.

Deployment, sharing, and governance practices

Creating a functional custom connector is only part of the journey. To maximize its value, you need to deploy it effectively, share it with the right users, and establish governance practices that ensure its ongoing management and security.

Deployment Approaches

There are several approaches to deploying custom connectors in Power Automate:

Manual Deployment

The simplest approach is manual deployment through the Power Automate portal:

1. Create the connector in the target environment.
2. Configure authentication and other settings.

3. Test the connector to ensure it functions correctly.
4. Share the connector with appropriate users or groups.

This approach works well for simple connectors or small teams but becomes cumbersome for complex enterprise scenarios.

Solution-Based Deployment

For more structured deployment, use solutions:

1. Create a solution in the source environment.
2. Add your custom connector to the solution.
3. Export the solution as managed or unmanaged.
4. Import the solution into the target environment.

Solution-based deployment offers several advantages:

- Packages related components together
- Supports versioning and updates
- Enables environment-specific configurations
- Provides deployment history and tracking

Automated Deployment with DevOps

For enterprise scenarios, implement a DevOps approach:

- **Source Control**: Store your OpenAPI definitions and related artifacts in a git repository.
- **CI/CD Pipeline**: Automate building, testing, and deployment.
- **Environment Management**: Define development, testing, and production environments.
- **Automated Testing**: Include automated tests in your deployment pipeline.
- **Monitoring**: Implement monitoring to detect deployment issues.

Note: *While implementing a DevOps approach, separate the connector's configuration from its implementation. Use environment variables or configuration files to manage environment-specific settings like endpoint URLs or authentication details.*

Sharing and Access Control

Controlling who can use your custom connector is essential for security and governance:

Sharing Options

Power Automate offers several options for sharing custom connectors:

- **User-Level Sharing**: Share with specific users.
- **Security Group Sharing**: Share with Azure AD security groups.
- **Environment-Wide Sharing**: Make available to all users in an environment.
- **Solution Sharing**: Include in a solution shared with specific users or groups.

Connection Management

Users who have access to your connector will need to create connections to use it:

- **Connection Credentials**: Determine who provides and manages authentication credentials.
- **Connection Policies**: Define who can create and use connections.
- **Connection Monitoring**: Track who is using the connector and how.

Data Loss Prevention (DLP) Policies

Implement DLP policies to control how your connector interacts with other services:

- **Classification:** Categorize your connector based on data sensitivity.
- **Policy Application:** Apply appropriate DLP policies to environments.
- **Monitoring:** Track policy violations and exceptions.

Versioning and Lifecycle Management

Managing the lifecycle of your custom connector ensures its continued reliability and relevance:

Versioning Strategies

Several versioning approaches can be used:

- **Solution Versioning**: Increment solution version with each significant update.
- **API Versioning**: Support multiple API versions in the same connector.
- **Separate Connectors**: Create distinct connectors for major versions.

When planning your versioning strategy, consider:

- Backward compatibility requirements
- Impact on existing flows
- Communication with users
- Transition periods for migration

Update Management

Establish a process for managing updates:

- **Change Communication**: Inform users about upcoming changes.
- **Testing**: Thoroughly test updates before deployment.
- **Rollback Plan**: Prepare for potential issues post-deployment.
- **Impact Analysis**: Assess how changes affect existing flows.

Deprecation and Retirement

Eventually, some connectors or connector versions will need to be retired:

- **Deprecation Notice**: Provide advance warning of retirement.
- **Alternative Recommendations**: Suggest replacement options.
- **Migration Support**: Help users transition to new solutions.
- **Grace Period**: Allow time for users to update their flows.

Governance Best Practices

Implement these governance practices to maintain control over your custom connectors:

- **Documentation**: Maintain comprehensive documentation, including:
  - Purpose and functional overview
  - Authentication requirements
  - Operation details and examples
  - Error handling guidance
  - Security considerations
- **Monitoring**: Implement monitoring for:
  - Usage patterns and trends
  - Performance metrics
  - Error rates and types
  - Authentication failures
  - Resource utilization
- **Audit and Compliance**: Establish audit procedures:
  - Regular security reviews
  - Compliance checks
  - Access control verification
  - Configuration validation
- **Support Process**: Define how users can get help:
  - Issue reporting channels
  - Troubleshooting guidance
  - Feature request handling
  - SLAs for response and resolution

Real-world Challenge: Enterprise Connector Governance

Imagine you are implementing a custom connector for a critical internal API that processes sensitive customer data. Design a governance framework that addresses:

- How will you control who can use the connector?
- What security reviews should be performed before deployment?
- How will you monitor usage and detect potential issues?
- What process will you establish for updates and changes?
- How will you ensure compliance with data protection regulations?

Next, let us explore integration with enterprise systems and services to expand the capabilities of your custom connectors.

Integration with enterprise systems and services

Custom connectors become even more powerful when they are integrated with enterprise systems and services. This section explores how to integrate your connectors with various enterprise components to get the best out of them.

Azure API Management Integration

Azure API Management (APIM) provides a comprehensive platform for publishing, securing, transforming, maintaining, and monitoring APIs. Integrating your custom connector with APIM offers several benefits like:

Importing APIs from Azure API Management

Power Automate can import APIs directly from Azure API Management:

1. In Power Automate, create a new custom connector.
2. Select "`Import from Azure API Management service.`"
3. Choose your subscription, resource group, service, and API.
4. Configure connector settings and complete the import.

This approach leverages your existing API management infrastructure while making the API available through Power Automate.

Advanced API Features for Connectors

Azure API Management provides additional capabilities that enhance custom connectors:

- **API Versioning**: Manage multiple versions of your API.
- **Access Control**: Implement fine-grained access control with API keys or OAuth.
- **Request/Response Transformation**: Modify requests and responses using policies.
- **Monitoring and Analytics**: Track API usage, performance, and errors.
- **Developer Portal**: Provide documentation and interactive testing.

Note: *Use Azure API Management for complex APIs with multiple consumers beyond Power Automate. This approach provides a centralized management point while allowing Power Automate users to access the API through a custom connector.*

Identity Provider Integration

Integrating with enterprise identity providers ensures secure authentication for your custom connectors:

Azure Active Directory Integration

Azure AD is commonly used for enterprise authentication and has the following capabilities to support it:

- **App Registration**: Register your connector in Azure AD.
- **Permission Configuration**: Define required permissions and scopes.
- **Consent Management**: Handle admin consent for organizational permissions.
- **Token Validation**: Validate tokens and claims in your API.

Other Identity Providers

For non-Microsoft identity providers, here are a few supporting capabilities for enterprise authentication:

- **OAuth Configuration**: Sets up OAuth 2.0 integration with providers like Okta, Auth0, or Ping Identity.
- **Federation**: Establishes trust relationships between identity providers.
- **Token Exchange**: Implements token exchange for cross-provider scenarios.
- **Claims Mapping**: Maps external identity claims to your API's authorization model.

Integration with enterprise systems and services

Many organizations need to connect Power Automate to on-premises systems:

On-Premises Data Gateway

The On-Premises Data Gateway enables secure communication with on-premises resources:

- **Gateway Installation**: Install the gateway in your on-premises environment.
- **Gateway Registration**: Register the gateway with Power Automate.
- **Connector Configuration**: Configure your custom connector to use the gateway.
- **Authentication**: Set up Windows Authentication or other authentication methods.

Here are some key considerations for gateway integration:

- Network configuration and firewall rules
- High availability and redundancy
- Monitoring and management
- Security and access control

Hybrid Connection Scenarios

For complex hybrid scenarios:

- **API Proxies**: Use on-premises API gateways as intermediaries.
- **Relay Services**: Implement Azure Relay or similar services.
- **VPN/ExpressRoute**: Establish direct network connectivity.
- **Message Queues**: Use queuing mechanisms for asynchronous communication.

Integration with Security Services

Enterprise security services help protect your custom connectors and the data they handle:

Azure Security Center Integration

Azure Security Center can monitor and protect your connector infrastructure:

- **Vulnerability Assessment**: Identify security vulnerabilities.
- **Threat Protection**: Detects and responds to threats.
- **Compliance Monitoring**: Ensure compliance with security standards.
- **Security Recommendations**: Receive actionable security guidance.

Key Vault Integration

Azure Key Vault securely stores and manages sensitive information via:

- **Credential Storage**: Store API keys, certificates, and secrets.
- **Key Rotation**: Implement automatic key rotation.
- **Access Control**: Control who can access secrets.
- **Audit Logging**: Track secret access and usage.

Implementation example for Key Vault integration:

```
// Example backend code for retrieving a secret from Key Vault
var keyVaultName = Environment.GetEnvironmentVariable("KeyVaultName");
var kvUri = $"https://{keyVaultName}.vault.azure.net";
var client = new Secrand so onlient(new Uri(kvUri), new DefaultAzure
Credential());
KeyVaultSecret secret = await client.GetSecretAsync("ApiKey");
string apiKey = secret.Value;
```

Note: *Never hardcode secrets or credentials in your connector definitions or policies. Always use secure storage solutions like Azure Key Vault and reference the secrets dynamically.*

Enterprise Integration Patterns

Apply these enterprise integration patterns to enhance your custom connectors:

- **Message Transformation**: Convert message formats between systems.
- **Content-Based Routing**: Direct messages based on content.
- **Scatter-Gather**: Distribute requests and aggregate responses.
- **Circuit Breaker**: Prevent cascading failures during API issues.
- **Retry with Exponential Backoff**: Intelligently handle transient failures.
- **Idempotent Receiver**: Ensure duplicate messages are handled correctly.

Hands-on Exercise: Enterprise Integration

In this exercise, you will integrate a custom connector with Azure API Management and Azure AD:

1. Create a simple API in Azure API Management.
2. Register an application in Azure AD for authentication.
3. Configure the API to use Azure AD authentication.
4. Create a custom connector in Power Automate that imports from APIM.
5. Test the connector with Azure AD authentication.

With enterprise integration covered, let us turn our attention to performance optimization and monitoring.

Performance Optimization and Monitoring Strategies

Performance is critical for custom connectors, especially in enterprise environments. This section explores techniques for optimizing connector performance, monitoring behavior, and troubleshooting issues.

Performance Optimization Techniques

Several techniques can improve the performance of your custom connectors.

API Design Optimization

Start with optimizing the underlying API in these ways:

- **Efficient Endpoints**: Design endpoints that return exactly what is needed.
- **Pagination**: Implement pagination for large result sets.
- **Filtering**: Support server-side filtering to reduce data transfer.
- **Projection**: Allow clients to specify which fields to return.
- **Compression**: Enable response compression to reduce bandwidth usage.

Connector Configuration Optimization

Optimize your connector configuration for performance via the following measures:

- **Streamlined Schemas**: Define precise schemas that avoid unnecessary properties.
- **Appropriate Data Types**: Use the most efficient data types for your parameters.
- **Operation Design**: Structure operations to minimize the number of API calls needed.
- **Default Values**: Provide sensible defaults to reduce user input requirements.

Caching Strategies

Implement caching to reduce API calls and improve response times:

- **Response Caching**: Cache API responses for frequently accessed data
- **Token Caching**: Cache authentication tokens to reduce authentication overhead
- **Metadata Caching**: Cache schema and metadata information
- **Configuration Caching**: Cache connector configuration details

Example caching policy:

```
<policies>
  <inbound>
    <base />
    <cache-lookup vary-by-developer="false" vary-by-developer-groups="false">
      <vary-by-query-parameter>category</vary-by-query-parameter>
      <vary-by-header>Accept</vary-by-header>
    </cache-lookup>
  </inbound>
  <outbound>
    <base />
    <cache-store duration="3600" />
  </outbound>
</policies>
```

Batch Processing

Implement batch operations for scenarios involving multiple items:

- **Batch Requests**: Allow multiple operations in a single request.
- **Bulk Data Transfer**: Optimize for transferring large amounts of data.

- **Asynchronous Processing**: Use asynchronous patterns for long-running operations.

Monitoring and Analytics

Effective monitoring helps you understand connector usage and identify potential issues.

Key Metrics to Monitor

Focus on these key metrics:

- **Usage Metrics:**
    - Number of calls per operation
    - Number of distinct users
    - Call frequency patterns
    - Peak usage times
- **Performance Metrics:**
    - Response times (average, minimum, maximum)
    - Throughput (requests per second)
    - Resource utilization
    - Latency breakdown (network, processing, authentication)
- **Error Metrics:**
    - Error rates by operation
    - Error types and distribution
    - Authentication failures
    - Timeout occurrences
- **Compliance Metrics:**
    - Data access patterns
    - Regulatory compliance status
    - Security policy adherence
    - Data residency conformance

Monitoring Tools and Approaches

Several tools and approaches like the following can help you monitor your custom connectors:

- **Azure Monitor**: For connectors hosted in Azure
- **Application Insights**: For detailed application telemetry
- **Power Platform Analytics**: For Power Automate-specific metrics
- **Azure API Management Analytics**: For APIs managed through APIM
- **Custom Telemetry**: For specialized monitoring requirements

Implementation example for custom telemetry:

```
// Example backend code for tracking custom telemetry
public async Task<IActionResult> ProcessRequest()
{
    var stopwatch = Stopwatch.StartNew();
    try
```

```
        {
            // Process the request
            var result = await _service.ProcessAsync(request);

            // Track successful operation
            _telemetry.TrackEvent("OperationSuccess",
                new Dictionary<string, string>
                {
                    { "OperationName", "Gand so onustomerData" },
                    { "UserId", GetUserId() }
                },
                new Dictionary<string, double>
                {
                    { "ProcessingTime", stopwatch.ElapsedMilliseconds }
                });

            return Ok(result);
        }
        catch (Exception ex)
        {
            // Track operation failure
            _telemetry.TrackException(ex,
                new Dictionary<string, string>
                {
                    { "OperationName", "Gand so onustomerData" },
                    { "UserId", GetUserId() }
                });
            return StatusCode(500, "An error occurred");
        }
    }
```

Troubleshooting Performance Issues

When performance issues arise, follow this structured approach to troubleshooting:

- **Identify the Problem:**
    - Which operations are affected?
    - Is the issue consistent or intermittent?
    - Are there patterns related to time, load, or specific users?
    - What changed before the issue began?
- **Isolate the Cause**:
    - Is it the API backend?
    - Is it the connector configuration?
    - Is it related to authentication?
    - Is it related to network conditions?
    - Is it related to specific data or parameters?
- **Implement Solutions**
    - Optimize API performance.
    - Implement or tune caching.
    - Revise connector configuration.
    - Adjust timeouts and retry policies.

    - Scale underlying infrastructure.
    - Implement asynchronous processing.
- **Verify the Resolution**
    - Monitor performance after changes.
    - Test under various load conditions.
    - Collect user feedback.
    - Document the solution for future reference.

Note: *Create a performance baseline when your connector is functioning well. This baseline provides a comparison point when troubleshooting performance issues later.*

Performance Testing

Proactive performance testing helps prevent issues before they affect users:

- **Load Testing**: Simulate multiple concurrent users to identify bottlenecks.
- **Stress Testing**: Push the system beyond normal capacity to find breaking points.
- **Endurance Testing**: Run tests over extended periods to detect memory leaks or gradual degradation.
- **Spike Testing**: Introduce sudden increases in load to test system resilience.

For each test type, establish clear performance targets and acceptance criteria based on your organization's requirements.

Think about It: What performance metrics are the most important for your custom connector? How will you monitor them? What thresholds can trigger alerts or intervention?

Now that we have covered all aspects of custom connector development, we will conclude with best practices and a look toward the future.

Best Practices and Future Directions

As we conclude our exploration of custom connectors in Microsoft Power Automate, let us summarize best practices and consider future directions in the connector ecosystem.

Custom Connector Best Practices

Apply these best practices to create robust, secure, and user-friendly custom connectors:

Design Best Practices

- **Start with the User Experience**: Design your connector from the perspective of flow creators.
- **Follow Naming Conventions**: Use clear, consistent names for operations and parameters.
- **Provide Comprehensive Documentation**: Include detailed descriptions, examples, and use cases.
- **Support Progressive Disclosure**: Use visibility settings to manage complexity.
- **Design for Reusability**: Create operations that can be combined in various ways.
- **Consider the Entire Lifecycle**: Plan for versioning, updates, and eventual retirement.

Development Best Practices

- **Follow API Design Standards**: Adhere to RESTful principles and industry best practices.
- **Implement Proper Error Handling**: Return meaningful error messages and appropriate status codes.
- **Use Strong Typing**: Define precise schemas for requests and responses.
- **Test Thoroughly**: Cover all operations, parameter combinations, and error conditions.
- **Implement Logging and Telemetry**: Capture information needed for troubleshooting and optimization.
- **Use Source Control**: Maintain your OpenAPI definitions and related artifacts in a version control system.

Security Best Practices

- **Implement Least Privilege**: Request only the permissions needed for operations.
- **Secure Authentication**: Use modern authentication protocols and secure credential storage.
- **Protect Sensitive Data**: Encrypt sensitive data in transit and at rest.
- **Implement Rate Limiting**: Protect your API from abuse or unintentional overload.
- **Regular Security Reviews**: Conduct periodic security assessments of your connector.
- **Monitor for Suspicious Activity**: Implement detection for unusual access patterns or potential attacks.

Governance Best Practices

1. **Document Everything**: Maintain comprehensive documentation for developers and users.
2. **Establish Clear Ownership**: Define who is responsible for the connector's maintenance.
3. **Implement Change Management**: Control how and when updates are deployed.
4. **Monitor Usage and Performance**: Track how the connector is being used and how well it is performing.
5. **Collect User Feedback**: Establish channels for users to report issues and suggest improvements.
6. **Regular Reviews**: Conduct periodic reviews of connector design, security, and performance.

Custom Connector Development Checklist

Use this checklist when developing custom connectors:

Planning Phase

- Identify API requirements and capabilities.
- Define connector scope and functionality.
- Document authentication requirements.
- Identify target users and use cases.
- Determine governance and support model.

Development Phase

- Create or obtain OpenAPI definition.

- Configure authentication.
- Define operations with clear names and descriptions.
- Implement appropriate policies.
- Test all operations with various inputs.
- Document usage examples and common scenarios.

Deployment Phase

- Determine deployment approach (manual, solution, DevOps).
- Configure environment-specific settings.
- Establish sharing and access control.
- Implement monitoring and analytics.
- Create user documentation and training materials.
- Plan for updates and version management.

Maintenance Phase

- Monitor usage and performance.
- Collect and respond to user feedback.
- Apply security updates.
- Optimize based on usage patterns.
- Plan for future enhancements.
- Review governance compliance.

Future Directions in the Connector Ecosystem

The Power Automate connector ecosystem continues to evolve. Watch for these emerging trends and capabilities:

- **AI-Enhanced Connectors**: Integration with AI services for intelligent processing
- **Low-Code Connector Development**: Simplified tools for creating connectors without extensive coding
- **Enhanced Security Features**: More sophisticated authentication and authorization options
- **Expanded Policy Capabilities**: More powerful transformation and integration policies
- **Cross-Platform Compatibility**: Broader interoperability across the Microsoft ecosystem and beyond
- **Community Connector Marketplace**: Expanded sharing and discovery of community created connectors

As Microsoft continues to invest in the Power Platform, you may expect custom connectors to become even more powerful and easier to create.

Conclusion

Custom connectors represent a powerful extension point in Microsoft Power Automate, enabling integration with virtually any system that exposes an API. By following the principles and practices outlined in this chapter, you can create connectors that are secure, performant, and user-friendly.

We have covered the entire lifecycle of custom connectors, from initial planning and development through deployment, monitoring, and governance. We have explored the technical foundations, including OpenAPI specifications, authentication methods, and policy implementation. We have also addressed important considerations such as security, performance, and integration with enterprise systems.

As you embark on your custom connector development journey, remember that the goal is to create a bridge between Power Automate and your APIs that empowers users to build sophisticated workflows without having to understand the underlying API complexities. A well-designed custom connector abstracts these complexities while providing the full power of your API in a user-friendly package.

In the next chapter, we will explore how to extend Power Automate even further through custom actions and app integration, building on the foundation we have established with custom connectors.

Questions

1. What is the primary purpose of a custom connector in Power Automate?
2. What are the key components of an OpenAPI definition?
3. Which authentication methods are supported by Power Automate custom connectors?
4. How can you implement error handling in a custom connector?
5. What are the advantages of using policies in custom connectors?
6. How can you monitor the performance of your custom connector?
7. What are the best practices for securing a custom connector?
8. How should you approach versioning for custom connectors?
9. What is the role of Azure API Management in custom connector scenarios?
10. How can you optimize a custom connector for performance?

Additional Resources

To strengthen your knowledge of custom connectors in Microsoft Power Automate, explore these resources:

Microsoft Documentation

- Create a custom connector from scratch
- Create a custom connector from an OpenAPI definition
- OpenAPI extensions for Power Automate custom connectors
- Secure your custom connectors in Power Automate

Tools and Templates

- OpenAPI (Swagger) Editor
- Microsoft Power Platform Connectors CLI
- Azure API Management
- Postman for API testing and documentation

Community Resources

- Power Automate Community
- Microsoft Power Platform GitHub repositories
- Power Platform Blog

Training

- Microsoft Learn modules on custom connectors
- Power Platform Developer videos

Best Practices Resources

- REST API guidelines
- OAuth 2.0 specifications
- Microsoft API Management policies

CHAPTER 15
HTTP Requests and API Integration

Introduction

In today's interconnected digital landscape, the ability to seamlessly communicate between different systems and services is no longer a luxury, but a necessity. As organizations expand their digital footprint, they often find themselves working with several applications, each with its own specialized functionality. While Microsoft Power Automate offers an impressive array of pre-built connectors for popular services, the true power of automation is unleashed when you can extend beyond these boundaries.

This is where HTTP requests and APIs (Application Programming Interfaces) become indispensable tools in your Power Automate arsenal. By mastering HTTP requests, you effectively remove the limitations of pre-built connectors, opening up your automation workflows to virtually any system or service that exposes an API, which means almost everything in today's cloud-centric world.

In previous chapters, we explored how Custom Connectors (Chapter 14) allowed us to create reusable, shareable connections to specific APIs. We also delved into essential Security Measures (Chapter 12) to protect our sensitive workflows and data. The Data Operations concepts we have covered throughout the book have prepared you to manipulate and transform the information flowing through your automations. Now, we will take a step forward by directly harnessing the power of HTTP requests, which is the universal language of web communication.

This chapter will equip you with a comprehensive understanding of HTTP concepts, RESTful principles, and practical implementation techniques specifically within Power Automate Cloud Flows. Whether you want to integrate with a niche service that does not have a dedicated connector, implement complex authentication flows, or simply gain more granular control over your integrations, mastering HTTP requests will dramatically expand your automation capabilities.

By the end of this chapter, you will confidently build flows that can communicate with virtually any modern API, handle responses effectively, implement robust error handling, and follow industry best practices for API integration. Let us begin our journey into the world of HTTP requests and APIs in Microsoft Power Automate.

Structure

In this chapter, we will cover the following topics:

- HTTP and API Fundamentals
- The HTTP Connector in Power Automate
- Working with Request and Response Bodies
- Authentication Methods for APIs
- Handling Responses and Errors

- Practical Implementation Examples
- API Security Best Practices
- Performance Optimization and Best Practices
- Hands-on Exercises
- Real-world Challenge Scenarios
- Think About It: Discussion Questions
- Knowledge Check
- Conclusion
- HTTP Request Implementation Checklist
- Additional Resources

HTTP and API Fundamentals

Before diving into the practical implementation of HTTP requests in Power Automate, it is essential to understand the fundamental concepts that underpin web APIs. This foundation will help you design more effective, efficient, and robust integrations.

Understanding HTTP

HTTP (Hypertext Transfer Protocol) is the foundation of data communication on the World Wide Web. It defines the format of messages, how they are transmitted, and what actions web servers and browsers should take in response to various commands. Think of HTTP as the postal service of the internet; it defines the ground rules for how packages (data) are addressed, formatted, delivered, and received.

When your Power Automate flow communicates with an external service, it typically does so using HTTP as the transport protocol. Understanding HTTP concepts is thus crucial for effective API integration.

Understanding APIs

An API (Application Programming Interface) acts as an intermediary that allows different software applications to communicate with each other. APIs define the methods and data formats that applications can use to request and exchange information.

In the context of web services, APIs typically expose endpoints (specific URLs) that accept HTTP requests and return data in structured formats like JSON or XML. These web APIs enable your Power Automate flows to interact with external systems, retrieving, creating, updating, or deleting data as needed.

HTTP Request Implementation Checklist

Before implementing a new API integration in Power Automate, use this checklist to ensure you have covered all the essential aspects:

- API Documentation Reviewed
    - Endpoints and methods identified
    - Authentication requirements understood
    - Request/response formats documented
    - Rate limits and quotas noted

- Authentication Configured
  - Appropriate authentication method selected
  - Credentials securely stored
    - Token management implemented (if using OAuth)
- Request Construction
  - Correct HTTP method selected
  - URL properly formatted with required parameters
  - Headers configured correctly
  - Request body structured according to API requirements
- Response Handling
  - Success responses correctly parsed
  - Error responses identified and handled
  - Status code checking implemented
  - Data validation performed on responses
- Error Handling Strategy
  - Retry logic configured for transient errors
  - Logging implemented for troubleshooting
  - User-friendly error messages defined
  - Critical error notifications configured
- Performance Considerations
  - Batch operations used where appropriate
  - Pagination handled correctly for large datasets
  - Rate limit handling implemented
  - Response caching considered
- Security Measures
  - Data transmission encrypted (HTTPS)
  - Sensitive data handled appropriately
  - Principle of least privilege applied to API credentials
  - Compliance requirements addressed
- Testing Completed
  - Happy path scenarios verified
  - Error handling tested
  - Performance under load evaluated
  - Edge cases considered

HTTP Methods Explained

HTTP defines several request methods (that are also called "verbs") that indicate the desired action to be performed on a resource. The most commonly used methods in API interactions are:

HTTP Method	Purpose	Typical Use	Example in Power Automate
`GET`	Retrieve data	Fetching information without modifying anything	Retrieving customer details from a CRM
`POST`	Create new data	Submitting data to create a new resource	Creating a new ticket in a support system
`PUT`	Update existing data	Replacing a resource entirely	Updating a product's complete information
`PATCH`	Partially update data	Modifying specific attributes of a resource	Updating just the status field of an order
`DELETE`	Remove data	Deleting a resource	Removing an outdated record

Table 15.1: *HTTP Methods*

Understanding which method to use is crucial for correctly interacting with APIs. Using the wrong method may result in errors or unexpected behaviour.

Anatomy of an HTTP Request

An HTTP request consists of several components:

- **URL (Uniform Resource Locator)**: The address that identifies the resource you want to interact with. For example: https://api.example.com/v1/customers
- **HTTP Method**: As discussed above, this indicates which action will be performed.
- **Headers**: Key-value pairs that provide additional information about the request or the client making it. Common headers include:
    - **Content-Type:** Specifies the format of the data in the request body (such as, application/json)
    - **Authorization:** Contains authentication credentials
    - **Accept:** Indicates what content types the client can process in the response
- **Query Parameters**: Additional data appended to the URL after a question mark (?), used to filter, sort, or paginate results. For example: https://api.example.com/v1/products?category=electronics&sort=price
- **Request Body**: The payload containing data to be sent to the server, typically used with `POST`, `PUT`, and `PATCH` requests

HTTP Response Structure

After sending an HTTP request, you will receive an HTTP response containing.

- **Status Code**: A three-digit number indicating the outcome of the request. Status codes are grouped into five categories:
    - **1xx:** Informational responses
    - **2xx**: Successful operations (such as, 200 OK, 201 Created)
    - **3xx**: Redirections
    - **4xx**: Client errors (such as, 400 Bad Request, 404 Not Found)
    - **5xx**: Server errors (such as, 500 Internal Server Error)
- **Headers**: Similar to request headers, these provide additional information about the response.
- **Response Body**: The payload returned by the server, often containing the requested data or confirmation of the requested action.

REST Architectural Principles

REST (Representational State Transfer) is an architectural style for designing networked applications. RESTful APIs adhere to certain constraints mentioned as follows:

- **Client-Server Architecture**: Separation of concerns between the client (requesting resources) and the server (providing resources).
- **Statelessness**: Each request from a client contains all the information necessary to process it. The server does not store client state between requests.
- **Cacheability**: Responses should indicate whether they can be cached.
- **Uniform Interface**: Resources are identified by URLs, manipulated through representations, and include self-descriptive messages.
- **Layered System**: A client cannot ordinarily tell whether it is connected directly to the end server or an intermediary.
- **Code on Demand (optional)**: Servers can temporarily extend client functionality by transferring executable code.

Understanding REST principles helps you design more predictable and maintainable API integrations in your Power Automate flows.

The HTTP Connector in Power Automate

Power Automate provides a dedicated HTTP connector that allows your flows to send HTTP requests to any API endpoint. This connector is your gateway to unlimited integration possibilities.

Finding and Adding the HTTP Connector

Power Automate's HTTP connector is the primary tool that enables your flows to communicate with external APIs and web services. Understanding how to locate and configure this connector is the first step toward building powerful, custom integrations that extend beyond standard connectors.

1. In your flow editor, click the "New step" button.
2. Search for "HTTP" in the connector search box.
3. Select the "HTTP" action from the results.

Configuring Basic HTTP Requests

Let us examine the essential configuration options for an HTTP request in Power Automate:

- **Method**: Select the appropriate HTTP method from the dropdown (`GET`, `POST`, `PUT`, `PATCH`, `DELETE`).
- **URI**: Enter the complete URL of the API endpoint you want to call. This can include dynamic content from previous steps.
- **Headers**: Add necessary headers as key-value pairs. Common headers include:

```
Content-Type: application/json
Accept: application/json
```

Figure 15.1: *Header Setup for HTTP Actions and APIs*

- **Body**: For **POST**, **PUT**, and **PATCH** requests, provide the request payload. This is typically a JSON object when working with modern APIs.
- **Authentication**: Configure authentication details if the API requires it (we will cover authentication in detail later).

Let us look at a basic example of a **GET** request to retrieve a list of products from a fictional e-commerce API:

```
Method: GET
URI: https://api.example-store.com/products
Headers:
  Accept: application/json
Authentication: None
```

***Figure* 15.2:** *Basic GET Request to Ecommerce API*

This simple configuration will send a GET request to retrieve product data from the specified endpoint.

Handling Query Parameters

Query parameters allow you to filter, sort, or paginate results when making API calls. In Power Automate, you can add query parameters directly to the URI or use the dedicated "**Query parameters**" section in the HTTP action.

For example, to retrieve only electronic products sorted by price:

```
Method: GET
URI: https://api.example-store.com/products
Query parameters:
  category: electronics
  sort: price
  order: asc
```

***Figure* 15.3:** *Using Query Parameters in HTTP Actions*

This is equivalent to calling:

https://api.example-store.com/products?category=electronics&sort=price&order=asc

Using the dedicated query parameters section helps keep your URI clean and makes it easier to dynamically set parameter values using expressions.

Working with Request and Response Bodies

When interacting with APIs, you will frequently need to send data in the request body and process data from the response body. Understanding how to properly format and parse these bodies is essential for successful API integration.

Formatting Request Bodies

Most modern APIs expect request bodies to be formatted as JSON (JavaScript Object Notation). In Power Automate, you can specify a JSON request body in the "**Body**" field of the HTTP action.

Here is an example of creating a new product using a **POST** request:

```
Method: POST
URI: https://api.example-store.com/products
Headers:
  Content-Type: application/json
  Accept: application/json
Body:
{
  "name": "Wireless Headphones",
  "category": "electronics",
  "price": 89.99,
  "stock": 120,
  "features": ["Bluetooth 5.0", "Noise cancellation", "20-hour battery"]
}
```

Figure 15.4: *HTTP Action JSON Body Example*

Using Dynamic Content in Request Bodies

One of Power Automate's strengths is the ability to dynamically construct request bodies using data from previous steps. For example, you might want to create a product based on form submissions:

```
{
  "name": "@{triggerBody()?['product_name']}",
  "category": "@{triggerBody()?['category']}",
  "price": @{triggerBody()?['price']},
  "stock": @{triggerBody()?['initial_stock']},
  "features": @{json(triggerBody()?['features'])}
}
```

Figure 15.5: *POST Request with Dynamic Form Data*

This approach allows you to build dynamic API requests based on user inputs or data from other systems.

Note: *When working with complex JSON structures, consider using the "**Compose**" action to build your JSON object first, then reference it in the HTTP request body. This approach makes your flows easier to read and maintain.*

Processing Response Bodies

After sending an HTTP request, you will receive a response that typically includes a body containing the requested data or confirmation of the requested action. Power Automate automatically parses JSON and XML responses, making the data available for use in subsequent steps.

To access data from the response body, use the dynamic content from the HTTP action. For example, if your HTTP action is named "**Get Products**" and returns a JSON array of products, you could access it in a "**For each**" loop:

```
For each item: body('Get_Products')
```

Figure 15.6: *Using For Each Loop to Process API Response Data*

To access specific properties from the response, use the following syntax:

```
body('Get_Products')?['products'][0]?['name']
```

Figure 15.7: *Working With JSON Properties in HTTP Response*

This would retrieve the name of the first product in the response.

Handling Different Response Formats

While JSON is the most common response format, you might encounter APIs that return data in different formats:

- **XML**: Power Automate can automatically parse XML responses, making the data available through the **`body()`** function.
- **Text**: For plain text responses, you can access the entire response body as a string.
- **Binary**: Some APIs return binary data (like images or files). You can handle these using the binary output of the HTTP action.

Authentication Methods for APIs

Most APIs require some form of authentication to ensure that only authorized users or applications can access their resources. Power Automate's HTTP connector supports various authentication methods to securely connect to protected APIs.

Basic Authentication

Basic authentication is one of the simplest forms of HTTP authentication, where credentials are sent as a base64-encoded string in the request header.

To configure Basic authentication in Power Automate:

1. In the HTTP action, expand the "**`Authentication`**" section.
2. Select "**`Basic`**" from the authentication type dropdown.
3. Enter the username and password.

Power Automate will automatically encode these credentials and add the appropriate Authorization header to your request.

Warning: *Basic authentication sends credentials with minimal protection. It should only be used with HTTPS connections to ensure the credentials are encrypted during transmission.*

API Keys

Many APIs use API keys for authentication. These are unique strings that identify the calling application or user.

API keys can be included in different parts of the request:

- **As a header**: Most common approach

```
Headers:
  X-API-Key: your_api_key_here
  api-key: your_api_key_here
```

Figure 15.8: *Including API Keys in HTTP Headers Power Automate*

- **As a query parameter**:

```
URI: https://api.example.com/data?apikey=your_api_key_here
```

Figure 15.9: *Power Automate HTTP Request with API Key in URI*

- **In the request body**: This is less common but may be required by some APIs.

Note: *Store API keys and other sensitive credentials in Power Automate environments or Azure Key Vault rather than hardcoding them in your flows. This enhances security and makes credential management easier.*

OAuth 2.0

OAuth 2.0 is a more complex but highly secure authentication framework widely used by major API providers like Microsoft, Google, and Salesforce.

To use OAuth 2.0 in a custom HTTP request, follow these steps:

1. In the HTTP action, expand the "`Authentication`" section.
2. Select "`OAuth 2.0`" from the authentication type dropdown.
3. Configure the OAuth settings according to the API provider's documentation:
    - Authority
    - Client ID
    - Client Secret
    - Scope
    - Grant Type

Power Automate will handle the OAuth flow, obtaining and refreshing tokens as needed.

Note: *For commonly used services that support OAuth, consider creating a Custom Connector (as covered in Chapter 14) rather than configuring OAuth manually in each HTTP request.*

Bearer Tokens

Bearer token authentication involves including a token (typically a JWT - JSON Web Token) in the request headers. This approach is commonly used with OAuth 2.0, where the bearer token is obtained through the OAuth flow.

To use a bearer token in Power Automate:

1. First, obtain the token (either from a previous OAuth step or from another system).
2. In the HTTP action, add a header:

```
Authorization: Bearer your_token_here
```

Figure 15.10: *Bearer Token Authentication in Power Automate HTTP Request*

Note: *If you are repeatedly calling an API that uses bearer tokens, store the token in a variable and reuse it across multiple HTTP requests to improve performance.*

Custom Authentication Schemes

Some APIs implement custom authentication schemes that do not fit the standard patterns. In these cases, you will need to construct the appropriate headers or parameters as specified in the API documentation.

For example, AWS API calls often require a complex signature process:

Headers:

```
  X-Amz-Date: 20230915T123456Z
Authorization:AWS4-HMAC-SHA256 Credential=AKIAIOSFODNN7EXAMPLE/20230915/us-east-1/
s3/aws4_request, SignedHeaders=host;x-amz-date, Signature=fe5f80f77d5fa3be-
ca038a248ff027d0445342fe2855ddc963176630326f1024
```

For complex authentication schemes, you might need to use "**Compose**" or "**Initialize variable**" actions to build the authentication values before including them in your HTTP request.

Handling Responses and Errors

Properly handling API responses and errors is crucial for building robust and reliable flows. This section covers strategies for processing responses, detecting errors, and implementing appropriate error handling.

Understanding Status Codes

HTTP status codes provide immediate feedback on the success or failure of your request. Here is how to interpret common status codes:

Status Code Range	Meaning	Common Examples	Handling Strategy
200-299	Success	200 OK, 201 Created, 204 No Content	Process the response data as expected
300-399	Redirection	301 Moved Permanently, 302 Found	Configure your HTTP action to follow redirects automatically
400-499	Client Error	400 Bad Request, 401 Unauthorized, 404 Not Found	Check your request parameters, authentication, or resource path
500-599	Server Error	500 Internal Server Error, 503 Service Unavailable	Implement retry logic or graceful failure handling

Table 15.2: *Status code table*

Checking Response Status in Flow Logic

Power Automate allows you to branch your flow based on the HTTP response status. You can use the **`outputs('HTTP_action')['statusCode']`** expression to check the status code and take appropriate action.

For example, you might use a Condition action to check if the request was successful:

Condition: `outputs('HTTP_action')['statusCode']>=200andoutputs('HTTP_action')['statusCode'] < 300`

If yes: Process the successful response

If no: Handle the error condition

Implementing Retry Logic

APIs can occasionally fail due to temporary issues like network problems or service outages. Implementing retry logic can help your flows handle these transient failures gracefully.

Power Automate provides built-in retry policies for HTTP actions:

1. In the HTTP action, click the ellipsis (three dots) in the top-right corner.
2. Select "`Settings`".
3. Configure the retry policy:
    a. **Default**: Retries up to 4 times with an exponential backoff strategy
    b. **Fixed**: Retries a specified number of times with a fixed interval between attempts
    c. **None**: No automatic retries

For more control, you can implement custom retry logic using "`Do until`" loops:

Initialize variable 'attempts' to 0

Do until:

```
attempts>=3oroutputs('HTTP_action')['statusCode']>=200andoutputs
('HTTP_action')['statusCode'] < 300
```

Actions:

Increment variable 'attempts' by 1

HTTP request

If condition (checks if status indicates retry needed)

Delay for calculated time

This approach allows you to implement more sophisticated retry strategies, such as exponential backoff with jitter.

Extracting Error Details from Responses

When an API returns an error, it often includes valuable information in the response body that can help diagnose the issue. To extract these details:

```
If HTTP request failed:
  Create a variable 'errorDetails' with value: body('HTTP_action')
  Log or process the error details
```

Figure 15.11: *Extracting Error Details from API Response Power Automate*

Many APIs follow standard formats for error responses. For example, a typical JSON error might look like:

```
{
  "error": {
    "code": "RESOURCE_NOT_FOUND",
    "message": "The requested resource could not be found.",
    "details": [
      {
        "field": "productId",
        "issue": "No product exists with ID 12345"
      }
    ]
  }
}
```

Figure 15.12: *Typical API Error Response Format JSON*

You can extract specific error information using expressions like:

```
body('HTTP_action')?['error']?['message']
```

Figure 15.13: *Using Expressions to Read API Error Fields*

Graceful Failure Handling

When API requests fail, it is important to handle the failure gracefully to maintain a good user experience. Strategies include:

- **Displaying user-friendly error messages**: Transform technical API errors into messages that users can understand.
- **Fallback mechanisms**: If a primary API is unavailable, try a secondary source of data.
- **Partial success handling**: If a batch operation partially fails, process the successful items and report on the failures.
- **Logging and monitoring**: Record API failures for later analysis and troubleshooting.

Note: *Use Power Automate's "**Scope**" action to group related HTTP requests. This makes it easier to implement try/catch-like error handling for a series of related operations.*

Practical Implementation Examples

Now that we have covered the theoretical aspects of HTTP requests and APIs, let us look at some practical examples of implementing API integrations in Power Automate. These examples demonstrate common patterns and best practices for different types of API interactions.

Example 1: Retrieving Data from a REST API

In this example, we will build a flow that retrieves a list of products from an e-commerce API and processes the results.

Scenario: Daily product inventory report

Implementation:

1. **Trigger**: Recurrence (daily at 8:00 AM)
2. **HTTP Request** (`GET`):

```
Method: GET
URI: https://api.example-store.com/products
Headers:
  Accept: application/json
Authentication: API Key
  Header name: X-API-Key
  Value: your_api_key_here
```

Figure 15.14: *Automated Daily Inventory Report Using HTTP GET*

3. **Parse Response**:
    a. Apply to each item in `body('HTTP_request')?['products']`.
    b. Inside the loop, extract relevant product details.
4. **Filter for Low Stock**:
    a. Condition: `items('Apply_to_each')?['stock'] < 10`
    b. If yes, add to a "`Low Stock Items`" array variable.
5. **Generate Report**:
    a. Create HTML table from the "`Low Stock Items`" variable.
    b. Send email with the report.

This simple flow demonstrates how to retrieve data from an API, process it using Power Automate's built-in actions, and generate actionable insights.

Example 2: Creating Resources via a REST API

In this example, we will build a flow that creates a new support ticket in a ticketing system when a form is submitted.

Scenario: Support ticket creation from Microsoft Forms

Implementation:

1. **Trigger**: When a new response is submitted in Microsoft Forms
2. **HTTP Request** (`POST`):

```
Method: POST
URI: https://api.ticketing-system.com/tickets
Headers:
  Content-Type: application/json
  Accept: application/json
Authentication: OAuth 2.0
  (configured according to the ticketing system's requirements)
Body:
{
  "subject": "@{triggerBody()?['r1234567']}", // Form question ID for subject
  "description": "@{triggerBody()?['r7654321']}", // Form question ID for description
  "priority": "@{triggerBody()?['r1122334']}", // Form question ID for priority
  "requester": {
    "name": "@{triggerBody()?['r2233445']}", // Form question ID for name
    "email": "@{triggerBody()?['r3344556']}" // Form question ID for email
  }
}
```

Figure 15.15: *Power Automate Flow Create Ticket from Form Response*

3. **Check Response**:
   a. Condition: `outputs('HTTP_request')?['statusCode'] equals 201`

      If yes: Extract the ticket ID from the response and proceed.

      If no: Handle the error.
4. **Send Confirmation**:
   a. Send an email to the requester confirming the ticket creation.
   b. Include the ticket ID and expected response time.

This example demonstrates how to create resources via API, handle the response, and provide feedback to users.

Example 3: Implementing Pagination for Large Datasets

Many APIs limit the number of results returned in a single response, requiring pagination to retrieve the complete dataset. This example demonstrates how to handle pagination in Power Automate.

Scenario: Export all customers to a SharePoint list

Implementation:

1. **Initialize Variables**:
   a. `pageNumber`: 1
   b. `hasMorePages`: true
   c. `allCustomers`: array []

2. **Do Until Loop**:
   a. Condition: **hasMorePages** equals false
   b. Inside the loop:
3. **HTTP Request** (**GET** with pagination):

```
Method: GET
URI: https://api.crm-system.com/customers
Query parameters:
  page: @{variables('pageNumber')}
  pageSize: 100
Headers:
  Accept: application/json
Authentication: Bearer Token
```

Figure 15.16: *Iterative GET Request with Pagination Example*

4. **Process Page Results**:
   a. Append current page results to **allCustomers** variable: **setVariable('allCustomers', concat(variables('allCustomers'), body('HTTP_request')?['customers']))**
   b. Check if there are more pages: **setVariable('hasMorePages', body('HTTP_request')?['pagination']?['hasNextPage'])**
   c. If more pages, increment page number: **setVariable('pageNumber', variables('pageNumber') + 1)**
5. **Process All Customers**:
   a. After the loop completes, apply to each item in **variables('allCustomers')**.
   b. Create a SharePoint list item for each customer.

This pattern can be adapted for any API that implements pagination, though you will need to adjust the specific parameters and response handling according to the API's documentation.

Example 4: Implementing Webhook Integration

Webhooks allow external systems to notify your flows when events occur, rather than your flows having to poll for changes. This example demonstrates how to set up a webhook receiver in Power Automate.

Scenario: Process inventory updates from a supplier

Implementation:

1. **Trigger**: When an HTTP request is received
   a. Method: **POST**
   b. Relative path: **/inventory-updates**
   c. Request body JSON schema:

```
{
  "type": "object",
  "properties": {
    "supplier": { "type": "string" },
    "products": {
      "type": "array",
      "items": {
        "type": "object",
        "properties": {
          "sku": { "type": "string" },
          "quantity": { "type": "integer" },
          "price": { "type": "number" }
        }
      }
    }
  }
}
```

Figure 15.17: Request Body JSON Schema

2. **Process Webhook Data**:
    a. Apply to each item in **`triggerBody()?['products']`**.
    b. Inside the loop, update your inventory database.
3. **Send Response**:
    a. Response action: Status code: 200 Body:

```
{
  "status": "success",
  "message": "Inventory updates processed",
  "itemsProcessed": @{length(triggerBody()?['products'])}
}
```

Figure 15.18: Successful API Response

Once this flow is saved, Power Automate will generate a unique URL for your webhook endpoint. You will need to provide this URL to your supplier so they can send inventory updates to it.

API Security Best Practices

Security is a critical consideration when working with APIs. This section covers best practices for ensuring your API integrations are secure and compliant with organizational policies.

Securing API Credentials

Properly managing API credentials is fundamental to API security:

- **Use Power Automate's secure inputs**: When configuring HTTP actions, use secure connections and environment variables to store sensitive values such as API keys, client secrets, and passwords.

- **Implement Azure Key Vault**: For enterprise scenarios, store API credentials in Azure Key Vault and retrieve them as needed in your flows.
- **Regularly rotate credentials**: Establish a process for regularly updating API keys and tokens to minimize the impact of potential breaches.
- **Use appropriate authentication**: Choose the most secure authentication method that the API supports. OAuth 2.0 is generally preferable to API keys, which are preferable to basic authentication.

Warning: *Never hardcode API credentials directly in your flows, as this creates security risks and makes credential management difficult.*

Data Protection Considerations

When transmitting data via APIs, consider these data protection measures:

- **Always use HTTPS**: Ensure all API communications use encrypted connections. Power Automate's HTTP connector should only connect to HTTPS endpoints.
- **Implement data minimization**: Only request and transmit the data you actually need for your process.
- **Handle sensitive data appropriately**: Be cautious when processing Personally Identifiable Information (PII), financial data, or other sensitive information through APIs.
- **Comply with data residency requirements**: Be aware of where API providers store and process your data, especially for regulated industries.

Implementing Proper Authorization

Authentication verifies who you are, while authorization determines what you are allowed to do. Implement these authorization best practices:

- **Use minimal-privilege accounts**: API credentials should have only the permissions necessary for your flow's functionality, not administrative access.
- **Implement IP restrictions where possible**: Some APIs allow you to whitelist specific IP addresses for added security.
- **Validate responses**: Do not assume that authenticated API calls will always return safe data. Implement validation on received data before processing it further.

Monitoring and Auditing API Usage

Maintaining visibility into your API integrations is essential for security:

- **Implement logging**: Record key information about API interactions, including times, endpoints accessed, and response codes.
- **Set up alerts**: Configure alerts for unusual patterns, such as high failure rates or unexpected volumes of requests.
- **Regularly review API usage**: Periodically audit your flows' API interactions to ensure they align with expected patterns and comply with API provider terms of service.

Performance Optimization and Best Practices

Optimizing your API integrations ensures they run efficiently and reliably. This section covers best practices for performance, maintainability, and troubleshooting.

Optimizing API Calls

Efficient API usage improves performance and reduces costs:

- **Batch operations where possible**: Instead of making multiple API calls for individual items, use batch endpoints if the API supports them.
- **Implement caching**: For frequently accessed data that does not change often, consider implementing caching to reduce API calls.
- **Use filtering and field selection**: Many APIs allow you to specify exactly which fields you need or filter results on the server side. For example:

```
https://api.example.com/users?fields=id,name,email&department=sales
```

Figure 15.19: *HTTP Request Filter and Select Fields*

- **Optimize pagination**: When retrieving large datasets, use appropriate page sizes to balance between making too many small requests and requesting overly large pages.

Rate Limiting and Throttling

Most APIs impose limits on how many requests you can make in a given time period. Exceeding these limits typically results in errors or temporary bans. Handle rate limits by:

- **Understanding the API's limits**: Thoroughly read the API documentation to understand rate limits, such as requests per second or daily quotas.
- **Implementing exponential backoff**: When rate limit errors occur, wait progressively longer between retry attempts.
- **Scheduling high-volume processes**: For large batch operations, schedule them during off-peak hours or spread them over time.
- **Monitoring usage**: Track your API consumption to ensure you stay within limits and plan accordingly for growth.

Debugging and Troubleshooting Techniques

When API integrations do not work as expected, use these troubleshooting techniques:

- **Use the run history**: Power Automate's run history provides detailed information about each step, including the actual request sent and response received.
- **Implement logging**: Add "`Compose`" actions before and after HTTP requests to log important details for troubleshooting.
- **Test with Postman or similar tools**: Before implementing complex API calls in Power Automate, test them in API tools such as Postman to ensure they work as expected.
- **Check common issues**:
    - Incorrect authentication
    - Malformed request bodies
    - Missing or invalid headers
    - URL encoding issues
    - Timeout settings

- **Use HTTP response headers**: Many APIs include helpful debugging information in response headers, such as remaining rate limits or request IDs that can be referenced in support tickets.

Maintainability Best Practices

Create API integrations that are easier to maintain and adapt over time:

- **Document your flows**: Use notes and descriptive names to explain the purpose of each action, especially complex HTTP requests.
- **Modularize with child flows**: For reusable API operations, create child flows that can be called from multiple parent flows.
- **Centralize configuration**: Store API endpoints, credentials, and other configuration in environment variables to make updates easier.
- **Version control**: When possible, export important flows and store them in a version control system like Git.
- **Implement proper error handling**: As covered earlier, robust error handling makes debugging easier and improves reliability.

Hands-on Exercises

Now it is time to put theory into practice with some hands-on exercises. These structured exercises will help you build confidence in working with HTTP requests and APIs in Power Automate.

Exercise 1: Basic GET Request

Objective: Create a flow that retrieves and displays current weather data using a public API.

Steps:

1. Create a new instant flow with a manual trigger.
2. Add an HTTP action with these settings:
   a. Method: `GET`
   b. URI: https://api.openweathermap.org/data/2.5/weather?q=London&appid=YOUR_API_KEY&units=metric (You will need to sign up for a free API key at OpenWeatherMap)
3. Add a Condition action to check if the request was successful:
   a. Condition: `outputs('HTTP')?['statusCode'] equals 200`

   If successful, add a "`Show notification`" action:

   b. Title: Weather Update
   c. Text: The current temperature in London is `@{body('HTTP')?['main']?['temp']}°C` with `@{body('HTTP')?['weather'][0]?['description']}`

   If not successful, add a different notification displaying the error message.
4. Test your flow and observe the results.

Challenge: Modify the flow to allow the user to input any city name when triggering the flow.

Exercise 2: Working with POST Requests

Objective: Create a flow that sends data to a REST API and processes the response.

Steps:

1. Create a new instant flow with a manual trigger that collects:
    a. Customer Name
    b. Email
    c. Product Interest
2. Add an HTTP action with these settings:
    a. Method: **POST**
    b. URI: https://reqbin.com/echo/post/json (this is a test endpoint that echoes back your request)
    c. Headers:
        - Content-Type: **application/json**
    d. Body:

```
{
  "customer": {
    "name": "@{triggerBody()['text']}",
    "email": "@{triggerBody()['text_1']}",
    "interest": "@{triggerBody()['text_2']}",
    "timestamp": "@{utcNow()}"
  }
}
```

Figure 15.20: HTTP Action Body

3. Add a Condition action to check if the request was successful:
    a. Condition: **outputs('HTTP')?['statusCode'] equals 200**

    If successful, parse the response body and display a success message.

    If not successful, create an error handling path that logs the error details.
4. Test your flow with different inputs and observe the results.

Challenge: Extend the flow to validate the email format before submitting the request, and handle validation errors appropriately.

Exercise 3: Implementing Authentication

Objective: Create a flow that connects to an API using OAuth 2.0 authentication.

Steps:

1. Create a new scheduled flow that runs daily.

2. Add an HTTP action to obtain an OAuth token:
   - Method: POST
   - URI: https://login.microsoftonline.com/{tenant-id}/oauth2/v2.0/token
   - Headers:
     - Content-Type: **`application/x-www-form-urlencoded`**
   - Body:

```
client_id=your_client_id
&scope=https://graph.microsoft.com/.default
&client_secret=your_client_secret
&grant_type=client_credentials
```

Figure 15.21: *HTTP Action JSON Body Setup*

3. Add a "**`Parse JSON`**" action to extract the access token from the response.
4. Add another HTTP action to call the Microsoft Graph API:
   a. Method: **`GET`**
   b. URI: https://graph.microsoft.com/v1.0/users
   c. Headers:
      i. Authorization: Bearer **`@{body('Parse_JSON')?['access_token']}`**
5. Process the response to extract user information.
6. Test your flow and verify that it successfully authenticates and retrieves data.

Note: *For this exercise, you will need to register an application in Azure Active Directory to get the client ID and client secret.*

Challenge: Modify the flow to handle token expiration by implementing a token refresh mechanism.

Exercise 4: Error Handling and Retries

Objective: Create a robust flow that implements proper error handling and retry logic for API calls.

Steps:

1. Create a new instant flow with a manual trigger.
2. Add an "**`Initialize variable`**" action to create a counter:
   a. Name: **`RetryCount`**
   b. Type: **`Integer`**
   c. Value: **`0`**
3. Add a "**`Do until`**" action with the condition:
   a. **`@variables('RetryCount')`** greater than 3
   b. OR
   c. **`@and(greater(outputs('HTTP')?['statusCode'],199), less(outputs('HTTP')?['statusCode'], 300))`**

4. Inside the "`Do until`" loop, add:
   a. An HTTP action to call an API endpoint
   b. A "`Condition`" to check if the request failed
   c. If failed, add:
      i. An "`Increment variable`" action to increase RetryCount
      ii. A "`Delay`" action that waits progressively longer (such as, RetryCount * 30 seconds)
      iii. A "`Create HTML table`" action to format error details
   d. If succeeded, add actions to process the successful response
5. After the loop, add a final condition to check if the maximum retries were exceeded.
6. Test your flow with both successful and failing scenarios.

Challenge: Implement different retry strategies based on the specific error status code received.

Real-world Challenge Scenarios

Now let us explore some more complex, real-world scenarios that demonstrate how HTTP requests and APIs can solve business problems in Power Automate. These challenges will help you apply the concepts from this chapter to realistic situations.

Scenario 1: Multi-system Data Synchronization

Business Need: A manufacturing company needs to keep product data synchronized between their ERP system, e-commerce platform, and warehouse management system. Each system has its own API with different authentication methods and data formats.

Solution Approach:

1. **Source Data Extraction**:
   a. Create a scheduled flow that runs daily to extract product updates from the ERP system using its REST API.
   b. Implement OAuth authentication for the ERP system.
   c. Use query parameters to filter for only products that have changed since the last synchronization.
2. **Data Transformation**:
   a. Parse the ERP response and map fields to the target systems' expected formats.
   b. Handle special cases like unit conversions and category mappings.
   c. Generate appropriate payloads for each target system.
3. **Target System Updates**:
   a. Implement separate HTTP actions for each target system:
      i. E-commerce platform (using API key authentication)
      ii. Warehouse system (using basic authentication)
   b. Use `PUT` or `PATCH` requests to update the existing products.

   c. Use **POST** requests for new products.

4. **Comprehensive Error Handling**:

   a. Implement system-specific error handling for each target.

   b. Create a synchronization log that tracks successes and failures.

   c. Send notifications for critical failures.

5. **Reconciliation Process**:

   a. Add a final step that verifies synchronization by retrieving and comparing product data from all systems.

   b. Flag discrepancies for manual review.

Implementation Highlights:

```
# ERP Data Extraction
Method: GET
URI: https://erp-api.company.com/products/changes
Query parameters:
  lastSync: @{variables('LastSyncTimestamp')}
  fields: id,name,description,price,stock,category
Authentication: OAuth 2.0

# E-commerce Update (for each product)
Method: PATCH
URI: https://ecommerce-api.company.com/products/@{items('Apply_to_
each')?['product_id']}
Headers:
  X-API-Key: your_api_key
  Content-Type: application/json
Body:
{
  "name": "@{items('Apply_to_each')?['name']}",
  "description": "@{items('Apply_to_each')?['description']}",
  "price": @{items('Apply_to_each')?['price']},
  "inventory": @{items('Apply_to_each')?['stock']},
  "category": "@{variables('CategoryMapping')[items('Apply_to_each')?
['category']]}"
}
```

This scenario demonstrates how to integrate with multiple systems using different API patterns and handle the complexity of cross-system data synchronization.

Scenario 2: API-based Approval Workflow

Business Need: A financial services company needs to implement a loan approval process that integrates with their core banking API, credit check service, and document management system.

Solution Approach:

1. **Loan Application Intake**:

   a. Create a flow triggered by a form submission.

   b. Validate application data using schema validation.

2. **Credit Check Integration**:
    a. Send applicant information to a credit bureau API.
    b. Retrieve credit score and history.
    c. Implement secure handling of sensitive personal information.
3. **Document Verification**:
    a. Call the document management API to retrieve uploaded identification documents.
    b. Process document status and verification results.
4. **Risk Assessment**:
    a. Calculate risk scores based on application data, credit information, and document verification.
    b. Determine if manual review is required.
5. **Banking System Integration**:
    a. For approved loans, create a new loan account in the banking system API.
    b. Generate loan documents and payment schedules.
    c. Handle account creation confirmation.
6. **Communication Workflow**:
    a. Send appropriate notifications to applicants based on decision.
    b. Schedule follow-up actions for incomplete applications.

Implementation Highlights:

```
# Credit Check API
Method: POST
URI: https://credit-api.bureau.com/check
Headers:
  Authorization: Bearer @{variables('CreditAPIToken')}
  Content-Type: application/json
Body:
{
  "firstName": "@{triggerBody()?['firstName']}",
  "lastName": "@{triggerBody()?['lastName']}",
  "ssn": "@{triggerBody()?['ssn']}",
  "address": {
    "street": "@{triggerBody()?['street']}",
    "city": "@{triggerBody()?['city']}",
    "state": "@{triggerBody()?['state']}",
    "zip": "@{triggerBody()?['zip']}"
  },
  "requestType": "loan-application",
  "requestId": "@{workflow()?['run']['name']}"
}

# Conditional: Manual Review
If @{body('Calculate_Risk_Score')?['score']} > 50 and @{body('Calculate_Risk_
Score')?['score']} < 75:
  # Create approval task
```

```
Else if @{body('Calculate_Risk_Score')?['score']} >= 75:
  # Auto-approve
Else:
  # Auto-decline
```

This scenario demonstrates integration with multiple secure systems, handling sensitive data, and implementing complex business logic based on API responses.

Scenario 3: IoT Sensor Monitoring and Alerting

Business Need: A smart building management company needs to monitor environmental sensors, trigger alerts, and adjust building systems when conditions exceed thresholds.

Solution Approach:

1. **Sensor Data Collection**:
    a. Create a flow triggered by an HTTP webhook receiving sensor data.
    b. Validate incoming data for required fields and formats.
    c. Store readings in a database for historical analysis.
2. **Threshold Analysis**:
    a. Compare current readings against defined thresholds.
    b. Implement time-window analysis for pattern detection.
    c. Calculate severity based on multiple factors.
3. **Building System Control**:
    a. For temperature exceptions, call the HVAC control API.
    b. For humidity issues, adjust dehumidifier settings.
    c. For air quality concerns, increase ventilation.
4. **Alert Notification**:
    a. Based on severity, send notifications via different channels.
    b. Include sensor details, current readings, and recommended actions.
    c. Implement alert aggregation to prevent notification fatigue.
5. **Incident Tracking**:
    a. Create incidents in the service management system for persistent issues.
    b. Track resolution status and effectiveness of automated responses.

Implementation Highlights:

```
# Webhook Trigger (sample incoming data)
{
  "buildingId": "B123",
  "floor": 3,
  "zone": "East",
  "sensorId": "TEMP-301",
  "type": "temperature",
  "value": 78.5,
  "timestamp": "2023-09-15T14:22:15Z",
```

```
    "battery": 76
  }

  # HVAC Control API (if temperature exceeds threshold)
  Method: POST
  URI: https://building-controls.company.com/hvac/adjust
  Headers:
    Authorization: Bearer @{variables('BuildingAPIToken')}
    Content-Type: application/json
  Body:
  {
    "buildingId": "@{triggerBody()?['buildingId']}",
    "floor": @{triggerBody()?['floor']},
    "zone": "@{triggerBody()?['zone']}",
    "adjustment": "@{if(greater(triggerBody()?['value'], variables
  ('TemperatureMax')), 'cool', 'heat')}",
    "targetTemp": @{variables('OptimalTemperature')},
    "priority": "@{variables('AlertSeverity')}"
  }
```

This scenario demonstrates handling streaming data from IoT devices, implementing real-time analysis, and controlling physical systems via APIs.

Conclusion

In this chapter, we have explored the powerful capabilities that HTTP requests and APIs bring to Microsoft Power Automate Cloud Flows. By mastering these concepts, you have expanded your automation toolkit far beyond the limitations of pre-built connectors, enabling integration with virtually any modern web service or system.

We began with fundamental HTTP and API concepts, explored the anatomy of requests and responses, and delved into authentication methods that secure your integrations. We examined techniques for handling responses and implementing robust error handling, ensuring that your flows remain resilient even when external services encounter issues.

Through practical examples and hands-on exercises, you have seen how these concepts apply to real-world scenarios across different industries and use cases. The knowledge check and discussion questions have helped reinforce key concepts and encourage deeper thinking about API integration strategies.

In the next chapter, we will build upon this foundation as we explore advanced data transformation techniques that will help you bridge the gap between different systems and data formats in your Power Automate flows.

Key Takeaways

- HTTP requests serve as a universal integration mechanism, allowing your flows to communicate with any system that exposes an API.
- Security should always be a primary consideration when working with APIs, from credential management to data protection.
- Robust error handling and retry strategies are essential for building reliable integrations that can recover from transient failures.
- Performance optimization techniques like batching, pagination handling, and caching can significantly improve the efficiency of your API integrations.

- Following best practices for maintainability ensures your flows remain manageable and adaptable as your organization's needs evolve.

Questions

As you continue to develop your skills with HTTP requests and APIs in Power Automate, consider these thought-provoking questions:

API Design Considerations

1. How would you approach the decision between using a custom connector versus direct HTTP actions in Power Automate? What factors would influence this choice?
2. When integrating with multiple related APIs (such as, Microsoft Graph, SharePoint, Teams), what strategies can you implement to maintain consistency and reusability in your flows?
3. How might the choice of API authentication method impact the security, performance, and user experience of your Power Automate solutions?

Security Implications

1. What additional security measures would you consider when integrating with financial or healthcare APIs that handle sensitive data?
2. How would you implement proper separation of duties when creating flows that interact with high-privilege APIs?
3. What strategies can you use to securely manage and rotate API credentials in an enterprise environment?

Performance Optimization

1. How would you approach the implementation of caching for API responses in Power Automate?
2. What techniques can you use to minimize the impact of API rate limits on business-critical processes?
3. When working with large datasets returned by APIs, what strategies can help optimize performance in Power Automate?

Error Handling Strategies

1. How would you design a comprehensive logging system for API interactions in Power Automate?
2. What approach would you take to handle dependency chains, where one API failure affects subsequent API calls?
3. How might you implement different error handling strategies based on the criticality of the business process?

Multiple Choice Questions

1. Which HTTP method is most appropriate for updating a subset of fields in an existing resource?
   a. GET
   b. POST
   c. PUT
   d. PATCH
2. When implementing OAuth 2.0 authentication in Power Automate, which of the following is NOT typically required?
   a. Client ID
   b. Client Secret
   c. Server IP Address
   d. Scope
3. What is the primary purpose of using query parameters in an API request?
   a. To authenticate the request
   b. To filter, sort, or paginate results
   c. To specify the response format
   d. To compress the response data
4. Which HTTP status code range indicates a client-side error?
   a. 100-199
   b. 200-299
   c. 300-399
   d. 400-499
5. When implementing pagination in Power Automate, which flow control is most appropriate?
   a. Switch
   b. Do until
   c. Apply to each
   d. Scope
6. Which of the following is a best practice for handling API credentials in Power Automate?
   a. Hardcoding them in the HTTP action
   b. Storing them in environment variables
   c. Including them in flow comments
   d. Sharing them across all flows

7. What is the main advantage of using bearer tokens for API authentication?
   a. They never expire.
   b. They can be used across different APIs.
   c. They separate the authentication concern from the API requests.
   d. They work without HTTPS.
8. Which Power Automate action is the most useful for transforming JSON data received from an API?
   a. Compose
   b. Parse JSON
   c. Select
   d. Filter array
9. When implementing retry logic for API calls, which approach is generally recommended?
   a. Fixed interval retries
   b. Exponential backoff
   c. Immediate retries
   d. Manual retries
10. Which of the following is NOT a common component of a RESTful API URL?
    a. Base URL
    b. Resource path
    c. Query parameters
    d. Request body

Answers

1. d
2. c
3. b
4. d
5. b
6. b
7. c
8. b
9. b
10. d

Additional Resources

To further expand your knowledge of HTTP requests, APIs, and their implementation in Power Automate, consider exploring these resources:

Official Documentation

- Microsoft Power Automate HTTP Connector Documentation
- REST API Design Best Practices
- OAuth 2.0 Authentication for Microsoft Power Automate

API Standards and Specifications

- OpenAPI Specification
- JSON:API Specification
- Microsoft API Guidelines

Tools

- Postman - API development and testing environment
- Swagger UI - Interactive API documentation
- JSON Schema Validator - Validate JSON against a schema

Community Resources

- Power Automate Community
- Power Automate Blog
- Stack Overflow - Power Automate Tag

CHAPTER 16
Real-World Case Studies

Introduction

Real-world case studies provide invaluable insights into how theoretical concepts translate into practical implementations. In the rapidly evolving landscape of business automation, Microsoft Power Automate Cloud Flows have emerged as a transformative solution, enabling organizations of all sizes to streamline operations, reduce manual workload, and achieve significant cost savings. This chapter bridges the gap between the technical knowledge you have acquired throughout this book and its practical application in diverse business environments.

By examining actual implementations across various industries and organizational scales, you will gain a deeper understanding of how Power Automate Cloud Flows can address specific business challenges and deliver measurable benefits. These case studies will not only reinforce your technical knowledge but also inspire innovative applications in your own organizational context. Building on your comprehensive journey through Microsoft Power Automate Cloud Flows, from foundational concepts and interface navigation to advanced techniques including triggers, actions, data operations, and enterprise governance, this final chapter synthesizes these learnings into actionable best practices and strategic recommendations for successful automation implementation.

By the end of this chapter, you will not only understand the technical aspects of Power Automate Cloud Flows but also gain insights into the business considerations that drive successful automation initiatives.

Structure

In this chapter, we will cover the following topics:

- Implementation Strategies for Small, Medium, and Enterprise Businesses
- Industry-Specific Automation Solutions and Their Outcomes
- Cost-Benefit Analysis of Power Automate Implementations
- Scaling Automation across Organizational Departments
- Integration with Existing Business Systems and Infrastructure
- Measuring ROI and Efficiency Gains
- Change Management and User Adoption Strategies
- Performance Optimization in Complex Workflows
- Security and Compliance Considerations in Real-World Deployments
- Future-Proofing Automation Investments

Small Business Implementation: Streamlining Operations with Limited Resources

Small businesses often face unique challenges when implementing automation solutions, primarily due to limited IT resources, budget constraints, and the need for quick returns on investment. However, these constraints can also drive focused, high-impact implementations.

Case Study: Regional Real Estate Agency

Background: A regional real estate agency with 15 agents and 3 administrative staff was struggling with manual processes for listing management, client communications, and document processing. These inefficiencies were limiting their ability to scale operations and compete with larger agencies.

Implementation Approach: The agency identified three critical processes for initial automation:

- **Property Listing Workflow**
  - Automated the transfer of listing information from their CRM to multiple listing services
  - Created notification flows for new listings, price changes, and status updates
  - Implemented document generation for property information sheets
- **Client Communication Management**
  - Developed automated follow-up sequences for property inquiries
  - Created appointment scheduling and confirmation workflows
  - Implemented automated satisfaction surveys after property viewings
- **Document Processing**
  - Automated contract generation based on CRM data
  - Implemented digital signature workflows with status tracking
  - Created document archiving and retrieval processes

Technical Implementation Details:

The agency used the following Power Automate components:

```
Trigger: When a new record is created in Dynamics 365 CRM
Action: Get record details
Condition: If listing status = "New"
    Action: Create SharePoint folder with property ID
    Action: Generate property information document (Word template)
    Action: Post to Teams channel with property details
    Action: Send welcome email to property owner
Condition: If listing type = "Premium"
    Action: Create social media posting schedule
    Action: Assign photography task
```

Figure 16.1: *Regional Real Estate Agency Power Automate Flow Components*

Results:

- 70% reduction in administrative tasks related to listing management

- 45% faster document processing
- 30% increase in client responsiveness
- $27,000 annual cost savings in administrative overhead
- Gained the ability to handle 40% more listings without employing additional staff

Note: *When implementing Power Automate in small businesses, start with high-volume, repetitive tasks that directly impact customer experience or revenue generation. This approach delivers visible benefits quickly and builds momentum for broader adoption.*

Common Implementation Challenges for Small Businesses

While Power Automate offers tremendous potential for small businesses, the implementation journey often presents unique obstacles that differ significantly from those faced by larger organizations. Understanding these challenges and their solutions within the Power Automate ecosystem helps small businesses navigate their automation journey more effectively and avoid common pitfalls that could derail their initiatives.

Challenge	Solution Approach	Power Automate Features
Limited IT expertise	Start with template-based flows and gradually customize	Ready-to-use templates, intuitive designer interface
Budget constraints	Leverage included licenses with Microsoft 365 subscriptions	Pay-as-you-go pricing options for additional needs
Data silos	Prioritize integrations with existing systems	400+ pre-built connectors
Resistance to change	Begin with non-disruptive automations that enhance rather than replace existing processes	Parallel testing capabilities
Scaling concerns	Design flows with modularity in mind	Child flows, reusable components

Table 16.1: *Small Business Challenges*

Common Pitfall: *Small businesses often underestimate the importance of documentation and knowledge transfer. Even simple flows should be well-documented, as staff turnover can result in automation "orphans" that no one understands or maintains.*

Medium Business Implementation: Balancing Complexity and Resources

Medium-sized businesses typically have more complex requirements and greater resources than small businesses, but still face significant constraints compared to enterprise organizations. Their automation strategies often focus on departmental efficiency while building toward enterprise-wide integration.

Case Study: Regional Healthcare Provider

Background: A regional healthcare provider with 200+ employees across three facilities needed to streamline patient intake, insurance verification, and appointment management while ensuring HIPAA compliance and data security.

Implementation Approach: The organization adopted a phased approach:

1. **Phase 1: Front Office Automation**
    a. Implemented appointment confirmation and reminder workflows

b. Created insurance verification processes
c. Automated new patient intake documentation

2. **Phase 2: Clinical Workflow Enhancement**
    a. Developed patient visit documentation workflows
    b. Implemented lab result notification systems
    c. Created medication refill request handling
3. **Phase 3: Back Office Integration**
    a. Automated billing and insurance claim submission
    b. Implemented payment processing workflows
    c. Created reporting and analytics dashboards

Technical Implementation Example: Insurance Verification Workflow

```
Trigger: When a new appointment is scheduled in the EHR system
Action: Get patient insurance information
Parallel Branch:
    Branch 1:
        Action: Query insurance eligibility API
        Condition: If eligibility = "Active"
            Action: Update patient record with verification status
            Action: Add verification details to appointment notes
        Condition: If eligibility = "Inactive" or "Unknown"
            Action: Create task for billing specialist
            Action: Send insurance update request to patient
    Branch 2:
        Action: Check for previous visits and outstanding balances
        Condition: If balance > $0
            Action: Generate payment reminder
            Action: Update appointment notes with balance information
Action: Send appropriate confirmation to front desk staff
```

Figure 16.2: *Regional Healthcare Provider - Insurance Verification Workflow*

Results:

- Observed 60% reduction in insurance verification processing time
- Recorded 35% decrease in claim rejections due to eligibility issues
- Achieved 25% improvement in appointment utilization
- Saved $125,000 annually in administrative costs
- Improved patient satisfaction due to streamlined check-in process

Note: *Medium-sized businesses should establish a Center of Excellence (CoE) for Power Automate, even if it is just a part-time responsibility for a few team members. This group can develop standards, provide internal support, and ensure consistent implementation across departments.*

Implementation Strategy for Medium Businesses

- **Departmental Approach with Enterprise Vision**
    - Start with departmental workflows but design with cross-departmental integration in mind.
    - Establish governance standards early to prevent "flow sprawl".
    - Create a roadmap for progressive integration of departmental solutions.
- **Building Internal Capabilities**
    - Identify and train Power Automate champions across departments.
    - Develop internal knowledge-sharing mechanisms.
    - Create a library of organization-specific templates and components.
- **Integration Planning**
    - Map data flows between systems to identify optimization opportunities.
    - Standardize naming conventions and documentation requirements.
    - Implement monitoring and analytics to measure automation impact.

Common Pitfall: *Medium-sized businesses often create department-specific flows that duplicate functionality or create data inconsistencies. Establish central governance early to ensure flows align with organizational data management practices.*

Enterprise Implementation: Scaling Automation across Complex Organizations

Enterprise organizations require structured, scalable approaches to Power Automate implementation, with robust governance, security controls, and integration with existing enterprise architecture.

Case Study: Global Manufacturing Company

Background: A global manufacturing company with 5,000+ employees across 12 countries needed to standardize and automate procurement, inventory management, quality assurance, and customer service processes, while integrating with their existing ERP and CRM systems.

Implementation Approach

The company established a comprehensive Power Platform strategy:

- **Governance and Infrastructure**
    - Created a dedicated Power Platform Center of Excellence (CoE)
    - Established environment strategy aligned with business units
    - Implemented Data Loss Prevention (DLP) policies
    - Developed approval and certification processes for production flows
- **Enterprise-Wide Implementation**
    - Procurement automation with approval workflows and vendor management
    - Quality management processes with defect tracking and resolution
    - Global inventory synchronization and demand forecasting
    - Customer service case routing and resolution tracking

- **Integration Architecture**
  - SAP ERP integration for financial and inventory data
  - Salesforce CRM integration for customer information
  - Microsoft Teams integration for collaboration and approvals
  - Power BI integration for analytics and reporting

Technical Implementation Example: Global Procurement Workflow

```
Trigger: When a purchase requisition is submitted in the procurement portal
Action: Get requisition details
Condition: Check requisition type and amount
    Action (Low value): Route for department manager approval
    Action (Medium value): Route for department manager and finance approval
    Action (High value): Route for department manager, finance, and executive approval
    Action (Strategic): Route to strategic sourcing committee
Action: Apply regional business rules based on requisition location
Condition: If approved
    Action: Generate purchase order in SAP
    Action: Send notification to vendor
    Action: Create tracking record in procurement dashboard
Condition: If rejected at any level
    Action: Return to requester with comments
    Action: Log rejection reasons for analytics
```

***Figure 16.3**: Power Automate-Driven Workflow for Global Procurement*

Results:

- Saved $3.2 million annually in procurement through process optimization
- Reduced purchase order processing time by 75%
- Recorded 40% decrease in inventory carrying costs through improved forecasting
- Achieved 90% reduction in manual data entry errors
- Standardized global processes while maintaining regional compliance requirements

Note: *Enterprise organizations should leverage premium connectors and API integration capabilities to connect Power Automate with legacy systems. Custom connectors can extend Power Automate's reach to virtually any system in your technology ecosystem.*

Enterprise Implementation Best Practices

- **Centralized Governance with Distributed Development**
  - Establish central standards, security controls, and certification processes.
  - Enable business units to develop their own flows within governance boundaries.
  - Implement flow templates for common business processes.
- **Security and Compliance Integration**
  - Incorporate security reviews into the flow development lifecycle.
  - Implement data classification and handling procedures.
  - Create compliance documentation templates for regulated processes.

- **Scaling Strategy**
  - Develop reference architectures for common integration patterns.
  - Implement monitoring and alerting for critical flows.
  - Create capacity planning models for flow volume and performance.

Common Pitfall: *Enterprise organizations often underestimate the importance of business process standardization before automation. Automating inconsistent processes merely scales inefficiency. Invest time in process optimization before implementing enterprise-wide flows.*

Industry-Specific Implementations

Different industries have unique requirements and regulations that shape Power Automate implementations. Here are examples from three diverse sectors:

Financial Services: Regulatory Compliance and Risk Management

The financial services industry presents unique challenges for Power Automate implementation, where automation must balance operational efficiency with stringent regulatory requirements and comprehensive audit trails. Power Automate's built-in security features, combined with its ability to integrate with compliance management systems, makes it particularly well-suited for creating workflows that not only streamline operations but also ensure adherence to regulations such as SOX, GLBA, and various banking compliance standards.

Case Study: Regional Bank

A regional bank implemented Power Automate Cloud Flows to address regulatory reporting requirements and streamline loan processing:

- **Regulatory Reporting Automation**
  - Automated data collection from multiple systems for regulatory reports
  - Implemented review and approval workflows with audit trails
  - Created validation checks against regulatory requirements
- **Loan Processing Workflow**
  - Automated document collection and verification
  - Implemented credit scoring integration and decision workflows
  - Created closing document preparation and review processes

Technical Highlight: The bank used Power Automate's security and compliance features, including:

- Connection references for secure credential management
- Integration with Azure Key Vault for sensitive information
- Encryption for data in transit and at rest
- Comprehensive audit logging for regulatory requirements

Results:

- Reported 65% reduction in regulatory reporting effort
- Recorded 40% faster loan processing times
- Reduced compliance-related errors by 30%
- Improved customer experience through faster service delivery

Healthcare: Patient Care Coordination and Compliance

Healthcare organizations require Power Automate implementations that prioritize patient data security while facilitating seamless communication across care teams and departments. Power Automate's HIPAA-compliant infrastructure, combined with its ability to integrate with Electronic Health Record (EHR) systems and healthcare-specific applications, enables healthcare providers to automate patient workflows while maintaining the strict privacy and security standards required for Protected Health Information (PHI)

Case Study: Multi-Specialty Clinic

A multi-specialty clinic implemented Power Automate to enhance patient care coordination while maintaining HIPAA compliance. They enacted the following actions with improved results:

- **Referral Management System**
  - Automated referral intake and routing
  - Implemented insurance verification workflows
  - Created appointment scheduling and preparation processes
- **Care Plan Coordination**
  - Developed care team notification and update workflows
  - Implemented follow-up reminder systems
  - Created patient communication templates and delivery mechanisms

Technical Highlights: The clinic leveraged these key Power Automate capabilities:

- Integration with healthcare-specific APIs and systems
- HIPAA-compliant data handling with encryption
- Secure document generation and storage
- Role-based access controls for PHI

Results:

- Reduced referral processing time by 50%
- Improved care plan compliance by 70%
- Reported 45% decrease in missed appointments
- Enhanced coordination between specialists

Manufacturing: Supply Chain Optimization

Manufacturing organizations leverage Power Automate to create responsive, data-driven supply chain workflows that connect production systems, inventory management, and supplier networks in real-time. Power Automate's ability to integrate with ERP systems, IoT sensors, and third-party logistics platforms enables manufacturers to build automated workflows that respond dynamically to supply chain disruptions, demand fluctuations, and inventory changes, transforming reactive supply chain management into proactive optimization.

Case Study: Industrial Equipment Manufacturer

An industrial equipment manufacturer implemented Power Automate to optimize their supply chain operations:

- **Supplier Management System**

  - Automated purchase order generation and tracking
  - Implemented supplier performance monitoring
  - Created exception handling and escalation processes
- **Inventory Optimization**
  - Developed demand forecasting integration
  - Implemented reorder point automation
  - Created inventory exception alerting and resolution workflows

Technical Highlights: The manufacturer utilized these advanced features:

- Integration with IoT sensors for real-time inventory tracking
- AI Builder for demand forecasting models
- Complex business rules using expressions and conditions
- Mobile notifications for critical supply chain events

Results:

- Reduced inventory carrying costs by 30%
- Achieved 60% faster response to supply chain disruptions
- Reported 25% improvement in on-time delivery performance
- Saved $1.8 million annually in procurement costs

Cross-Industry Implementation Patterns

Despite industry-specific requirements, certain implementation patterns emerge across sectors:

Business Process Automation Pattern

This pattern focuses on automating structured, repeatable business processes:

```
1. Process Trigger (form submission, email, scheduled)
   ↓
2. Data Collection (gather information from relevant systems)
   ↓
3. Business Rules Application (apply conditional logic)
   ↓
4. Approval Routing (if required)
   ↓
5. System Updates (update relevant systems with results)
   ↓
6. Notification (inform stakeholders of completion)
```

Figure 16.4: *Structured Business Process Automation Pattern*

Example Implementations:

- Employee onboarding processes
- Expense approval workflows
- Contract review and approval

- Service request handling

System Integration Pattern

This pattern focuses on connecting disparate systems to share data and functionality:

```
1. Data Change Trigger (record created/updated)
   ↓
2. Data Transformation (map fields between systems)
   ↓
3. Validation (ensure data meets target system requirements)
   ↓
4. Error Handling (manage exceptions)
   ↓
5. Target System Update (create/update records)
   ↓
6. Synchronization Logging (record successful operation)
```

Figure 16.5: *Disparate Systems Integration Pattern*

Example Implementations:

- CRM to ERP integration
- E-commerce platform to inventory system
- HR system to directory services
- Marketing platform to sales system

Document Automation Pattern

This pattern focuses on the creation, processing, and management of documents:

```
1. Document Request Trigger (form, email, system event)
   ↓
2. Data Collection (gather information for document)
   ↓
3. Template Selection (based on document type)
   ↓
4. Document Generation (populate template with data)
   ↓
5. Review/Approval (if required)
   ↓
6. Distribution (deliver document to recipients)
   ↓
7. Storage/Archiving (save to document management system)
```

Figure 16.6: *Smart Document Handling Pattern*

Example Implementations:

- Contract generation
- Invoice processing
- Certificate issuance
- Report distribution
- Technical Requirements

Implementation Best Practices

Regardless of organization size or industry, certain technical best practices ensure that you can implement Power Automate with remarkable efficiency. Some of them are mentioned as follows:

Power Automate Implementations

Environment Strategy

Implement a clear environment strategy to separate development, testing, and production:

Environment	Purpose	Access Control	Deployment Approach
Development	Flow creation and initial testing	Flow creators, developers	Individual development
Test/UAT	Validation before production	Flow owners, testers, key users	Solution-based deployment
Production	Live business processes	Limited to necessary service accounts	Controlled deployment with change management

Table 16.2: *Environment Strategy Table*

Note: *Use solution-based deployment between environments to ensure consistency and enable version control of your flows.*

Connection and Data Security

Implement robust security practices for connections and data handling:

- Use connection references to manage credentials securely.
- Implement data loss prevention policies to control connector usage.
- Apply the principle of least privilege for connection credentials.
- Encrypt sensitive data using secure variables or Azure Key Vault.

Common Pitfall: *Avoid hardcoding credentials or sensitive information in flow definitions. Always use secure references and environment variables for credentials.*

Error Handling and Monitoring

Implement comprehensive error handling and monitoring:

```
Try-Catch Pattern:
Scope: Try
    [Main flow actions]
Scope: Catch (Run after: Try scope has failed)
    Action: Get error details
    Action: Log error to monitoring system
    Condition: Check error type
        Action (Recoverable): Implement retry logic
        Action (Non-recoverable): Send alert to support team
    Action: Send appropriate notification
```

Figure 16.7: *Monitoring and Exception Management Framework*

Monitoring Implementation:

- Create a central error logging system (like SharePoint list, Azure Log Analytics).
- Implement flow run history retention appropriate for your industry.
- Set up alerts for critical flow failures.
- Create dashboards for flow performance and reliability metrics

Optimize your flows for performance and reliability

Technique	Implementation Approach	Benefit
Parallelization	Use parallel branches for independent operations	Reduced execution time
Batch processing	Process multiple items in single API calls	Reduced connector calls
Concurrency control	Manage run limits for high-volume flows	Prevention of throttling
Scoped error handling	Implement granular try-catch blocks	Targeted error recovery
Caching	Store frequently used data in variables	Reduced redundant queries

Table 16.3: *Flow Optimization Technique Table*

Note: *Use the "`Run after`" configuration to create sophisticated error handling that can recover from specific failure types without restarting the entire flow.*

Governance and Documentation

Implement the following governance practices to ensure maintainability and compliance:

- Standardize naming conventions for flows and connections.
- Document business purpose, owner, and support process for each flow.
- Create data dictionaries for complex flows with multiple systems.
- Implement approval processes for production deployment.
- Perform regular audits and cleanup of unused or inefficient flows.

Integration Strategies

Most real-world implementations require integration with existing systems. Here are some key integration strategies:

Direct API Integration

For systems with well-documented APIs, use direct HTTP actions as demonstrated in the following figure:

```
HTTP Action Configuration:
Method: POST
URI: https://api.example.com/endpoint
Headers:
    Content-Type: application/json
    Authorization: Bearer [token]
Body:
{
    "property1": "@{variables('value1')}",
    "property2": "@{triggerBody()?['fieldName']}"
}
```

Figure 16.8: *API Integration Pattern for Documented Systems*

Note: *For complex APIs, create a collection of HTTP request template flows that can be called as child flows, creating a reusable API library.*

Custom Connector Development

For frequently used systems without standard connectors, develop custom connectors:

1. Define the API specification (OpenAPI/Swagger).
2. Configure authentication methods.
3. Define actions and triggers.
4. Implement request/response templates.
5. Configure connector policies for rate limiting and caching

Implementation Example: A manufacturing company created a custom connector for their legacy MES (Manufacturing Execution System), enabling bidirectional data flow with standardized actions for order status updates, quality checks, and production reporting.

Middleware Integration

For complex integration scenarios, use Azure middleware services:

Middleware Service	Use Case	Integration Approach
Azure Logic Apps	Complex orchestration with enterprise systems	Direct connector from Power Automate to Logic Apps
Azure Service Bus	Message queuing for reliable system communication	Service Bus connector with publish/subscribe patterns
Azure Functions	Custom processing beyond Power Automate capabilities	HTTP trigger or direct Azure Functions connector
Azure API Management	API façade for complex backend systems	HTTP connector with standardized API calls

Table 16.4: *Middleware Integration Table*

Case Study Example: A financial services company used a combination of Power Automate and Azure Logic Apps to process mortgage applications. Power Automate handled user interactions and document collection, while Logic Apps managed the complex integration with credit bureaus, underwriting systems, and document generation services.

Interactive Elements

Try It Yourself: Implementing a Business Process Automation

Exercise: Create an Expense Approval Workflow

In this exercise, you will implement a basic expense approval workflow with these requirements:

1. **Trigger**: When a new expense form is submitted
2. **Process**
   a. Check expense amount and category.
   b. Route to appropriate approver based on amount.
   c. Send notifications to submitters and approvers.
   d. Update expense status based on approval decision.
3. **Completion**
   a. Update expense record with approval status.
   b. Notify the finance department for approved expenses.
   c. Provide feedback to the submitter.

Implementation Steps

1. Create a new cloud flow with a Microsoft Forms trigger.
2. Implement approval routing logic based on expense amount.
3. Configure approval actions with dynamic approvers.
4. Create notification templates for different scenarios.
5. Implement status update actions for tracking.
6. Test the flow with different expense scenarios.

Extension Challenge: Add advanced features like receipt processing with AI Builder or integration with an accounting system.

Think About It: Strategic Implementation Considerations

Consider these questions as you plan your own Power Automate implementations:

- **Process Selection:** What criteria should be used to identify the best processes for initial automation? How would you prioritize automation opportunities in your organization?
- **Change Management:** How would you approach user adoption challenges when implementing automation for established business processes? What strategies could minimize resistance?
- **Scaling Strategy:** How would you evolve from departmental solutions to enterprise-wide automation? What governance structures would you need to implement?
- **ROI Measurement:** How would you measure the success of your automation initiatives beyond simple time savings? What metrics would demonstrate business value?

- **Future-Proofing:** How would you design your automation architecture to accommodate future business changes and technology evolution?

Scenario-based Challenge: Cross-Departmental Automation

Scenario: Customer Onboarding Process

You need to design an automated customer onboarding process that spans multiple departments:

- **Sales:** Initial customer information collection and contract details
- **Legal:** Contract generation and approval process
- **Finance:** Account setup and initial billing configuration
- **Operations:** Service provisioning and resource allocation
- **Customer Success:** Welcome process and initial training scheduling

Challenge Requirements:

- Design the overall process flow with appropriate department handoffs.
- Identify potential integration points with existing systems (CRM, ERP, and so on.).
- Define error handling and exception management strategies.
- Develop a monitoring approach for process visibility.
- Create a user adoption plan for cross-departmental implementation.

Deliverables:

- Process flow diagram showing the end-to-end workflow.
- System integration architecture.
- Implementation roadmap with phasing strategy.
- Risk assessment and mitigation plan.

Knowledge Check: Implementation Fundamentals

Test your understanding of real-world implementation concepts:

- What are the primary considerations when selecting between a cloud flow and a desktop flow for a business process?
- How does the environment strategy differ between small businesses and enterprise organizations?
- What governance controls should be implemented before allowing widespread Power Automate development in an organization?
- How do data loss prevention policies impact Power Automate implementations, and when should they be applied?
- What role does process standardization play in successful automation implementation, and how would you approach it?

Practical Application

Case Study 1: Financial Services - Mortgage Processing Automation

Mortgage processing represents one of the most document-intensive and time-sensitive workflows in financial services, requiring coordination across multiple departments, external services, and regulatory checkpoints. This case study demonstrates how Power Automate Cloud Flows can orchestrate complex, multi-stage processes while maintaining compliance requirements, integrating with external data sources, and providing real-time visibility into application status throughout the entire mortgage lifecycle.

Organization: Regional Mortgage Lender (250 employees)

Challenge: The lender was struggling with manual mortgage processing, resulting in:

- Average processing time of 27 days per application
- High error rates in document collection and verification
- Inconsistent communication with applicants
- Compliance risks due to manual oversight
- Limited visibility into application status and bottlenecks

Solution Implementation:

The lender implemented a comprehensive mortgage processing system using Power Automate Cloud Flows:

- Application Intake Automation
  - Created a unified application portal with Microsoft Forms and SharePoint
  - Implemented document classification and verification workflows
  - Developed automatic checklist generation for required documentation
- Underwriting Process Orchestration
  - Automated credit report retrieval and analysis
  - Implemented property valuation service integration
  - Created underwriter assignment based on application characteristics
  - Developed structured decision documentation workflows
- Closing Process Automation
  - Automated closing document preparation with dynamic templates
  - Implemented scheduling coordination workflows
  - Created closing checklist verification processes
  - Developed funding release workflow with multi-level approvals

Technical Implementation Highlight

The solution leveraged these key Power Automate capabilities:

```
Document Processing Flow:
Trigger: When a document is uploaded to the application folder
Action: Get document metadata and content
Action: Submit to AI Builder Document Processing
Condition: Check document type
    Action (Known document): Extract specific fields based on template
    Action (Unknown document): Classify document using AI model
Action: Validate extracted information against requirements
Condition: If validation successful
    Action: Update application record with document information
    Action: Mark document requirement as fulfilled
    Action: Check if all documents are received
Condition: If validation failed
    Action: Create exception record for manual review
    Action: Notify processor of validation issue
```

Figure 16.9: *Cloud Flow Based Mortgage Processing Model*

Integration Points:

- Credit bureau services via custom connector
- Property valuation services via HTTP actions
- Banking systems for funding via secure API integration
- E-signature platform for closing documents
- Compliance reporting systems for audit requirements

Results:

- Reduced average processing time from 27 days to 12 days
- 60% reduction in document processing errors
- 80% reduction in compliance exceptions
- 40% increase in processor productivity
- 35% improvement in customer satisfaction scores
- $1.2M annual cost savings through efficiency and error reduction

Implementation Lessons:

- Begin with process standardization before automation
- Implement strong exception handling for non-standard applications
- Create comprehensive audit trails for compliance requirements
- Develop detailed dashboards for process visibility
- Implement progressive rollout by application type

Case Study 2: Healthcare - Patient Journey Orchestration

Patient care coordination involves complex workflows that span multiple touchpoints, departments, and systems throughout a patient's healthcare journey, from initial appointment scheduling to post-visit follow-up and ongoing care management. This case study illustrates how Power Automate

Cloud Flows can create seamless, automated communication pathways between clinical and administrative systems while maintaining HIPAA compliance, ensuring that patient information flows securely and efficiently across care teams to deliver coordinated, high-quality healthcare experiences.

Organization: Multi-Location Healthcare Provider (500+ employees)

Challenge: The healthcare provider faced significant challenges in coordinating patient care:

- Fragmented communication between departments
- Inefficient scheduling and resource allocation
- Manual follow-up processes leading to missed opportunities
- Inconsistent patient experience across locations
- Limited visibility into patient journey metrics

Solution Implementation:

The provider implemented a comprehensive patient journey orchestration system:

- **Initial Patient Engagement**
  - Automated new patient onboarding with personalized information collection
  - Implemented insurance verification and financial clearance workflows
  - Created pre-visit preparation processes with custom instructions
- **Care Coordination Automation**
  - Developed cross-department communication workflows
  - Implemented test and procedure scheduling coordination
  - Created clinical documentation routing and notification system
  - Automated care plan tracking and compliance monitoring
- **Post-Visit Management**
  - Automated follow-up appointment scheduling
  - Implemented satisfaction survey distribution and analysis
  - Created outcome tracking and reporting workflows
  - Developed referral management and coordination processes

Technical Implementation Highlight:

The solution illustrated in the following figure utilized these key Power Automate components:

```
Care Plan Monitoring Flow:
Trigger: Scheduled (daily)
Action: Get active care plans from EHR system
Apply to each care plan:
    Action: Get patient details and plan requirements
    Action: Check for completed items in EHR
    Condition: If outstanding items exist and due date approaching
        Action: Send reminder to care coordinator
        Action: Create follow-up task in coordinator dashboard
        Action: Generate patient reminder message
    Condition: If plan milestone reached
        Action: Generate progress report for provider
        Action: Update care plan status
        Action: Schedule review if required
```

Figure 16.10: *Patient Care Pathway Automation*

Integration Points:

- Electronic Health Record system via secure API
- Scheduling system for appointment management
- Patient portal for direct communication
- Medical device systems for monitoring data
- Billing system for financial clearance

Results:

- Achieved 45% reduction in care coordination time
- Reported 30% improvement in appointment adherence
- Reduced missed follow-ups by 50%
- Achieved 65% decrease in communication delays between departments
- Improved patient satisfaction scores by 28%
- Achieved $2.1 million annually through improved efficiency and capacity utilization

Implementation Lessons:

- Prioritize HIPAA compliance in all automated workflows.
- Implement robust error handling for clinical processes.
- Create clear escalation paths for exceptions.
- Design for both clinical and administrative users.
- Start with high-impact patient populations.

Case Study 3: Manufacturing - Supply Chain Resilience

Organization: Global Manufacturing Company (with 5,000+ employees)

Challenge: The manufacturer faced significant supply chain vulnerabilities:

- Limited visibility into supplier risks and performance

- Reactive approach to supply chain disruptions
- Manual procurement processes with long cycle times
- Inconsistent inventory management across facilities
- Experienced difficulty adapting to changing demand patterns

Solution Implementation:

The company implemented a comprehensive supply chain resilience system:

- **Supplier Risk Management**
  - Automated supplier performance monitoring and scoring
  - Implemented early warning detection for supplier issues
  - Created alternative supplier identification workflows
  - Developed proactive risk mitigation processes
- **Intelligent Procurement Automation**
  - Automated purchase requisition and approval workflows
  - Implemented dynamic sourcing based on availability and cost
  - Created contract compliance monitoring
  - Developed spend analytics and optimization recommendations
- **Inventory Optimization**
  - Automated inventory level monitoring across locations
  - Implemented predictive replenishment based on demand patterns
  - Created cross-facility balancing workflows
  - Developed exception management for critical shortages

Technical Implementation Highlights:

The solution illustrated in the following figure leveraged these advanced Power Automate capabilities:

```
Supply Chain Disruption Response Flow:
Trigger: When disruption alert received from monitoring system
Action: Get affected materials and impact assessment
Action: Identify affected production orders and customers
Parallel Branch:
    Branch 1 (Mitigation):
        Action: Query alternative suppliers database
        Action: Check inventory at other facilities
        Action: Generate reallocation recommendations
        Action: Create expedited procurement requests if needed
    Branch 2 (Impact Management):
        Action: Identify affected customer orders
        Action: Generate production reschedule options
        Action: Create customer communication drafts
        Action: Notify sales and customer service teams
Action: Create war room Teams meeting with relevant stakeholders
Action: Generate comprehensive impact and options report
```

***Figure 16.11:** Supply Chain Resilience System Implementation*

Integration Points:

- ERP system for inventory and production data
- Supplier portal for performance metrics
- IoT sensors for real-time inventory tracking
- Transportation management system for logistics
- Market intelligence services for external factors

Results:

- Achieved 70% faster response to supply chain disruptions
- Reduced stockouts of critical materials by 40%
- Improved procurement cycle time by 35%
- Reduced inventory carrying costs by 25%
- Increased visibility into potential supply chain risks by 60%
- Saved $4.7 million annually through improved efficiency and disruption mitigation

Implementation Lessons:

- Design for both routine operations and exception handling.
- Implement real-time monitoring for critical supply chain elements.
- Create clear escalation pathways for different disruption types.
- Develop scenario-based response templates.
- Balance automation with human judgment for complex decisions.

Conclusion

In this chapter, we have explored real-world implementations of Microsoft Power Automate Cloud Flows across various industries and organizational sizes. These case studies illustrated several key principles such as: successful automation initiatives depend on having a well-defined implementation strategy that aligns with clear business objectives. The approach must be carefully tailored to match the organization's size, available resources, and operational complexity, with progressive implementation focusing on quick wins to build momentum and encourage user adoption. Integration is the cornerstone of real-world automation value, as the true potential of Power Automate emerges when it effectively connects disparate systems across the organization. However, integration strategies must carefully balance technical requirements with robust security considerations, often requiring hybrid approaches that leverage multiple Microsoft technologies to deliver optimal results. Governance frameworks play a critical role in enabling scalable automation by preventing "automation sprawl" through clear guidelines and standards. Standardized development practices ensure long-term maintainability of automated processes, while comprehensive security and compliance controls must be built into the foundation of any automation program to protect organizational assets and meet regulatory requirements.

Index

A

B

C

D

G

H

I

J

L

R

S

T

V

W